Theatresports DOWN UNDER

Theatresports™ DOWN UNDER

Lyn Pierse

A GUIDE FOR COACHES AND PLAYERS

Second edition

Improcorp Australia
ish production & design
Sydney

publishers

Improcorp Australia Pty Ltd
PO Box 688
Kensington NSW 2033
Australia

ish production & design
11 Power Ave
Alexandria NSW 2015
Australia

editor Irma Havlíček

designers Aristedes Maniatis & Linden Goh, ish production & design

illustrator Arnum Endean

National Library of Australia
Cataloguing-in-publication entry

Pierse, Lyn, 1955— .
Theatresports Down Under

Bibliography.
Includes index.
ISBN 0 646 23861 2
1. Improvisation (Acting). 2. Acting — Study and teaching. I. Title
792.028

printed by Southwood Press

10 9 8 7 6 5 4 3 2 1

ACKNOWLEDGEMENTS

This book could not have been written without the counsel of Penelope Wells. Thanks, P.

I owe much to the guidance of my editor, proofreader and colleague, Irma Havlíček.

Also I am indebted to my friend, computer consultant and editor Peter Fyfe for advice, support and generosity.

To my parents Bill Pierse and June Jones, and to Eileen Clarke, Jenny Lovell, Irene Maniatis, Lorraine Stacey and Belvoir Street Theatre, thanks for your encouragement.

Keith Johnstone, Dennis Cahill and Deborah Iozzi of The Loose Moose Theatre, Canada, thanks for your work and trust.

I am ever grateful to Christine Carlton and the teachers of the Educational Drama Association of New South Wales for supporting the idea of this book for over three years. I am also grateful to the late Ron Danielson, a teacher of teachers.

Thanks to Maureen Barron for your assistance.

Thanks to Joseph Mifsud of Qantas Australia.

My grateful thanks to editor Janet Healey, Arnum Endean for illustrations, Paul Haber for the original cover design and additional illustrations, Terumi Sakaki for additional illustrations, Theodore Maniatis for scanning, and Aristedes Maniatis and Linden Goh for design, typesetting and publishing consultancy.

Thanks to John Hughes, Dr Amanda Morris and Michael Robinson for editing advice; and readers: Joyce Conte, Phil Joseph, Gillian Richards and Elizabeth Whitty; and David Brett Springett for consultancy.

Thanks to: Chris Gregory, Lou Bennetto, Megan Garrity, Steven MacPhail, Suzanne Bennie, Suzanne Brown, NIDA library staff, Zita Denholm, Lois Moffat, and to all the Australian and New Zealand players for your thoughts, comments, time, memories and philosophy, especially Christine Keogh, Kate Herbert, Russell Fletcher, David Toranto, Gary McCaffrie, Dennis Watkins, Steven Ford, Anne Jones, Robert Jarman, Christine Best, John Wood-Ingram, Annie Burbrook, Adam Couper, David Callan, Berryn Schwerdt, Brett Wood, David Wood, Robyn Butler and Gabby Millgate.

Thanks to Derek Nicholson and the members of the inaugural Theatresports Inc Board and Artistic Council for your everything.

Finally, thanks to all who invested in the first edition, without whom there would be no second.

For my parents
Bill and June

Thanks for believing.

ABOUT THE AUTHOR

Lyn Pierse was born in Melbourne and educated at the Star of the Sea Presentation Convent Gardenvale. Trained as both teacher (B.Ed Drama Melbourne State College 1976) and actor (National Institute of Dramatic Art 1983), Lyn began teaching improvisation in Victorian high schools ten years before Theatresports as we know it evolved in Australia.

As an actress and comedienne she has performed in theatre, film, television and radio: in productions such as Rex Cramphorn's *Measure for Measure*, as the Sphinx in the Australian premiere of Berkoff's *Greek*, and as the sole performer in *Divinely Irresistible*. Her character, Sister Mary Leonard, is well known to Theatresports fans and has appeared on stage and television, including the ABC's *Big Gig*.

Lyn has written stand-up comedy and devised and co-written three plays: *The Radio Show, The Money or the Box, Write It Down and Don't Forget It*. She has also co-written a stage adaptation of Susan Johnson's novel, *Messages From Chaos*.

In 1986 she captained the Australian National Theatresports team at the first International Theatresports Tournament, Expo '86 Vancouver; and, with the support of the Australia Council, she worked with Theatresports creator Keith Johnstone at the Loose Moose Theatre and the University of Calgary, Canada. On her return to Australia she was appointed Theatresports National Coach by Belvoir Street Theatre.

Since then, Lyn's energy and expertise have been among the driving forces behind the extraordinary surge in the popularity of Theatresports and improvisation in Australia. She has taught community and professional Theatresports nationwide, leading in-service training programs for teachers, actors, and professionals. These workshops have supported literacy, oracy, language, drama and personal development programs in primary and secondary schools, teachers' colleges, universities and centres for actor training.

She introduced Theatresports to New Zealand theatre and television in 1987, directed International Theatresports at Expo '88 Brisbane, Radio Theatresports 2BL, Cranston Cup Grand Finals at the Enmore Theatre and the Sydney Opera House, Theatresports Ringside, Mixed Doubles, and Theatresports Superleague.

Lyn has been at the grass roots level of Theatresports, and with a team of veteran players has nurtured the growth of Theatresports to an international level Down Under.

In 1994 Lyn introduced Theatresports to Japan. Since then she has directed three seasons including bilingual Theatresports for the Asia Screen Network Association and special performances at the Canadian Embassy Tokyo.

Based in Sydney, Lyn writes, directs and performs, teaches improvisation at the National Institute of Dramatic Art (NIDA) and teaches Theatresports for Theatresports Inc and Theatresports Japan.

PREFACE

In 1958 my mother took me to see the Christmas pantomime *Cinderella* at the Melbourne Tivoli. It was my first experience of live theatre. I was three years old. I remember sitting in the seat. My feet could not touch the floor. The compere sang *You're all mine in buttons and bows* and threw a handful of caramels into the audience. I looked up. Lollies were flying all around me. I put up my hands. From nowhere one landed in my glove. I couldn't believe it! I looked at the stage. I was convinced that the man on the stage knew I was there. He must have. He threw me a lolly and I caught it!

In October 1986 I was watching a game of Theatresports at Belvoir Street Theatre. There was a roar from the crowd and a block of about forty people in front of me stood up. I looked up at the shower of Minties flying over my head. I put up my hand and one of the Minties landed right in it. It was then that I remembered *Cinderella.*

PREFACE TO THE SECOND EDITION

In 1994 I was at Tokyo Kabuki-za for the first time. I was transfixed by Kabuki magic: acting, sets, costumes, music, acrobatics, characters flying on strings... Suddenly, someone from the audience shouted words to the stage. The actor was not perturbed. In fact he held his pose with pride. The audience was smiling. A few more shouts rang out, then subsided. The performance continued.

A few weeks later, about one hundred of us were sardined into the tiny Tsutsujigaoka studio watching the first season of Theatresports Japan, and the same thing happened. The compere was opening the show when suddenly there were spontaneous shouts from the audience. People around me sat forward in their seats. The compere smiled and blushed. Another voice echoed the shout, then a third. The audience errupted with laughter. I couldn't figure it out.

'It's an old Japanese Kabuki tradition,' Yoko translated reassuringly. 'They're calling out his yago or stage name. It's a form of respect. To do this at Theatresports is very funny.'
'Does he have a stage name?' I asked bewildered.
'He does now. They just gave him one.'

The Japanese had embraced Theatresports.

Contents

SECTION 3 Programs 77

Introduction

This book is a culmination of my improvisation and Theatresports work in Australia and New Zealand. It is based on the teaching principles and methods of Theatresports inventor Keith Johnstone; it has been enriched by David Lander, my first improvisation teacher, and draws from my experience as a player, teacher and coach. It is both collection and invention.

Writing it has given me the opportunity to describe the beginnings of Theatresports in Australia and New Zealand, to share some memorable Theatresports moments, and to name some of the pioneers who have shaped the way we play and teach the game Down Under.

For years I resisted teachers' and players' requests for written material and Theatresports games sheets. It concerned me that simply describing the performance games would limit their educational value. Theatresports games are undoubtedly a recipe for success when teachers need sure-fire activities and students want quick results. But under these circumstances Theatresports becomes the fast food of classroom drama.

Instead, I wanted the Theatresports games to be seen in their best light. I wanted to outline the valuable communication and theatre skills they teach and their relevance to the drama and other curricula, and to share my discoveries from having performed, taught and experimented with them (helped by literally thousands of child and adult players) since first taking notes in teacher training in 1974.

To emphasise the educational value of improvisation, I have down-played the competitive element of Theatresports. The communication, language, literacy, theatre and social skills inherent in learning Theatresports games have educational value that is easily overlooked when players and teachers concentrate on competitive improvisation and Theatresports in performance.

The teamwork and goodwill that players experience in the training room is more valuable than their performance in a Theatresports competition. It is more important that players experience the joy and freedom of improvising than place too much emphasis on competitive performance. Good Theatresports relies on a supportive and cooperative spirit. Competitive playing will be richer and more valuable when the players perform from a foundation of solid improvisation skills.

I cannot stress strongly enough that after reading the whole book you support your teaching from it by participating in a follow-up Theatresports workshop with an accredited coach. Working with a coach will allow you to hear the improvisation vocabulary in action (as outlined in Basic terms and skills). It will clarify the teaching process and give you an opportunity to have first-hand player experience. To gain easy access to the programs, read How to use the programs. I recommend you also read Competitions and tournaments.

When the text refers to a game or exercise played in English, I differentiate between the working language and gibberish. Of course your working language may be German or Japanese. Whatever — play these games in your working language.

Within this context, here, finally, are the games. I have chosen those most appropriate to provide a foundation for teaching improvisation in preparation for playing Theatresports. This book offers ideas for teachers and for players mature enough to coach themselves. Use it as a guide. As your experience and confidence increase, experiment and invent. Trust your instinct. These are suggestions from my experience; your experience may be different.

In 1994 I was invited to introduce Theatresports to Japan. The thrill of seeing a theatre form for the first time made a double impression. For me it was the Kabuki, for the Japanese it was Theatresports.

Teaching and directing Theatresports through an interpreter in another language and culture strengthened my conviction in the value of improvisation as a teaching method and learning tool. I was reminded of the freedom improvisation gives actors.

Inspired by the Japanese experience and celebrating a decade of Theatresports in Australia, the second edition adds a handful of games, endowment scene exercises, magic moments, photographs, teacher accreditation news, various text changes and, in response to the culturally diverse Theatresports community, Section five – Global Network.

In June 1995 Sydney Theatresports celebrated its 10th birthday with an audience of 1700 at the Enmore theatre. The night began with a rookie round heralding the future and finished with returned veteran players who proved they have not yet passed their use-by date. Teams dispensed with the judges and scored themselves: a fitting tribute to the theatre game that was predicted to last six months.

So here's to the next decade of Theatresports in Australia and its subsequent international growth and bilingual performances. Remember, please support all teaching from this book with Theatresports accredited workshops.

I hope the work gives you as much joy as it has given me. Good luck!

section 1

origins rituals *and* traditions

Robert McFarlane

Cranston Cup

Origins, rituals and traditions

WHAT IS THEATRESPORTS?

Theatresports is improvised theatre entertainment played as spectator sport. It is the marriage of theatre and sport. It is competitive improvisation. Teams of players invent scenes from given suggestions, which are prewritten or taken from the audience. They play their scenes in structures we call games. The players know the specific requirements of each game, but they do not know what will happen during the scene or what the final outcome will be. Everything is improvised: story, dialogue, song, music and lighting. The players come from a variety of backgrounds: classical acting, stand-up comedy, writing, music and opera. Some are keen amateurs and others have no formal theatre training or experience.

The scenes are judged by a panel of three judges who each give a score out of 5 after the scene is played. Teams challenge each other to spontaneously tell a better story, deploy their players more fruitfully, and to generally improvise and solve problems with more invention, wit and skill than each other in the presentation of comedy and drama. The team with the highest score wins.

An audience is entertained by the comic and dramatic storytelling skills and the risks taken by the players to complete the games within time limits. For many spectators, the sporting element and the improvisation mode of Theatresports bridges the gap between audience and stage. The audience interacts with the performance on a number of levels. They give suggestions for scenes, are encouraged to barrack for teams and, as they watch, they identify with the players, asking themselves, 'What would I do in that situation?' They share the sense of risk and excitement with the players as the scenes are created before their eyes for the first time. Unlike scripted theatre, the audience sees unrehearsed performance, warts and all.

When a scene is good spectators are inclined to think, 'I could do that'. When a scene fails they cringe, thinking, 'I'm glad it's not me up there'. And when the improvising is wonderful they sit in awe, recognising the skill of crafted playing. Whatever the outcome, the audience wants the players to succeed and tends to side with the players rather than the judges. They watch the scenes, wait for the judges' scores and vocalise their response immediately. When the audience disagrees with the scores, they boo the judges, and when teams succeed and are rewarded with high scores, they stamp and cheer. In this way improvised performance and Theatresports are unlike any other performance experience for audience and players. The raw energy and excitement generated by truly improvised theatre creates magic. Today an audience seeks the same thrill at Theatresports as did their early European counterparts when they watched the Christians and the lions in ancient Rome, Arlecchino and Pantelone in Italy, and Punch and Judy on the streets of Europe.

While it seems contradictory that a collaborative theatre process should be competitive, the competition element is part of the theatrical presentation and is usually more important to the audience than to the players.

Where did it come from?

Theatresports as competitive improvisation began in Canada at the University of Calgary, when director, teacher and writer Keith Johnstone and his improvisation and acting students developed rules and playing structures for their improvised scenes within a theatrical presentation not unlike championship wrestling. Although Keith Johnstone's work had begun in Britain at the Royal Court Theatre a decade before, improvisation as competitive sport did not occur until the middle 70s; it has been developing at the Loose Moose Theatre, Calgary, and at Theatresports centres worldwide ever since. It is now played with a variety of cultural interpretations in many languages and countries: Canada, the United States, Norway, Sweden, Denmark, Holland, Great Britain, Germany, France, Italy, Australia, New Zealand and Japan. [See Section five – Global Network.]

Where is it today?

There is nothing new about improvisation or the concept of theatre games. Many have been in existence for hundreds of years, and new games are constantly being invented. The games stem from the root traditions of the Commedia dell'arte and Elizabethan theatres, and have entertained western cultures since the 15th century. It is from these scenarios that most of our western comedy and tragedy has developed.

In the Commedia dell'arte, the players were skilled physical storytellers and musicians. The players wore masks, each representing an archetype and their position in the social pecking order. The comedy was created within loosely scripted scenarios that were familiar to the audience. The players improvised much of the dialogue and comic business (*lazzi*) as they created theatrical mayhem by reversing the master/servant relationships that existed not only between a master and servant but also between characters such as husband and wife, teacher and pupil, and parent and child.

Theatresports comes from this style of improvisation. No part of the Theatresports scenes are scripted, but as in the Commedia dell'arte the players and the audience are familiar with the requirements of the games. Each game demands specific skills of the players. For example, one Theatresports game stipulates that the scene be mimed, another that all the dialogue be spoken in rhyme; one that the story be told in a specified genre, another that it be sung as grand opera.

There are many games, and some are easier than others. The audience comes to recognise the degree of difficulty in each game and what is good Theatresports and what is not. The content of the scenes is topical and usually relevant to and reflective of the immediate local culture. This further endears the audience to the onstage action.

The sporting element of Theatresports captivates the modern audience. The pace of the performance, the spectacle of the production, the robust nature of the onstage action and the noise and integration of the audience have made Theatresports theatre for everybody. It is popular theatre that appeals to a wide age group and a diverse general public. As with many sports, the spectators believe they are experts. At interval they discuss the tactics and speculate on the final outcome, and they relive the onstage moments long after the production is over.

AUSTRALIAN BEGINNINGS

Sydney — Belvoir Street Theatre

Theatresports began in Australia in 1984 when 500 members of the Australian entertainment industry formed a syndicate to buy the old Nimrod Theatre building in Surry Hills, Sydney. We named the theatre 'Belvoir Street Theatre' and considered ideas for new productions. Syndicate members Ray Lawrence and Noni Hazlehurst had seen performances of Theatresports in Canada and suggested Theatresports to draw the syndicate together and attract a new audience to the theatre. Belvoir Street Theatre applied for the Theatresports Australian and New Zealand stage, radio and television rights and appointed Dennis Watkins producer.

Workshops began on Sunday afternoons in the Downstairs Theatre at Belvoir Street Theatre in January 1985. Teams formed to decipher a list of 27 games and ten commandments that Watkins had received from Theatresports Vancouver. Actors played and theatre directors judged. John Turnbull led the teaching. Dennis Watkins directed the performance, gathered the production team and recruited the players. The rest was improvised. We were flying blind.

The production that developed from those afternoons became the basis of the ritual known as Classic Aussie Rules Theatresports and the blueprint for Theatresports Down Under. While there are similarities between Theatresports worldwide, the interpretations of the Theatresports rituals and the traditions are culturally specific. Down Under Theatresports developed a style and production surprisingly different from any other.

Dennis Watkins divided the 27 games into time categories of one, two and four minute games. He introduced the concept of a timekeeper to enforce time limits and take the scores. He cast a musician to play live improvised accompaniment for the improvised scenes and support the production. He divided players into teams of four, each with a name, an identity and a captain, and cast a compere to host the proceedings.

The original production team was Melody Cooper (design), Paul Chubb (compere), Dennis Watkins (timekeeper), Chris Harriott (Mr Music), Trevlyn Gilmour (stage manager, sound and lights), Kevin Palmer (the hanging judge) and 32 players (eight teams).

The board

Melody Cooper designed a portable Sydney Skyline Games Board. On it are written the original 27 games known as the Theatresports Classics, and the secret topics and titles are pre-set on the board.

The compere

Paul Chubb initiated the role of the compere. His relaxed, affable 'What's going on here, because I don't know?' style gave the original Sydney production a sense of improvised mayhem.

The Minties throw

Legend has it that Chubby was nervous on his way to the theatre on opening night — no wonder! There was no rehearsal, none of us knew what would happen, and he was the one up front. On the way to the theatre he stopped to buy something to chew. During the performance an audience member who saw him eating yelled, 'Give us a lolly!' Chubby obliged, throwing one of his Minties into the audience. The great Minties throw had begun. The next week, he brought two packets. Now 12 kilos are consumed every season.

The timekeeper

The role of the timekeeper was originally created and performed by Dennis Watkins. He educated the audience in the ways and vocabulary of Theatresports by naming the infringements such as blocks and wimps as they occurred, calling them out from the stage. His other function was to run the topics, titles and game explanations to the compere. This role was later perfected by the incomparable Jenny Lovell.

Corrie Ancore

Paul Chubb, compere

Mr Music

Live and original improvised music was pioneered by Chris Harriott in the role of Mr Music, who filled gaps, paced scenes, yielded to offers and supported the production on the electronic keyboard. He was the original fifth player of every team. Chris composed the Theatresports theme music for the ABC Theatresports television series. It became the stage theme and later the theme for Radio Theatresports. This theme occasionally intros Theatresports in Calgary, Canada.

The anthem

The Theatresports anthem is another Dennis Watkins invention. Traditionally, the audience sings the anthem and recites the commandments at the opening of the performance. The familiar sight of audience and cast united in arm-swaying (as pictured on the cover) is rooted in the Sydney Theatresports ritual. The first anthem, *My City of Sydney*, was replaced when Chris Harriott and Dennis Watkins wrote an anthem for the ABC Theatresports television series in 1986. This anthem is still sung today:

We are here in the name of our favourite game,
We each support the team we thought would gather the most fame.
But if our team should fail,
Let common sense prevail,
Remember, it's only a game.

So Theatresports fans arise, with stars in your eyes,
We're gathered here to see how well our team can improvise.
But win, lose or draw,
Don't be a bore,
Remember, it's only a game,
Remember, it's only a game.

The Ten Commandments

The world over, Theatresports players agree to ten principles and guidelines. Down Under they are referred to as *The Ten Commandments*. They are:

1. Thou shalt not **block**.
2. Thou shalt always retain **focus**.
3. Thou shalt not **shine** above thy team-mates.
4. To **gag** is to commit a sin that will be paid for.
5. Thou shalt always be **changed** by what is said to you.
6. Thou shalt not **waffle**.
7. When in doubt, **break the routine**.
8. To **wimp** is to show thy true self.
9. S/he that tries to be **clever**, is not; while s/he that is clever, doesn't try.
10. When thy faith is low, thy spirit weak, thy good fortune strained, and thy team losing, be comforted and smile, because **it just doesn't matter**!

It is not known where the commandments originated. They came to Australia via Vancouver Theatresports, but no one knows who wrote them. They are ten sensible, clear rules, essential for any creative teamwork enterprise. They are usually recited in part or full by the audience, players and compere at the beginning of the performance. Sometimes the three major commandments — numbers 1, 8 and 10 —

Andrew Denton

are repeated, and wimping and blocking are generally demonstrated before the match.

Judges

Three judges are each allocated one of the following categories:

- technique
- story-line
- entertainment

They evaluate the improvisation and score the scenes between 0 and 5:

0 Leave the stage
1 Poor
2 Just OK
3 A good scene
4 An excellent scene
5 Outstanding: take it on a national tour

If a scene is boring judges honk it off stage with a horn or gong it with a gong. The judge who sounded the horn or gong must hold up a zero card. The other two judges score at their own discretion. Their decision is final. The scores are tallied and the team with the most points wins.

The hanging judge

The world over, Theatresports judges serve the same function: to save the players. All have a head judge, who is traditionally a hard marker and generally contentious and mean. Down Under we call this judge the 'head', 'chief', 'technique' or 'hanging' judge. Kevin Palmer was the first Australian hanging judge. Every Sunday night for nearly three years he delighted in entering, swinging a golden noose to the jeers of the crowd. Although his scores were particularly low, he saved many scenes and teams from disaster by unashamedly 'honking' them off the stage. He knew it was better that the audience boo him, rather than the onstage players. [See Process – Introducing judging of scene-work for players 15+.]

(left to right) Georgie Parker, Steve Johnston, Lyn Pierse
— Cranston Cup Grand Final judges 1991

The sin bag

Theatresports infringements such as interruptions to scenes and offensive behaviour or language are punishable in different ways around the world. In Canada, players are literally 'basketed' (a cane waste-paper basket is put over the offender's head). Sydney has a sin bag, into which offending audience members or players are placed for up to 60 seconds.

Topics and titles

Theatresports players worldwide collect topics and ideas for scenes from the audience. They construct their 'ask fors' according to the needs of an improvised scene. Down Under, Watkins began with secret, prewritten titles carefully constructed by the timekeeper. They were witty, and provided variation and inspiration. This had a remarkable effect on the scene content and the performance style. Content generally tended to be fresher, more varied and less predictable than when gathered from the audience. It decreased set-up time, increased improvisation time and kept players spontaneous. The responsibility for fronting the show and keeping the audience in check became that of the compere. All the players had to do was improvise. [See Appendix B – Topics and titles.]

The night

Sunday night became the traditional Theatresports night. It was the only night of the week that actors were available and the theatre 'dark'. As the saying goes, 'Theatresports is just like church: you go on Sundays'.

The set

Most Theatresports performers improvise on the set of the current mainstage production. This involves adjusting playing every few weeks to accommodate the changing stage spaces and set configurations. Improvised scenes have taken place on sets in kitchens, bedrooms, boats, bars, outside, inside, on the moon, and with all manner of things centre stage: grand pianos, clams, lights, washing lines, a train set and even a pole. Theatresports has been played with puppets hanging from above, with trees, penny-farthings, drapes, on bare boards, sand, red dirt, carpet, glass, gravel, and on a 45 degree raked stage. Down Under Theatresports plays on anything and everything, and the players improvise under some very unusual conditions.

The moment of the match

Moment of the match originated in Melbourne. This prestigious commendation is awarded to a player for courageous yielding. In football terms it is akin to 'mark of the day', when a player fearlessly risks all in pursuit of the ball. When a Theatresports player fearlessly risks all to embrace an onstage idea, the result is usually physically spectacular. This moment is awarded by the judges, announced at the end of the match and replayed in slow motion.

Opening night

The first production opened on 2 June 1985, with the eight team format. Thirty-two players, a compere, a timekeeper and a musician comprised a cast of 35 — an astonishing number in anybody's language.

I remember waiting nervously in the well-named vomitory. Huddled in the semidark, I saw several very famous faces turn a light shade of green as each team entered to a terrifying roar from the audience who had paid four or two dollars and wanted blood! Like Christians to the lions we ran down the vomitory on to the stage.

The atmosphere was electric. No one knew what was going to happen. None of us knew what we were going to say or do. We would simply improvise!

I was so scared I only recall two things from that night. Our team, the *Southern Cross All Stars*, did a fancy entrance involving silver stars and aluminium foil knives, choreographed by Julie Haseler. We sang the anthem, recited the commandments and took our places on the benches. By this time the audience was frothing at the mouth. One by one the captains went to the stage for the tossing of the coin and the calling of the game.

I don't remember what we did out there but I do remember we won. That week I received my first Theatresports payment. Mark Owen-Taylor, Dean Carey, Julie Haseler and I split the winning cheque. We each received $2.68.

The following week we returned to defend our position. We played one game at the end of the night and were honked off. For our efforts we were publicly pied. Somehow I managed to convince the others to play again. Julie left the team to star in a musical, and Mark, Dean and I formed the first three person team and won the Cranston Cup [see Global network – Sydney]. We then asked Gia Carides to join us in the first national finals, and represented Australia at the first international tournament at Expo '86 Vancouver.

The impact of Theatresports

While the audience loved it, Theatresports was not without its detractors. It created a furore with theatre purists, who disagreed with its competitive element and said so. For many theatre traditionalists, Theatresports was uncouth in its presentation. They rejected Theatresports as a form of theatre. They thought it crass that amateur and professional players performed side by side, and were disgusted by the mob mentality of the vocal audience who yelled and scrambled for lollies. One critic likened a Theatresports performance to a Goebbels rally. Critics in general shone little light on the situation. They described the theatrical presentation as being energetic and exciting, but few understood the improvisation mode, the theatrical style or how to assess and comment on the skills and standard of the playing.

But the general public loved it. Within three months of opening in Sydney, Theatresports was playing in three states in Australia to capacity weekly audiences. [See Global network – Australia.] It brought a new audience of general public to the theatre. For a generation of children and young people, Theatresports became their first live theatre experience.

For the Australian public, Theatresports filled the gap left in live theatre by the introduction of television in 1956 and the close of the Tivoli in the 60s. It combined elements of music hall, burlesque, vaudeville, variety, circus and stand-up comedy with sport and the concept and pace of a television game show. It was entertaining and accessible. Like the sign outside the Tiv, Theatresports players and audience asked, 'What will happen this evening?'

For many performers the very idea of public improvisation was terrifying. Many well known actors were not inclined to have a go. But for others, Theatresports provided the freedom to invent and play, the opportunity to cast their own teams, make their own decisions, write their own material on the spot and to play in front of a responsive and vibrant audience. Theatresports demanded new skills from actors. It put improvisation back at the forefront of the creative process and performance. A generation of new performers cut their teeth on Theatresports stages all over the country. If Roy Rene and George Wallace were alive, they may well have been playing with us.

Meanwhile, the effect Theatresports was having on the Australian theatre-going population was completely different from the experience in North America and Europe.

In every other country Theatresports had started quietly, with unknown players in fringe venues and small, loyal audiences. There were, and still are, rarely more than twelve players on stage in any one performance. While some of the performers have since become well known writers, actors and stand-up comics in North America, most began Theatresports as virtual unknowns.

On the other side of the world, Theatresports Down Under started with a bang. The Sydney, Adelaide and Melbourne productions began with well-known actors playing and compering and celebrities judging. [See Global network – Australia.] The games were the same but the ritual of the singing of an anthem, the onstage compere and timekeeper, the throwing of Minties, and the sheer size and number of teams combined with the capacity audience, made Australian Theatresports a unique experience.

From the first performance this drew enormous crowds. The growth of Belvoir Street Theatre, the support of the industry and Dennis Watkins' pacy production exploded Theatresports like a bomb under Australian theatre. Curious, audiences flocked to the theatre in record numbers. [See Global network – Australia.] Love it or hate it, improvisation, the bastard son of theatre, was back!

The first Australian national finals

By the end of 1985 New South Wales, South Australia and Victoria fielded teams for the first Australian national finals, held in Sydney at Belvoir Street Theatre. All the teams consisted of the classic four player teams of two men and two women.

Adelaide: *The Plastic Max*, with Isobel Kirk, Richard Margetson, Glynn Nicholas and Maureen Sherlock.

Melbourne: *4 x 4's*, with Kate Herbert, Carole Patullo, Ian Shrives and John Thompson.

Sydney: *The Southern Cross All Stars*, with Dean Carey, Gia Carides, Mark Owen-Taylor and Lyn Pierse.

The audience went wild when a tie between Melbourne and Sydney resulted in an EXPERT DOUBLE FIGURES play-off. Sydney team, *The Southern Cross All Stars*, shaved in by one point and went on to represent Australia at the first International Theatresports Tournament at Expo '86, Vancouver.

Since then, Australian teams have competed in four national finals and on the international Theatresports circuit at the Calgary Winter Olympics '88, Expo '88 Brisbane, The Commonwealth Games Auckland 1990, the New York International Tournament 1991, and the 1992 International Tournaments in Orlando, Florida and Bay Area, San Francisco.

National coach and the leagues

Requests for Theatresports teaching came from community theatres, universities and schools around the country. In 1986 Dennis Watkins appointed a national coach to implement production and teach workshops. Teaching began all over the country and Theatresports spread like a bushfire. By the end of 1988 the original Classic Australian Rules Theatresports production was being played in 25 professional and community theatres in Australia and in five New Zealand capital cities. [See Global network.]

(left to right) Lyn Pierse, Mark Owen-Taylor, Dean Carey, Gia Carides — *Southern Cross All Stars*

There was a thriving University League, the Melbourne Next Wave Festival had begun its Theatresports in Schools Program and the ABC had pioneered a Theatresports television series. By 1987 Theatresports had introduced a corporate program and schools programs were flourishing in three states, and in 1990 2BL piloted Radio Theatresports.

Theatresports became more than a cult hit of the 80s. Its effect on Australian and New Zealand comedy, theatre, film, television and education is undeniable.

Theatresports provided a meeting place for like and unlike minds and has been a training ground and stepping stone for a surprising number of artists and writers.

Community Theatresports

As community theatre, Theatresports provides a unique opportunity for amateur theatre, opera and school drama groups to share skills and participate in a combined theatre event. Community theatre licences have been held by Deck Chair Theatre Perth, the Mackay Arts Festival, Now Theatre Orange, Murray River Performing Group Albury, and by amateur groups in Ballarat, Bendigo, Mallacoota and Albany. [See Global network – Australia.]

NEW ZEALAND AND THE GLOBAL NETWORK

The first New Zealand national finals

Theatresports crossed the Tasman in July 1987 and commenced with professional actors, as it had in Australia. Two day workshops were held in five major theatre centres across the country. The standard of playing was exceptional and Theatresports opened across New Zealand to sell-out houses.

New Zealand subsequently formed a national network. In July 1988 Christchurch hosted the first New Zealand national finals at the James Hay theatre where 1000 people saw spectacular improvisation. John Givins directed the event for television. It was compered by Nick Blake, with Bryan Aitkin as timekeeper, and Theatresports theme music was composed by John Gibson and David Stott.

The winning team, the *Von Trapp Family* (Mari Adams, Bruce Hopkins, Jay Laga'aia and Michael Mizrahi) won the hearts of New Zealand with probably the greatest OPERA I have ever seen, 'Hamlet of Larnach Castle'. This phenomenal team went on to represent New Zealand at the international Theatresports tournament at Expo '88 Brisbane. New Zealand Theatresports took off like a rocket and continues to thrive as a major force in improvisation. [See Global network – New Zealand.]

Global network and Theatresports Down Under

By 1988 rumours of the Aussie Rules Theatresports style and the size of Theatresports Down Under had filtered through the international Theatresports network. Players in Canada, the United States, Denmark, Sweden, Holland and Great Britain were curious about the number of teams, the lolly throwing, the anthem, the time limits, the format and the size of the Down Under audiences.

At that time only two Aussie teams had played Theatresports in North America and had experienced the culture shock of playing the North American open format challenge rounds, without time limits and collecting all suggestions for scenes from the audience. It was time for some international exchange.

At Brisbane Expo '88 Theatresports International Tournament, 50 improvisors from six different countries celebrated the individual playing styles and formats of Australia, New Zealand, Sweden, Denmark, the United States of America and

Canada. We had Aussie rules, Danish judging, Canadian reffing and New York games, playing Theatresports as an international sport. Each team carried a token trophy across the Pacific. To win the 'Danish Ham' we played Danish style; to win the 'Moose and Mounty Cup' we played the Canadian way; to win the Koala Kiwi Cup the Canadians and Europeans played Classic Australian Theatresports.

(left to right) Michael Mizrahi, Bruce Hopkins, Mari Adams (seated), Jay Laga'aia — first New Zealand national champions — *The Von Trapp Family*

As a direct result of this cultural exchange, some New Zealand and Australian centres loosened traditional time limits and opened up game structures, formats, judging and scoring systems in exchange for the North American open challenges and other international Theatresports customs. While most Down Under Theatresports centres play Classic Theatresports, they also experiment with a variety of judging styles, scoring systems and games from all over the world as players continue to push the limits and boundaries of improvisation.

As part of this exchange, New York and San Francisco stage special performances of Australian Rules for American audiences. Overseas Theatresports players marvel at audiences of more than 1000 at the New Zealand National Finals in Christchurch, and 2000 at grand final performances in Melbourne and Sydney, and at the size and popularity of the Down Under Theatresports in Education program. At all this Keith Johnstone (The Moose) scratches his head.

The Moose speaks

'They're crazy in Australia.'

Robert McFarlane

(left to right) Josie O'Reilly, Michael Gregory and Sister Mary Leonard lead players and audience in the closing anthem — Sydney Opera House grand final 1989.

Theatresports in education

Classroom teachers and their students have been attending Theatresports performances since the first game was played in Australia at Belvoir Street Theatre. The students loved it, and began playing Theatresports games in the playground, at home, at scouts, at youth centres, on the weekends, after school and in school time, and pressed teachers to play it in the classroom.

Initially, teachers saw Theatresports in the theatre and attempted to transfer the games and competitive structure directly to the drama and English classroom. Unfortunately, in many cases this emphasised the competitive aspect of the performance rather than the process. Most were unaware of the skills required and their sequential development, and were inexperienced in the techniques of sidecoaching.

The potential of Theatresports as an educational catalyst was obvious. When teachers introduced Theatresports games in the classroom, most students wanted to play or at least watch. The game structures and the immediacy of peer feedback harnessed group energy. Teachers recognised marked changes in the behaviour and attitude of their students, and a consequent change in the group dynamics. In situations where students had previously been unstimulated and difficult to motivate, teachers found the students were energised and committed to 'having a go'. Self-consciousness and fear of failure were replaced by confidence and a sense of achievement. A general sense of positivity and good-will prevailed. The students communicated with each other. They laughed. They had fun.

The potential for the exploration of language, communication and personal development skills encouraged many teachers to investigate Theatresports further. The danger at this point, however, was that 'Theatresports' would become the generic term for improvisation. The need for improvisation training programs and Theatresports workshops for teachers was obvious and pressing. These began in 1987 in association with a variety of professional organisations: the NSW Educational Drama Association, the Disadvantaged Schools Program, the Next Wave Festival Melbourne, La Boîte Theatre Brisbane, Carclew Adelaide, and various departments of education and teacher training institutions. As a result thousands of teachers in Australia have added improvisation and Theatresports skills to their professional development and teaching craft.

From classroom to Theatresports

Theatresports has a different role to play in the classroom from the role it plays in the professional and community theatre arenas. The competitive team structure seen in theatrical performance is relevant only within the educational drama process when students have the appropriate training and when their coach is informed and skilled. I recommend that competition is relevant only for players over fifteen years of age who have had three years of a full drama curriculum at secondary school level. Until then, all the games described in this book are played without competition.

For Theatresports to reach its full potential in the classroom, coaches need a complete understanding of the processes and philosophies involved in the teaching of improvisation. There are no short cuts. They must understand how the games work when not played in competition before they attempt competitive improvisation. When classroom improvisation is taught clearly, and placed in a non-competitive theatrical, social and educational perspective, it is a valuable part of an expressive arts and personal development program.

Teacher workshops

An improvisation teacher and Theatresports coach needs an understanding of the fundamentals of improvisation. It is best to have experienced these on a practical level. Solving problems 'on your feet' with other adult players, experiencing the thrill and frustration of learning to offer and yield and other foundation skills allows us to be clearer in our teaching and coaching.

Tip

Doing it is better than watching it if you want to teach it.

We know education is more active when the teacher is flexible and listens to the needs of students. However, the pressure of leading groups each day can block our spontaneity. Improvisation workshops refresh our listening skills and challenge us to understand, interpret, and say 'yes' to offers given by other people. These are powerful teaching skills.

Theatresports and related improvisation techniques empower both student and teacher. The process of 'offer and yield' not only allows a student to 'make an offer' but affirms their belief that they have something to offer. Student and teacher share a common vocabulary. The class unites as a team, completing tasks within a given time frame. There is a link between participation and observation. Valuable skills develop, such as lateral thinking, team leadership, team responsibility, spontaneity, creative problem solving, artistic and managerial discipline, respect for other people's ideas and self-trust. Players further language and vocabulary skills while enjoying themselves.

Theatresports workshops conducted by accredited coaches are available through the Theatresports licensor in your state, territory or province. A two day workshop will provide a basic introduction to improvisation and the games. However, the tools and skills required to understand the teaching of improvisation, train teams, sidecoach and direct improvisation will require further study.

Preparing for an in-service workshop

Be an active participant during improvisation teacher in-service sessions. Observation and note taking will not give you a practical experience. Remember you do not need to be a brilliant player. Playing simple games and training exercises will introduce you to the process, and chances are you will have a lot of fun.

Read Keith Johnstone's *Improvisation and the Theatre.* It is not a Theatresports manual, it is the source from which Theatresports sprang. Also read his second book *Don't be prepared* which explores Theatresports ideas and methods specifically for teachers. Viola Spolin is the mother of modern improvisation. Her game structures have laid the foundations for drama improvisation since the 1950s. Read her books for further clarification. [See Appendix C – Suggested reading.] Historically, these are important works and certainly worth reading.

Teacher accreditation

A school teacher accreditation course has been introduced to keep teaching standards in schools high and to support teachers with skills and refresher courses. Teachers who successfully complete the course are certificated as accredited Theatresports school coaches.

Competitions and tournaments

Remember, tournaments and judged work are only part of the process and should be introduced only when players have a working knowledge of skills and scene-building. If introduced too early, competition can be detrimental to a joyful learning experience and irrelevant to the creative process.

For information about competitions and tournaments, contact Theatresports Inc or the Theatresports licensor in your state, territory or province. [See Appendix A – Contact list.]

Theatresports and improvisation across the curriculum

This work is vocational for those students who may pursue a career in the performing arts. But improvisation skills are beneficial for students whatever their future career path. Adult players from a variety of backgrounds find the training programs assist their work in a range of fields by increasing their communication and lateral thinking skills, and their confidence.

The agility of the open, youthful mind devours this work, which supports literacy and language through self-expression. Valuable socialisation skills such as group interaction, eye contact and commitment have long term benefits for the group's working relationship. Individuals experience a growth in self-confidence when they follow their instinct, value their own ideas and find the language to articulate and express them.

Theatresports teaches the principles of theatre and related performing and expressive arts. When placed in a well rounded drama syllabus, Theatresports activities support other drama and text-based studies. They provide a framework for the teaching of theatre skills: storytelling, focus, musicianship, status, physicalisation, dance, mime, timing, singing, theatre history, stage presence, stage craft, voice training, characterisation, play building, discipline and good sportspersonship. These open the door to a basic understanding and appreciation of all the arts subjects while also having application for use in other core subjects when drama is used as a teaching method across the curriculum.

The role of the coach

The role of the coach is most important. It demands responsibility, commitment, consistency and craft. Coaching Theatresports clarifies and strengthens your personal teaching method. It provides an opportunity for the coach to learn as much from teaching as do the students from playing. As your observation skills increase, you learn to recognise the creative impulse of players and assist them to find and develop it. You might find that for the first time you do not have to actively control a class. You will be responsible for it and share the control with the students.

You may begin to laugh with your students, be moved by their work and experience a new relationship with them. Your status relationship with the group might change. You may discard tired old teaching habits and experience a new teaching method.

As young teachers we struggle to develop a personal teaching style. Some of us find we have absorbed the habits, vocal rhythms and inflections of the teachers who taught us and are shocked when we hear their clichéd responses rolling off our tongues. Our untrained voices screech to assert our status in the room. Most of us learn to teach by watching other teachers. We need to learn to teach by watching students.

I was working as a drama teacher at an inner city Melbourne high school — land of the brave! This high-rise area was a shock to a middle class second year out drama teacher who fancied herself as a bit of an actress. Their previous drama teacher resigned because of stress after one term. They had destroyed him and were proud of it! On my first day I was greeted with, 'We got ridda' him, and we're gonna' get ridda' you!'

Diary entry — Melbourne

I sit between two year 9 students, Rocky and Tsoula. The other 20 students lie on the drama room floor or sit in chairs as we watch. They are a volatile group and easily disrupted. Their concentration span is usually about 15 seconds but this work has grabbed them for more than a double period. Their grasp of status structures is compelling to watch. Three players, Shane, Cosimo and Graham, perform a THREE WAY STATUS HAT GAME *with clarity, precision and intelligent energy.*

Their characterisations of boss–worker relationships are spot on. They are 15 years old. Tsoula laughs so much she reaches for the hand of the person sitting next to her. It is mine. Tears of laughter roll down big Rocky's face. We roar with laughter until we ache. The lunch bell rings. 'Oh, Miss!' says Rocky, pulling a hanky from his pocket wiping away the tears. To my shock I realise first that Rocky has a handkerchief and second that he is looking at me. We hold eye contact for more than three seconds. I see his face for the first time. I also realise that the lunch bell has gone and no one has moved. For the first time at the sound of the bell they do not stampede! Tsoula continues to hold my hand. The STATUS HAT GAME *continues. 'Find an ending to the scene,' I call. It is seven minutes into lunch time when the 25 leave, still clutching their stomachs. Something has happened. I have never seen them like this before.*

Until then the class had not functioned well as a group. It was a constant, painful battle for them to respect each other's work. The status exercises clinched their commitment. They crossed the threshold laughing together and luckily took me with them. Drama became a positive force in the timetable.

It is important to note that these students never improvised in competitive structures. It was inappropriate for them, as they needed to build group trust and cohesion. We worked towards cooperation rather than competition.

Diary entry — Melbourne

Cosimo is Spanish, 15 and very short. He loves to play high status. I guess drama provides his only opportunity, considering his self-consciousness about his height. He stands between Rocky and Spiro ordering them — his servants. 'Up boys!' They lift him by the elbows. His feet swing two feet off the floor. He is now six feet tall and at their eye level for the first time. They move him into the imagined poolroom and begin the improvisation they love to play. The 'servants' dust the seat on which 'Boss Cosimo' will sit. The 'servants' take their shots.

The 'servants' lift Cosimo and hold him over the pool table while he takes his shot. When his shot is completed the servants lift him down gently and place him on the dusted seat.

They play the improvisation over and over. The mimed 'pool shooting' is flawless. I did not know they saw life in this much detail. When I come into the poolroom they endow me as a character in their reality. The lunch bell goes. Cosimo hits the ground with a thud as real life status returns.

Diary entry — Melbourne

Shane is 15. His self-esteem is low. He is the fastest, funniest improvisor I have ever seen. Today he played the two–person HAT TRANSITION GAME *and taught me how it should be played. He changes from character to character, male to female, faster than the eye can move. He instinctively creates a performer's focus. His timing is impeccable. In drama he is a hero. He leaves the class in fine spirits. The others have nothing but the utmost respect for his work. I feel I know a secret about him. The other teachers do not believe me when I describe what happened today.*

My empathy and respect for this year nine's work soared. The class recognised the change and responded. The status work was the catalyst that changed the relationship between teacher and students. The subject matter united us in our observation of society. Performance provided the opportunity for their expression of the pecking order.

As you brave sidecoaching by practising offside stimulation for scenes, you too will develop ways of satisfying the narrative — dealing with the focus of the scene and finding ways to maximise their ideas rather than your own. You may also experience a change in your teaching method in other subject areas.

The empowering experience of this teaching is that teacher and student are not bound by trying to find the 'correct' answer. There is no correct answer. At last teacher and student are free to share responsibility for the outcome. The individuality of each student's work has value. No student is compared with another.

Christchurch press

Christchurch 1989 secondary school champions — *Avante Garde*

Our children have a lot of things to say. Improvisation provides a method of expression and Theatresports gives them a forum within a structure they can access and understand. The Theatresports framework is a flexible, economic beast. It functions regardless of sex or race. It knows no geographic or language boundaries. It is as informed as those who teach it, as skilled as those who play it, and as rich and as complex as the society it mirrors.

The Moose speaks

'If you learn to unblock other people's ideas, you may learn to unblock your own.'

Basic terms and skills

Every sport has its vocabulary. In tennis, we have serves and returns, and faults; in Theatresports we have offers and yields, and blocks. In football we have marks, in cricket catches — in Theatresports we have moments.

The following is an alphabetical list of the terms we use when we improvise and play Theatresports.

Advancing

Advancing is developing the plot and giving new information. To advance we may:

- Change the focus
- Change the status
- Introduce a new offer
- Introduce a new character
- Change the rhythm, mood and timing of the scene

Commandment

Thou shalt not waffle.

Ask fors

Ask fors refer to topics, titles or ideas for scenes and games that are solicited from the audience.

Audience

In the programs an audience usually refers to classroom players watching their peers in scene-work rather than a theatre audience watching teams competing in Theatresports games.

Robert McFarlane

The audience sings the anthem, Grand Final, Enmore Theatre, Sydney 1991

Bench

The bench refers to the players' seating area in training or performance. They may not necessarily be sitting on a bench but are waiting to go on stage if required. We call players waiting to go on stage 'benched' players.

Blocking

Blocking

A block occurs when an offer is stopped, rejected, negated or ignored.

Blocking stops the action. It breaks down the communication and steals the focus from another offer. It grinds the story to a halt.

It is the opposite of yielding, and usually occurs when a player is afraid of accepting another player's ideas. On many occasions a blocking player is afraid to share the responsibility of the scene and prefers total control. This shows a lack of trust and is based on fear.

A block often occurs when players cannot hear or see the offer made in the scene. Blocking does not support the focus. A block creates a different focus or it may split the focus.

Offer: 'That dog has three legs.'
Block: 'That's not a dog.' Or: 'What dog?'

Saying 'No' is not always a block.

Offer: 'Stick 'em up!' (Holding fingers as gun.)
Yield: 'No, don't shoot.' (Hands up in surrender.)

In this instance player B has agreed to be in danger, and yielded to the offer of the gun and the status of player A. Player B can overaccept the danger by adding, 'The money is in my back pocket'.

The hand signal for blocking is one clenched fist hitting the palm of the opposite hand.

Commandment

Thou shalt not block.

Breaking the routine

Breaking the routine creates an advance. It occurs when a new offer is introduced to break the rhythm and action of the scene. For example, two (of the countless) options for breaking the routine of one player miming tossing pizza dough are: 1) a second player enters shouting, 'There's a fire!'; or 2) the pizza dough tosser mimes the dough landing on his/her face. There are many ways to break the routine, including changing the rhythm of the scene, vocalising after silence, moving after stillness.

The timing of knowing when to break the routine is important. Too often, players break the routine before a routine has been firmly established.

Beware of players who continually break the routine for motives other than serving the scene.

Commandment

When in doubt, break the routine.

Bridging

Bridging is a useful storytelling technique but does not necessarily encourage sponteneity. A bridging player builds a story from point A to point B, anticipating the conclusion at point B from the outset. For example, FIRST AND LAST is a bridging game because players aim to build the story from the first line to the last line.

Bringing down the lights

AKA 'pulling down the lights' or 'flagging a scene'.

When players want to finish a scene, they signal to the lighting operator by holding both hands up in the air and quickly lowering them. This is the signal for bringing down or pulling down the lights. On this signal, the lights fade down or go to black.

Bulldozing

When players enter a scene and destroy the established ideas with their own, we say they are bulldozing the scene.

Cap off

This refers to a punch line, witty finish or slick ending to a scene or game.

Clever

Clever is a term used to describe a choice made by a player who is trying to be funny and impress the audience rather than going with an idea that supports the story.

Endowment

When players endow offers they give them value — for example size, weight, shape, attitudes, relationships. They endow their environment, the weather, and other players. Endowment allows players to imagine, 'What if this player were the queen/a hairy monster/my brother, etc' and treat the other player accordingly. Endowment encourages players to express opinions and deepens their commitment to the ideas and other players in the scene. Endowment games are especially enjoyed by the audience when they know the secret endowment in games such as ENDOWMENTS and MURDER ENDOWMENT.

Event

An event is something that happens in a scene. It causes a development in the plot.

Extending

Extending occurs when players provide detail. It:

- Supports and maintains the existing offer
- Develops the current information in the scene
- Supports and maintains the existing focus
- Broadens the potential of the existing focus
- Prolongs the moment
- Maintains the existing status relationship in the scene
- Establishes and continues a routine
- Establishes and maintains a consistent rhythm

Fielding

Fielding refers to the way a team chooses to deploy its team members on stage and off stage. Teams may utilise their players in a number of ways. Some teams, for example, play ONE-WORD-AT-A-TIME-STORY with all four players, others play it with two or three players. Good fielding is having the optimum number of team members on stage in roles that best serve the scene, with other team members staying off the stage ready to come on if required or end the scene by bringing down the lights. [See Process – Bringing down the lights.]

Focus

The focus is the point of concentration shared by players and audience. It is what the players and audience see and hear. It is important that all players serve the focus in the scene at all times.

Commandment

Thou shalt always retain focus.

Freeze

When players freeze, they stop their movement and hold their position, including eyeline, as still as possible. The freeze has a number of functions, including helping players locate focus. Take care that players are not uncomfortable or in danger of any injury (eg losing balance) in a freeze.

Function

When players serve a function in a scene, they know when to come on stage, what to come on as, what to do when they get there and when to leave. When a player steps into the scene, the player's function is to serve the scene. In some instances, the scene is best served by a player staying off stage. Some characters are required only momentarily. Functional players are a rare breed.

Gagging

Gagging

A gag is a line or physical action played for a laugh at the expense of the scene.

Gagging:

- Blocks the action
- Breaks the reality
- Hinders or disrupts the storyline
- Breaks, splits or destroys the existing focus
- Breaks the dramatic tension
- Disrupts teamwork, causing improvisors to compete with each other and play for audience approval
- Breaks team trust
- Encourages self-gratification

Gagging occurs when players lose their belief in the scene. It is usually caused by fear and occurs when a player comments on the action rather than responding to the principal offer in the scene.

Offer: 'That puppy's been hit by a car. Let's help it.'
Gag: 'What a dog of an idea.' Or

Offer: 'Do you know the vet's telephone number?'
Gag: 'Yes. K, nine, nine, nine.'

The sign for gagging is made by cupping your hand around your own throat and opening your mouth to reveal your teeth and tongue.

Commandment

To gag is to commit a sin that will be paid for.

Game

A game is a structure for play. The structure and the rules are known and followed by all the players. The outcome is unknown at the outset and known at the end.

For our purposes the games stimulate spontaneity, and develop improvisation and scene-work skills.

There are three types of games:

Warm-up games are ice-breakers, energy raisers and skill builders that involve all the players.

Training games are structures that are useful for skill-building. They link skills to scene-work and prepare players for performance games.

Performance games refer to the Theatresports games, of which there are 27 classics and countless others that are suitable to perform in front of an audience.

Game on game

Game on game playing occurs in competitions and tournaments when two teams compete for the judges' scores, each playing the same Theatresports game. The first team plays the scene and is scored. This is followed by the opposing team playing the same game with a different topic or title, and their scene is scored.

Gibberish

Gibberish is a language made up of vocal sounds of different pitches, accents and inflections. It is nonsensical in that no such language exists. But when players improvise in gibberish, they believe they understand everything that is said by themselves and the other players. Many games are played in gibberish.

We use gibberish in warm-up, training and performance games to release energy and encourage players' emotional commitment to the content without relying on words.

Given circumstances

Given circumstances refer to the prevailing conditions in a given situation; they tell us one or more of the following: who, what, where, when, why. For example, two French soldiers, scrubbing the floor, in the barracks, in winter of 1914, because the General is coming.

Handle

A handle is an additional element introduced to the playing of a game. For example, a team plays TYPEWRITER, choosing to add the handle of a rhyming couplet. This means that at some point in the improvisation the team plays the TYPEWRITER in rhyming couplets. A list of possible handles includes: POEM; RHYMING COUPLETS;

SONG; MIME; GIBBERISH; IN THE STYLE OF; EMOTIONS; SCENE WITHOUT QUESTIONS. Do not use handles until all players are ready for this additional element. Do not play more than one handle with any one scene; you may overload the scene.

Hedging

Hedging lies somewhere between blocking and wimping. It is failure to deal with the offer by making excuses or asking questions which evade the issue. Hedging derails the scene.

Hogging

When players do not share the scene with other players but insist on controlling the scene by talking and staying on stage even if they are not required, we say they are hogging.

Image

When players image, they picture their circumstances. They see their environment, experience the weather, and use their senses to create the specifics of size, weight, shape, colour, smell, texture, etc. Imaging supports belief for both the players and the audience.

Improvisation

When we improvise, we act spontaneously, without preplanning, using whatever is at hand to invent stories and characters to create a world of make-believe. [See Process.]

Instinct

When we say players trust their instinct, we mean they act on their intuitive response.

In the moment

When players are in the moment, they are not preplanning the future. They are genuinely responding to every offer as it arrives.

In the space

'In the space' has two meanings in the context of improvisation and general drama activity: one refers to the room in which the players train, eg the coach may ask players to find their own place 'in the space'. The other way the phrase is used relates to the space determined as the performance area (it may be on stage); eg, the coach may ask two players to begin a scene 'in the space'.

'It'

'It' refers to the chaser in chasing games. One player, 'it', pursues the other players in an effort to catch another player and make another player 'it'.

Moment

A moment refers to a specific offer, yield, transition or interaction that is memorable played by one or more players in a story, scene or game. When the sidecoach reminds players to 'stay in the moment', they mean for players to find the focus of the present moment and yield to it.

Moment of the match

Moment of the match is awarded to a player for overaccepting an offer and embracing an onstage idea. It is awarded by the judges and replayed by the players in slow motion at the end of the match. [See Origins, rituals and traditions.]

Objective

An objective is something to achieve. When a player wants something, they play an objective; eg to ask your father for $100.

Offer

An offer provides a beginning as the first action which starts the scene. It may be verbal, non-verbal or both. An offer initiates a commitment to an idea. It needs to be clear, simple and brief. Offers then continue to be made through the scene.

To make an offer is to make a positive suggestion, movement, physical shape or expression (silent or spoken) which starts or develops a story or a scene.

Clear offers are simple responses. They are not clever, but obvious reactions or ideas. They build the foundation for basic communication. Some offers are richer than others. Strong offers are vocally and physically clear, and provide a focus quickly and efficiently. Offers give us who, what and/or where. Offers provide the structural pegs for the narrative.

There are six points to remember about an offer:

1. Make it
2. Yield to it
3. Name it
4. Extend it
5. Advance it
6. Shelve it

An offer is only as good as its yield.

Commandment

**S/he who tries to be clever is not,
while s/he who is clever doesn't try.**

Write on the blackboard:

offer + reaction = yield

Off stage

Off stage refers to the area that has been determined as being outside the performance area. Offstage players usually watch the onstage action from the sidelines. They wait, sitting or standing, out of the playing action in preparation to go on stage if required.

On stage

On stage refers to the area determined as the performance area. It is the area at which the audience looks. Onstage players are those performing in the scene. For the most part when I refer to on stage I mean the playing space within the training room rather than a stage with lights and audience.

Open scenes

Open scenes are scenes which allow free improvisation. They are not played within game structures. Players begin scenes without specific requirements. Sometimes we call these scenes, 'scenes from nothing'.

Overaccepting

An overacceptance is unconditional yielding.

Offer: 'Look, here's a dog.'
Overaccept: 'A dog! I've wanted a dog all my life. I love dogs.' Or
'A dog!' (Sneezing.) 'I'm allergic to dogs.' (Coughing.) 'Once I was bitten and caught rabies.' (Starts frothing at the mouth.)

An overacceptance involves a commitment to the whole idea of the offer.

Overload

When players offer or try to deal with too many ideas, they overload the scene.

Pulling down the lights

[See Bringing down the lights.]

Railroading

Railroading occurs when a player steers the scene towards their own prefixed ideas rather than going with the current scene ideas and sharing the scene ideas spontaneously with other players.

Responsibility and control

When players share the responsibility for, and control of, the scene, they are yielding to one another's ideas and sharing the improvising.

Risking

It is a risk at any time to speak or perform in front of other people. With improvisation, the risk is heightened because the outcome is not known. That anything can happen is the appeal and terror, the double-edged sword, of improvisation. When the sidecoach says, 'Take a risk', they mean trust your impulse and surrender to it, dare to let go of the known and go towards the unknown. Dare to become the carrot if it is called for in the scene.

Risking is also associated with saving the scene or saving another player. It is then an act of bravery. Players take a big risk when they enter a scene that is not going well and change the energy, focus or direction of a scene for the sake of the scene.

If players feel safe in the physical environment (they know they will not bump into things or fall over), when they trust the other players not to hurt or ridicule them, and when they have deep confidence in the coach and their sidecoaching, they will be more inclined to take risks.

Robert McFarlane

Ross Daniels dares to become a carrot

Sabotage

Sabotage does not occur very often, but when it does it is worse than blocking. It happens when a player refuses to accept another player's idea, railroading the scene or belittling the other player's offer. It is usually associated with sexism or placing oneself at a higher status than the other players, the scene, the audience or the offer. [See Program five part D.]

Saving

Saving is the basis of teamwork. All players can be coached to save other players and the scene. Saving relies on yielding, overacceptance of other people's ideas and selfless team-spirited playing. As they say in Canada: 'When a scene is good, everybody wants to be in it. When a scene is not good, nobody wants to be in it.' Be alert for cries for help from players in scenes. 'I'll just get some help', 'Oh, this is boring', 'I don't know what to do', 'I think the phone's ringing' — these comments are warnings. Help the onstage player. Go on and save them.

Commandment

Thou shalt not shine above thy team-mates.

Scene

For our purposes, scenes refer to improvised scenes unless they are specified as text scenes. A scene involves a story presented by one or more players in which something happens, and may directly include the audience (if there is one). It can be spoken, moved and/or sung. We refer to improvised scenes as being short (up to one minute), medium (two to three minutes) or long (four to ten minutes). Scenes are usually watched but can be played without spectators. An improvised scene may take place within a game structure or as an open scene.

Serving

To serve a scene is to give value and precedence to the ideas, characters and environment already established. It includes coming on stage when needed and staying off stage when not needed.

Shelving

Shelving is a comic and dramatic storytelling device. When a player shelves an idea, they take an offer introduced earlier in the story and put it 'on the shelf', as it were — saving it till later. Reincorporation of the idea (or taking it from the shelf) towards the end of the plot creates a satisfying conclusion. Good shelving provides the missing link, gives the story reason and a sense of completion (although reincorporation of a shelved idea need not occur only at the end of a scene).

Good shelving is a rare talent. It demands listening, skilful dealing with offers, and usually not too many ideas. It harnesses the storyline and disciplines the improvisation.

Good shelving promotes good storytelling.

Sidecoaching

Sidecoaching is offside vocal calling from the coach to the players while they are in action and the scene is in progress.

Status

When characters form a hierarchy, the pecking order becomes clear and status relationships are formed. When the status of characters changes, there is a turning point and an advance in the scene, as when Cinderella is fitted with the glass slipper. A change in status denotes an event and is a potential moment of comedy or tragedy.

Commandment

Thou shalt always be changed by what is said to you.

Status — keeping the status of the group even

While our aim is to explore a range of status positions for characters in performance, it is important that we work towards the status of all players in the group being as even (or equal) as possible, so that, overall, no player feels any more or less important than another. Value each member of the group so each player feels that they have a contribution to make. Encourage the achievements and self-worth of all.

Subtext

The subtext is the unspoken meaning that lies underneath the dialogue. It is conveyed through body language and mood.

Tag

For our purposes, there are three meanings for 'tag':

- In chasing games one player tags another player by tapping them on the back or shoulder. Tagging passes the role of 'it' on to the tagged player — eg CIRCLE TAG.
- In still focus games, tagging passes the scene responsibility on to the tagging player. One player tags another, taking their physical position to continue the scene, eg FREEZE TAG, or tagging the storyteller, which passes on the storytelling to the tagging player, eg TAG SPITFIRE. The tagged player leaves and the tagging player takes up the scene playing.
- A tag also refers to an improvised punch line or witty finish to a scene or game.

Task

A task gives players something specific and active to do in a scene, eg hanging the washing on the line, making a hat.

Time-out

Time-out

Time-out is the preparation time given to players before they improvise. In most Theatresports performances, teams are permitted ten seconds time-out to confer before they play the game or scene. Should teams wish to take the time-out, they make the appropriate signal; left hand horizontal, right hand vertically under it forming the 'T' to the timekeeper.

They then huddle together to discuss their tactics. They may decide the scene location, how to field players and cast the main protagonist. However they never decide the outcome of a scene during time-out. To maximise a spontaneous response to a given suggestion, warm-up games, training games and most scenes do not require time-out. Theatresports performance games that permit time-out are clearly marked throughout the programs in this book.

Topics and titles

Topics and titles are ideas for starting points for scenes or games. They may be locations, events, activities, endowments, etc, or any combination of these. The title for a DEATH IN A MINUTE could be: In a pig pen. The DEATH IN A MINUTE game is then played at this location. [See Appendix B – Topics and titles.]

Training

Players train to develop improvisation and Theatresports skills. Training sessions include warm-up games, voice and body work, training games, scene-work and Theatresports performance games.

Transition

A transition is a moment of change between one part of a story and the next. A transition usually occurs when a story or character undergoes a shift in emotion, location, status, mood or atmosphere. A transition advances the plot.

Upping the stakes

Upping the stakes raises the dramatic tension and provides an opportunity for advancing the plot by increasing the risk factor in the scene. In *Macbeth*, Shakespeare ups the stakes by bringing King Duncan to Macbeth's castle, which places Duncan's safety at risk.

Wimping

Wimping

A wimp occurs when a player refuses to take their share of responsibility for the developing scene. A wimp usually results in:

1. An offer not being named:
   Offer: 'Look at that thing.'
   Wimp: 'Yeah… look at it.'
2. The over-description of an offer, rather than the naming of it:
   Offer: 'Look at that!'
   Wimp: 'Yes… it's green, hairy, brown and…'
3. An offer being watered down rather than being maximised:
   Offer: 'Look at that incredible man-eating dog!'
   Wimp: 'Yes, but it's not real.'
4. A lack of emotional commitment to an offer:
   Offer: 'Look out, that car is going to hit that dog!'
   Wimp: 'Yes, it might.'
5. Unnecessary questioning of an idea — passing the buck:
   Offer: 'Where do you think that dog came from?'
   Wimp: 'I don't know, where do you think?'
6. Unnecessary stalling, lack of physical commitment or lack of acceptance of the other player's sense of reality of the developing scene.

A wimp occurs when the most recent offer is not given priority or focus, or is not placed at top status in the scene.

To make the hand signal for a wimp, raise the palms of both hands and drop them simultaneously from the wrists.

Commandment

To wimp is to show thy true self.

Yield

A yield is an acceptance of an offer. Yielding is saying 'yes' to another person's ideas. Yielding accepts the offer however obvious, ordinary or bizarre, names it and develops it. Yielding enables players to share the scene. It allows players to take their equal share of responsibility and control of the developing scene. Yielding requires listening to an offer and giving an honest reaction. Yielding supports the focus and serves the scene.

Offer: 'Look, that dog's got three legs.'
Yield: 'Yes, and it has three eyes too.' Or

Offer: 'I feel sick in the stomach.'
Yield: 'Yes… and your face is turning pale.'

Yielding does not always require players to be on stage. Does your team-mate need you? If not, yield and stay off. If they need you, go on.

The Moose speaks

'The art of improvisation is to make the other person look good.'

section 2

process

Process

IMPROVISATION

As necessity is the mother of invention so improvisation is the process through which we create. When we improvise, we act spontaneously, without preplanning, using whatever is at hand.

Whether we are improvising sitting at a piano, standing at an easel, or as a character from a play, writing, or playing a Theatresports game, it is the process of improvisation which releases our intuitive responses. Improvisation is the engine room of creativity.

For the purposes of this text, when I refer to improvisation in drama and theatre I mean the process through which we spontaneously invent stories and characters to create the world of make-believe.

Improvising is instinctive. It is play. Like children, we use our imagination to spontaneously play, making everything up as we go. We find ways of listening to each other, sharing ideas and solving problems; when we don't, the playing stops. To improvise productively with other people we need to agree on a set of principles which encourage play. The concept of offer and yield is integral to this process.

It is important that players understand the process and the fundamentals of improvisation before they play timed, competitive Theatresports games. I first learned the process through Madhat Theatre.

Madhat days

I began my work in improvisation at Melbourne State College in 1974 with seven other trainee drama teachers under the guidance of David Lander. We worked in a non-competitive environment, exploring the process of improvisation for three years.

We called ourselves Madhat Theatre after the status transition hat games. [See Program five – Status.] We performed the games now called the Theatresports classics. We performed in mask and with puppets. We improvised scenes, improvised from set texts and took our work into the classroom, team-teaching primary and secondary students in Victoria and South Australia.

After Madhat, each of us — Margaret Cameron, Raffi Ghazarian, Steven Gration, Johnno Joannides, Ian Rolland, Denise Scott, Nadia Tass and I — took the skills into a variety of creative pursuits, including theatre-in-education; stand-up comedy; writing; editing; teaching, directing for theatre, film and television; acting for theatre, film and television — comedy and drama; puppetry; music; photography; and more.

Madhat Theatre 1974 – 1976

We walked around the room simply describing what we saw. We named everything. We rambled in English and gibberish about the brick-work, the wooden floor, the holes in the ventilators. We played children's games and the energy level in the room transformed. We were not criticised, judged or scored. Nothing was wrong. It was like being on permanent holiday. We learnt to respond immediately to any stimulus — a ball, a hat, the space in the room, the space between the legs of the chairs, the space between our heads and the ceiling. We developed an acute awareness of space, shapes, size, texture and a sense of our own bodies in space. The first sessions were devoted to status, yielding, storytelling and creating environments. We taught each other when to advance and what to extend. If we were bored, it was time to advance. We taught ourselves to trust our instincts.

At the beginning of a session, David asked us to describe in one word how we felt — 'good', 'great', 'okay', 'tired'. The answers were important to him. He used the information to structure the session. He was facilitating the process. I had never seen another teacher do this. We learnt to listen to our instinct and voice our response.

We saved questions until the end of the sessions. By the end we couldn't remember the questions or we'd answered them ourselves. Time was dedicated to the release of impulse and scene playing through game structures. Most sessions were divided into sections devoted to warm-up games, scene building and performance games skills. Daily we sharpened our status, character building and storytelling skills. We put on masks and noses and discovered characters and families of characters who improvised pecking orders. As the characters developed, we taught them to speak text from prewritten plays. Each of us experienced the process as players and as audience for each other.

The work was energetic, committed and raw. We played as a company rather than in teams. We never knew what we were going to do, how we would do it, or with whom we would play until we stood.

We played scenes voluntarily. We were rarely named to play. 'Two people up', David would say, and then name the game to be played. In our excitement, five of us leapt to our feet to be the first players up to play the scene. There was a constant sense of 'thrill' and a complete sense of surrender. The set-up was the same whether we were training or in performance. No one missed a session. The work was too compelling.

Scenes were sidecoached (see below for explanation of sidecoaching) towards achieving the scene objective rather than towards the time frame. Except for objective-based scenes such as DEATH IN A MINUTE and I LOVE YOU IN A MINUTE, there were no time limits. Scenes ended because they were finished. We slowly faded the lights to propel the players towards the objective and to find the natural end of the scene.

As untrained actors we played from a sense of truth, which was encouraged and demanded at all times. In my first ten years of improvising theatre games, I never improvised in a competitive situation. (Indeed, until 1985 I was not aware that improvisation could be competitive.) We improvised without the pressure of a judge's zero or sounding of a horn. We were never accused of gagging as we didn't gag. We had no need to win approval by gagging. The sense of achievement we all experienced from simply improvising was more than enough.

If the scene was not working, we saved each other or David stopped the scene. We were compelled to save each other at all times. We risked because we felt safe. We were encouraged and expected to yield and did so, enjoying the rewards it brought. We beat rhythms, we sang whole scenes, and laughed till we cried. I remember I dreamed a lot during this time.

It was three months before we could find the endings to our scenes. We'd come to a point when we would just stop. We did not have the skills to take the story any further.

David sidecoached all the way through training sessions and performances. The audience laughed so much they couldn't hear him. We were hilarious.

David's sidecoaching was persistent:

'Pick up the offer.'
'Accept the offer.'
'Yield to the moment.'
'Advance the scene.'
'Extend.'
'Advance the offer.'
'Extend the new offer.'
'Drop the status.'
'Share it with us.'

At first I found David's sidecoaching helpful. As I gained confidence it began to annoy me. One session I was playing a scene and his persistent voice continued to distract and interrupt me. I stopped playing, looked out at him and screamed, 'I can't hear them if you keep speaking'. Without breaking the rhythm of the scene or scolding me for the outburst, he redirected my energy and focus back into the scene, sidecoaching: 'Pick up the offer Lyn and continue the scene'. I did. His sidecoaching was so clear and direct, I did as I was told.

Eventually the sidecoaching became inaudible and functioned as a subliminal reminder to our developing skills. David crafted our technique with precision and accuracy. All the choices we made in the scenes were ours!

SIDECOACHING

AKA 'calling'

Sidecoaching is offside vocal guidance from the coach to the players while the players are in action. It is a most active and effective method of improvisation teaching and Theatresports training when the sidecoach is skilled and confident in the process. Sidecoaching requires the coach to remain subjectively involved in every scene as if they were a player and, at the same time, to remain objective as an outside eye, able to 'call' what the scene needs throughout every training session. Through sidecoaching the coach is the extra player on every team, in every scene and game.

Sidecoaching can be an intensive and exhausting process because the coach needs to be 'in the moment' with eyes on the focus of every offer, every step of the way. For the sidecoaching to have a positive effect on skills building, the coach requires a practical working knowledge of all terms, games and exercises, and an understanding of the process of improvisation. The coach must believe in the potential of every scene and every player, and remain open to the microcues (the slightest nuances) offered by players.

The role of the coach is to build players' belief and confidence, assess their energy, interpret their body language and literally coach on the spot with the scene. The coach helps to open the communication channels between players as they improvise. The coach is an 'unblocker'.

The aim of sidecoaching is to maximise the potential of players' ideas rather than introduce the coach's. Unlike the theatre director with a clear vision of a script, the improvisation and Theatresports coach assists players to write, perform and direct their own words and actions in the moment on their feet while they improvise.

Clear sidecoaching assists players to:

- Make an offer
- Value their own ideas
- Clarify and support someone else's offer
- Say 'yes' and yield
- Name offers
- Find locations
- Save each other
- Pick up dropped offers
- Extend an offer
- Advance an offer
- Break the routine
- Clarify and build narrative
- Advance the scene
- Clarify the status in the scene
- Make smooth transitions
- Invent an event
- Raise the stakes
- Create dramatic tension
- Slow the scene down

- Use the space
- Endow other players and the environment
- Wrap up the story

The coach assists players to trust their intuitive responses and to believe that obvious reactions and ideas are interesting and of value.

Sidecoaching strategies — dos and don'ts

There are dos and don'ts for coaches, but coaches only call dos for players.

•

Good idea

Do talk as little as possible during the session. Allow players to have a practical experience rather than describing the experience to them.

Call the agreed Theatresports terms:

'Yield to the offer.'
'Pick up the offer.'
'Name the offer.'
'Yield to the focus.'
'Take a risk.'

Don't stop a scene, talk about it, and then go back to the scene.	**Do** sidecoach the scene while it is in progress.
Don't call the words 'block' or 'wimp' as negative reinforcement, especially during the first weeks of training.	**Do** find a positive alternative. Sidecoach towards the positive aspect of the scene, reinforcing skills rather than identifying negatives.
Don't call, 'Boring'.	**Do** sidecoach the scene or bring it to a close.
Don't criticise individuals or devalue content.	**Do** guide the improvisation and sidecoach the scene with positive reinforcement towards truthful responses.
Don't tell players what to feel.	**Do** give players things to do.
Don't tell players, 'That was wrong'.	**Do** keep the energy flowing.
Don't talk too much after an exercise or scene.	**Do** collect relevant feedback and move on.

•

Remember

Theatresports is a contact sport. Players make physical and eye contact with other players and, at times, with the audience. When players lose their concentration or the thread of the story, sidecoach them towards making eye contact with each other. Eye contact connects players and keeps them safe in the scene.

Theatresports and improvised scenes do not have to be funny. They can be comic or tragic and all the degrees in between.

•

Good idea

Do demand a sense of truth in every scene. The hilarious and bizarre moments will be richer if born of truth.

Do be prepared for players to adapt to this work at a faster rate than you anticipated. They may devour games at great speed, but continue to coach skills.

Do encourage players to express their own culture. Remind players to use their own accents and express their ideas with their own intonations and dialects. This, of course, does not apply to specific character choices where an accent may add to character. However, if a player uses any accent for no apparent reason (in my experience the most common gratuitous accent is American), sidecoach — 'Use your own accent'.

Don't use the word 'try'. Don't give the starting point: 'Try to fly a kite'.	**Do** give the starting point: 'Fly a kite'.
Don't say the words 'skit' or 'sketch'.	**Do** say players improvise 'scenes'.
Don't talk about 'tricks'.	**Do** encourage more risks, less jokes. **Do** teach truth and communication. **Do** encourage characterisation.
Don't pressurise players with time frames.	**Do** assess the group energy and adjust the times accordingly.

•

Remember

Physically disabled and visually impaired players may need to work to different time frames. The suggested playing times are indications only. Time frames for adult players are not relevant to primary and secondary students, whose cognitive processes vary according to individuals and ages.

•

Good idea

Find positive alternatives for:

- Commenting on characters
- Punch-lining
- Too many props
- Engineering or preplanning
- Cluttering scenes with too many players

Don't practise the Theatresports games first.

Don't ask players to show, repeat or demonstrate work. Improvisation is not show and tell. All work, including performance while training, is improvised. The majority of exercises or games may be repeated, but the topic and/or combination of players must be different every time.

Do practise skills.

Do keep the status of all players even during training sessions.

Do minimise the competitive element of the work whenever possible.

Do maximise energy level and fun.

•

Remember

- Encourage natural laughter. Most laughter is constructive. Permit it. Encourage it. Laugh too!
- Balance the sessions. Alternate between Theatresports and other drama activities. Use Theatresports to support the other work and the other work to inform Theatresports playing.
- There are as many solutions to a problem as there are players solving it. The joy of improvising and playing Theatresports games lies in the players discovering their own playwright, director and performer. The coach's task is to assist players to think quickly, take risks, follow impulses, use their life experiences as a resource, release their own personality, work as a member of a team, and achieve a sense of creative independence.
- The audience will see and believe what the player believes and imagines.
- The coach is an unobtrusive but active leader who provides an offer if one is not present in the scene or reminds players when an offer is present in the scene.
- When offers are not forthcoming from the players, always suggest offers of activity and place — give players something to do and somewhere to be.

If a scene is physically stagnant and the players are merely 'talking the scene':
Sidecoach: 'Continue the scene without words' or
'Continue the scene in gibberish.'

If the scene is lacking an environment or place:
Sidecoach: 'Find the place' or give the players an offer of place.

If players suggest an activity, but continue to wimp:
Sidecoach: 'Do it!'
Continue to call 'Do it!' until they do.

Coach from the offers given by the players. Yield to the possibilities the players come up with in the scene.

When the scene is physically jumbled and overloaded with offers:

Sidecoach: 'Go into slow motion.'

When the scene has clarified:
Sidecoach: 'Return to normal speed.'

This is particularly effective for situations when four players are required in a scene, such as the middle one minute section of Space jump.

When players are emotionally detached and uncommitted to the scene:
Sidecoach: 'Go to gibberish.'

Gibberish is particularly effective when players are not listening to offers or are not being changed by what is said to them in endowment and transition scenes and games, such as Emotions, Emotional replay, Death in a minute, Status transition scenes, Slow motion commentary, Four square emotions and Statues. Gibberish will release the emotional commitment to the scene and engage listening and shared delight. [See Program one – The present game step four – gibberish; Program four – Endowment; and Program six – Transition. Read Viola Spolin's section on gibberish in *Improvisation for the Theatre.*]

When players are physically and vocally under-energised and lack commitment:
Sidecoach: 'Sing the scene.'

When players' vocal level is inaudible:
Sidecoach: 'Share it with us.'

If you hear players straining their voices, reinforce the work with appropriate vocal warm-up exercises prior to the activities.

When you hear players speaking in unnecessary accents:
Sidecoach: 'Go to your own voice.'

When players panic and overload the scene:
Sidecoach: 'Breathe,' or 'Breathe out.'

•

Remember

Blocked playing is usually associated with holding the breath.

Reward players' successes. Some players may not be confident at first. Encourage and reward the scene, small victories as well as large.

It is important that all members of the group are attentive to the work and are permitted to give input at any time should the scene require it. They can:

- Provide offstage sound effects or music for the scene
- Come into a scene should a new character be required
- Come into the scene as inanimate objects, ie furniture, doors, etc
- Finish the scene and/or bring down the lights

Flexibility and instinct

The session itself is an improvisation. While a session plan or outline is vital, yield to offers made by the group. Be prepared to change your plan. The results may surprise you. Have plans B, C and D up your sleeve, ready to put into action. You will be required to identify 'moments' in split seconds as if you are another player in every scene, exercise and game. Boldly take this lead. You need not be loud or obtrusive when sidecoaching. Your ability to read the moment is reflected in the quality of the improvisation.

Be prepared to:

- Assess the dynamic of the group 'in the moment' as they walk in the door/make a circle/find eye contact
- Balance and harmonise the group in the space
- Harness the energy of the group
- Raise the energy of the group
- Change the mood
- Deflect counterproductive energy

TRAINING SESSIONS

The length of training sessions varies. In the primary classroom, ten minutes of improvisation between activities, for example after reading or before lunch, is an excellent introduction. In the secondary classroom, training sessions usually last one or two periods. In a specialised program such as a school camp, training sessions run successfully for two to three hours (even longer in some cases).

The room

If you are training in a school, in the best of all possible worlds you will be in a drama room with carpet, black-out facilities on all the windows, a small lighting rig, a selection of props and costumes, a tape deck, a video recorder, percussive musical instruments, a piano and a lockable cupboard.

Whether you are in a school or not, you need a functional space large enough for each player to lie spread out on the floor and not touch another player. The room should also be some distance from other classrooms so noise levels will not be an issue. While some schools enjoy a functional drama room, many teachers and students work in unsatisfactory, cramped conditions. Make the most of the facilities available to you. Overcome the limitations of the space as quickly and efficiently as possible.

The hall

If this is a huge space, shape it to suit your needs. Clear away all the chairs and use the whole space for warm-ups, group work and noisy activities. Find a section of the room, corner, or stage area with closed curtains when doing scene-work.

A classroom

Conquer the space however you can. Turn the desks around, stack them up. Ask three reliable students to meet you in the room prior to the class to prepare the space before the mob of thirty arrives.

Before the close of the session, put chairs back and assign three different students the task for next week. Remind them twice during the week. Shared responsibility and simple careful planning will overcome the obstacles the space may present.

A theatre

Keep the group tight. Use the auditorium and the stage but do not separate the group into audience and players. Keep them all on the stage or all in the auditorium. This keeps the status of all players even and reduces the pressure of performance.

Outside

Do not teach or perform outside unless players and coach are proficient in outdoor performance and street theatre skills.

General notes for all spaces

Check and clear the space

Whatever the working space, clear it of all breakables. Place all personal belongings at one end of the room away from the main working area. If possible place them off the floor away from running feet. Safety is paramount. Be sure to give all work enough space to expand and become physical.

Gathering

At the beginning of each session bring the group together. Gathering promotes trust and allows for clear communication. It harnesses the energy and establishes control. Name games are useful if group members do not know each other. [See Warm-up games.]

Trust and control

As leader you must have control and group trust within three minutes of beginning the session. Your role is to lead and guide the group. You are the facilitator and catalyst for learning and clear communication.

Warm-ups and ice-breakers — the whole group

Begin each training session with a whole group physical and vocal warm-up. Warm-ups harness the energy and channel the excitement. Choose chasing and tag games that do not eliminate players. [See Warm-up games.] Games which have a winner early in the session split and deflate the energy of the players who have dropped out. Choose a warm-up to match the energy of the group and needs of your session plan.

The circle — the whole group

The circle is a perfect formation for beginning training sessions. A circle:

- Keeps all group members at even status

- Allows the coach to be a part of the group
- Encourages eye contact
- Provides a sense of safety
- Provides an in-built discipline
- Channels energy
- Establishes the ensemble

When players are working in a circle the coach can stand with the group in the circumference of the circle for announcements, group games and exercises. There, you hold the reins. You can see every player, and direct the energy into the centre of the room to the whole group.

Maintaining concentration

Improvisation demands channelled concentration and every measure needs to be taken to achieve results, fun and good theatre. There are many interruptions in a classroom — bells, announcements, door-knocking, message-bringers. Sometimes you may not want to be interrupted during sensitive, demanding work. Appoint a door monitor from time to time, when necessary, to deal with interruptions. Save your concentration for the group.

Pairs

Work in pairs often; it maintains and concentrates the energy and allows players to work on a one-to-one basis. Change partners at regular intervals to provide an opportunity for players to experience working with a variety of people. [See Scene-work next page and Tip p 100.]

Threes

All exercises and games designed for pairs can be modified to work with groups of three, provided the coach makes small adjustments to directions and instructions.

Small groups — four to eight players

Groups this size develop a different type of decision making because players have to accept a variety of opinions as they solve problems. The more people in a group, the more ideas players must listen and yield to.

A group of four to eight players is a good size for training and games practice. Two teams, each of four players, can work together: one team playing, the other team as audience. Both teams have equal shares of playing time with a fast turn-around.

When you break the group into pairs or small groups to complete exercises, work the room yourself, sidecoaching groups, checking that:

- They understand the instructions
- They are not being 'clever'
- They are actively involved in the task

Use this time to observe the group and watch personalities. If there is a group outsider, take this person with you and have them help you as you sidecoach. Ask them to give feedback about what they saw during the exercise. This will give them a function in the room and the process.

Wind-downs, centring and deroling

Always bring the group together at the end of a session, and spend five minutes for players to cool down. This will calm the energy after exuberant activities, allow enough time for their bodies to cool down, derole characterisations and sum up the session's work. This is particularly important if the session has been vigorous and the group is easily excitable. If you are training in a school it is especially important to calm the group before they go to the next class. Other teachers will appreciate relaxed ready-to-work students, rather than rowdy, boisterous students who are too hyped up to concentrate. Use the five minutes for the group to lie on the floor and concentrate on breathing. Sending sounds from different parts of the body and shaking out all over with vigorous sounds is another good way of cooling down, deroling and preparing for the rest of the school day.

SCENE-WORK

Scene-work is a natural progression from warm-up and training games, developing them one step further. Most scene-work takes place with two or more players playing the scenes in front of the rest of the group.

Ease players into working in front of the whole group after they have experienced a degree of success working in pairs and small groups and feel confident with their work without spectators. Keep the scenes short.

Let's say you have completed a whole group warm-up, set your skills task, and the group is divided into smaller groups of pairs, threes or fours, working at their own pace on a specific skill: offering and yielding, naming offers, advancing and extending, etc.

Now is the time to bring the group together for scene-work.

Place scene-work against a clear unencumbered background. Place the class sitting together on the floor or in chairs where they can all see the work, sharing a common focus. Do not put scene-work on a stage while others sit in the auditorium seats; this puts unnecessary pressure on the players and separates the players from the watchers. All class members should be available to move into the scene at any time.

For the most part, the smaller groups will have been made up of friends. Now the coach can make some different choices. Take the opportunity to use scene-work to encourage players who haven't previously chosen to work together to do so now. Select two players who would benefit from the experience. Choose a girl and a boy, or a confident player and a player who lacks confidence. Place this unlikely combination together in the same scene. This could provide a positive opportunity and challenge for both players. Set the same task they were working on in small groups, eg THE PRESENT GAME, SIMULTANEOUS TALKING or YES AND…, but give a new scene, topic or title. This pair now plays the game in front of the whole group. Before they know it, they are playing a scene.

Sidecoach this pair through the scene. This will:

- Clarify the exercise or task for the rest of the group
- Allow you to focus on specific skills in front of the whole group

- Provide a common focus for a brief discussion on the skills explored
- Broaden the awareness of the whole group and their concepts of each other

The most surprising and rewarding improvisations often result from unlikely player combinations.

•

Remember

Scene-work is much more than just game playing.

Choose two different players. Set up a new scene. Play the same exercise or game but add a new challenge — eg gibberish, or no words at all.

Some scenes require intensive coaching. Generally, sit where you are able to see every offer made by the scene players. The coach must trust the rest of the group to focus on scene-work. If you cannot sit at the front for fear of disturbances and interruptions from the back of the room, then move to the back of the group.

Encourage group members who interrupt scene-work to sit at the front where they can see the work or to play in the scenes. Encourage the whole group to concentrate on the scenes. If observers interrupt, stop the scene-work. Find an alternative. Always be in a position where you can switch to plan B. It is no use saying: 'If you people can't take this seriously…'. They hear this in other classes. It stigmatises individuals and reinforces counterproductive behaviour. Place the attention-seekers in the scene. Sidecoach their energy into the work. If interruptions continue, return to working in pairs and small groups.

Change scene-work configurations from end-on to semicircle to in-the-round. [See Program two part D.] If working in a theatre, use the stage as a stage only when players are fully skilled and in preparation for a Theatresports performance.

'Two people up'

This is the phrase David Lander used when coaching Madhat. I still use it. It provides an opportunity for anybody and everybody to take the risk of playing in front of an audience. Two players arrive in the space. The combinations are then unplanned.

After they have jumped to their feet and are ready to play a scene, give them a simple starting idea/offer/place/instruction/activity/task/scene/title. They will have no preconceptions. This creates an exciting element of risk. When the group becomes familiar with this method of working, they will soon be leaping into the space to have a go.

If there is a continual reluctance from the group to work in front of each other, they may not be ready for scene-work. Return to group work or working in pairs or threes.

Feedback

Feedback

Feedback is part of the process. Keep it positive. A comment such as, 'What you could have done there was…' is of no help at all. It is too easy after the event to assess the scene by what should or could have happened or criticise content. As players' skills improve they will develop better stories.

Introducing judging of scene-work for players 15+

Theatresports is judged in three categories: story-line (character development and plot); technique (improvisation skills and risk); and entertainment (comedy and drama).

As players become more confident in their scene-work, appoint three judges after a good scene has been played, each judge to score in one of the above categories. Good scenes aren't necessarily funny. Praise a good scene, drawing attention to the strength of its narrative, character development, clarity of focus, yielding, endowment and transitions. Judging all scenes is unnecessary. Allow success and failure to pass unscored. Then, from time to time, unexpectedly ask different members of the group:

> 'How would you score that scene for story-line from zero to five?'
> 'What about risk and technique? How did they go yielding to the offers and naming the ideas in the scene?'
> 'Was the scene entertaining?'

Soliciting responses to questions such as these gives the onstage players positive feedback. Sum up the total response.

> 'So, we've said four for risk and technique, three for story-line and two for entertainment; four, three, two. That's a good scene.'

Minimise competition. Don't judge the next scene. It will be compared to the last.

When players are proficient, set up judges before the scene begins. Give each judge one of the three specific categories. Then have the judges come up and play a scene. Rotate this judging role constantly.

•

Beware

Do not appoint a hanging judge. It is not appropriate to have a ruthless judge at this point in the process.

The coach in the scene

I always participate in at least one exercise in every three hour class, just for 10 to 20 seconds. I perform alone and with other players. My reasoning is that if I expect players to take a risk, I will take it too. It evens the status between the players and me, and allows me to further assess the skills of individual players and focus the group energy. Players are always curious to see how the coach performs. Sometimes my performing can clarify an instruction. I sometimes preface the performing with, 'I'm terrified'. Then we all laugh.

Some scenes that are particularly good for the coach to play are: THE PRESENT GAME, SPEAKING IN GIBBERISH, SONG, MASTER/SERVANT GAME, SPITFIRE, ADVANCING AND EXTENDING physical and verbal.

I play chasing games. They warm me up! You may have other favourites. If you feel confident to play, keep your performance limited to about 20 seconds for every three hours of teaching. If you do not succeed, laugh. If you don't feel confident there is no pressure to play. However, a good coach is usually a good player.

Mark Ferguson, an actor and a player coach in Australia and New Zealand, enters scenes as an extra player for short moments to advance the scene. He is always in character, brings on news that develops the scene, then leaves. He becomes a facilitator in the scene. If this works for you, make it short, sharp, effective, then get out!

Do not play to win student approval or show what a good improvisor you are. Play to inform yourself and learn more about the skill levels of the group or to substantiate content. For the most part, stay out of the scenes and sidecoach towards what the scene needs.

Sidecoach: 'They need a doctor/mother/customer.'
'Someone in to save them.'

Your personal coaching style will develop. Choose the method with which you feel most comfortable.

Developing and sustaining belief

Staying in the scene 'Get lost, Keith!'

In the early days of training, some players consistently look out of the scene to the coach during skills training. The terrified player, unused to being given permission to play and succeed alone without the teacher, feels lost, so checks your response to monitor their own success. This is usually a result of lack of confidence and fear. Players who do this are breaking their belief in the scene.

During a class at Calgary University, Canada, Keith Johnstone was watching his students play a scene. A player glanced out and the following took place:

Keith: 'Say — "Get lost, Keith".'
Player: 'Pardon me?' (Canadians are very polite.)
Keith: 'I said, say — "Get lost, Keith".'
Player: 'Get lost, Keith.'

The player looked embarrassed, shocked, and continued the scene. After ten seconds or so he glanced at Keith again.

Keith: 'Say — "Get lost, Keith".'

This continued until the player realised that he was interrupting his own work by continually looking out the front. After four times, the player spontaneously yelled, 'Get lost, Keith!' and never looked out again.

The need for teacher approval is a problem. It does not facilitate 'creative independence', but its existence is not surprising given that most of our education is based on getting it right and keeping in the teacher's good books.

My suggestion is that you:
Sidecoach: 'Stay in the scene.'

Releasing players from the need to seek teacher approval frees them from seeking high point scores from the judges and from the desire to please and win.

Stopping a scene

Generally, we prefer to allow a scene to run its natural course. However, you will need to stop scenes if:

- Players become unsafe in any way
- There are indications of possible physical violence [see Dealing with physical violence at the end of this chapter]
- A player's emotional well-being is threatened
- Sidecoaching no longer helps develop the scene. This usually occurs when:
  - the scene has run dry of ideas
  - dropped offers are falling out of the scene like water overflowing a sink [See Program one – Dropped offers]
  - continual blocking occurs regardless of sidecoaching
  - subject matter or content is inappropriate
  - players don't have the skills to find scene endings

•

Tip

Stopping a scene just past its peak protects players from becoming disheartened — they are left with a sense of achievement rather than a sense of failure.

If scenes fall apart, tell the players:

- 'Good work! Skills are coming along.' Take this opportunity to name the skill that is developing, and also name the skill that needs further development.
- 'That was the beginning of a good scene. Good naming of offers. Now we need to do an extending and advancing exercise.'

When scenes slump, remind players that it is not important that they cannot 'do' it yet, as long as they understand the objective of the exercise and are clear about the principles and guidelines of the process.

When you stop a scene:
Sidecoach: 'Good! Two more people up!'

Keep the scenes short. Leave the analysis to the feedback part of the session.

•

Good idea

If a scene has worked and is brilliant, do not follow it with another similar scene as it will rarely live up to the expectations set by the previous scene in the same session.

Finishing a scene

As storytelling skills develop, encourage players to follow their instinct and recognise the natural endings of their scenes. If a scene has dragged on without an ending and you finished it for them, ask the players, 'When was the natural ending for that scene?' For the most part they will name the exact spot. Laugh and say, 'See — you knew when to end the scene'.

Sidecoach: 'Find an ending to the scene!'

If a scene is slow to round off, count down from ten, indicating that players have ten seconds to finish the scene.

•

Global

Do not hold players to the exact time of 10 seconds until they have the skills to complete a scene or end a game in 10 seconds. Vary the timing of your count-down according to the needs of particular players and scenes.

Encourage players to find their own scene endings.

Bringing down the lights

The recognised method of ending scenes is to 'bring down the lights' or 'pull down the lights'. Signalling by holding both hands up in the air and quickly lowering them is the clearest, simplest way to indicate lights down and end a scene. Initially, the coach 'brings down the lights'. As the narrative draws to a close:

Sidecoach: (Very loudly, signalling with your arms raised to the ceiling and dropping them to your side as you call) 'A...a...a...and — lights down!'

Aim for the players to recognise their own scene endings and indicate bringing down the lights themselves.

When playing Theatresports on a stage, the signal for 'lights down' is directed to the lighting operator. Be careful that this signal is not confused with part of the action of a scene. One night at Belvoir Street Theatre three players were saluting Mecca in a scene which was confused with 'lights down'. Players must be clear about this signal, and in performance the timekeeper should support it with a whistle. In a classroom, it is not necessary to turn off the lights. However, if a dimmer board is available, use it.

At first, players may be reluctant to finish scenes. In their excitement, players want to stay in the scene and on the stage. Reward teams and players who end scenes. In the excitement of playing Theatresports, especially in front of an audience, it is often difficult when playing a scene to know when to end it. An offstage team member can watch for a scene ending and perform the valuable function of indicating lights down for the team. Scene endings are sometimes difficult to recognise when all team members are on stage.

In Edmonton, Canada, I saw a member from one team leap out and finish the scene for another team by indicating lights down to the bio box (where the lighting operator sits). It was an example of a selfless player. Obviously the final score was less important than the successful finishing of a scene.

Time limits

Time limits should not be applied to the work during initial skill building or scene-work in the early days of training, when scenes dictate their own length or are being stopped by the coach. Introduce 'bringing down the lights' before you introduce time limits.

Time limits for each game are merely suggested structures for performance and competition playing. They are relevant only if you are using them for a specific purpose, such as preparing for or playing in a tournament, or a Theatresports demonstration in which teams play scenes within time frames.

Introduce time limits slowly. Tell the group, 'I'm going to time this at two minutes and give you a ten second call at the end'. [See below.] Cheat the times at first. It is preferable for the group to achieve a satisfactory scene and exceed the time limit by four seconds than to be stopped by a whistle just before completion.

A good timekeeper will do this even in performance. I have heard audiences groan with disappointment when teams have just missed out on achieving a death in a DEATH IN A MINUTE or MURDER ENDOWMENTS, or rhyming the last couplet in a POEM or SONG by being interrupted by an intrusive whistle. If left for two or three seconds, the team would have achieved success. In a good Theatresports production, the whistle is unobtrusive to audience and players. It becomes part of the music and the rhythm of the entertainment.

Working to time limits can be a blessing in disguise. Many Australian and New Zealand Theatresports players work in professional radio and television. Having the skills to meet the demands of time limits supports voice-over work, commercials, interviewing and reporting work, writing, producing and acting.

When used with care and for a specific purpose, time limits can provide a skill and accuracy that keeps the work succinct and clear. It is also important to work occasionally without the panic and pressure they create, developing longer scenes.

Halfway calls and the ten second bell

You may also wish to give a halfway call. This indicates that the scene has reached its middle, and encourages players to look for a scene resolution and find an ending. Teams may ask for 'halfway' to be called by the coach in scene-work or the timekeeper in performance.

The ten second bell clearly reminds teams that they have ten seconds to finish the scene. In training the coach calls 'ten seconds'. In performance the timekeeper rings the bell.

Content

You cannot control the content of improvisation. When we improvise, anything is likely to arise. However, the coach can contribute to the content by offering titles for scenes and starting places for ideas that guide players towards specific subject matter and issues.

Sometimes, unexpectedly, scene content arises that shocks the coach and the players, especially when personal thoughts and incidents from players' lives are revealed. On these occasions group trust and understanding will be a valuable asset. A player's spontaneous reaction to a given suggestion must be respected.

By its very nature, improvisation is stream of consciousness. If, for example, a player's mother is in the audience, a mother is likely to be played out or spoken about.

Similarly, swearing and particular words can appear unexpectedly. It is important for a coach to understand these processes. [Read the chapter, 'Spontaneity/Obscenity', in Keith Johnstone's *Improvisation and the Theatre*.]

When these incidents arise, use your discretion. If 'the word' was a slip of the tongue and not a deliberate ploy to sabotage the scene or test the coach, ignore it and allow the scene to continue. Sidecoach players and steer the scene towards more valuable content if necessary.

When playing in front of an audience fear can provoke the 'four letter word' syndrome. Some warm-up exercises allow teams to privately exorcise words and phrases that may not be appropriate on stage. Players can warm up with word games such as word association, ONE-WORD-AT-A-TIME STORY, POEM, SONG. This clears the subject matter that could float through a scene. If they say the word before they go on stage, they are less likely to say it while they are on stage.

Noise levels

This work, by its very nature, is energetic and lively. Be prepared for laughter, shouting, singing and the enthusiastic exuberance that raw energy creates.

Over a period of time, establish a series of training habits which will build into a ritual. The group will learn the signs and signals that indicate your need to recapture their attention. State this clearly at the beginning of your relationship with them. Building a consistent ritual is very important.

You must have ultimate control of the space for their safety and your sanity — and preferably without having to scream above the group. A noisy teacher is a noisy classroom!

You may choose to walk to each group in the room and give them a time frame in which to finish. Or you may choose to use a signal. Suggested signals to recapture their attention are:

- A whistle or drum beat
- Playing chords on a piano
- Flashing lights on and off

The lights are probably the easiest and most efficient attention-seeker as, however noisy they have become, players will see the lights and come to a halt.

Props and costumes

When used to serve characterisation and the scene, props and costumes are a valuable asset for improvisation and Theatresports performances. However, most Theatresports companies choose to use them selectively.

Don't introduce props or costumes until players are capable of completing scenes without them. Introduced too early, they can create an overload of offers. When overused they can block lateral thinking and spontaneity, as players reach for the same props to repeat gags. This creates habits and predictability.

Players sometimes spend too much time head down and tail up in the props box selecting their favourite wig. Their attention would be better spent supporting their onstage team-mate. This is a signal for the coach. Players habitually searching for

Melbourne players make use of a prop — Frank Wood (left) and Julian Branagan

props may be an indication that they are putting their funny clever ideas first rather than serving those on stage, or are desperately seeking an idea through a prop. If this occurs:

Sidecoach: 'Yield to the focus on stage.'

However, all this aside, I have seen some extraordinary lateral use of props in scenes. I remember one night in Calgary, Canada, when an aardvark appeared before our eyes, courtesy of a cloak and a piece of tubing. The player was fulfilling the offer in the scene, and the audience went wild.

Do not make a props box available all the time. Allow it to come and go. Change the props from time to time.

A props box, clothes rack and hat-stand should contain only those items you would give as toys to a child under three years: soft toys; soft, flexible tubing; dolls; cloaks; textured pieces of material that can be donned in one big sweeping motion; dressing gowns; wigs (limit these); a variety of hats, eg police and army hats, old ladies' hats, chef's hat, stetson, and wide-brimmed hats for status hat transition games [see Program five – Rules for hat games]; a fan; feather; feather boa; handbag and the like.

•

Beware

Never put glass or breakables in a prop box. An eye or a tooth is irreplaceable and too easily lost.

Developing a common vocabulary

There is nothing secretive about this work. There are no tricks. It is a good idea to coach players to use the language and terms of improvisation and Theatresports. Developing a shared vocabulary allows the coach and the players to discuss the work and the scenes with objectivity, and provides criteria for assessment.

All sports have an agreed vocabulary. In tennis we have a 'fault'. In Theatresports we have 'block' or 'wimp'. [See Basic terms and skills.]

Theatresports terms hold worldwide. Swedish and Danish teams, for example, play a slightly different format and variations of the games, but scenes are judged by the same criteria and the same vocabulary is used.

Build the vocabulary. Write it on the blackboard or on butchers' paper. Keep it visible in the training room.

Dealing with physical violence

Watch for players who resort to pushing and shoving in scene-work. Sidecoach these players to yield to the offer by dropping status. This will advance the scene. Sidecoach players away from physical aggression by calling, 'Go to slow motion!' This will tame the physical aggression and allow you to clarify the focus. Then sidecoach towards an offer that will 'break the routine' and advance the scene.

Physical aggression is usually a sign of blocking and controlling the ideas in the scene. The fear of accepting another person's ideas or dropping status is extremely confronting for some players who think that yielding is a sign of weakness. Sidecoach these players towards an alternative means of communication. Although conflict is the basis of drama and comedy, Theatresports should not create unnecessary aggression. While characters may disagree within the scene, players need to agree on the offers rather than fight about them.

In Edmonton, Canada, I watched a young Theatresports company come to terms with the amount of physical violence and number of dangerous weapons that continued to surface in their scenes and games. As a part of their warm-up prior to Theatresports performances, the players mimed and used as many different dangerous weapons as they could think of. They named them, made sound effects for them and piled them at the front of the stage in a huge invisible mountain.

Players mimed chainsaws, knives, machine-guns, pistols, hand grenades — all manner of weapons. The players instigated this as a method of content control. It was their idea, not the idea of their teacher/director. Players agreed to leave the weapons on the pile rather than use them in their scenes. Some scenes warrant weapons, but if players often resort to violence or use it as a way of wimping out of the improvisation or gaining cheap laughs and gags, try this method. Rid their work of these items and encourage them to make different choices.

The burden of comedy

When we first improvise, the results are usually comic. Some improvisors tire of being funny. They want to be serious; to be released from the burden of comedy. Most improvisors seek new challenges. They want to explore the subtleties of character, dramatic tension and conflict. Do not be afraid to explore comedy and drama. One company in Canada tried 'Serious Theatresports'. The players loved it. They played it in the training room to develop dramatic skills to play an occasional serious scene on stage.

Saving

Sidecoach towards 'saving' when coaching a scene. If a scene needs another player or the routine needs breaking or the scene needs an advance:

Sidecoach: 'Someone save them.'

Continue to call 'Save him/her' until a player comes to the rescue. It is the coach's task to sound this alarm during the scene rather than stopping the scene and discussing what should or could have happened. It is more beneficial to 'save' the scene in the moment while it is taking place than to talk afterwards about what could have occurred.

Improvisation and acting

Improvisation is an important element of actor training. Improvisation keeps the actor alert and open to new responses and ideas. Many young acting students deny their initial response to text. They fear ideas that come too quickly. They believe them too simple or obvious. Improvisation helps actors to trust their instinctive responses. It also enriches their imaging. When improvisation is used to explore a text, it is an important actor's tool.

Improvisation and writing

Improvisation has been criticised for seeming to make writers redundant. This is not so. Traditionally, the writer is the first part of the play production process. When we improvise, all the players become storytellers. The skills of building and telling a story are inherent in the scene-building and game-playing. The process taps the writer in us all. The result is that many improvisors find the process inspires them to write.

Most of the Theatresports games can be adapted to become writing games. Individual writers and teams of writers find playing the Theatresports games opens writing channels. The process of 'offer and yield' encourages a flow of ideas and releases writers from writer's block. When teams of television and script writers improvise together, they develop new ways of yielding to, and advancing and extending, each other's ideas. Writers who write alone find improvising in teams enables them to accept the flow of their ideas and encourages them to trust their intuition.

Risks and safety

Individuals begin to take risks when the coach provides a feeling of safety within a group and the working space. When players feel safe, they are less inclined to fear failure.

Teams

Forming a regular set team

Theatresports is a team sport. Better than watching a good team is playing in one. To play with other people and have a good time is undoubtedly the best part of the Theatresports experience. But forming a set team is not always as easy as it seems, nor is it always necessary or helpful. Knowing when to form teams and when to play without set teams is an important part of training.

It takes time before players are ready to form teams. Do not hurry the process of finding a regular team. It is more beneficial for beginner players to learn the skills of improvising and enjoy the games working with a variety of players than to play with a specific team. It is a good idea for coaches to keep the training sessions flexible so players can experience playing with all the members in the group. Friends, family and spouses are not always the best choices for fellow team members. Sometimes players enjoy improvising with people they would otherwise have never considered as team-mates.

When to play Theatresports

When players have a solid working understanding of the foundations skills covered in all the programs, are proficient in scene-building, have played all 27 classic Theatresports games and can find scene endings for the majority of their scenes and games, they could be ready to form teams and play a classroom Theatresports competition. I do not recommend team competition for players under 13 years. If, however, players are over 13 years and fulfil the above criteria, they could be ready to form teams and play a friendly Theatresports classroom competition. If players are over 15 years and extremely skilled, they may be ready to form teams and play a Theatresports performance for an audience other than classmates. [See Competitions and tournaments – Organising a school performance.]

Forming school teams

Don't let TEAM become that Theatresports four letter word. When too much emphasis is placed on forming teams, particularly with players under 18 years, sometimes the joy of improvising suffers. Don't let team forming cause competitive rifts. It can divide friendships and build the type of negativity not in keeping with the spirit of the drama classroom — learning, having fun and good communication. Remember the drama class operates as one whole team. Under no circumstances force players to pick and choose their team-mates where one or two players could be placed in a position of rejection. Generally, keep players rotating in a variety of combinations for classroom improvisation, forming teams only when appropriate. The 'two people up' coaching strategy [see Process – Scene-work] supports spontaneous player rotation.

By the same token, use your discretion as a coach. Sometimes player combinations just click. When players share the same sense of humour and idea of theatre (or whatever it is that happens when players click), they usually want to continue playing in the same combination. Before they know it, they have formed a team. Good teamwork builds friendships and develops trust through good sportspersonship. If players enjoy playing together and are consistently having a good time, continuing to learn together and improvising, encourage this development. Under these circumstances it would be foolish to deny players the team experience. If you think specific players would benefit from playing as a regular team, keep them working as a team for skills-building and scene-work. Remember, the remainder of the group does not have to be divided into teams; keep rotating the majority of players, each working at their individual level, continuing to benefit from playing with a variety of other players.

Number of players

While there is no set ruling on the number of players permitted to form teams, the majority of Down Under teams have a maximum of four players. North American teams have as many as five players. Some professional Theatresports teams comprise two or three players. Different team sizes introduce different elements of teamwork and skills, and the function of each team member adjusts accordingly. I highly recommend four player teams for all players under 18 years and for all players forming a first team in the first two years of adult training. Teams with fewer than four players require individual players of considerable ability and experience. Think carefully before forming or playing in teams with less than four players.

Four player teams

A four player team is the best combination to gain the most from teamwork and to play most of the games. This is a good number to sustain the narrative, encourage player support and play the full range of games, many of which are designed for four players.

Four player teams allow for easy player deployment, particularly in the split focus games such as SPACE JUMP, SLOW MOTION COMMENTARY, SUBTITLES, VOICES OFF. [See Program two.] By the same token, not all the games and scenes require all four players to be on stage at the same time. Many scenes require only two players.

Sometimes it is difficult for players in four player teams to stay off stage. When all the players are on stage they tend to overload scenes with too much information. Under these circumstances four player teams are advised to play the specific games and scene set-ups that require all four players so that all their players share the stage time.

Three player teams

Three player teams require all players to understand the full workings of all the games. A high degree of skill is required by the individual players to adjust all games and scene-work to a three player combination. All players must be prepared to save every scene and every other player at all times. Players must listen carefully and be particularly mindful of when to enter a scene and when to leave. They may be required to enter the same scene at different times as more than one character or with new information. Do not attempt three player teams until all players are solid in their narrative skills and have been playing well and often for at least two years in four player teams.

Two player teams

While it is in some ways easier to communicate well with only one other player, good two player teams are rare. It takes exceptional skill and talent to play all the games and challenges with only two players. Players must have a thorough working knowledge of improvisation and enjoy improvising with the other player.

Two player teams need to communicate with each other as improvisors. They plan strategies to complete the tasks ahead of them. They co-opt audience members, players from other teams and all manner of fancy work to play games and scenes that require more than two characters. Two player teamwork has a high degree of difficulty and is reserved for exceptional players under exceptional circumstances.

Some players who have ventured the doubles partnership include: Geoff Kelso and Phil Thompson — Western Australian Champions; Marko Mustac and Michael Gregory — *Lonely Guys* and *Three Guys*, who charmed the Sydney audience and the judges in consecutive years as Cranston Champions; and Sydney's Murray Fahey and Ewan Campbell, who have given the two person team a good run in *Two Sandwiches Short of a Picnic*, Cranston Cup winners 1992 and 1993. Brisbane and Sydney Theatresports both enjoy seasons of mixed doubles playing.

As players dare more and their skills refine, professional two player teams could well become a favourite.

One player teams

On the rarest occasions, very skilled professional players have formed one player teams. They do not usually play alone for the whole performance but only for selected games and scenes. During a Theatresports Festival of Sydney performance, Berynn Schwerdt formed a one player team and won the hearts of the audience for bravery. I recommend it for veteran players only.

Teamwork

Teamwork is the basis of improvising with other people. How we communicate with other players, read their signals and dare one another in the twinkle of an eye creates the magic, excitement and terror that makes playing in a team a wonderful experience.

What makes a good team is difficult to define and often intangible. Knowing your function in the team sets the team in motion. The team is working well when players are listening to and being affected by each other, sharing the responsibility for the scenes, communicating, enjoying themselves, producing quality work and taking risks.

Good teamwork results when all team players are skilled and prepared to play all and any of the following functions at any time. Good teams change these roles every scene and are not predictable.

Player 1

In a four player team, player one usually sets up the narrative, making clear offers that give a solid beginning. They are wise to create a sense of location. They either play the main protagonist or set the scene for the main protagonist. They know when to leave the stage and when to re-enter.

Player 2

Player two overaccepts everything and extends or advances the ideas set up by player one. They may be the main protagonist. They usually have a definite status relationship with player one. They are a yielder.

Player 3

Player three is usually the extender and advancer. This is where team players are sorted from the non-team players. Good third players are rare. They are players who do selfless things such as enter a four minute scene at the three minute twenty mark, say two lines which extend the current idea, advance the plot and then leave or die, giving the other two players time to wrap up the story and complete the relationships they have created. Player three does the support work and keeps the narrative moving. Sometimes player three simply watches a scene and if not required does not come on: they wait for the scene ending and bring down the lights.

Player 4

This player takes incredible risks. They create the scene magic and consolidate and support the style and tone of the scene. In a long scene they usually enter and leave the scene a number of times playing a variety of characters. If they make wild and wacky choices they do not steal the scene but boost its energy, creating scene conflict and resolution, developing the scene content.

The blocker from hell

Whether in an adult or school team, one day you could be in a team with a blocker from hell. Some players take longer to let go of blocking. These players are scared. It is possible to change their playing habits with positive sidecoaching and patience.

•

Beware

There are Dr Jeckyll players who yield in training and railroad on stage.

Hoggers

Some players stay on stage too long or talk too much. They are afraid to share the scene or to lose control of it. Some desperate-to-come-on-stage players enter a scene too close to the end or even after the ten second bell. They introduce irrelevant information or new ideas too late in the plot. If a player needs to be told when to leave the stage, tell them so, or the team will have trouble working. It is part of team talk.

Good players know:

- When to come on
- How long to stay
- When to speak and for how long
- When to listen
- When to shut up
- And when to leave

The Moose speaks

'You know how good you are by the number of people who want to play with you.'

TEAM COMBINATIONS

Theatresports is one of the few sports where women and men play exactly the same rules in the same competition with and against each other. This diversity is exciting and part of the valuable social function Theatresports plays in education and society. Many teams include players of both sexes, while others are single-sex teams. There are no restrictions on how teams are comprised. There is something to be said for all the following combinations. Each has its own personality and provides exciting learning opportunities.

All men

All-male teams provide an opportunity for men to play all the characters, including the women. This can be educational and extremely entertaining. There have been some memorable all-male teams: Sydney's first all-male team *Pack of Men*, champions *Writers' Bloc*, and *Four Sensitive Guys*; Adelaide's *Get Her*; Christchurch's *Handy Andies, Esther Williams* and *Spontaneous Combustion.*

Robert McFarlane

Esther Williams — (left to right) Matthew Gould, Ross Gumbley, Simon Peacock, Patrick Duffy

All women

All-female teams provide an opportunity for women to play a variety of status positions and to break the pattern of stereotyped choices they often make when playing in a mixed sex team. [See Program five part D – Status, sexism and the politics of gender.]

The all-women teams have certainly had their triumphs. The following will long be remembered: *Little Gloria Happy At Last* — Laurel McGowan's ABC Theatresports television team, who played in black evening gowns and entered with champagne glasses; *Natural Normans* — Melbourne's all star women's comedy team; *Big Bad Mommas* — a team of mums who became local heroines in Albany; *Horrid Girlie Swats*, Mackay's 1989 Champions; Sydney's *Redfern Mob* with 'London, New York, Paris, Redfern' on their T-shirts; *The Indestructibles* from Sydney University, who won the hearts of the Belvoir Street Theatre audience in 1988; *The J Curves*; and many more. Some of these women performed when up to eight months pregnant.

Three and one

In professional Theatresports, teams of three men and one woman have been a more common combination than teams of three women and one man. The three men/one woman combination provides an opportunity for a strong female player to play all the female roles. It also allows the female to challenge three men for stage time. Finding the function of four players in this combination can be an exciting learning experience for the males and the female. Teams who found unique teamwork in this combination include champions: Sydney's *The Funky Chickens*, *Once In a Lifetime*, and *Utter Codswallop*; Brisbane's *Carnival Knowledge*; Melbourne's *Gutless Wonders* and *Koyann And Squatzi*; Auckland's *The Von Trapp Family*; and Perth's *Zerobusters*.

Two and two

Many of the first Down Under teams were comprised of two men and two women players. The three teams to compete in the first Australian national final enjoyed the balance of this combination. It remains a popular choice for players experiencing team playing for the first time because it allows for ease of player deployment and fielding, particularly in split focus games, where the girls can provide the arms or the voices for the girls and the boys for the boys. It provides an opportunity for mixed sex playing when two male friends can team up with two female friends. It also encourages a range of characters in narrative scene-work by giving the male and

Robert McFarlane

Australian National Champions 1987 — *Koyann And Squatzi* —
with the Peter Cook Perpetual Cup. Legend has it that this trophy ,
found by an overzealous cleaner the morning after, was meticulously scrubbed.
(left to right) Russell Fletcher, John Thompson, Christine Lucas, Michael Blaire

female players the opportunity to be the main protagonist and to be supported by players of both sexes. I highly recommend it for new players.

Scratch teams

Traditionally these were formed literally minutes before a performance. Players decided to draw names from a hat and play together just for fun or because there was a team vacancy. Generally speaking, scratch teams work best when skilled players are caught off guard and do not have too much time to think about the playing but simply have a good time. Sometimes scratch teams are formed during international competitions to give players from different countries an opportunity to play together.

TRAINING RITUALS

Not all teams click spontaneously. Even after playing well together most teams need to work to retain the magic. In preparation for a performance, some teams simply like to sit and talk about what they might like to play. However, most players feel more comfortable if their team warms up and trains regularly together to clarify skills and understand the games, as well as discussing their strengths and weaknesses.

Each team builds its own warm-up and training ritual. Some confess to spending most of their energy and time deciding what they will wear and how they will stage their entrance. While it is good to look like a team and have a team theme, skills training and scene playing with fellow team members is an important part of team preparation.

Remember

You cannot practise the games or the content, but you can work on skills.

The following is a sample training session of approximately two and a half hours. For players who do not have such large blocks of time, it may be preferable to divide the session into two 80 minute sessions per week.

Use it as a menu and select skills appropriate to training needs and according to the length of the training session.

Tips for team training — coaching yourselves 15+ years

All team members can enjoy planning a training session. If possible, work in a clear space such as a garage, local hall or warehouse. If these are not available it is possible to achieve good results in the loungeroom. Clear the space, pull out the phone, put away the breakables, coffee, food and cigarettes. Set a time frame. While some great team combinations have occurred with players who meet only when they play, on the whole the majority of teams will work better if they train. Train together rather than talk about it.

Build a training ritual. At the commencement of each session, play the same warm-up game — one which you all love. This will harness group energy and prepare all players for the training session. Then proceed to a physical and vocal warm-up and scene-work before playing Theatresports performance games.

Some teams invite a skilled coach to work with them during a training session. This is a good idea, as it provides the team with an outside eye and gives all team members the opportunity of concentrating on playing during the session. Some teams nominate one of the team as coach for a particular training session. These teams must give their team-mate the permission to plan the training session and to coach them during the session, and then give him or her feedback after the session.

If your team is sharing the responsibility of coaching, plan your sessions together. Have at least one player sitting out observing and sidecoaching for each scene or game. It is more beneficial to have one team member sidecoaching and finishing scenes with only two or three players in each scene than four players in every scene. The objective eye of the player/coach can be very helpful.

•

Beware

Sidecoaching is only helpful if the person sidecoaching understands the process and has the skills to do so. Do not appoint a team-mate as sidecoach unless the decision to do so is agreed by the whole team. If sharing the coaching rotate the role of the coach during the session.

Too much talking during the training session will stop the process and diffuse the energy. It is better to leave all feedback discussion or assessment of the work to the end of the session and use training time for improvising.

Team training session outline — for players 15+ years

1. **Vocal warm-up** (15 minutes)
- Spine drops
- Body alignment
- Breath
- Relax jaw, tongue, hard and soft palates, face, etc
- Humming
- Vowels and consonants

[See Appendix C – Suggested reading for voice texts]

2. **Warm-up game/s** (5 minutes)
- WHERE DO YOU COME FROM?
- YES LET'S

3. **Physical warm-up** (10 minutes)
- Making shapes
- KNIFE AND FORK
- MARKO'S GAME

4. Skills

Offer and yield (15 minutes)
- Word association
- SHARED STORY
- ONE-WORD-AT-A-TIME
- Group singing

Overacceptance (15 minutes)
- THE PRESENT GAME (gibberish and mime)
- NO-BLOCKING SCENES x 4
- MASTER/SERVANT x 2

Focus (15 minutes)
- THANK YOU
- Two person STATUES
- WHAT ARE YOU DOING?

5. Scenes and games (60 minutes)
- FREEZE TAG
- VOICES OFF
- ENDOWMENTS
- SPICS 'N' SPECKS
- HE SAID/SHE SAID
- TYPEWRITER
- Group SONG (with instruments — optional)
- OPERA

Feedback/discussion (20 minutes)
Close
Eat together (optional)

Notes and comments

Notes and comments are beneficial if they are skills related. Beware of making personal comments, which can be hurtful to players and destructive to the team.

Good feedback includes praise as well as sharing notes on areas that may require improvement. Positive reinforcement deepens team trust and enjoyment.

When teams are experiencing communication blocks in the training room and/or in performance, players need to air their grievances. The most common gripes are:

- General unreliability
- Lateness to training
- Continual blocking of offers
- Continual gagging
- Continual sexist responses
- Refusal to stay off stage (hogging)
- Lack of sensitivity to other people's offers

- Holding back — wimping
- Taking it all too seriously

Failure to deal with any of the above will eventually result in bad play on stage.

•

Remember

Do not stay in a team if you are not happy or the team is not functioning well. If you are not enjoying yourself at least 90 per cent of the time, something is wrong. Players should never feel trapped in a team. Playing is a joyous experience. Find players with whom you can have fun.

Check

General notes for teams in scene-work

- Where are you? Find the scene location.
- The first offer establishes the style and focus of the scene. Know what it is and yield.
- Overaccept the current offer before introducing your own.
- Extend the current idea. Follow its progression rather than bridging to the end with prefixed ideas.
- Reach the event in the scene.
- Deal with the repercussions.
- Take your time. Beware of giving too many offers too fast.
- Answer the obvious questions the audience wants to know. Where are you? Who are you? What are you doing?
- When in doubt place the focus of the scene at the front facing the audience.
- If you cannot see the offers and the focus, move to a place where you can.
- Physicalise an idea rather than talk about it.
- Endow each other.
- Play a variety of status positions.
- Have an opinion in the scene.
- Field players carefully. Avoid unnecessary players in the scene. Most scenes need only two players.
- Remember, slow motion means S-L-O-W M-O-T-I-O-N.
- Use props, but think laterally about their use. Avoid using too many and spending time searching for props instead of listening to the onstage offers. When props overload a scene they derail the story and scene issues.
- Avoid too much talking. If you have been speaking for more than five seconds at any one time, you have probably been talking too long.
- Use the space.
- Make transitions.
- Recapitulate. Reintroduce earlier material from the narrative to tie up the loose ends. (The audience loves this.)
- Think of ways to help your colleagues — not ways to shine.
- Find scene endings.
- Like the audience.
- Take your bow after the judges score. Be gracious and charming. The audience will love you for it.

Robert McFarlane

The 1987 Perth champions — *Zerobusters* (left to right) Paul Barker, Angela Sanderson-Green, Eugenio Carroll, Michael Sanderson-Green — and compere Jon Firman

The Moose speaks

'If you don't want to train, find three other players who feel the same.'

Competitions and tournaments

Commandment

When thy faith is low, thy spirit weak, thy good fortune strained and thy team losing, be comforted and smile, because it just doesn't matter.

Theatresports competitions and tournaments provide an opportunity for impromaniacs to get together, exchange ideas, stretch their performance muscles and have fun. Competitions are held by international, national, community, university and school leagues.

International tournaments bring together the champion teams from different countries. These are usually professional adult players called 'vets' (veterans).

A national tournament pits the best team from each state, territory or province against the others to determine the national champion team.

A competition between local townsfolk — usually held at an annual community theatre event or festival — brings community players (adults and children) together for social playing.

A friendly inter-school get-together provides the opportunity for students to meet each other and broaden their theatrical horizons.

Whatever the reason, careful planning and staging of a Theatresports tournament is essential. Tournaments should be joyous celebrations that foster friendship and communication, rather than stressful events that overemphasise the competitive element. [See Teams – When to play Theatresports.]

We live in a competitive society. Inherent in competition is the desire to win. Winning is exhilarating and a natural part of competitive sport. When playing Theatresports it is most important, however, to keep the competitive element in perspective, especially when working with young players.

The competitive sporting element of Theatresports evolved as a training tool. Keith Johnstone introduced the concept of taking points off players for blocking or inaudibility. As a result he found that suddenly players yielded and could be heard. Thus judging originated as a means of enhancing performance. Judging then developed as a theatrical device to protect players. Judges save players by gonging them off stage before they die on stage. The result is that the audience sides with the players against the judges, booing the judges rather than the onstage players.

•

Beware

The concept of the hanging judge, as described in Origins, rituals and traditions, is a theatrical device for adult performances and should not be included in school Theatresports performances.

Tournament torture

There is no denying the sense of achievement and inner glow that comes from having played well with your team. Sometimes a team just clicks. Everything they do is perfect. They leap around the stage, rhyme as if they were Shakespeare, they even sing in harmony. As if by telepathy the team members read each other's offers. Every idea they have turns to gold.

Then they travel off to another school, another state or even another country to play a competition. Boy, are they ever going to show this bunch how to improvise! But when they run out on to an unfamiliar stage in front of a new audience, everything feels different. The audience clap and cheer but the lights are not the same. They play their first scene and that familiar team brilliance isn't there. One member of the team doesn't hear the first offer. The story doesn't develop. At interval the team is tense and they fear returning to the stage. The other teams seem happy and relaxed. Yes, good old tournament torture can hit when you least expect it. It saps you of your spontaneity and robs you of your wit.

Even professional and veteran players experience tournament torture, especially when they are not playing on home turf. The first tournament I played was in Vancouver. As Australia's champion improvisors we were shocked to find ourselves in a very different Theatresports culture, with open challenges, ideas solicited from the audience, no time limits, no whistles or bells to begin and end scenes; everything was different. The home team usually has the advantage. It can take years of practice and craft to improvise well when playing away.

Organising a school performance

It is important that all players are proficient and practised in the agreed principles and skills of improvisation before they embark on a competitive Theatresports performance in front of an audience. Footballers cannot kick goals before they can bounce, pass and kick the ball with some accuracy. Players will only be disheartened and frustrated if they don't have the necessary foundation skills to enable them to improvise before playing Theatresports in front of an audience. Begin with classroom and intra-school matches before embarking on an inter-school competition. I advise that players younger than 15 years, or Year 10, should not compete against students from another school in front of an audience. Do not rush students into competitive playing.

As teachers we need to be aware of the excitement and frenzy that often accompanies competitive improvisation. We must be careful not to place players under further pressure by wanting them to win. Sometimes, if our team doesn't win, we think we have failed as teachers. Remember — it just doesn't matter! What does matter is that players enjoy improvising. [See Teams – When to play Theatresports.]

There are ways of structuring a Theatresports event that reduce the competitive element. It is possible to make every team a winner by, for example, awarding a trophy to each team emphasising their strengths.

Competition licensing

It is illegal to hold a Theatresports competition without a licence. For information regarding competitions and tournaments, or to obtain a licence, contact the Theatresports licensor in your state, territory or province. [See Appendix A – Contact list.] Licences are available for anything from whole seasons of shows to single events, and are granted to groups ranging from professional theatre companies to community groups and schools. However, the Theatresports licensing package includes two very strong stipulations:

First, no competition or event is licensed unless the minimum teaching prerequisites are met:

- For professional theatre companies, community theatre groups, universities and other groups, this means a two day workshop plus a production meeting with an accredited Theatresports teacher/director.
- For primary and secondary school students, it means preparatory classes run by either an accredited teacher or a school teacher if, and only if, the school teacher has attended Theatresports in-service classes run by an accredited Theatresports trainer and the individual has satisfied the requirements of the Theatresports evaluation to undertake this responsibility.

Second, for the first competition event, a Theatresports representative or accredited trainer must be present to either host or act as head judge for the event. At the conclusion of this first event, a scheduled after-show debrief or notes session is conducted with this representative.

Finally, licence fees are applicable: a percentage gross box office fee is charged with ticket sales, and a flat fee for charity and free events. Contact your local Theatresports office for information and advice.

programs

How to use the programs

The following seven programs contain the method, principles and content for teaching improvisation and Theatresports games for players eight years and over.

The seven programs

There is significant overlap between each of these programs, none of which really functions in isolation. Making an offer, for example, cannot be separated from Finding the focus, and Status cannot be separated from Making a transition or Endowment. Building a character is inherent in all the programs. You will need to familiarise yourself with the Theatresports vocabulary. Definitions are found in Basic terms and skills.

Commence each session with appropriate warm-up games. They are an essential part of almost every training session and performance. Do not overlook them; they harness the energy and prepare the group. [See Warm-up games.]

THE GAMES

There are three types of games:

1. Warm-up games
2. Training games
3. Performance games

Some games serve as both training and performance games.

The games do not operate in isolation. They are inter-related. Each game informs the others. The coach must know the function of the games and when to use them. Games appear in small capitals: NAME OF GAME.

Each program develops both physical and verbal communication skills. It is important to balance the games in order to develop skills in the following areas:

- Verbal
- Physical
- Music
- Focus
- Endowment
- Transition
- Emotion
- Narrative
- Status
- Characterisation

It is important to introduce skills first and then develop scene-work before playing Theatresports performance games, so the programs contain sections as follows.

Part A: Foundation skills

These exercises provide the terms and skills that are the foundations and principles of improvisation. They allow players to build the simple verbal and physical exchanges that are the basis for later scene building.

Teach the foundation skills in the sequential order suggested before moving on to training and then performance games.

Part B: Training games and/or scene-work

Training games begin without an audience and develop the foundation skills into longer exchanges. They are the kick-board that keeps the fledgling improvisor afloat.

Not all of the training games work in performance; those which do are marked as such in the game structures.

Do not perform training games until all players have experienced them in pairs and small groups without the pressure of an audience.

Slowly build the training games into scene-work as players become confident in their foundation skills.

Scene-work enables players to build the skills they have learned in training games into narrative structures. It also provides an opportunity to create characters and locations.

Players must have the skills to play scenes before they play Theatresports performance games.

Part C: Theatresports performance games

Theatresports performance games provide structures for scenes. Some emphasise the physical, some the verbal, some both.

The challenges imposed by these structures promote lateral thinking and problem solving and stimulate the spontaneous creative process, necessity being the mother of invention.

For example, a simple interview scene with the additional challenge of playing it in gibberish taps players' ingenuity and invites unexpected possibilities as players strive to articulate their thoughts, unable to rely on their usual mode of communication. Their understanding of verbal and body language is enhanced in the process as they read the microcues given by other players.

There are 27 foundation performance games, which are referred to as the 'classics'. It is from these that all the other performance games are derived. Teach the classics first when choosing from the performance games.

Understanding the game structure

Below is an explanation of the standard game structure used throughout the seven coaching programs.

SPACE JUMP
classic

performance game
4 players
4 minutes
12+ years

- The most common title.
- Person who invented the game. Classic denotes one of the 27 games on which Theatresports in the southern hemisphere was built.
- Type of game. Whether a game is a training game, scene-work or performance game is indicated here. Some games may fit more than one of these catergories.
- Suggested number of players to reap the maximum benefit for the players and the storytelling. (Use as a guide only.)
- Training games and group activities can last from 3 to 45 minutes. Adjust playing time according to situation and age of group.

Performance games usually run approximately 1 to 4 minutes. While these times have been suggested, use them as a guide to indicate 1 minute = a short scene; 2 minutes = medium length scene; 3 to 4 minutes = a longer, more developed scene.

- Recommended age group.

AKA: Any other names by which the game may be known.

Description: This is the game description. If it is a performance game, it is the description as read out by the compere during a Theatresports performance to introduce the game.

Resource: Space/props/costume/music requirements or suggestions.

Time-out: Indication of whether ten seconds discussion time is helpful among team-mates prior to playing.

Example of a title: Place/activity/character starting points.

Aim: Educational goal.

Degree of difficulty: Expressed by 0.5 increments from 0.5 to 5, roughly as follows:

1. Simple introduction for beginners:
   Introducing offer and yield; focus; simple plot; simple endings; simple problem solving; completing a task.
2. Building skills:
   Offer and yield; focus; simple plot; longer time span; simple resolution; problem solving; introducing an event; basic endowment; simple transition; introducing status; actioning an objective.
3. Developing craft:
   Developed focus; structured scenes; developed narrative; development of characters; a clear event; clear endowment; subtext introduced; clear transition; satisfactory resolution to plot.
4. Craft in action:
   Highly developed plot; developed functional characters; location changes; time shifts; developed problem solving; subplot; subtext; comedy/drama; advanced dealing with an event; developed teamwork; risks taken; developed transitions; moral or tag; satisfactory ending.
5. Breaking new ground:
   Highly developed skills in place; maximum risk; extraordinary teamwork; playing to perform.

One of the two following skills headings appears in each game structure:

Skills to be developed: Skills to be developed playing the game.
Skills required: Prerequisite skills necessary to attempt the game.

Suggested preparation: Warm-up games, training games and performance games advised as prerequisites for skill building. In planning each session, use these as a guide and select according to the needs of the group, the time and space available, and the age of the players.

How it works: Detailed explanation of the game and how to set it up and coach it.

ICONS AND TERMS EXPLAINED

Tip

Advice.

Tips for tots

Recommended adjustments for young players whose motor coordination, language and life skills may not as yet make it possible to play the game or exercise as written.

Tips for text

Thoughts and adjustments for working with improvisation on text and for developing acting technique.

Beware

Take heed.

Global

Universal comment that applies as a general thought for all improvisation.

Magic moment

Indelible memories of delightful moments. An opportunity to tell a yarn. Examples of the Moment of the match and the three judges' perfect score — 5-5-5!

Good idea

Try this.

Bad idea

A different choice is more productive.

Feedback

Gathering players' responses to the work.

Remember

Write it down and don't forget it.

Summary

Drawing the threads together.

Check

Questions to assess players' readiness to progress to the next stage.

The Moose speaks

Words of wisdom from Keith Johnstone.

Commandment

The ten basic agreed Theatresports principles.

It is important to have read and understood all seven coaching programs before beginning to teach the first. The overlapping of the programs and the growth of the skills will be appreciated only when the coach has an overall perspective of the entire craft.

EXAMPLE LESSON PLANS

The following two lesson plans prepare players' foundation and scene-work skills to play one classic performance game, Expert double figures. They outline skills progression in two one-hour sessions. We assume the group has completed Parts A and B of both Programs one and two, and at least four low-degree-of-difficulty classics (below difficulty level 3.5) from Programs one and two, and is ready to advance and extend the storyline and develop their ideas further.

Lesson plan one

Aim: To introduce the skills of advancing and extending for scene-building.

Method: Warm-up; group activity into scene-work developing offering and yielding, focus and function skills. Then work in pairs, developing scene-work towards a performance game.

Activities:

1. Warm-up: Circle tag (emphasis on advancing the playing with quick turnover and saving). Yes let's (to stimulate agreement and offer-making). What are you doing? (full circle then build into collage and scene-work to emphasise focus and function). 15 minutes.
2. In pairs, the whole group working at the same time: Advancing and extending the verbal offer. 10–12 minutes.
   In pairs, the whole group working at the same time: Extending and overextending the physical offer. 10–12 minutes.
3. Scene-work: choose a succession of two different players to play new scenes from the above in front of the whole group. 10–12 minutes.
4. Wind-down and summary. 5 minutes.

Total: 55 minutes.

Lesson plan two

Aim: To continue advancing and extending skills for scene-building, and to introduce a classic performance game — Expert double figures.

Method: Warm-up; group activity into scene-work developing offering and yielding, focus and function skills. Then work in pairs, developing scene-work towards a performance game.

Activities:

1. Warm-up: What are you doing? developing into collage and scene-work. Advancing and extending the physical offer in pairs. 10–15 minutes.

2. Sidecoached scene-work: one player ADVANCING AND EXTENDING THE PHYSICAL OFFER [see Program three – Trusting your instincts advancing and extending]. Build the scene with two characters, sidecoached towards speaking. 10 minutes.
3. In pairs, the whole group working at the same time: YES AND... EXPERT. 10 minutes. THAT'S RIGHT. 10 minutes.
4. Scene-work — players play scenes in front of the rest of the group: using YES AND... EXPERT and THAT'S RIGHT as a basis and starting point, introduce EXPERT DOUBLE FIGURES scenes with four players in front of the whole group. Sidecoach towards extending and overextending physical offers and verbal agreement through YES AND..., YES BUT... and THAT'S RIGHT. 10 minutes.
4. Wind-down and summary. 5 minutes.

Total: 55-60 minutes.

•

Tip

- Do not teach with this book in your hands. Use it as a starting point, planning the session from it in advance. Learn the lesson plan by heart. Keep all your energy directed towards the players. Make notes after the session.
- It is important to value the skills. They are the basis of scene-work. Good scene-work lies at the heart of good improvisation and Theatresports playing.
- Read Keith Johnstone's *Improvisation and the Theatre.*

•

Beware

Players with medical conditions are advised to consult professional medical advice before undertaking strenuous games and activities. If players experience pain or discomfort, they should cease the activity immediately and consult a doctor.

Final words

Words cannot express the energy, vitality and fun the games and scenes produce. Be prepared for some exciting surprises.

Making an offer

program 1

Commandment

Thou shalt not block

Making an offer is the first step towards improvising. An offer communicates an idea to another player. It can be spoken, moved, or both.

Making offers is a natural part of human communication.

> 'Hey, let's go down to the shed and get out the bikes.'
> 'Yeah, and let's take some money with us and get a drink on the way down to the park.'

These children are making offers to one another and building on each other's ideas.

We don't need to speak to make an offer. Crossing the road, we hold out our hand and our child takes it. With this simple gesture we have conveyed something of our relationship, the potential danger and our natural instinct to protect.

When we improvise, we communicate our ideas and hope they will be accepted. Improvisors call accepting an idea 'yielding'. We call not accepting an offer 'blocking'.

There are six points to remember about an offer. Our aim is to develop skills to:

1. Make an offer
2. Yield to the offer
3. Name the offer
4. Extend the offer
5. Advance the offer
6. Shelve an offer

Some players find making an offer easy and seem to be brimming with ideas. They respond quickly and are full of energy. For these players, improvisation is a means of self-expression and communication. They always have something to say and rely on other players to yield to them. They initiate everything. They need to learn new ways of listening to, and yielding to, other people's ideas. They need to trust that other people have good ideas too.

Other players are reluctant to make offers. They lack confidence in their ideas or think they have no ideas at all. These players appear underenergised, slow to respond and lacking in commitment. They tend to look around the room comparing their work to other people's, embarrassed by their inability to express their thoughts. They distract other players or give up. They do not want to play. They think they have nothing to offer. For these players, improvising presents a new way of working. The possibility of having an idea, making an offer and having someone yield to it is an empowering process. It reinforces to these players that **they have something to offer**.

For both types of players, and for all the other players in between, the process of offer and yield provides an opportunity to express ideas and have them respected. Players must be encouraged to value their first response and go with their first idea. Some offers are richer than others, but there are no bad offers. No longer are players searching for the secret or correct answer that only the teacher knows.

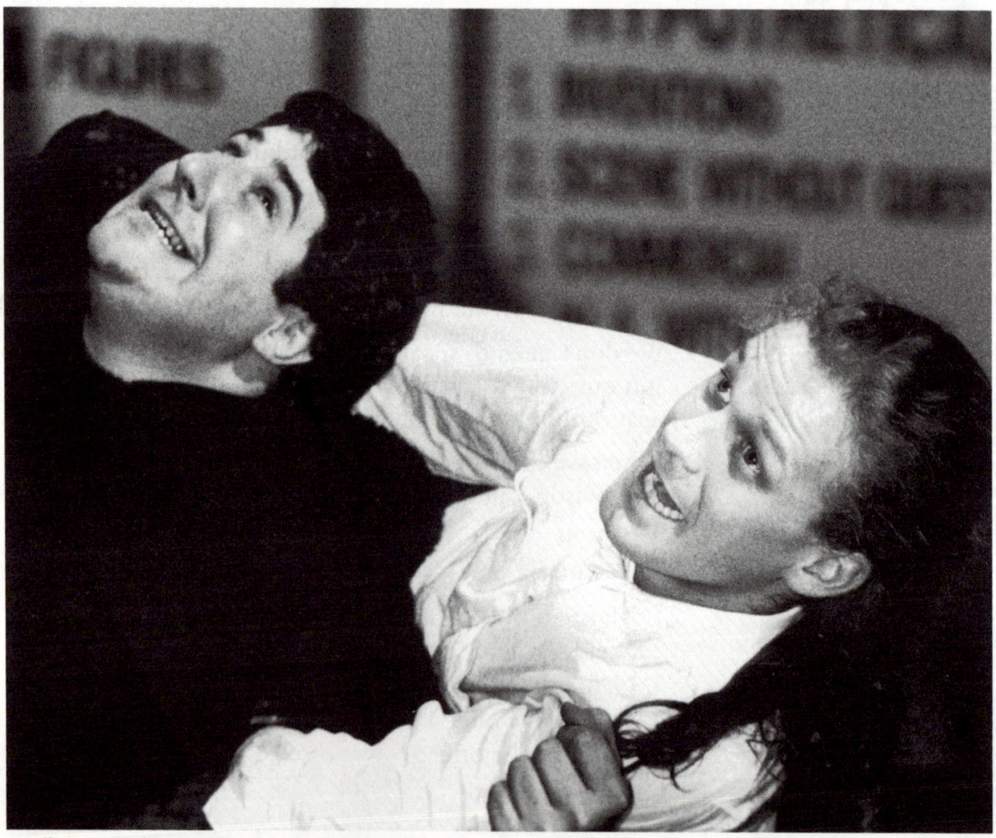

Melbourne players Tim Smith (left) and Andrew Bayly enjoying teamwork

Offers are the pegs for the narrative. They give us place, time, characters and events. We try not to drop them or block them. If there are no offers, there is no scene.

The in-built structures in the following training games provide opportunities to offer and yield.

Players work first as a whole group, then in pairs, then small groups, and return to work as a whole group again.

At this early stage, players do not perform. Their work is not compared with other players' work. There is no better answer than another. The work is shared and respected by the whole group. Sometimes the work is very fast. At other times it is quite slow. Begin with physical, unspoken work, and gradually introduce speech after players have experienced yielding to unspoken ideas.

In preparation for offer and yield work, choose warm-up games that remind players to say 'yes' to their own and other people's ideas: CIRCLE TAG; YES LET'S; ALL THOSE PEOPLE WHO; WHERE DO YOU COME FROM?; PERFORMANCE GAME. [See Warm-up games.]

The following exercises allow all players to experience the thrill of making offers and the joy of having their ideas accepted and yielded to. Trust and respect in other people's ideas are inherent in the work. Improvisation demands it! Players are encouraged to make eye contact with other players and to work in partnership and as a team.

The following Part A introduces offer and yield.

part A FOUNDATION SKILLS

MAKING A PHYSICAL OFFER

KNIFE AND FORK

Madhat Theatre

2–32 players
10–20 minutes
8+ years

Description: Players form shapes with their bodies.

Resource: A very clear space sufficient for players to swing their arms and lie on the floor without touching another player.

Time-out: No.

Example of a title: See suggestions below.

Aim: To provoke a spontaneous physical response to a given suggestion. To introduce basic Theatresports vocabulary of terms and skills.

Degree of difficulty: 0.5

Skills to be developed: Making and yielding to a physical offer, peripheral vision, eye contact, physical contact, spatial awareness, teamwork, reading physical signals.

Suggested preparation: MEETING AND GREETING (if players don't know each other); CIRCLE TAG.

How it works: In this exercise the players form shapes with their bodies. They work as a team building on each other's ideas. They do not talk or make signs to each other or interfere with the position made by another player. Instead, they communicate through their movement. They work together as quickly and efficiently as possible until the shape is complete. Each player is responsible for him or herself and shares the responsibility for the whole work.

Step one

Begin working with the whole group. The group combines to make simple geometric shapes and alphabetical letters using as much space as required. They lie on the floor or stand. These decisions are made in silence. As soon as one player has an idea they physicalise it. The others see it and find their place in the shape.

Contain the energy and ensure a smooth transition from the warm-up. Give the following instructions while the group holds a circle formation: 'Without talking, without making signs to each other or signalling to another person in any way, move into the space in silence. I'm going to call some shapes. Make these as a whole group before the count of ten.'

Shapes to call:

- A circle
- A square
- A triangle
- A rectangle

Count out loud, introducing each offer immediately after the previous one has been physicalised. Sidecoach the group to recognise strong physical offers. Encourage players to build on the strongest ideas. If one player lies on the floor or makes a strong physical offer to create the beginning of a shape, draw the group's attention to this offer.

Sidecoach: (as often as necessary) 'Yield to the strongest offer. Go with the strongest idea.'

For example, if three players form the three points of a triangle, encourage the others to identify the offers.

Sidecoach: 'Look to see where you are needed.'
'Find your function in the scene.'

Now call letters:

- Capital letter P for Peter
- Capital letter T for Tasmania
- Capital letter Q for Queensland
- Capital letter S for Sam
- Capital letter W for Wellington
- Capital letter Z for Zelda

Some people respond better to a physical image, others to the written word, others to an aural stimulus. Naming the letters and giving a noun as an example, eg 'Capital T as in Tasmania', clarifies the direction.

As the group comprehends and moves with speed, increase the pace, hasten the count from 1 to 10. (For slow groups, count backwards 10 to 1 to increase the sense of urgency.)

Sometimes, if players lie on the floor end to end, there will be insufficient space for the whole group. This could indicate a lack of spatial awareness. Encourage them to solve the problem.

Sidecoach: 'Use another level. Use the space in a different way. You don't have to lie on the floor.'

Continue to keep the room silent. Extend visual and physical skills.

Sidecoach: 'No talking.'

Good idea

- Encourage their sense of achievement. If players have difficulty forming a particular shape, leave it, call another shape and return to the difficult shape later.

Bad idea

- Do not judge the work. Do not say, 'You can do better than that', or 'That's the worst T I've ever seen'.

Allow the group to find its own creative direction. The artistic discipline is inherent in the exercise. If you want to make positive comment, call 'Great!' and continue without stopping.

Step two

Break the group into pairs. The pairs now make shapes of objects (see list below) on a one-to-one basis. They continue to work in silence. The partners yield to each other's ideas. The shapes now involve closer physical contact, require more imagination and allow for individual interpretation.

Even the status of all players and establish trust by instructing each player to look their partner in the eye, shake hands, say their partner's name and for both to simultaneously say, 'I promise to save you'. [See Basic terms and skills – Saving; Status.]

Now give these instructions: 'Without signing or talking, with your partner make these shapes. Become the things I name. Freeze after you have made each of them.'

Shapes to call:

- Pair of chopsticks
- Knife and fork
- Rose in a vase
- Stamp on an envelope
- Cup and saucer
- Egg on toast

Some players look around the room to check that their work is correct or compare theirs to that of others. These players could be trying to please the coach.

Keep the energy moving. Build their trust.

Sidecoach: 'No one is watching.'
'Make eye contact with your partner.'
'Save your partner.'
'Go with what you know.'
'Nothing is wrong.'

•

Tip

Keep them on their toes. Pace the calling a microbeat ahead of the group's movement. Allow shapes to complete and reach stillness, but do not let them settle, rest or lose their energy.

Shapes to call:

- Same rose, same vase, 15 years later
- Pair of hiking boots
- Two front teeth of a six-year-old
- Thread through a needle
- Ears of a six-day-old baby
- Pair of thongs/jandles
- Two boiled eggs, one with its head chopped off
- Button and button-hole unbuttoned
- Button and button-hole buttoned up
- Paste on a toothbrush
- A pair of new Mother's Day slippers
- Groucho Marx's eyebrows
- Cup and saucer — from which one drinks a cappuccino
- Two black crows sitting on a power line
- Volkswagen
- Baby seat on a car seat
- Towel on a towel rack
- Head lights of a Porsche turned on–off
- Compact disc player — playing

- Pair of contact lenses
- The last two hairs on a bald man's head
- China cup and saucer — 200 years old
- Fern in a pot
- Standard lamp
- Pair of bookends
- Banana
- Brush and comb
- Telephone
- Rudder on a boat
- Fan belt in a car engine
- Pair of grey suede high-heeled ladies' boots
- Burning match
- Coffee table
- Computer screen and keyboard
- Two-bar radiator
- Pair of pillows
- Easter egg with chook
- Television set
- Torch switched on
- Ancient ceramic bowl
- Photo in a frame
- Sliding door — opening
- Bear rug on a floor

Use 15 to 18 of these at any single session. This list represents a few thoughts. It contains specific offers to promote physical contact and empathy, spark the essence of character, introduce imaging of colours/textures, encourage use of a variety of spatial levels and planes. [See Program two – Focus zones.]

All the coach's suggestions should be easily identifiable so that all players are free to imagine them and make an immediate physical response. Adjust the list according to the age of the players. Select ideas which stimulate a number of choices. Vary the list to suggest a range of textures, sizes, weights, shapes, colours, etc. As players respond to more complex images, the physical shapes become more detailed.

•

Good idea

Be prepared for laughter. Let them have fun. Keep a sense of humour during the exercise. Encourage them to combine humour and hard work and associate both with concentration.

Step three

Now that pairs have built a working relationship, keep the partners together but join two pairs to form a group of four.

The following shapes are more complex requiring players to look for, and yield to, a greater number of offers. They will be required to use more space and a variety of heights, shapes and sizes as players deal with more complex problem-solving. Some players could lift each other off the ground. Be prepared for anything, but remember that player safety is paramount.

Shapes to call:

- Sydney Harbour Bridge/Westgate Bridge/Story Bridge
- Sydney Opera House/Parliament House
- A pyramid/sphinx
- Overhead ceiling fan (in motion)
- Pair of telegraph poles
- Statue of Liberty
- Big Ben striking the hour of three
- Respiratory machine
- Eiffel Tower
- Uluru
- The Big Banana
- Wedding photo
- Giant octopus
- Coat on a coat hanger
- Cocktail cabinet
- Fluorescent light
- Child's nursery mobile
- Security screen door
- Aboriginal paintings on a cave wall

Without stopping to discuss, continue to the next step.

Step four

Bring the whole group together again and have them create shapes as a whole group. Challenge them with more complex ideas that require more sophisticated problem solving.

Call these shapes:

- An upright piano (someone playing and a candelabra)
- A rowing boat
- A guitar
- A speedboat pulling water skiers
- A Viking ship
- A helicopter with fluffy woollen seat-covers

The list is endless.

•

Tips for tots

Players 8 to 10 years work best beginning their shapes as individuals, then in pairs, fours, and finally as a whole group. Begin lying on the floor working as individuals making the shapes of capital letters of the alphabet: T, O, Q, B, etc. Players stand as they gain confidence to explore different spaces. After they have experienced making a number of shapes, bring the group together to spell out whole words, each player taking one letter of the word. They then work in pairs to make cups and saucers, knives and forks, etc. Choose objects that challenge but are within their grasp. In fours they make bridges, etc. Then the whole group can make capital letters, shapes and objects — eg a rowing boat with oars. Younger players need more time for their decision-making.

•

Summary

At the end of this exercise, players have worked for 10–20 minutes using their bodies in a variety of ways. They have explored the space and had a working relationship with every other member of the group. They have solved simple and complex problems and should be pleased with their achievements. The skills covered are many. No part of this work exists in isolation. While the main concentration has been making and yielding to non-verbal physical offers, players have also been introduced to focus, endowment and character skills. Now develop parallel verbal skills.

MAKING A VERBAL OFFER

NAMING THE OBVIOUS

Keith Johnstone

2–32 players
5–7 minutes
8+ years

Description: Players name objects in their environment.

Resource: A clear space.

Time-out: No.

Example of a title: Not applicable.

Aim: To provoke a spontaneous vocal response to a given suggestion and reinforce the Theatresports vocabulary.

Degree of difficulty: 0.5

Skills to be developed: Making, giving, receiving and naming the offer, language and listening, player to player contact, teamwork, confidence, artistic discipline, accepting other people's ideas.

Suggested preparation: MEETING AND GREETING (if players don't know each other); CIRCLE TAG; KNIFE AND FORK.

How it works: This exercise encourages players to name everything they see within their environment. Wanting to name things is natural. We name dogs, cars, ships, cyclones. It is important to name offers when we improvise. Naming allows us to claim and identify our ideas. It clarifies and specifies our ideas to ourselves and to other players.

Step one

All individuals in the group move around the room at the same time but work individually, pointing to objects and naming them. They use simple language. They point as they look at and name things, eg wall, floor, brick, carpet, window.

Encourage players to be simple and name ordinary things that are tangible rather than trying to be clever.

•

Tip

If necessary, vary the pace of movement throughout the exercise, especially for younger players or those with a limited concentration span. Start at a moderate speed, change to fast movement and naming, then slow players down as the work progresses.

Suggest different ways to move.

Sidecoach: 'Walk, run, hop, skip.'

Suggest players explore naming objects from a variety of levels in the room, eg up high, down low, underneath, on top, between. Players continue to point as they name.

Step two

Now the naming is second nature, they describe what they see in short sentences; for example, 'The carpet is brown. The wall has grey bricks. The blackboard is dirty. The doorknob is broken.'

Suggest different ways of naming the objects — calling loudly, whispering, speaking in gibberish, another language, singing. This strengthens the skills demanded by Theatresports performance games.

•

Global

Continue to encourage players' physical connection to all verbal naming. When players develop the habit of pointing and touching when naming and physically moving to the same level as the object, eg on the floor, they associate movement with talking. This will help combat the 'talking heads' syndrome that often appears in Theatresports games based on verbal offers.

Step three

Challenge players' observation skills while building their language skills. Instruct them to name each object and describe it in detail — colours, shapes, textures. Encourage players to take the description as far as possible, keeping the information totally factual. They now stop in parts of the room describing a brick, or the leg of a chair, in minute detail. Introduce the concept of players being experts in their field

— eg, 'The brown carpet is a wool blend. The weave is approximately one centimetre.' And so on.

Sidecoach: 'You are an expert. Describe it in detail. You cannot be wrong.'

Players continue to touch the objects they are describing. They may be quite close to the object as they examine it in minute detail, talking all the while.

•

Check

- All players are actively involved in their own work
- No group member is excluded
- No player is heard above or seen as separate from the others
- All players share equal status
- The coach is the only observer in the room

HERE AND NOW

2–32 players
5–7 minutes
8+ years

Description: Players describe their environment and their activity in it.

Resource: A clear space.

Time-out: No.

Example of a title: Not applicable.

Aim: To place players in the present moment and sharpen their awareness of their environment.

Degree of difficulty: 0.5

Skills required: Ability to work as individuals.

Suggested preparation: All work in this program so far.

How it works: This follows on from Naming the obvious, in which players have described their environment. Here and now emphasises the player's relationship to the space.

Again, all players work at the same time. They describe what they see and do, naming everything in the present or present continuous tense, in short sentences: 'I am walking across the wooden floor. I see little nails sticking out of the floorboards.' This exercise eradicates everything but the present moment. It places the player in the here and now. It prepares the player for spontaneity. Continue the exercise until players have fully explored the space and described their environment and their actions in it.

NAMING THINGS AS THEY ARE NOT

Keith Johnstone

2–32 players
5–7 minutes
8+ years

Description: Players name things as they are not.

Resource: A clear space.

Time-out: No.

Example of a title: Not applicable.

Aim: To make a spontaneous offer.

Degree of difficulty: 0.5

Skills required: Ability to name offers.

Suggested preparation: GIBBERISH CIRCLE. All work in this program so far.

How it works: Now players name everything, but name things as they are not. They point to a chair and call it a car. This stimulates the imagination. They begin at a quick pace, naming aloud and pointing. Slow down the pace, lengthening the phrases as the description becomes more detailed.

Players tell complete fabrications as if they are experts in their field: for example, they point to a door — 'Behind this hatch is the hidden passageway to the tomb of Bozo the Great. It leads to a…'.

Encourage minute detail to be explored. Players can describe a crack in the wall, a one centimetre square or a speck. The possibilities are endless.

Variations: Continue to develop a sense of risk and challenge language skills. Change to gibberish [see below] for 30 seconds, then return to English. Describe in rhyming couplets and then sing the words.

INTRODUCING GIBBERISH

Gibberish is a language made up of a collage of vocal sounds of different pitches, accents and inflections. It is nonsensical in that no such language exists. But when players improvise in gibberish, they believe they understand everything that is said by themselves and the other players. Many games are played in gibberish. Use gibberish in warm-up, training and performance games to release energy and encourage players' emotional commitment to the content without relying on words. Some players find using gibberish confronting. With these players, begin using a simple 'Blah, blah, blah,' sliding through on a range of pitches. Slowly introduce new vowels and consonants as confidence increases. Goo-da, bool-a-busha, zano. Remember when speaking gibberish — continue to think the thoughts in your head. Play with a variety of accents in gibberish — Aussie Ocker gibberish, American gibberish, French gibberish, Japanese gibberish, Slavic gibberish. Play the warm-up game GIBBERISH CIRCLE and when all players have made a range of sounds and enjoy speaking in gibberish, introduce it regularly through foundation, scene-work and performance games.

•

Check

It is important that during these exercises players are not aware of being watched or judged. Their immediate responses to suggestions are valuable and personal. Encouraging permission to play with respect and without judgment is particularly important at this point in training. It evens the status and values the work of all players.

•

Summary

Players have stimulated their basic verbal improvisation skills. They have described their environment and their relationship to it in a variety of ways. They have accepted the first idea that came into their mind and chosen ideas that were obvious and not clever. They have stimulated their imagination without the pressure to be funny or perform. They have worked on their own. Now extend these skills. Players combine the verbal and the physical, and work with other players.

TRAINING GAMES

Now players are ready to string their ideas together and to combine the physical and the verbal. The following exercises are played one-word-at-a-time. Working one-word-at-a-time with a partner provides the essence of the improvisation experience. Every word the other player says must be accepted. If not, the thoughts are disparate and do not make sense. Players share responsibility and control of the developing ideas. The value of the game is that all players experience 'offer for offer' playing. This initiates spontaneous improvisation. Players cannot preplan or think into the future. This training game then develops into a Theatresports performance game.

ONE-WORD-AT-A-TIME

training game
2–32 players
5–7 minutes
8+ years

Description: Players speak one word at a time.

Resource: An extremely clear space.

Time-out: No.

Example of a title: Not applicable.

Aim: To introduce the verbal offer and yield.

Degree of difficulty: 1

Skills required: Ability to listen and yield.

Suggested preparation: All work in this program so far.

How it works: Each player finds a partner. They place their arms around each other's waists, or link arms or hold hands, or at least stand in close proximity, perhaps shoulder to shoulder. Arms around the waist may not be appropriate for some groups or for pairs of uneven sizes — very tall with short. Make sure linking does not constrict the upper torso. Players need to be physically open and available to move. Form a trio if the group has an odd number. Trios speak down the line in rotation.

Pairs find a comfortable walking rhythm, establishing an even pace and become used to the movement before they begin to speak.

Begin by simply walking around the room pointing to objects and naming them. Each player speaks only one-word-at-a-time. For example, one of the pair points to the door and says, 'This', the other player reads the indication from the pointing and says, 'door', the first player adds, 'is', the second player completes the thought, 'brown'. Players do not prepare their speech. All this work is improvised and found on the spot as they work.

As they gain confidence they describe things as they see them in detail, one-word-at-a-time. For example, '[This] chair [is] brown. [It] has [a] plastic [cover] on [it]'.

Robert McFarlane

The J Curves field Julia Zemiro (left) and Jenny Lovell to tell a two person ONE-WORD-AT-A-TIME STORY

Tip

Change partners at regular intervals. Give each pair three to five minutes, then change partners again. For some groups (players 8–12 years in particular), changing partners can be threatening. Allow these players to keep the same partners rather than interrupt the flow of the work. Sometimes it is more beneficial to work for a longer time with the same partner than to work for shorter periods of time with a variety of partners. Try both ways and adopt the method that suits your group.

Sidecoach: 'Share a common focus by pointing to the object being described.'
'Find objects at different levels in the room.'
'Have your outside arms work in unison' (when pointing to or touching objects).
When players are losing concentration: 'Make eye contact.'

Granting permission and reading the room dynamic

The energy level of the room will rise. Laughter begins as players soon enjoy the experience of spontaneous improvisation and the joy of accepting the unexpected. Be prepared to allow 'working joy'. The nature of this work gives the impression that players are having too much fun to be working. This is not the case: it is possible to have fun while learning.

Time note: Increase the amount of time spent on ONE-WORD-AT-A-TIME in relation to the group's concentration span. Spend more than 5 to 15 minutes on this exercise only if the players continue to gain value from it. Some groups will want to continue for 20 minutes or even longer. Be prepared to advance to the next exercises as soon as their skills and concentration span reflect the need.

For players 10+ who crave more: When offer and yield skills are solid, extend the activity of NAMING THINGS AS THEY ARE NOT from an exercise played as individuals to working in pairs one-word-at-a-time describing objects in great detail. Players are free to invent detailed stories of fantasy about mundane objects in the room. Time — as appropriate.

MEETING ANOTHER PAIR ONE-WORD-AT-A-TIME

training game
2–32 players
5–10 minutes
8+ years

Description: Pairs of players meet other pairs speaking one-word-at-a-time.

Resource: A clear space.

Time-out: No.

Example of a title: Not applicable.

Aim: To build short scenes one-word-at-a-time.

Degree of difficulty: 1.5

Skills required: Ability to offer and yield one-word-at-a-time.

Suggested preparation: All work in this program so far.

How it works: Players remain in their one-word-at-a-time pairs. They meet other pairs. They develop a simple dialogue with the other pair. Players are now identified in 'pairs' as 'two people sharing the same experience'.

I or we: There is some division of thought about whether players speak one-word-at-a-time as a singular unit — 'I' or 'me' — or in the plural — 'we' or 'us'. Both have their value. For specific characters, for example the two-headed monster 'Diurgan', the players would refer to themselves in the singular: 'My [name] is [Diurgan]'. However, in general, I recommend that players use the plural form, particularly in the early days of training. Rather than saying 'I', 'me', 'my', they say 'we', 'us', 'our'. This promotes sharing.

Encourage players to use the present tense or present continuous tense rather than the past tense, eg 'We [open] the [door].' Or, 'We [are] opening [the] door.'

This supports belief, commitment and shared subjectivity. It also supports the notion that the work is happening 'here and now', in the present moment, for the first time.

Pair A: 'Hi, [our] name [is] Cheryl. [What] is [your] name?'
Pair B: 'Our [name] is [Max]. Do [you] want [to] dance?'

Sidecoach: 'Continue eye contact wherever possible.'
'Share equal responsibility and control in the scene.'
'Remain actively involved at the same time.'
'Stay in the present tense.'
'Say "we".'
'Save each other.'

Small scenes and interchanges develop as partners become familiar with the structure. Laughter, joy and skills develop at the same time.

These interchanges and greetings can continue for up to 10 minutes as players have a coffee, go to the pinball parlour, travel on a holiday, etc.

Extend the exercise to involve the whole group at a common meeting place or shared environment, eg a party, an airport, a courtroom, a swimming pool. To stimulate the playing of characters, choose an environment where a range of characters could meet. All this work is spoken one-word-at-a-time. With some groups this exercise can continue for a whole 40 minute period.

INTRODUCING A TASK

Introducing a task ONE-WORD-AT-A-TIME

Until now the players have improvised without a specific task. A task gives players something specific to do — washing the car, buying a pet. Players should have developed a mutual understanding and rhythm, so that they no longer need to work holding hands or with arms around each other. They may play side by side, one in front of the other as a shadow, close together or at great distances — even on different sides of the room. They are two separate bodies experiencing the same movements, telling the same story, completing the same task. They are both active.

At this point it is impossible to identify which idea comes first — the physical movement or the spoken word. Both impulses usually move together. Therefore a balance of physical and verbal offering and yielding is necessary.

•

Tip

If players stop moving when they speak, interchange one-word-at-a-time activities with non-verbal one-movement-at-a-time activities. THE MIRROR GAME is an excellent exercise to redress the balance. [See Warm-up games – THE MIRROR GAME.]

FIND, OPEN AND READ A LETTER ONE-WORD-AT-A-TIME

2–32 players
10–15 minutes
8+ years

Players form pairs speaking one-word-at-a-time. They move together. They improvise entering a room and finding a private letter in a drawer, on the floor, in a safe, under a mat. They endow it with secrecy, intrigue, gossip, mystery. They pick up the letter as one body with their outside arms. They open/unseal/unroll it, and read it aloud one-word-at-a-time. The information in it changes them.

The letter could be a simple love letter, or written in Elizabethan verse, eg '[My] Dearest [Love] thou [art] …'. Or IN THE STYLE OF Jane Austen, Thomas Hardy, Sartre, nonsense poetry etc. Vary choices according to the age and skill of the players.

•

Tips for tots

Players 8 to 11 years sit in a circle. Two players read a letter to another pair, who send a letter in reply, or read a letter to yet another pair. Pairs speak one-word-at-a-time. Continue this around the group.

•

Feedback

Now might be a good time to sum up with group feedback. Ask what happened rather than how they felt working one-word-at-a-time. They may relate stories and details of their work they found amusing. Ask them to name the difficulties they had to overcome working one-word-at-a-time.

The major challenge is to concentrate on offering and yielding one-word-at-a-time. Listen to the feedback. Comments such as 'She would not say what I wanted her to say,' or 'I kept saying two words,' are natural, recurring comments. Discuss these and remind the group that saying two words instead of one is okay. It takes time to learn the game! It is more important to understand the game first and have fun with it. Encourage players to enjoy stumbling and finding the words with their partner.

•

Bad idea

Never tell players what they did was wrong, or judge what they 'should' or 'could' have done. [See Coaching strategies – Dos and don'ts.]

•

Global

Remind the group that improvisation involves accepting other people's ideas, remaining in the present moment and not thinking into the future. Although forward planning is natural, it is not helpful when improvising. The improvisor throws away all preconceived ideas and accepts the one currently being offered. We take all the information with us and build the story.

The Moose speaks

'You don't know where you are going,
you only know where you came from.'

•

Tip

Write on the blackboard:

offer + yield = listening
offer + yield = idea + yes

Remind the group that this exercise gives players the opportunity to have an equal share of the **responsibility** and the **control** of each story.

•

Global

Improvisation and Theatresports require a team effort. The strongest teams are those that deal with the ideas presented by all players. The happiest players are those whose ideas are listened to. The fun of improvising is listening to and being changed by another person's ideas, as well as being listened to and affecting other players' ideas.

Commandment

Thou shalt always be changed by what is said to you.

Remind players to overaccept each other's ideas. When you overaccept another person's idea, you commit yourself to it totally. You give it all your attention. You make it the focus of the scene. You throw away any idea you may have thought of, and not only yield but double yield to the other player's offer. Even the most ordinary ideas become exciting and lead to interesting developments when they are overaccepted. [See the game IT'S TUESDAY in Keith Johnstone's *Improvisation and the Theatre.*]

INTRODUCING AN OBJECTIVE

Linking the task to an objective ONE-WORD-AT-A-TIME

An objective is something to achieve.

Introduce a quest or journey, eg quest for world peace; journey to the centre of the earth; search for gold at the end of the rainbow.

These titles give scenes an objective and usually an offer of place. Players have something to do (a task), somewhere to be (a place) and something to achieve (an objective).

Players begin their journey, search or quest speaking one-word-at-a-time and moving at the same time. Actions inform words and vice versa. Placing the scene in a specific location allows players to do the scene rather than talk about it.

'We [are] getting [into] the [spaceship] to [fly] to [Mars]. Buttoning [up] our [jackets] we…' etc.

Observe players' concentration and commitment to the focus. Sidecoach accordingly.

TREASURE MAP ONE-WORD-AT-A-TIME

Jenny Lovell

2–32 players
5–7 minutes
8–14 years

This exercise further links the task to the objective. It provides the step that links the 'letter' to the 'quest'. The information players find in their imaginary map directs them to finding their treasure. It provides a sense of place, action and adventure. It is particularly good for players of 8 to 14 years.

How it works: Players name the quest before they begin. Working one-word-at-a-time, players find a treasure map. They read the directions one-word-at-a-time. The map leads them on a hunt/quest for the treasure.

When allowing players to set their objective — eg 'finding buried treasure' — sidecoach them to begin to hunt immediately so that they improvise towards achieving the objective without preplanning.

•

Beware

Players who discuss how or where they will find the treasure and what will happen when they get there are scripting. While scripting may promote a good story, it does not promote spontaneity or risk [see Basic terms and skills] or build team skills.

It is more valuable to do it first. They can discuss the story, write it down, or use it as a starting point for follow-up work later.

Set the task and objective. Read the map and hunt for and find the treasure.

This is the most complex work players have had to date. Here are some ways of avoiding the most common pitfalls:

Sidecoach: 'Present tense.'
'Present continuous tense.'
'Use *ing* words, for example, walking, hunting.'
'Say we.'
'Say us/our.'
'Tell the story.'

•

Beware

If the work sounds like this — 'Hello [Mr] Pirate. [Hello] sailor,' the players have created two characters and dialogue. This tells the coach the players have separated. They have stopped imaging together.

Sidecoach: 'Make eye contact!'

Use of the past or the conditional and subjunctive tenses — should, would, could — tells the coach that players are prejudging and asking for permission and approval. For example: 'Should [we] pick [up] the [shovel]?'
Sidecoach: 'Pick up the shovel!'

Note: Some players develop a flow with their partner very quickly. Others experience short bursts of achievement. The coach's role is to use verbs (doing words) to kick-start those who are experiencing difficulty when the action stalls. They should do it rather than talk about it.

•

Tips for tots

Some players under 12 years require solid and consistent sidecoaching. They tend to run out of ideas every 20–30 seconds. Keep their confidence in their ideas high. Sidecoach pairs to keep their ideas flowing.

Encourage players to action the verb.

When players need to make a commitment or a new decision:
Sidecoach: 'Let's!' or 'Say let's.' (Indicating players begin their next sentence with 'Let's'.)

'Let's…' facilitates an agreement. [See Warm-up games – YES LET'S.]

Asking questions: When players are asking questions, they are searching for answers. '[What] is [this]? I [don't] know, [what] is [this]?'
Sidecoach: 'Name it!'

Asking questions: '[Where] are [we]? I [don't] know, [where] are [we]?'
Save them: They want to know where they are! Suggest a location/place/environment. Take the suggestion from the obvious. Give players somewhere to be.
Sidecoach: 'See the door in front of you and open it.'

•

Feedback

Now is a good time for feedback. When they have finished, bring the group together. Ask players if they achieved their objective. 'Did you find gold at the end of the rainbow? Achieve world peace? Find the treasure?'

Ask them what happened. Listen carefully to their stories. Did they do what the title implied? If they did not, or if they say, 'No, we didn't get there yet,' or, 'We were just about to,' they may be wimping. Rather than telling them they are wimps, give them something to do. They need to action the title. Give them topics that require more action and which have an inherent task (eg cracking a safe) and objective (finding valuables).

Are they improvising?

Check

Learn to read their improvisations. For example, 'Cracking a safe':

If they cannot get out of the car, cannot find the room, cannot find the safe or lose their way in the house, they are having trouble improvising. They are blocking and stalling. They need intensive sidecoaching to achieve yielding. Return to basic skills. Set another task and sidecoach them all the way — eg 'panning for gold'.

If they arrive at the house and forget the safe but find a valuable painting instead, they are not dealing with the task (cracking the safe) but they are improvising. Set another task and sidecoach towards their dealing with it.

If they find the safe, crack it but find nothing, they are improvising but they have wimped. Set another objective and sidecoach towards their achieving it.

If they arrive at the safe, crack it but blow themselves up with dynamite and end up in hospital, they have achieved their task (but not the objective) and they are improvising.

If players overcame obstacles and, through their adventures, arrived at the safe, cracked it and found the diamonds, they have succeeded in:

1. Completing a task (arriving at and cracking the safe).
2. Achieving an objective (finding the loot).

Ask them what happened after that. If they say, 'Nothing, that was the end,' they have successfully bridged to the end of the scene. [See below.]

If they say, 'We got diamonds and were just about to leave when the light went on and a security guard arrested us,' they have actioned an event.

In both cases, players are ready to move on and 'deal with an event'. In both cases, players reached their objective.

Objectives can be achieved in two ways:

1. Early in the story. Players then have to deal with what happens as a result of achieving the objective (ie finding the valuables).
2. At the end of the story. Players build the narrative towards the objective (ie finding the valuables). This is called bridging.

Although the first way involves more risk, both are valuable. At this early stage of skills development the coach's role is to skill players to improvise both ways.

•

Tips for text

Find a scene from a well structured text. Consider the offers made by the writer. How do the characters interact? Do they block each other's offers or yield to them? When characters deal with offers, they make choices. Choices reveal character. These characteristics are always evident in a good script.

INTRODUCING AN EVENT

An event is something that happens. It is a big offer that provides a moment of transition between one part of the story and the next. It breaks the routine. Players usually spend 10 to 30 seconds establishing an activity or setting up a routine. The routine is broken when something new occurs to interrupt the activity. For example, two players begin the task of washing the car, one-word-at-a-time. They spend time washing the outside and enter the car, polishing the interior. They are busy polishing everything when they accidentally polish and release the hand brake. When the car starts to roll, the routine has been broken. They have actioned an event. They now need the skills to support the developing scene and deal with the effects of the event.

A discussion about the development of plot line and narrative relevant to the texts they are reading could be beneficial at this point.

Events occur in different places in the plot for different reasons. In *Romeo and Juliet,* the lovers die towards the end of the story. In *Hamlet,* the death of Hamlet's father occurs before the play begins. Each event affects the rest of the plot.

Storytelling is built on events. Scenes are rich when they involve various aspects of the event — **before** the event, **during** the event, **after** the event. Then a story is more likely to have a **beginning**, a **middle** and an **end**.

Discovering the effects of the event is exciting. We improvise towards the unknown and we wait to see what happens next, daring not to think into the future. The further we dare, the more we risk and improvise.

Commandment

When in doubt, break the routine.

INTRODUCING AN EVENT ONE-WORD-AT-A-TIME

2–32 players
3–7 minutes
12+ years

Description: Title given. Players action an event speaking one-word-at-a-time.

Resource: A clear space.

Time-out: No.

Example of a title: The best titles introduce a simple activity and objective. Titles are more helpful when they name the basic offer. Then what happens is implicit in the title.

Searching is good. It facilitates finding. Finding actions an event.
Questing is good. It facilitates epic experiences. Experiences action events.
Journeying is good. It facilitates arriving. Arriving actions new events.

Titles and starting suggestions that offer quests, journeys or crimes spark our adventurous impulse.

Titles that suggest suspense, plots of action and drama are more beneficial at this stage than those which purely imply description.

'Bill the bikie butcher wins the race' is more beneficial than 'Bill the bikie butcher' because players are challenged to move as Bill rather than stand still and talk about Bill.

Titles are more active in the present or present continuous tense.

Aim: To build a story, introduce an event, deal with the results and find an ending.

Degree of difficulty: 1.5

Skills required: Ability to speak and make offers one-word-at-a-time.

Suggested preparation: All work in this program thus far.

How it works: Working in pairs players begin a searching, questing or journeying story one-word-at-a-time. Stop the players after about three minutes. Ask them if an event has occurred. Has something happened? If it hasn't, they are probably wimping. If it has, ask them where the event occurred. Was it at the beginning, the middle or the end?

Now choose two players to tell a one-word-at-a-time story in front of the rest of the group. Provide a new title. Sidecoach the scene as appropriate. Bring two different players up to tell another story. Discuss the different stories and the effects of the events on the plot. Vary the possibilities by placing the event in a variety of positions within the scene (ie at the beginning, middle, end).

•

Summary

In the exercises to date, players have called upon the foundation skills of all the programs. They have made and accepted spoken and unspoken offers, created and dealt with a variety of focus shifts, advanced and extended ideas while developing simple and sometimes quite complex stories, made and accepted simple endowments, and some will have experienced transitions and developed simple characters. More importantly they have worked with other players and experienced the joy of improvising.

There are now two options for the coach to take. If the group is anxious to play Theatresports performance games, capitalise on the one-word-at-a-time story work and introduce the game ONE-WORD-AT-A-TIME STORY as outlined in Part C of this program. Be sure to keep players physically active and the storytelling simple. Other Theatresports performance games in Part C which are good choices at this stage are SHARED STORY and DIE GAME. Spend no more than one hour playing these performance games. It is more important that the players build skills towards scene-work and continue further exploration of making an offer as outlined in this program than play too many Theatresports performance games.

Making offers and repeating them

To date, all offers have been made on the spot, spontaneously. At this point it is a good idea to vary the pace and style of the improvisation. The next exercise introduces another way of making an offer. It builds on skills from the above exercises but slows the pace, providing an alternative to fast decision making. It introduces simple endowment and character work.

The players now return to working in small groups. They work towards building an environment from physical body shapes, but take time to discuss their ideas. Both coach and players take a rest from sidecoaching. The coach now has an opportunity to watch the players solving problems in another way.

ROOMS

2–32 players
15–40 minutes
(allow an extra 10 minutes for feedback)
8+ years

Description: Groups of players create environments.

Resource: A clear, large space.

Time-out: Yes, for discussion. See below.

Example of a title: Bedroom, bathroom, laundry.

Aim: To develop improvised choices and repeat them.

Degree of difficulty: 1

Skills to be developed: Physical and vocal offering and yielding, and team discussion.

Suggested preparation: Physical warm-up; CIRCLE TAG; WHERE DO YOU COME FROM?; KNIFE AND FORK.

How it works: Players become inanimate objects and bring them to life. They build on the physical skills discovered in KNIFE AND FORK and explore them in more detail.

Players form groups of 5–8 members. Each group chooses a room in a house — bedroom, bathroom, laundry, garage. One player is chosen to be the only human character in each scene. All the other members in each group will be the inanimate objects, furniture and all the other items required by the human. All the furniture and items are made physically by the players. They literally become the doors, window, curtains — anything that could be in the room. The human enters the room through a door formed by one or more players, turns on lamps, sits in the chair, etc. They use at least seven different items of furniture as they move through the room. Although the furniture is not human, every nuance can be expressed by the furniture; for example, the bean bag sighs and flattens as it is sat in, a light changes facial expression as it is turned on and off. Players are specific and detailed in their physical representations.

Detail is expressed in a number of ways. Each group defines the period in time in which their room is set. This informs furniture, colour, decor, general atmosphere. An ultra space-age bathroom in 2030 with sauna, spa, steam room and cellular phone is very different from a 1950s grey and pink tiled bathroom with enamelled, stained bath, shower curtain stuck to the bath and rose shower which coughs and splutters. A 1960s lounge room with bean bag, chairs, psychedelic lamp, black and white TV with indoor aerial and roll-over horizontal hold is vastly different from a 13th century room with flaming torch, stone and wood chairs, sundials and bear skin rugs. The possibilities are endless. Vary the content. Items are encouraged to be as physically simple or complex as required. Some items may need more than one member; for example, a washing machine, telephone or bar fridge could involve three players each.

Scenes may be silent or voiced. Humans speak. Furniture makes sounds. A simple story is revealed as the human moves through the space and relates to the environment. The furniture and the human are changed by the experience.

While the groups are working, the coach walks around the room to encourage groups to 'do' rather than talk about it too much and to be detailed in their presentations. Although discussion is important, encourage activity and problem-solving on their feet. In the preparation and to stimulate the imaging process the coach can suggest the following: 'What colour are you? How long have you been here? Are you rough or smooth? What happens when you are still? What happens when you are in motion? What sounds do you make?' Check that each member of the group agrees on the same details.

Encourage players to empathise with the characteristics of the furniture. For example (to a leather armchair): 'Feel the studs on your back. Endow the armchair with pride/tiredness,' etc.

Sidecoach: 'Find the first moment of stillness — the stillness before the action begins.'
'Find the object in motion.'
'Find the object's final resting point.'
'How was the object changed?'
'How does the human's use of the object change the object?'
'How does using each object change the human?'

Now each group presents their room to the others but does not tell them what room it is or in which period of time it is set. After the presentations, their classmates identify the room, name the objects they recognised and relate the details they imagined — the colour and textures of the items, period in time of the setting, etc. Each group presents their work in as much detail as possible.

Ask the observers:

- 'What colour was the floor?'
- 'What texture was the lampshade?'
- 'What century was the setting?'
- 'Describe the personality of the objects.'

Attention to detail is as important in the observation as it is in the playing of each item in each room.

This exercise is never the same twice. It is relevant to players of any age. I have marvelled at the invention of ceiling fans, pedal bins, and even a bedroom that travelled through time.

•

Global

Ask detailed questions to encourage imaging throughout the teaching of all the programs, whether at beginner, intermediate or advanced levels of work.

•

Tips for text

Choose rooms and environments from specific novels or plays.

•

Beware

As this work is not improvised, observe the new dynamic in the room. Players can become over-competitive, wanting their presentation to be as good as or better than the others. Beware of players in the audience who continue to discuss and plan their presentation rather than concentrate on the work being shown.

•

Tips for tots

To grasp the possibilities available with this exercise, players under 12 years require detailed modelling (ie a clear demonstration as an example). When they have grasped the concept, their work generally is detailed and highly imaginative.

Further environments: Build on the skills and explore more detailed work. Players build more detailed environments — a bank, fun park, factory, outer space, under the sea, etc. Play a long scene in this player-made environment.

Theatresports players are required to play a variety of inanimate objects as well as characters. Give players the permission to think laterally and use their bodies in unusual and unexpected ways in the early days of training. This stimulates the imagination and prepares them for a variety of future possibilities.

INTRODUCING OFFERS OF PLACE — VERBAL AND NON-VERBAL

An offer of place is a starting point, telling us where the scene takes place. It can be verbal, physical or both. In the following game, players build on the skills developed in KNIFE AND FORK, and ROOMS. Players begin very short scenes with an offer of place. They build the environment (people, furniture, nature and objects) in which the scene occurs. For the first time players work in, and are identified as, teams. The work is physical, spontaneous and very fast. It develops from frozen moments into short verbal scenes. Each group works in front of the whole group in quick turnaround.

MARKO'S GAME

Marko Mustac

training game for
STATUES, SPACE JUMP, TIME WARP, MIME
2–32 players
15 minutes
8+ years

AKA POSTCARDS

Description: Groups of players form frozen moments based on offers of place and activity.

Resource: A clear space. A preprepared list of at least 20 offers of place and at least 20 offers of activity.

Time-out: No.

Example of a title: On a desert island; At the unemployment office; Under the sea; At the blood bank; Christmas morning; In an all night diner; In a television studio; Mother's day; At the laundromat; In a space ship; On a float in a parade; At the zoo; At an audition; In the lolly factory; Bathing the dog; Sorting lollies; Christmas dinner; At the swimming carnival; Christmas night; Watching a parade; Playing pool; Building a bonfire, etc.

Aim: To invoke spontaneous reaction to a suggested offer of place or activity and to introduce teamwork.

Degree of difficulty: 1.5

Skills to be developed: Yielding, spatial awareness.

Suggested preparation: Circle tag; What are you doing?; Knife and fork; Rooms.

How it works — Step one: Form teams of four to five players and name or number each team. Making a random selection, call a team number and an offer of place from your list; eg 'Team number 2, in an aeroplane.' Team number 2 jumps up, comes to the front of the class and finds the frozen moment in an aeroplane. One player sits down and begins to fly the plane as pilot. Seeing this, a second player enters and becomes what is needed to the scene. (They find the focus — more on this next program.) They may become the wings of the plane, the instruments used by the pilot, a passenger, the steward — the possibilities are endless. They freeze the moment.

The team creates the frozen moment, representing the place/activity as quickly as possible. They hold the freeze until the coach calls another group; eg 'Team number 6 — on a desert island.' At this, team number 2 sits down to make way for team number 6. The freezes and the calls continue. 'Team 1 in Pharaoh's tomb,' etc. Players depict the full scene. They become trees, people, furniture, etc. They build on one another's ideas. These moments are made in front of the whole group with the rest of the group watching. Each group is given a new suggestion. No suggestions are repeated.

Sidecoach: 'Yield to the first offer.'
'Share the focus.'
'Build on the offers one at a time.'

Players enter one at a time. Each player is aware of, and yields to, the offers given by the previous player.

Step two: After each team has made at least three different freezes and has depicted clear locations with characters, furniture and so on, extend the above exercise. Bring the frozen moments to life. Begin short, short scenes from the frozen moments with movement only. Play a 5-10 second scene without speech. Players use their peripheral vision to see the offers made by the other players and yield to them.

Step three: Begin short scenes from the frozen moments, adding dialogue. Keep dialogue extremely simple, — no more complex than offer + yield + simple extension. Do not coach to an advance. Although some groups will automatically advance, do not expect it to occur. [See Basic terms and skills.] Keep scenes brief: 5-15 seconds. The coach calls the end of the little scene and calls up another team, 'Great, next.' These scenes are usually overloaded with offers at this early stage of the work. Most players want to talk all at once and forget to listen. Keeping the scenes short gives players an experience of playing a scene and a sense of achievement that may be lost if they attempt longer scenes at this stage.

THANK YOU

training game
2–4 players
4–10 minutes
8+ years

Description: Players yield to a frozen position given by a team-mate, endow it as a starting place for a new scene, freeze and are thanked for their endowment.

Resource: A clear space.

Example of a title: No title required.

Aim: To identify, yield to and endow a still focus.

Degree of difficulty: I

Skills required: Ability to identify focus and endow it with an idea.

Suggested preparation: All work from Program one part A.

How it works: Players form pairs or groups of three. Player A holds a frozen position. Player B enters the scene yielding to the focus and takes up a frozen position that gives meaning to the freeze of player A. If the first freeze looks as if player A is walking a dog, player B could kneel on all fours as the dog. Then player A says, 'Thank you,' unfreezes and leaves the scene. Player C, or player A, then enters the scene using the frozen moment of player B (the dog) as a new starting position for a new scene. After the frozen moment is complete player B says, 'Thank you,' unfreezes and leaves the scene. And so the freezes and the new endowed moments continue.

All scenes are played in silence except for the 'Thank you'. All offers and yields are non-verbal. Players do not guess what the previous player had in mind, but use their own ideas to make something of the previous player's position. This is similar to THE PRESENT GAME played non-verbally. The freezes occur in quick rotation and move as fast as players can enter the scene.

Play the game in a number of ways. When players understand how it is played begin with the whole group working in the space in groups of three or four. Players enter and leave the scenes in strict rotation. If entering players are stalling, the frozen player counts out loud to three. The next player is encouraged to enter with their freeze by the count of three. Sidecoach to keep players rotating quickly.

Extend the game by allowing player B to remain frozen and player C yields to both players entering to establish a frozen moment using both positions and player D then enters to add to the three frozen positions. At player D's entrance the other players say 'Thank you,' exit and leave player D frozen. They then re-enter one at a time to build their freezes on player D's position.

From this simple exercise introduce verbal offers when players are ready. Note: playing is ofter clearer, less complicated and more physical when it is non-verbal. Remind players to keep verbal offers to a minimum. Cut them completely if the scenes lose their physicality and vitality.

THANK YOU is perfect preparation for the following work and an obvious preparation for FREEZE TAG and SPACE JUMP.

Players remain in teams of three or four and work one group at a time in front of the whole class. Give each team a name or number and the first player an activity on which to base their freeze, eg building a shed, working in the garden, feeding a dolphin etc. From time to time introduce speech in short bursts. As skills progress encourage a full scene of up to four players with dialogue.

Summary

Offer and yield foundation skills

To this point the players can recognise and have experienced the following:

- The difference between making an improvised and a preplanned offer
- The economy of a silent offer and yield
- Physical and vocal (verbal or gibberish) offers
- Building stories with partners
- Short improvisations from offers of place
- Dealing with tasks, objectives, events
- Working with the whole group, small groups, pairs, alone
- Working towards scene endings
- Simple endowments
- Yielding to still and moving focus
- Developing very simple characters and expressions
- Working for short periods in front of the whole group

They are now ready to develop their skills and explore introductory scene-work.

part B

TRAINING SKILLS AND SCENE-WORK

When players accept, identify and name offers, establish a well-defined scene location, can action an event and develop simple ideas into a story, they begin to build short scenes. To this point, most of the work has developed in silence and, except for occasional moments, all verbal offers have been made one-word-at-a-time. Players now build short interchanges, speaking to each other in complete sentences as individuals.

Introducing scene-work requires accurate sidecoaching [see Process – Sidecoaching strategies and tips]. Scene-work begins in pairs with the whole group working at the same time. Then, when foundation skills are solid, introduce the group watching two players building a scene. [See Process – Scene-work.] The link to all scene-work is THE PRESENT GAME.

THE PRESENT GAME

training game
2–32 players
5–20 minutes
8+ years

The present game is at the root of the work from this point on. It operates as a foundation tool for every program and provides a solid structure for opening communication channels and building simple ideas into scenes.

Description: Players give each other gifts and name them.

Resource: A clear space.

Time-out: No.

Example of a title: Not applicable.

Aim: To give, receive and name a variety of offers.

Degree of difficulty: I

Skills to be developed: Giving, receiving and naming the offer.

Suggested preparation: All work in this program so far.

How it works — Step one: Begin with a demonstration in front of the whole group. This is one occasion when coach demonstration is required. Choose a player to work with you. Keep this informal. Have the rest of the group stand or sit around you rather than you standing out the front as if performing. The demonstration lasts about one minute. The coach picks up an imaginary mimed gift and gives it to the player. Endow the gift with size, weight, shape: 'Judy, I've got a present for you'. Stop the scene but keep the mimed gift in your hands. Ask the whole group what they think the present could be. If the gift looks big and heavy, suggestions such as a video, a television, a stove, are named. Now ask your partner what they think it is. Remind the group that all answers are correct. Ask your partner to accept the gift and name it. Now ask your partner to give you a gift in the same way.

Judy picks up an imagined gift. It can be small, big, heavy or light. She gives it to the coach, who accepts it, names it and adds, 'and…'.

Judy: 'Miss Pierse, I've got a present for you.'
Miss Pierse (coach): 'Oh, a light bulb and it glows red.'

Reiterate to the group the simple process that has occurred. The present has been accepted, named, and an 'and' has been added by the player who received the gift. What follows the 'and' tells us something more about the gift. In this simple two line exchange, both players have started a small scene. At this point, do not go beyond this two line exchange.

Step two: Break the group into pairs. Both players give each other gifts in this fashion. Players give each other at least six gifts each.

Always play The present game standing on your feet (unless players are disabled). Encourage players to believe and imagine (image and see) the gifts they receive.

Sidecoach: 'Accept the gift with the size, shape and weight with which it is given.'
Sidecoach: (if players look away from the gift) 'See the gift. Share the focus.'
Sidecoach: 'Name it.'
The receiver names the gift immediately.

When the gift is named, both players know what the offer in the scene is. They both have access to the information.

There are two ways of playing the exercise. If you give something and you have an idea of what the gift could be, you may be pre-empting the scene. Be prepared for the other player to name the gift as they imagine it, rather than hoping they name what you had in mind. When you give something and you do not know what it is, you can be affected by your partner's response. Then both players share the control of the scene. Listening to your partner then becomes second nature and a joy.

Sidecoach: 'Be changed by the gift.'
'Enjoy the gift.'
'Want to know what your partner has received. Want to hear their reaction.'
'Overaccept the other player's ideas.'
'Allow your partner's reaction to change you.'
'Make the present really enjoyable.'

Step three: Play THE PRESENT GAME without words. Players give each other a present and use the gift. The gift is not mouthed or demonstrated. It is named by being used, for example a player receives a vase and names it by filling it with water and placing flowers in it. The giver watches what the receiver does with the gift. This non-verbal naming encourages both players to look carefully at their partner. The exercise is quiet and has a calming effect on players.

Step four: Then play it in gibberish. Players give, receive and name the gift in gibberish. When speaking gibberish, players must be as clear in their physical presentations as they were when miming. The gibberish releases an emotional connection to the gift and builds the relationship between the players. If players are not confident in gibberish, warm up with GIBBERISH CIRCLE. [See Warm-up games.]

Tips for text

For players 15+ years

Write on the board:

offer + yield = idea + yes

offer + yield = action + reaction

The equations explain the process at work. THE PRESENT GAME provides a golden rule for acting. If one actor gives a line to another as if it were a gift, wanting to know how it affects the other actor, the acting becomes less self-conscious. The players begin to affect each other and each is more inclined to be changed by the other actor. Take a piece of text. Follow two characters speaking to each other. Does the dialogue reveal the effects one character has on another? If so, how?

Tips for tots

For players 8–11 years

Play THE PRESENT GAME sitting or standing in a circle. Player A chooses another player, crosses the circle and gives them a present. Player B names it and says, 'and…'. For example, 'It's a pen, and it writes with pink ink.' Player B gives a new present to a third player. Do not go around the circle in order because players, knowing that their turn is coming, may become anxious or preplan. Players give presents to any player in the circle.

Building THE PRESENT GAME into NO-BLOCKING SCENES 12+

With modification, the following can be enjoyed by players under 12 years, but be prepared for slow, simple work, as they may not yet be ready for longer scenes.

Introduce NO-BLOCKING SCENES (where players overaccept all offers) by developing THE PRESENT GAME a step further. [See Program two for a detailed description of NO-BLOCKING SCENES and THE PRESENT GAME.] Bring two players in front of the group. They begin with THE PRESENT GAME. They now extend past the gift and continue past the 'and' to build short scenes of 5–15 seconds.

Each player yields to every offer. Sidecoach when necessary. Stop the scene if blocks occur (ie when players are not accepting each other's ideas, not yielding). Keep these scenes very, very short. Allow players to have a positive experience improvising in front of their peers. They do not yet have the skills to play scenes longer than about a minute.

NO-BLOCKING SCENES 12+

Now develop the previous exercise by introducing a NO-BLOCKING SCENE without the structure of THE PRESENT GAME. Again, start with two players in front of the group. Player A gives player B an offer which is accepted and developed. Player A could give the offer of rowing a boat and player B yields by picking up the other oar and rowing too, or stands looking through binoculars to the shore. The scene continues with both players agreeing with all the ideas that arise in the scene. If there is a block, sidecoach the players past the block or replace the blocking player with another player and begin a new scene or continue the same scene. Actively involve the whole group in recognising the blocks and calling 'block' when they occur. Keep the spirit positive with a sense of fun. Down-play failure and criticism. Play the scene without words then with words. If players devour the work, play the scenes in gibberish, rhyming couplets and singing the lines.

BLOCKING SCENES 12+

If players have difficulty accepting each other's ideas, introduce a BLOCKING SCENE. This is set up in the same way as the NO-BLOCKING SCENE, but players must block every idea offered by the other player. Begin the scene without words. Both players negate each offer made by their partner. They destroy all mimed objects, walk through doors, etc. In most cases, players find it impossible to block more than two or three offers in a row. Blocking scenes build confidence. Players realise that intuitive yielding and saying 'yes' is easier than blocking. BLOCKING SCENES also raise the energy level and create laughter, which evens the status of the group and decreases the fear of failure.

One-word-at-a-time and the Present game

training game
2–32 players
10–15 minutes
9+ years

Now we combine the two training games One-word-at-a-time and The present game to consolidate skills already developed.

Description: Two pairs of players give each other a present speaking one-word-at-a-time.

Resource: A clear space.

Time-out: No.

Example of a title: Not applicable.

Aim: To give, receive and name offers, building a small scene.

Degree of difficulty: 1.5

Skills required: Ability to offer and yield one-word-at-a-time.

Suggested preparation: All work in this program so far.

How it works: Players form pairs and speak one-word-at-a-time. They meet another pair and offer them a present which is accepted, named, and used. All is played one-word-at-a-time. Allow scenes to develop as far as possible. Extend into a No-blocking scene. Both pairs give each other a present. Sidecoach towards a scene ending. [See Process – Finishing a scene; Bringing down the lights; Time limits.]

Agreement and conflict

To this point, the work has encouraged all players to agree with, and yield to, other players' ideas. How do we achieve conflict and drama in improvisation if players are training to agree with each other all the time? Conflict and disagreement are the essence of dramatic tension. However it is more important at this early stage of skills development that players agree to agree on the ideas in the scene. Argument about the scene and the offers in it leads to blocking. Concentrate on yielding and overaccepting until both become second nature. Keep agreement at a maximum until players have the skills to identify the difference between a blocked offer and characters having a difference of opinion. These require an understanding of status and other endowment skills yet to be developed.

Dropped offers

Dropped offers are ideas that are not dealt with. They occur for a number of reasons. They are usually an indication that players are not listening. Sometimes the excitement of the moment causes players to stop listening and looking. At other times offers are dropped when players flip through ideas at the rate of knots as they search for a better idea. Some players panic and attempt to control the scene by bulldozing it with their own ideas.

While the good news is that players are experiencing a flow of ideas, the bad news is that they are not following them through; they are dropping them. The abundance of ideas is terrific, but they only need one idea or offer at a time. If they are dropping offers, players need to work on the following skills:

- Slowing the scene down
- Listening and watching for offers given by the other player
- Dealing with one offer at a time
- Being changed by what is said by the other player

Sidecoach: 'Pick up the offer.'

If players cannot sustain the scene and continually drop offers, sidecoach the scene to a close or stop it. Go to ONE-WORD-AT-A-TIME STORY or THE PRESENT GAME. This will reinforce offer-for-offer playing and separate one idea from the next.

Sometimes continuing the scene in gibberish will allow players to concentrate on how the other player is relating to them rather than on what they want to say next.

YES AND.../YES BUT...

training game
2–32 players
3–12 minutes
8+ years

Description: Players answer 'Yes and...' or 'Yes but...' to a given offer and build short scenes.

Resource: A small space. Players may sit at desks or on the floor but better results are achieved when players move on their feet and do the scene rather than talk about it.

Time-out: No.

Example of a title: First line — 'Let's go to the beach'; 'Is this your pedigreed dog?'

Aim: To overaccept offers.

Degree of difficulty: 1.5

Skills required: Ability to make offers, listen and yield.

Suggested preparation: NAMING THE OBVIOUS; NAMING THINGS AS THEY ARE NOT; THE PRESENT GAME.

How it works: YES AND... assists in developing agreement and helps players to take their ideas further. Players learn to feed off each other's ideas and share the responsibility for them. No single player dominates or has greater control of the information. The game's inherent structure allows both players to share the scene equally. Players simply say 'Yes and...' to every idea the other player says. The simple YES AND... training structure is introduced at this stage and continued at all levels from here on.

Step one: One player asks the other a question that can be answered with 'Yes and...'. This sometimes takes time for players to become used to. Much laughter arises as they think of questions to ask each other.

Player A offers an idea:	'Let's go to the beach.'
Player B agrees and adds 'and':	'Yes, and I've got two beach towels.'
Player A:	'We can sit on the beach and watch the sun set.' ('Yes and' implied.)
Player B:	'Yes and there is a full moon tonight.'

Continue this Yes and... structure for about one minute. Players always agree with every idea. Remind players not to think too hard but to practise saying the first idea that comes into their head rather than trying to think up a clever idea.

Step two: When players are familiar with the structure, throw the training game away. Play short No-blocking scenes using the foundation 'yes and' as implied rather than saying 'yes and' every time.

Play the scene with two players in front of the whole group. Give an offer of place as a starting point — eg two friends meeting at a party. Sidecoach the scene and bring it to a natural conclusion. If a third character is required, send another player into the scene to join the other two. Instead of a conversation sounding like this:

Player A: 'Have you met my friend?'
Player B: 'Yes and her name is Georgie.'

The conversation now sounds like this:

Player A: 'Have you met my friend?'
Player B: 'Georgie, it's a change to see you out of uniform.'

In the latter, player B has implied 'yes and' rather than having stayed within the boundaries of the training game.

Step three: Yes but... Sometimes players are tempted to say 'Yes but...' and water down an idea or wimp on it. Encourage players to use 'Yes but...' as a way of yielding rather than blocking or wimping.

Divide the group into pairs to play the game. Then play the game with two players in front of the group as scene-work. Give players a starting place or activity.

Player A: 'Is this your pedigreed dog?'
Player B: 'Yes but I share it with my sister.'

Yes but... results in unusual and unexpected ideas which build into interesting scenes. Continue this structure; 'yes but' every idea.

Step four: Now build scenes which combine the two. Play No-blocking scenes in which players yield to every offer. They interchange 'Yes but...' and 'Yes and...' whenever they wish. Set up the No-blocking scenes beginning with offers of place, activities or relationships (siblings, friends, neighbours). Be clear in the sidecoaching of these early scenes and bring them to an end within a minute or two to ensure that players experience a sense of achievement rather than playing longer scenes before they have the skills to do so.

Offer and yield scene-building skills

Now is the time to assess your coaching skills and players' skills and understanding of the work to date.

•

Check

To assess players' scene-building skills, ask yourself the following questions of their work while their scenes are in action:

- Do they laugh when you sidecoach, 'Say yes' (in recognition of their blocking)?
- Do they say/imply 'yes' spontaneously to more than one offer in a row?

- Are their thoughts connected to a physical response?
- Do they yield with a physical response?
- Can they hear you sidecoach? Do they accept it?
- Are they imaging place?
- Do they recognise the focus and yield to it?
- Can they make an offer without speaking?
- Can they make an offer speaking for less than five seconds?
- Do they listen and yield to an offer when it is the first offer in the scene and the offer was made by the other player?

If the answer is 'yes' to all of these questions for the majority of players, the group is ready for more sophisticated scene-work and Theatresports games.

A 'no' answer on any of the above could indicate that basic foundation work is not complete. Reiterate skills as necessary before moving on.

part C

THEATRESPORTS PERFORMANCE GAMES

Many of these games are exactly the same as the training games. They function in both training and in performance. Make sure all players have experienced these in training before performing them for each other — class members as audience. No player is ready to perform before an audience other than their classmates until the seven training programs have been completed. Do not introduce any performance games until all players have completed all the components of Program one — parts A and B, unless you are introducing one or two games as discussed in Part A – Summary — this program.

Introduce simple Theatresports games such as Mime and One-word-at-a-time story as scene-work. Rather than introducing time limits, allow the scenes to find natural endings and sidecoach them carefully.

ONE-WORD-AT-A-TIME STORY

classic

training game
performance game
2–4 players
up to 2 minutes
8+ years

Description: Situation or title given. Team members tell a story one-word-at-a-time.

Resource: A clear space.

Time-out: No.

Example of a title: Curing the koala king; The journey of the time travellers; Quest for the killer bees.

Aim: To yield to all offers and overaccept them.

Degree of difficulty: 1.5

Skills required: Listening and speaking.

Suggested preparation: Circle tag; Knife and fork; Word ball; One-word-at-a-time training games.

How it works: Players stand next to each other telling a story, speaking one word each in order, one-word-at-a-time. Players move while telling the story. Physicalisation of the story is to be encouraged.

The story is of maximum importance. The structure gives players an opportunity to develop an idea with a beginning, a middle and an end. Begin with simple plot structures:

- Introduce theme or problem
- Develop theme or problem
- Solve theme or problem
- Sum up with a moral or conclusion

•

Tip

Vary the playing from pairs and trios to fours, and have players maintain regular eye contact with each other.

This is a wonderful team game. There are so many ways to play it. Players can stand close to each other or move across wide distances. This game keeps the status of all players equal because all players share equal responsibility for the story at all times.

Performance: When playing 'game on game' in performance, vary the presentation. If the previous team played with four players, play the next One-word-at-a-time story with two players.

For players 15+ who crave more: When skills are solid players spread out over the space, keeping eye contact with their partner. They physicalise the story but no longer make physical contact.

SPEAKING IN ONE VOICE

training game
performance game
2–4 players
up to 2 minutes
8+ years

AKA Simultaneous Talking

Description: Title or interview situation given. Two (or more) team members combine to become one voice.

Resource: A clear space; taped lyrical music as in The mirror game. [See Warm-up games.]

Example of a title: Parachuting; Buying a car.

Activities, characters, simple problems to solve are best.

Aim: To speak in unison with other players.

Degree of difficulty: 1.5

Skills required: Ability to listen, speak and overaccept all offers, keeping concentration and eye contact with fellow players.

Suggested preparation: Vocal warm-up; Yes let's; Where do you come from?; The mirror game — extended to voice.

How it works: This game requires the same skills of players as One-word-at-a-time, but players speak simultaneously. For those who have not seen this game in action it is surprising to imagine, but it is possible for players to speak simultaneously without preplanning.

Players form pairs (as skills increase, form threes or fours). They link up with arms around each other. They speak extremely slowly, over-emphasising every sound in an effort to speak at the same time. When players speak simultaneously, they speak as the same character.

Encourage players not to lead the speaking. Let the sounds form slowly and gradually develop into words rather than thinking of the words and then forcing the sounds.

Robert McFarlane

The Horrid Girlie Swats imaging and moving together as they tell a story — Mackay champions 1989

Step one: Introduce Simultaneous talking in pairs to the whole group at the same time. To build a sense of trust and concentration, keep the same partner for the duration of this session.

Begin with The mirror game to emphasise eye contact and concentration with a particular partner. Players stand close together facing each other and find a shared breathing pattern. They slowly move as one and then extend the shared movement into speech by concentrating on each other's breathing. The players work in harmony. It is impossible to know where each sound and movement starts. There is no leader. Both players move as one. They continue the physical movement of The mirror game, and allow a 'hum' to form on their lips, creating sound. They watch each other's mouths and faces closely until both mouths are moving at the same time and sound is being shared and mirrored. Remember that close eye contact such as this is confronting for some players and could take some time to develop.

Encourage the exploration of physical and vocal sounds — clapping, stamping, humming, etc.

Sidecoach: 'Explore different levels, eg walls, floor.'
'Change focus.'
'Develop sounds into words.'
'Look at each other, make eye contact.'

Step two: Pairs move around the space with each player linked or standing close to their partner. Take the same physical considerations into account as with One-word-at-a-time, that is, beware of players restricting their movements when combining with their partner to form one person. They are one person speaking as 'we'. They play Naming the obvious, speaking simultaneously. When they have achieved this, they play Naming things as they are not.

Step three: Now introduce The present game, using two pairs, each speaking in one voice. One pair gives the other pair a present. The whole group works at the same time. Short scenes develop between pairs and groups of pairs.

Step four: Develop from The present game with two pairs, each speaking in one voice, working in front of the whole group. Introduce scenes with an objective — something to achieve in the scene: to borrow one hundred dollars, or to reveal that you have crashed the other character's car. Give players a starting location and character — in the kitchen on a Sunday morning, father and daughter. Daughter tells father she has crashed the car. Give them only the bare bones. Don't tell them how to do it. Beware of scripting. Allow them to improvise.

•

Tip

From time to time, vary the number of players, grouping to form characters who speak in one voice. Increase pairs to threes and then to fours as skills progress.

Step five: This is a Keith Johnstone training game. Involve the whole group as two characters. Divide the group in half and place them on opposite sides of the room. There could be 15 players making up each character. One half becomes one character, and the other half another; for example, all males one group, all females in another group. Set an objective and location, perhaps at a party with the objective of getting to know one another.

Have one whole group meet the other whole group with simple objectives: to find out their name — ask them out to dinner — give them a present, etc.

Step six: When players are comfortable with the convention, introduce open improvisation involving the whole group. Players work in pairs who speak in one voice. Good situations are: at the market, buying a used car, fighting a fire, at a party, in a court-room. Some preplanning and decision-making about characters and discussion concerning some events and the specifics of the location are advisable before working with the whole group in a big improvisation such as this. A 40 minute period can be productively spent speaking in one voice if the group becomes interested in working in this way.

•

Tip

In all the above, planning what to say next is pointless. The value of the work is in meeting the problems and challenges on the floor in the moment.

Watch the group dynamics, and adjust the exercises to the needs of the group. Needs vary according to the group's skills and level of maturity.

SHARED STORY

classic

performance game
4 players
2 minutes
8+ years

Description: Team tells a story, one phrase or sentence at a time.

Resource: A clear space.

Time-out: No.

Example of a title: Revenge of the scout leader; I was a computer virus.

Choose titles which give the story an event, interesting character descriptions, mood, possible tension, dramatic plot line.

Aim: To tell a collective story.

Degree of difficulty: 1

Skills required: Ability to build a simple plot and tell a simple story.

Suggested preparation: Hospital tiggy; Yes let's; Where do you come from?; Die game (see below) without elimination.

How it works: This is the simplest of the story-telling games. Players experience a high degree of achievement within a short time. Team members form a line and tell a shared story down the line in turn, speaking a phrase or part of a sentence each. Players develop a continuous story, building on the ideas of the previous player. Players who merely say a sentence each are not enjoying the full potential of the game. Encourage further risk by leaving a sentence or thought incomplete as a cliff-hanger for the next team-mate to complete. Work towards the whole team thinking and imaging as one. Physicalisation of the story strengthens plot development.

DIE GAME

training game for
SHARED STORY
performance game
3–4 players
2–4 minutes
15+ years

AKA: STORY STORY DIE

Description: Title given. Players form a line and tell a shared story. They speak only at the indication of a conductor who points to the players, changing the storyteller at random. Players are eliminated if they pause too long, stumble, are grammatically incorrect or repeat the previous player's last word. The last remaining player wins.

Resource: A clear space.

Time-out: No.

Example of a title: My life as the two-headed zombie; Travelling through Europe.

Aim: To tell a story.

Degree of difficulty: I

Skills required: Ability to tell a simple story and yield to all offers.

Suggested preparation: HOSPITAL TIGGY; YES LET'S; WHERE DO YOU COME FROM?

How it works: The team of storytellers stands in a line facing the audience. The conductor is a player from the same team, another team, the coach (in training) or the timekeeper or compere (in performance). The conductor sits on the floor in front of the storytellers and points at random to the players to indicate which player will tell the next part of the shared story. Players speak only while they are being pointed at. Each storyteller picks up the story from where the previous player left off. When players hesitate, falter or lose their place, the audience calls 'Die!' at which the offending player steps gallantly out of the line and performs a mimed death. Players solicit death weapon, place and activity from the audience, or simply choose their own method of dying and drop to the floor. The story continues with the remaining players. The last remaining player wins.

In training, introduce the DIE GAME by playing SHARED STORY with the conductor and gradually introduce the death. This is terrific fun. In scene-work and performance the audience loves the game because they become the judges of the onstage players, determining the faults and calling 'Die!'

The main value of the game lies in its function as a training game for SHARED STORY. It gives players an opportunity to speak for short periods of time (sometimes only a few words). All players share the storytelling, speaking briefly and passing it on rather than controlling the story by speaking for a long time.

•

Beware

For some players under 15 years, the elimination factor can derail the story, disrupting the flow and the players' concentration. Every time a player is eliminated, the story is interrupted to the extent that the coach needs to reiterate the last point of the story made before the death. Use the competitive elimination with discretion.

Competition: In competition played in front of an audience, it is necessary for the compere to demonstrate the game in order for the audience to yell 'Die!' at the appropriate moment. This is usually played with 2–8 players. The last remaining player wins the predetermined number of points (usually one or two) for their team.

DIE GAME is an interesting performance game, but beware of it as tie-breaker. It can become very competitive. However, if players enter the spirit of the game, it is great fun.

•

Tips for tots

For some players under 12 years the game may not be appropriate as it creates too much pressure and fear of failure.

SHARED STORY MIXED GENRE

training game
performance game
4 players
2 minutes
14+ years

Description: Title and styles given. Players tell the same story, each telling it in a different genre.

Resource: A clear, small space.

Time-out: No, but allocate genres.

Example of a title: Climbing the southern alps; Journey through Toyland.

Example of genres: Mills and Boon; science fiction; instruction manual; Dr Seuss; a fairytale; Raymond Chandler; Aussie yarn. [See Appendix B – Genres.]

Aim: To explore story-telling, literary styles and story-telling genres.

Degree of difficulty: 3

Suggested preparation: HOSPITAL TIGGY; YES LET'S; STORY BALLS; DIE GAME without elimination; SHARED STORY.

How it works: Each player in the team is assigned a style or genre. The rest of the set-up is the same as that for SHARED STORY. Each player tells their part of the given story in their assigned style or genre — for example, one player tells the story in the style of an Agatha Christie story, the next in the style of the *Women's Weekly*, the next as a Thomas Hardy novel and the last as science fiction. The change of style usually helps to advance the story.

•

Tip

Use a conductor (as in DIE GAME) to increase spontaneity. Do not eliminate players.

•

Global

BALL GAMES are excellent training for story-telling and can be developed from word association exercises to complete story forms. Ball games are many and varied. [See Warm-up games.]

POEM

classic

performance game
4 players
1–2 minutes
10+ years

Description: Title given. Team members compose an original poem.

Resource: A clear space. A small space is acceptable. Simple musical instruments for developing rhythm and rhyme: drum, tambourine, triangle.

Time-out: No. Encourage immediate response to the title as a starting point. Talking about it could block or reduce the initial spontaneous impulse and response.

Example of a title:

Simple descriptive:	Red shoes; Rainy days.
Activity:	Walking to the beach at dawn.
Character:	The fishmonger's daughter, Bob the bully badger.
Hypothetical:	Maybe it's because I'm an alien.

Aim: To explore the language of poetry.

Degree of difficulty: 3

Skills required: Ability to listen and tell a story in rhyme.

How it works: Four members of a team stand in a line and tell a poem, one-line-at-a-time.

Step one: Finding rhythm and rhyme.

Not all players will find this easy to achieve. Here are some ideas for starting points.

Begin with the whole group standing close to each other in a circle so they can hear every other player. The coach or a player taps a steady slow beat softly on a drum, tambourine or triangle. Do not race. The group constructs a poem one-line-at-a-time around the circle, using the drum as a guide to establish the rhythm. Players physicalise the rhythm — beating a leg, head-swaying, clapping, tapping, etc. The shared rhythm helps the words of the poem to flow.

As skills develop, add other instruments to develop syncopation.

•

Tip

Extend this exercise into the Theatresports performance game SONG simply by singing the poem.

Encourage players to use physical formations as suggested by the images created by the title of the poem.

If a player cannot find a rhyme, allow other players to call a rhyme to 'save' the situation and continue the beat. Players share responsibility for the narrative and the rhythm. Players should not feel a sense of failure for not having found a rhyme. All players should feel safe at all times.

Some players experience the pressure of searching for the perfect rhyme. Rather than stop the spontaneous flow and rhythm, encourage 'made up' or gibberish words to complete rhymes. This will build confidence in early training and reduce the feeling of failure.

While rhyme is suggested, it is not obligatory. Simple rhyme gives the poem form. It is, of course, not essential if players are attempting a particular style, eg haiku.

Step two: Introduce rhyming schemes. Experiment with a variety of poetic structures. The simplest are the following:
The second and fourth lines rhyme, and there is no rhyme between the first and third lines:

I like to wear red shoes,
I wear them all the day,
And when I put them on my feet,
I want to skip and play.

Or, the first and second lines rhyme, and the third and fourth lines rhyme:

I like to wear red shoes,
They help me fight the blues,
I put them on my feet,
It's really quite a treat.

Or the limerick:

There was a young woman a singer,
Whose red shoes made her look like a swinger,
When on her feet,
She'd sing up a treat,
Then the barman a drink he would bring 'er.

Sonnet form and iambic pentameter are for more dextrous and older players.

Titles: Those which suggest imagery and description are the richest. They might include simple characters, alliteration and rhythm, and indicate style and form. Begin with simple titles and develop as skills grow.

Titles in the style of:

Sonnet: My lover's eye doth thrill me
Ode: Ode to a housefly
Limerick: There was an old lady from Canberra

Some advanced players enjoy developing poems from titles close to those of existing poems which they may be studying or other well known poems, eg 'Shall I compare thee to the milky way?' or 'The man with snowy liver'. For some players these can be great fun, but they could block the imagination of players who try to come close to the original style. They spend their time being clever rather than enjoying improvising.

Help players to develop the imagery in the poetry and advance the narrative. Encourage all players to image the poem as they speak. When players are physicalising, encourage them to see the same pictures and move toward the same scene. Sidecoach towards a shared common focus using the six focus zones. [See Program two.] Develop each poem as a story with a beginning, a middle and an end, regardless of its style.

Performing Poem

Most teams form a line shoulder-to-shoulder when playing word and story games. Poem is no exception. A basic structure for this line-up when four players are in a team is as follows:

Player 1: introduces the first offer of the narrative.
Player 2: develops and extends the offer given by player 1 and develops the plot line.
Player 3: extends the offer further or introduces a new element to advance the story (can rhyme with player 1).
Player 4: has little control over the story-line and needs to feel free to say whatever they can think of in order to rhyme.

On the second stanza, sidecoach player 1 to pick up the last offer or the main idea given by player 4. This will keep the narrative tight and reduce the possibility of dropped offers.

•

Tip

Poem is a game when there may seem to be one answer that is more correct than another, one rhyme more effective than another. Poem is not an easy game, even for the most experienced players. But it is terrific fun. Spontaneity is at an all-time high if players are given the permission to enjoy playing with the language and taking a risk rather striving to be right.

Poem can be introduced very early in training and developed as skills increase. It is a good team warm-up, especially before a performance.

RHYMING COUPLETS

classic

training game
performance game
2–4 players
1–2 minutes
13+ years

Description: Situation given. Team plays the scene speaking in rhyming couplets.

Resource: A clear space, props and costumes.

Time-out: Yes. Best used to decide one of the following: location, activity, characters.

Example of a title: Active — Digging to China; Escape from hell. Location — At the supermarket; At customs; The other side of the wall.
Degree of difficulty: 3

Skills required: Ability to play a simple scene and rhyme.

Suggested preparation: Word ball and story building; Shared story in a circle developing a rhythm as described in Poem step one; Gibberish circle played the same way; The present game played in rhyming couplets.

How it works: Players play a scene but speak in rhyming couplets. This is a narrative game. The story is very important.

When locations are given, sidecoach towards doing the obvious main physical activity associated with the location. For example: at the supermarket — shopping, stacking, pricing, checking-out. Encourage something to happen. Sidecoach towards an event.

Beware of having too many players in the scene. The excitement of the rhyme often disrupts team deployment. At least one player would best serve the scene by staying off. They will be needed as the rhyming scheme becomes more developed and new characters are required to develop the plot or to clarify the plot-line if it becomes confused.

It is easy in these wordy structures to forget physicality. Sidecoach players to physicalise the verbal suggestions they make and name in the scene. Talking about the scene stops the scene. Remember, not everyone in the scene needs to speak all the time, if at all.

Encourage players to spend time in the scene without speaking. This will allow the development of place and other physical offers that are often lost when the emphasis is placed on rhyming rather than on developing a scene.

Players can save each other by completing the couplet or rhyming scheme started by a team-mate.

Performing Rhyming couplets

This game is often used as a handle. [See Basic terms and skills – Handle.] Although often played in the one minute time frame, two or three minutes allow for clearer, less panicked scenes.

Some players enjoy rhyming the scene for its complete duration. Others enjoy changing from rhymed to unrhymed speech. Practise blowing a whistle at intervals of about 20-30 seconds throughout the scene, calling 'rhyming couplets' and 'stop rhyming couplets'. Call these changes as new elements of the story are introduced and the scene advances — eg the entrance of a new character, or a change of location or mood. The calls are never given at random or without thought. In performance, rhyme calls are given by the timekeeper. Listen to the narrative and support it with the call. When players enjoy a flow of rhyme, allow the rhyming time frame to increase until players rhyme a whole scene.

The handle of rhyming couplets can be applied to most scenes and games. Introduce a section of rhyme in a Space jump, Expert double figures or Truth.

Competition: Judges should reward these scenes for plot, character development and risk.

•

Tip

Coach a whole class speaking in rhyme yourself from start to finish.

Tips for text

For players 15+

Take a Shakespeare play and discuss the journey of the rhyming scheme through the story. Discuss the different effects of the rhyme on the plot development, the characters and our understanding of the status of the characters in the play.

•

Magic moment

In a Hobart competition, Nigel Curtain-Smith, needing an additional team member, brought the stage manager's phone to the stage to ring player Gary McCaffrie in Adelaide. They played RHYMING COUPLETS together over the phone, into the microphone and out to the audience.

MIME

classic

performance game
2–4 players
usually 1 minute
8+ years

Description: Situation given. The team plays a scene without words.

Resource: A clear space. Minimal props, if any. Improvised instrumental music may support the scene.

Time-out: If necessary.

Example of a title: At the weight-loss or weight-gaining clinic; In the trenches; Hanging wallpaper.

Aim: To tell a simple story without words.

Degree of difficulty: 1.5

Skills required: Ability to make and yield to physical offers.

Suggested preparation: WHERE DO YOU COME FROM?; THE MIRROR GAME; THE PRESENT GAME in mime.

How it works: Players improvise a scene in mime. Give the starting point of a location or an activity. Encourage players to begin with large physical offers and build simple scenes toward an event. Mimes are usually very short scenes, so keep the story simple. Encourage players to concentrate on a common focus and not to have too many characters on the stage at the same time. Remember that it is possible for the most domestic situations to reach epic proportions both comic and tragic when scenes are mimed.

Clear actions without words make for riveting scenes. You don't have to be Marcel Marceau to play and enjoy mime, but attention to the discipline of mime technique lends clarity and theatrical presentation. A session spent on the skills of miming opening and closing doors and windows, walking, running and experimenting with the size, weight and shape of objects will clarify the mime.

Styles: There is a variety of mime performance styles: pantomime/silent-picture/melodrama. Offstage music enhances the speed and rhythm of scenes in the style of 'silent picture'. Move to the pace and style of the music.

Performance: An excellent choice of game for a nervous team or when playing in a large auditorium where vocal projection is difficult. A mime galvanises a team early in a match because it encourages team members to keep eye contact and support a shared focus. [See Program two.]

SPICS 'N' SPECKS

training game
performance game
usually 2 players
2 minutes
12+ years

AKA Who what where?

Description: Situation given. One or more players encounter a 'voice' (provided by an offstage player), which must be located, named and dealt with.

Resource: A clear space. Sometimes in performance a microphone is used by the offstage player who provides the voice of the speck.

Time-out: No.

Example of a title: A place or activity: In a video parlour; At the agricultural show; Doing up your shoelaces.

Aim: To name offers.

Degree of difficulty: 1.5

Skills required: Ability to offer, yield, name and overaccept offers.

Suggested preparation: Where do you come from?; Naming the obvious; Naming things as they are not; Here and now; The present game; Yes and...

How it works: This game is helpful as an early training and performance game because it builds a simple scene between two players who are required to name and identify offers with clarity.

One player enters the space, sets up the scene and begins it. The other player stays offstage providing the tiny voice for the little 'speck', which advances the scene. The offstage player (providing the speck's voice) sits so as to see the onstage action. After the onstage player enters and sets up the scene, the speck breaks the routine with a vocal offer interrupting the onstage action. The onstage player establishes belief in the tiny invisible object by looking towards the place in the scene where the speck is — **not** at the offstage player providing the speck's voice. The speck guides the player to their whereabouts, being as pedantic as it wishes.

'Down here! I'm on your shoe. Ow! Lift up your foot, you moron, you're nearly squashing me!'

The speck names what they are: 'That's right, I'm the speck of dandruff on your shoulder.' Or, 'Yeah that's me, I'm the dust on your shoelace.'

The scene continues with the onstage player dealing with the speck and its demands. Encourage the onstage player to give the speck the focus and the status. Events in the scene could result in a change of status, but the speck usually requires attention and clear focus.

•

Beware

Confusion can occur when an additional onstage player enters the scene. Do they hear the voice? Do they ask questions about the voice? This player usually slows the scene down as the information is retold. Generally the clearest playing is achieved with one onstage player dealing with the speck. Do not encourage the presence of more than one onstage player until the mechanics of the game are understood.

Performance: This is a delightful performance game. However it rarely works when played game on game. Play it once as part of a narrative skills challenge. The best value from this game is in the training room because it demands that players clearly 'name' the offer. It also teaches a clear sense of visual and aural focus. [See Program two.]

Variations: Introduce the game using a small speck. However, the speck can also be enormous. Scenes have been played with a big booming offstage voice when the speck has been a mountain or a tree. For this reason the game is also known as WHO WHAT WHERE?

COMMERCIAL
classic

training game
performance game
1–4 players
1 minute
10+ years

Description: Product given. The team advertises it.

Resource: A clear space.

Time-out: If necessary.

Example of a title: A fur sink; Rubber bricks.

Vary the content by introducing a variety of products. You might choose titles that relate to work in other subjects across the curriculum; for example, set the scene in another historical period — an ancient Greek typewriter or a prehistoric dishcloth.

Aim: To introduce a simple objective.

Degree of difficulty: 2

Skills required: Ability to accept, overaccept, listen, name the offer, use props, play an objective, combine music and words, and tell an extremely simple story.

Suggested preparation: Warm-up game; KNIFE AND FORK; YES; SPICS 'N' SPECKS (see above); NO-BLOCKING SCENE.

How it works: This game combines many of the Program one skills: story-telling, mime, song, simple scene development and the playing of a scene objective. The objective of the scene is to advertise and sell a product. It does not have to be a television commercial. Encourage a variety of media and advertising techniques by exploring the avenues of radio, newspaper, billboard and live department store advertising.

Step one: Introduce the game in the early days of scene playing. Begin with a NO-BLOCKING SCENE in which one character has an objective — eg to sell a product.

Sidecoach the scene heavily towards playing and achieving the objective. Encourage the other player to yield and buy the product. If they overaccept the ideas, a transition could occur. They may be changed by the product.

Step two: Encourage players to explore the advertising techniques at work in radio and television advertising rather than just mimicking commercials that are well known. However, reward intelligent satirical comment. Use the game to explore the advertising processes at work. How effective are sex and social stereotyping, vocal inflections, aural and visual images, music and jingles, social conditioning and so on in advertising?

•

Beware

Beware of the team that preplans their advertising style. This does not encourage spontaneity.

SOUND ENVIRONMENT

training game
performace game
usually 2 players
2 minutes
8+ years

Description: Situation given. Onstage players play the scene with sound effects provided by player(s) offstage or by the audience.

Resource: A clear space, musical instruments, an audience.

Time-out: Yes.

Example of a title: Waiting for exam results.

Aim: To make clear, simple offers and build a simple story.

Degree of difficulty: 1.5

Skills required: Ability to make clear physical offers and to make and yield to sound effects.

Suggested preparation: SOUND BOARD; WHAT ARE YOU DOING?; Introduce offstage sounds to WHAT ARE YOU DOING? and MIME.

How it works: A team plays the scene. Team members, classmates or the audience provide offstage sounds for onstage players. They provide the sound effects for all the movements made by the onstage players and the objects they use, eg footsteps, opening doors, car sounds, pouring drinks. They do not provide voices for the onstage players.

Offers need to be clear, leaving plenty of time for the reaction to the sound. Split focus and offer overload will muddy the scene.

When working with an audience, divide it into sections. Designate one player to each half of the audience, so that the right side of audience makes one player's sounds and the left side makes the other player's sounds.

•

Tip

This is a helpful structure for developing environment and soundscapes for text, poetry and general story-telling.

Use this structure to support the playing of RADIO PLAY.

•

Magic moment

At the Cranston Cup '89 Grand Final at the Sydney Opera House, a two person team, *The Lonely Guys* (Marko Mustac and Michael Gregory), were challenged to Best use of the audience, which they chose to play as a SOUND ENVIRONMENT. The situation was given: 'Under Parliament House'. One player became a rat. The audience of 2100 made all the sound effects for both players, including the 'unzipping' of the rat's skin to reveal 'Sir Rodent Cutler', which won Moment of the match.

SONG
classic

performance game
4 players
2 minutes
12+ years

Description: Title given. Teams improvise an original song.

Resource: A clear space. Acoustic/percussive accompaniment is a good idea but not essential — piano, guitar, rhythm sticks, tambourine, maracca, etc.

Time-out: Yes.

Example of a title: Loving you is torture; Pancake baby; Skateboard rap.

Titles that suggest styles of music — blues, country and western, lullaby, punk, spiritual.

Aim: To explore improvised music and song.

Degree of difficulty: 2.5

Skills required: Ability to listen to, make and yield to musical offers.

Suggested preparation: Vocal warm-up, prepare as for POEM; rhythm and rhyme exercises in a circle, build to POEM in a circle, sing the POEMS.

How it works: Team members stand in a row or semicircle. They sing accompanied or unaccompanied, in unison or as individuals. They usually establish a chorus which solidifies the central ideas and establishes a style, rhythm and beat. Verses are usually sung by individuals who step forward from the group and return on completion. Some teams establish a style during the time-out. It is acceptable to confer with the musician if specific styles or beats are required. Solo singing is also acceptable. But backup singing is so much fun to do and enjoyable to watch that most teams contribute and sing as a team effort.

For most players, improvised singing is joyous. Yet some players find singing in front of other people confronting. Some may have had negative experiences being told they are tone-deaf, or cannot hold a tune or sound awful. Be sensitive to these players in your coaching. Remind players that improvised songs do not have to be perfect. There is much fun in simply singing and telling a story. Building up rhyming skills will reassure players who fear singing. Not all songs require a rhyme, but sometimes it helps. Begin improvised songs with the whole group. Experiment with a range of styles.

When working with an improvising musician, some teams prefer the musician to follow their lead and wait for the singing as the first offer in the song rather than allow the music to make the first offer. Some musicians are helpful by adjusting to the established key and aiding the singers to stay in key through the accompaniment. Some teams provide their own accompaniment with musical instruments such as tambourines, clap sticks or bells, or by sounds such as tongue clicking or thigh slapping.

Song in performance

Before a performance or competition, all coaches should decide, in consultation with the players and the tournament organiser, whether teams may accompany themselves on musical instruments such as the piano or guitar. Coaches convey this important information to the teams.

Mama mia — (left to right) Sue Cao, Eric 'Buck' Buckingham, Michael Wedemeyer, Andrew Foreman — performing Song in the round — La Boîte Theatre Brisbane 1991

The Madrigal

The madrigal is a 16th century song form in which players sing separately and together. Its simple structure builds confidence and provides an opportunity for all players to use their voices and experience sung improvisation.

How it works: Four players stand close together in a row. Each player is given (or asks for) a specific line to sing. Common ask-fors are:

- An advertising slogan, eg 'It's the real thing', 'Oh what a feeling', 'It's moments like these'.
- The name of a rock or pop star, eg Madonna, Elton John, Prince, Jenny Morris, John Farnham.

- Something your parents might tell you to do, eg 'Don't put your elbows on the table,' 'Be home before midnight,' 'Clean your teeth after meals.'
- A favourite dessert, eg bombe alaska, peach melba, cream tart, passionfruit pavlova.

Choose each 'ask for' from a different category.

The singers usually begin by cupping their hands on their chests in formal singing pose. They softly tune up, each selecting a note and humming it. This ensures that everyone has at least warmed their vocal chords before they sing. One player begins simply repeating their phrase or word over and over in a one, two or three note tune — the simpler, the better. The player with the fewest words is wise to start first to establish a simple regular beat, on a low note, on which the other players can build.

One by one, all the players sing their line and tune. As the layers of sound are established and all players are singing, one player steps forward and begins to improvise, incorporating their line with a word or phrase from another player's line: eg 'Madonna puts her elbows on the table'. We call this 'weaving'. The other players continue to sing their lines softly in the background. The weaving is repeated two or three times, and as the improvising player steps back, a second player steps forward. The weaving of lines and words continues, building a variety of possibilities which are often hilarious. As far as possible, players keep to the lines and phrases given; some words will be modified and added to clarify sense.

The madrigal is complete when every player has sung at least twice and many possibilities have been explored. The group concludes by bringing the volume to a crescendo or slowly fading out.

Tip

Some players enjoy being conducted. A conductor indicates the order of singing, who is to step forward, and when to 'weave', and signals volume changes and when to finish. The coach as conductor is a good idea in early training.

Da do ron ron

This song-game was invented by players Michael Gollege and Adam Couper in Brisbane, where it is a regular Theatresports feature performed for the audience after interval. All teams sing as one group and individuals are eliminated when they cannot complete the rhyme.

How it works: The audience selects a one syllable first name as the starting point, eg Sue, John, Beth, Bob. Players sing the tune of the 1960s popular song, *Da Do Ron Ron*, line by line, individually around the circle, substituting the new given name for 'Bill' and changing the song accordingly.

Player A: 'I met him on a Monday and his name was Bob.'
All: 'Da Do Ron Ron Ron Da Do Ron Ron.'
Player B: 'Somebody told me that he'd lost his job.'
All: 'Da Do Ron Ron Ron Da Do Ron Ron.'
Player C: 'Yeah he'd lost his job, oh the poor old slob.'
Player D: 'And he could be heard to sob.'
All: 'Da Do Ron Ron Ron Da Do Ron Ron.'

The song continues. All verses feature the same given name, eg 'Bob', as the basis for the rhyming pattern. Players search their vocabulary to find a number of words that rhyme with the name. All players attempt the rhyme and are eliminated when they cannot complete it. This is a Song warm-up rather than a performance game. It is a little like Die game without the conductor.

•

Magic moment

Wollongong player Julie Hockey, from the team *Fan Forced and Radiant*, sang up such a storm with a 'spiritual' one night that the audience stood (some on the seats) crying 'hallelujah'. I turned around to see a hat being passed through the audience — who were singing and filling it with money. But I couldn't believe my eyes when one audience member spontaneously donned dark glasses and tapped, as if blind, down the aisle to the stage and, after receiving a sung blessing, threw off the glasses. With his sight miraculously restored, he led the audience in the last refrain.

program 2

Finding the focus

Commandment

Thou shalt always retain focus.

Focus is a fundamental principle of improvisation. It is the pivotal skill for all improvised scenes and Theatresports games.

Focus is the central point of attention in the scene. It is what the players and the audience see and hear.

This sporting analogy may help. During a game of football or tennis, the ball is the focus of the players and the spectators. It is where the action is.

When improvising, our attention is on the invisible ball we call the focus.

Focus is created by the sound or movement that draws our attention.

Two players are having a conversation. We see the invisible ball passing between them. There is a knock at the door. Immediately the focus shifts. The two players and the audience now share a new focus.

When players support the focus of the scene, they are yielding (ie saying yes). When players do not support the focus of a given offer, they are blocking.

The focus and the offer are inseparable. The established focus always provides a possibility for a yield. Where players place their focus, they usually place their next offer.

Our aim is to develop skills to:
1. Establish focus
2. Recognise focus
3. Support focus

4. Yield to focus
5. Extend focus
6. Advance focus

As Viola Spolin says, 'It gives the control, the artistic discipline, in improvisation.' [See Spolin, *Improvisation for the Theatre.*]

In preparation for focus work, warm up with games which help sharpen concentration: Ball games; What are you doing?; Yes; You; Blindfold game.

All Theatresports games require the identification and understanding of still and moving focus. Games such as Statues rely on players finding the focus when it is still. Slow motion commentary relies on players identifying it when it is moving, and Space jump requires the skills to do both. Players need to understand focus and how to use it to improvise and to play Theatresports games.

FOCUS ZONES

As the focus ball moves, it travels within a space we call the 'focus zone'. Two players are having a conversation. The focus zone is created by where they are looking. If they are looking at each other, the focus zone is eye contact. If they are looking at the horizon, the focus zone becomes the horizon.

There are seven focus zones we use when improvising, acting, directing or playing Theatresports games:

- Body
- Eye contact
- Earth
- Underground
- Horizon
- Epic
- Inner landscape

Body

The most commonly used zone in all scenes and game playing is the area around the player's body. It is the realm of the domestic. It is usually concerned with objects, furniture, things within the grasp of the players as they complete day to day indoor or outdoor tasks.

Players tend to use this area from early days of playing, especially in exercises and games such as The present game, Yes and…, and No-blocking scenes as they complete simple tasks and activities.

A Theatresports coach keeps an alert eye on the focus when scenes develop in this zone because it is here that focus is most likely to become confused and split. Fledgling players need careful sidecoaching to believe in the objects they have created (walls, tables, car doors, steering wheels, glasses, coffee cups, crystal balls, tiny pets, telephones, or elevators) so they will not forget them and other players will not destroy them. This is one area where a knowledge of mime is useful.

Many games are played in this zone, the most common being Truth, Expert double figures, Spics 'n' specks, Mime, Voices off, Space jump and Endowments.

Sidecoach towards clear and articulate speech, well voiced simple offers (if speaking) and careful and precise use of peripheral vision when working in this zone.

Helpful warm-ups that build skills in this zone are You; Where do you come from?; ball games, eg Word ball; and games which involve mime, eg What are you doing?

Eye contact

This zone is created when players make eye-to-eye contact. When players look at each other, something is communicated between them.

Encourage players to extend moments of eye contact before advancing them. A look can be extended to reveal a range of emotions from great love to seething hate. Coach players to enjoy these moments and follow them through rather than send them up.

Unless required, generally keep off the stage when two onstage players are making eye contact. Focus can be easily split by players entering the scene who are insensitive to the possible extension of these moments of contact. If the players making eye contact do not extend or advance the scene, then another player may enter to save them.

Encourage eye contact in all scenes and game playing, but particularly in Truth, Voices off, One-word-at-a-time story, Shared story, Speaking in one voice.

Earth

This is the area on the ground at which the players are looking.

Encourage exploration of this level in training games and warm-ups. However, if playing to an audience use this level sparingly, as an audience needs to see the players' faces and eyes.

It is an area for surprise, change and quick discovery before a change of focus, for example, a player finds a letter on the ground. She bends down and picks it up, which changes the focus zone. The information in the letter advances the scene.

Moments of good earth focus can be found in games such as Space jump, Puppets, One-word-at-a-time story, Shared story, Statues.

•

Beware

If players and whole teams are heading to the ground too often, it is usually a sign that they are literally grinding to a halt. Sidecoach players to move to a new focus. For example:

Sidecoach to earth: 'See the letter on the floor. Pick it up. Read it.'
Sidecoach to epic: 'Look at the sky. Describe what you see.'
Sidecoach to underground: 'Open the trapdoor. Descend the stairs.'

Underground

This is the area underneath the ground. It is the area we cannot see.

There is a saying among Theatresports players in Edmonton, Canada: 'When in doubt, dig'. Many players literally dig for a new offer in the hope of finding something to save a scene. Exciting and wonderful offers can be found under the ground.

•

Tip

Keep eye level up as often as possible and allow the scene to 'surface' again.

If you dig to the underground, make sure an event occurs when you get there. It is terrific when players dig down to hell — as long as they meet the devil when they get there. Underground is common in scenes that involve quests, journeys and discoveries, eg ONE-WORD-AT-A-TIME STORY.

Horizon

This zone is created when players look towards a horizon — usually in or beyond the audience — painting a canvas of images in the distance for themselves and the audience. It may be from sea to land, land to sea, across a desert, and so on.

It is the realm of journey, adventure and travel. Anyone or anything may appear on the horizon. It holds the unknown. It is a theatrically powerful zone because it may envelop and include the audience and conquer the 'fourth wall', lifting the imaginary barrier between audience and player. It's thrilling! [See this program part D – The fourth wall.]

Audiences bristle with excitement when they are included in a scene. They have been known to enthusiastically provide sound effects, move their arms to become licking flames of fire or falling rain drops, and sing and speak in unison. They have even taken on a character en masse. In these moments improvised theatre holds the magic and risk audiences crave. On rare and wonderful occasions, players seize the opportunity to enter from the audience and incorporate them as part of the scene.

Encourage players to sustain their belief when working to the horizon. It takes strong concentration and bravery to sustain the enormous potential. It is also the zone for personal contemplation, song, and soliloquy. Shakespeare is the master of writing for the horizon.

Placing focus on the horizon gives a strong sense of location. The created sense of distance provides a terrific sense of expectation, excitement, discovery and suspense. There is a sense that someone or something is on the way and about to enter the scene. Horizon is therefore associated with creating moods of fear, danger, hope and excitement.

•

Tip

Once established, whatever is appearing on the horizon must be dealt with. Players travel to the horizon or what is on it travels to them. This advances the scene.

Some games that explore this zone are Song; One-word-at-a-time story; Opera; Sound environment; Poem; Shared story.

Epic

The epic zone is created when the player's eyes are raised to the heavens and there is a sense of surrender and availability in the upper torso and arms. It is the world of the gods, a realm beyond mortality where anything can happen.

It is the zone of eternal life, judgment, address and redress. In the classics (for example Shakespeare and the Greeks), monologues are delivered to this zone when we consider our mortality, address the gods, beg forgiveness, pray, and contemplate the great questions of life.

It is the realm of ascension and descension. Encourage players to climb there, leap there, ride up on an angel's wings or in a space ship. It is the area of magic and, as none of us have been there, we can cheerfully accept whatever players find there and allow anything to happen.

The epic takes us outside our everyday world. Everything becomes larger than life. To meet the size of the situations and to express the emotions we feel, at times our language reaches beyond the ordinary. We no longer simply speak, we speak in rhyme or we sing. Our movements are large and energised. The epic zone requires physical and vocal commitment from all players.

•

Tip

Encourage players to drop their status (sense of importance) and to yield to the status of the characters, voices or ideas that descend from above.

One-word-at-a-time story, Poem, Rhyming couplets, Opera, Typewriter, Mime, Soundtrack and Space jump frequently give rise to scenes of epic proportions.

Inner landscape

The inner landscape describes the area inside the player's mind. While a character may be gazing into the distance, the ground or up into the clouds, they may be deep in thought and not focusing their eyes on anything in particular. Although they appear to be in one of the other six focus zones, they are focusing on an inner emotion, thought or memory. Theatresports scenes that could benefit from this type of focus are Song, Inner song, Opera, Four square emotions, Emotions and scenes where a character has private thoughtful moments or thinks aloud.

•

Summary

Some games lend themselves to all the focus zones while others tend to favour one or two.

When players move from one of these zones to another, the focus shifts. This creates an advance in the scene.

Sidecoach players to recognise and use all the zones. Players should not become self-conscious of them but use them as reference points. Instinctive players move freely between zones, creating belief in all of them.

Sidecoach: 'See the horizon.'
'Keep eye contact.'
'Share the focus with the other player.'
'Yield to the focus.'

Careful establishment of the focus clarifies all scene-work and all games.

part A

FOUNDATION SKILLS

Focus warm-ups

Prior to focus work, choose warm-ups that prepare and sharpen focus skills — CIRCLE TAG; YES; YOU; BALL GAMES; THE PRESENT GAME.

After the warm-up, bring the group together in a scene-work formation. [See Training sessions.] This part of the session is spent concentrating on the specific details of finding and identifying the focus in a freeze. The work is quiet and requires full group concentration and respect for other people's ideas. Players are expected to contribute their ideas in discussion and to put their ideas into practice by going out in front of the group to improvise them. The work covered in these first focus sessions is fundamental to the rest of the work. Your clarity as you introduce the concept of focus is paramount.

Some players recognise the concept of focus more quickly than others. This is particularly evident among players 8-12 years old. Some see it and some don't. This may be due to their level of ability to deal with abstract concepts. When a player instinctively finds and yields to the focus, take this opportunity to clarify the concept of focus and explain how it has enhanced the improvisation.

STILL FOCUS CREATING BELIEF

2–32 players
20 minutes
8+ years

Description: Players identify the focus of a frozen moment.

Resource: A clear space and a chair.

Time-out: No.

Example of a title: Not applicable.

Aim: To identify and name the focus.

Degree of difficulty: 0.5

Skills to be developed: Ability to identify still focus and yield to it.

Suggested preparation: Keep the whole group together for most of the first focus session. Begin with warm-up games that sharpen focus skills and prepare the peripheral vision, eg CIRCLE TAG, YES, YOU, BALL GAMES, THANK YOU; THE PRESENT GAME.

How it works: Still focus is easier to identify than moving focus. This first exercise enables us to find the focus of a silent frozen moment.

Step one: Place a chair in an open space. Ask one player to take up a position on the chair and freeze it. They are usually more comfortable sitting than standing, and as they could be out the front for some time, the chair is a good idea. As focus is principally supported with the eyes, encourage the player to keep their eyes still (fixed but relaxed) during the freeze. The frozen statue remains silent.

The coach must be accurate and clear in this demonstration. Go into the space and point to the possible focus points. Encourage the group to find the most potent focus.

Ask the observers:

- Where is the focus? What do we (the audience) find ourselves looking at?
- Is it in front of the player?
- Is it to the side?
- Is it created by the player's eye level?
- Is it between their hands, above their heads, between their legs or feet?
- Which focus zone are they using?
- Is it on the horizon? If so, what do we imagine s/he is looking at?
- Is it on the ground?
- Is it close to his/her body?

Encourage the observers to be specific in their identification of the focus. If two ideas arrive, encourage the group to identify the most potent focus.

Ask the player to change position. Repeat the exercise a number of times with different players.

Step two: Now that the majority of players recognise the points of focus in a frozen moment, ask another player to come into the scene and take up a position to become the focus of the seated player. They can use any part of their body or any part of the space around the seated player to do so.

Ask the seated player to adjust their position to regain the focus. They do not have to remain on the chair. Repeat these readjustments. Players give the focus to each other and take it from each other. They use any position on or off the chair, around, behind or in front of each other.

When players understand and recognise the focus, they instinctively surrender to it. Now ask the entering players to use a variety of physical shapes and different body parts and positions to support the focus. They use their heads, backs, legs, hands, whole body. They use a variety of spatial levels and may become people or objects. They follow the eye level created by the first player, meet it and support the focus or they find a position that is the focus.

Continue this exercise until the group understands how focus is created, how we find and use it.

Robert McFarlane

Michael Gregory extends the focus, pulling the spear out of the side of Christ (Julie Dunsmore)

Step three: Now place two chairs in the space. Two players sit on the chairs. They each choose a separate frozen position — not relating to each other in the freeze. Ask the rest of the group which player has the focus. Which player do we find ourselves looking at? Why?

Ask player A to move so that s/he:
- Takes the focus from the other player
- Gives the focus to the other player

Ask player B to move so that s/he:
- Supports the focus of the other player
- Becomes the focus of the other player

When each new frozen position is created, ask the onlookers questions about what they see. Who has the focus and why? Who do we imagine would make the next offer? Who do we think would speak first and why? What would they say? Who do we imagine the players to be? What is their relationship: mother/daughter, employee/employer, master/servant, etc? Where do we imagine they are?

Ask a third player to enter and clarify the focus. The third player may share the focus of one of the players or become the focus of both players.

Repeat this exercise using a number of frozen positions until all players see the potential of yielding to the focus, ways to give it and take it and the wealth of information held in the focus of a frozen moment.

INTRODUCING STATUS

At this point there is value in introducing the concept of status because of its relationship to focus. Status is the hierarchy or pecking order of characters in a scene. It determines a character's sense of importance. [See Program five.]

A player may have the focus but not necessarily the status. That is, the onlookers may find their eyes drawn to one player but the other player may be of higher status and be giving the focus to the lower status player by looking at them.

Repeat the STILL FOCUS exercises as STILL STATUS exercises with two players. Ask the onlooking players to determine not only which player has the focus but which player has the status. Which player looks more important in the frozen moment?

Ask one player to leave the chair and stand in another position behind the other player, to the side of them, in front, kneeling, lying on the ground, or standing on the other chair. Ask them to freeze their position, looking at the other player, placing the other player as the focus, and then looking away from the other player creating a new focus. What do these new focus positions tell us about the status relationship between the two players?

When is the second player the protector? When are they a threat to the first player? Which positions give the status to another player and which positions take it away? How is the status affected by the focus?

Ask a third player to enter and clarify the status. They support the focus and the status created by the onstage players. Then they find a position that takes the status and the focus away from both players. Experiment with a variety of positions until the possibilities of, and the relationship between, status and focus are identified and understood by all players.

Remember, all these decisions have been made from frozen moments without speech. The work is clearer at this point in silence. [For more detailed status work see Program five.]

MOVING FOCUS SERVING A FUNCTION

training game and scene-work
4–32 players
10–15 minutes
12+ years

Description: Players identify and yield to the focus established by the onstage player(s).

Resource: A clear space.

Time-out: No.

Example of a title: Washing the car; Hanging washing on the line.

Aim: To identify focus as it moves and to serve the scene.

Degree of difficulty: 0.5

Suggested preparation: YOU; STILL FOCUS.

How it works: Having identified focus in a still moment, we start looking for the focus as it moves from one moment to the next.

Ask a player to enter the space and engage in a simple physical mimed activity, eg washing the car.

When the player has established the scene, ie the car exists and the player is washing it, freeze the action and ask another player to enter the scene.

•

Tip

Do not leave the first player alone in front of the group for too long — three to five seconds establishing the activity before the second player enters is ample in the first days of training. Keep them safe. Increase this time to ten to fifteen seconds as the skills develop.

The oncoming player identifies and yields to the established focus and continues the same scene without talking. When players support the focus they are playing a function in the scene. Player B, for example, may become the car or part of it.

Sidecoach: 'Yield to the focus and continue the same scene without talking.'

Now both players are involved in a scene about washing the car.

The mimed scene continues. Freeze it. Call a third player into the scene. The third player finds an activity that is involved with car washing. They polish it or create a tap and hose nearby, etc.

Sidecoach: 'Continue the same scene supporting the focus.'

Repeat with player D. Continue the exercise until all players are serving a function in the same scene, eg washing, polishing, filling the bucket with water, or becoming the car.

Give players B, C and D time, if they need it, to find the most potent focus. Some players find the focus instinctively. For others, rushing decisions may cause panic which breaks concentration. Allow entering players to wander through the frozen statues and take time to find the space they want to fill. Encourage them to look carefully and reward their decisions.

Remember up to this point the work is done without speech. Building scenes without words aids concentration and emphasises the physicality. Vocal offers during early focus training can split focus, derail the scene, slow it down and stop the action.

Allow the four players to live in the scene for up to ten seconds and then sidecoach players to speak only if they need to. Sidecoach players to keep moving while they speak. They may be tempted to stop all the activity and overload the scene with talking. Sidecoach players to continue the activity and find an ending to the scene.

Offers of place

We have dealt with offers that build on an activity and give players something to do. Now we find offers that give players a place to 'be'. We call these 'offers of place'.

Return to the Still Focus – creating belief, where one player sits on a chair or takes a position in the space and freezes it.

Turn the chair upside down. Ask player A to take up a position on the chair, using the chair in an unusual way (remembering that safety is paramount). Freeze the moment.

Ask the group to suggest where they think player A might be. What does this frozen moment suggest in terms of place? All sorts of answers may be given. There are as many answers as there are ideas:

- On a beach lying on a deck chair
- On a beach lying on a short-legged wading chair
- In a space ship

Ask different group members for their opinion. Some may have similar ideas. Others may see totally different possibilities. It is similar to seeing pictures and patterns in an open fire or clouds or patterns formed by stars. Gaining an insight into what is obvious for other people — their world view — is one of the joys of improvising. Remind the group that not one of these ideas is wrong. They are all perfectly acceptable.

Now ask the player to imagine where they think they are and to make an offer that clarifies the place. They let us know where they are by doing something that is associated with being in that place.

Let's say the player leans back in the upturned chair and sighs as they bask in the sun. They then lean over, pick up the suntan lotion and begin to rub it on their body. With simple unvoiced offers this player has established the place and atmosphere of a scene, in this case at the beach in the heat.

A single player needs time to establish the offer of place. They need time to image their environment and their relationship to it. Are they:

- Lying on the beach waiting for a friend?
- A parent anxiously watching their child in the water?
- On a holiday at the beach?
- A person who has never been to the beach before?

They need to find their immediate response to 'at the beach' — who they are and what they are doing. When players do not establish the place and their relationship to it, the scene is not grounded and has nowhere to come from and nothing to build on.

Setting up a routine

By 'setting up a routine' the player establishes the belief systems on which the scene is based. They may establish a routine of cooking in the kitchen, driving to work, or waiting for a train. The lone improvisor setting up the routine without advancing will hold the audience's attention for up to about thirty seconds. All oncoming players need to commit to the belief system established. If they don't, they are blocking. Too often oncoming players enter before they are required rather than trusting in and building on what is established by the first player in the first thirty seconds.

Beware

What happens when the belief is lost?

Some players experience pressure to be clever or to do something funny. Pressure and fear stop the process of play and spontaneity. When players fear they will not know what to do next, they lose their belief and jump ahead into the future. They try to make the scene work rather than living in the scene and waiting for the next idea to arrive from it. This manifests itself in two ways. They 'demonstrate the place' and/or 'talk the scene'.

Demonstrating the place: Demonstration is overtly showing the activity or place rather than simply creating it. Some players work hard expending energy showing they are at the beach. Frenetic setting up of imaginary props, putting up umbrellas and deck chairs, and making sounds for the props are signals that the player is demonstrating. This is particularly apparent in the performance game SPACE JUMP where one player is alone on stage for up to thirty seconds.

Cartoon-style improvisation may be very funny and is at times totally acceptable, but at this point of the training it holds little value because it can create one dimensional scenes. Sidecoach away from one dimensional activities and towards strong belief and three dimensional scene building: who, what and where.

Talking the scene: 'Ho hum, here I am at the beach. Now I'll get my suntan lotion…'. This voice-over quality is of no value at this stage of training. Talking the scene is another way of avoiding belief in the scene. Sidecoach players away from talking about the activity or place and towards doing the activity and believing in their location.

Talking the scene can lead to gagging, which occurs when players are not physically engaged and are not creating a physical focus. Coach away from gagging. Encourage a sense of truth as the basis of all work. Relieve players of the need to be funny and clever. Sidecoach to establish the place.

Sidecoach: 'Take your time.'
(Name parts of the location.) 'See the water/sand.'

Making sounds and noises

While talking the scene is not always helpful, the impulse to be 'on voice' is natural. Suggest players use breath and sound: sigh, grunt, exhale, hum tunes and so on during activities. Vocalisation releases the emotional response and connects the player with breath.

•

Tip

Blocked breath usually results in blocked offers.

Breathing is associated with yielding. Connecting the voice to breath and physical action grounds the work, deepens belief and relaxes the body, connecting the images created in the mind with physical movement.

Sidecoach: 'Make sounds.'
'Breathe.'

Introducing a second player

The onstage player continues the scene, and another player enters the scene in one of two ways:

1. The onstage player makes an offer for another player to come on and advance the scene. The second player does not enter until s/he is required. The sunbaking player may stand up, look at the horizon, wave to someone in the water. They have advanced the focus by shifting to a new focus zone, and have given an offer for another player to enter the scene. They have also given the oncoming player a lot of information. The oncoming player knows that they have been swimming and they are wet, and they know to enter from the horizon. When they do so they have overaccepted the offer of place. They are yielding to, and building on, the same scene. Unless the oncoming player sees all these offers and yields to them, they will be blocking. Offstage players must sit where they can see the focus created by the onstage player(s). Or:
2. The offstage player enters with an offer and advances the scene or breaks the routine. They may enter as the beach inspector, a seagull, or a friend joining in the sunbathing. Whatever their choice, they add to the place established. The scene continues as a No-blocking scene.

Build short scenes in both ways. One player establishes an offer of place. The second player enters to build on the established ideas in the scene, or to break the routine and advance the scene. Continue this exercise until clear scenes develop with all players giving clear offers of place and oncoming players are yielding to the location and serving a function in the established scene, whether invited on by the first player or coming on to add information to the place.

Begin from the starting point of using a chair in an unusual way for several scenes.

Then give locations as starting points, which the first player accepts and establishes. Some examples of locations are:

- In an art gallery
- In a library
- In a railway station
- Around a campfire

All these locations give a clear point of focus and a variety of focus zones.

When do you come on and what do you bring?

Rather than talk about the suntan lotion — 'Ho hum, here I am at the beach. Now I'll get my suntan lotion...' — the player on the beach would better serve the scene were they to relax, breathe out, look for their suntan lotion, search in their bag, sigh again and then perhaps talk, 'Oh darn! I've left it at home'. This is a perfect offer for another player to jump into the scene, lie on a towel next to the first player, accept all the offers of place and serve a function in the scene, 'Here use mine!' handing the first player some lotion. Now both players are in the same location, they share a common focus (the suntan lotion) and can begin to play a scene.

Blocking

Too often a second player enters a scene before they are needed, bulldozing the ideas and destroying the belief and place created by the first player. Freeze the scene and sidecoach the bulldozer. If blocking continues, sidecoach the bulldozer to get off. Reward players for staying off if they are not required in the scene. Encourage respect for the time needed to establish place and belief.

Saving

Sometimes one player alone in a scene can be vulnerable and may need support to play the scene rather than improvising alone. Some players cannot last for thirty seconds alone. Players join these players to 'save them'. Watch and listen for the telltale signs and sidecoach accordingly. Sometimes players call for 'help', even picking up the phone and dialling 'emergency'. They call out people's names, or say 'This is boring'. Send other players on to save them.

Status of player A

Remind players that one of the best ways to serve an already established scene focus is to keep the status of the onstage player higher than their own. This supports the focus and is helpful training for Theatresports performance games such as SPACE JUMP. Too often greedy, excited, nervous, desperate-to-please players enter, dominate and control the onstage focus rather than serving it. They enter scenes ordering other players around, and assume a dictatorial role rather than serving the scene.

Sidecoach: 'Yield to the focus.'
'Support the existing status.'

•

Beware

It is alright to play the controlling role or top status in the appropriate situation. However, watch for the player who continues to do it and sidecoach them towards making alternative choices by using the focus as a starting point rather than bringing on a preplanned idea. Introduce status exercises if these problems continue. [See Program five.]

Searching instead of believing

A player's first idea is usually their best. In the panic of the moment, some players lose their belief and block their own ideas searching for a better idea. When players are 'searching for the good idea' they go from one offer to the next without extending, advancing or dealing with any of them. They start sifting ideas and judging them along the way. Their eyes are not on the focus of the scene.

Sidecoach: 'Trust your instincts. Yield to the focus.'

It is helpful to freeze scenes momentarily. This helps players to locate the focus and re-establish it.

•

Tip

Some players tend to walk out of the scene and search for imaginary objects. Remind players that when improvising everything they need is handy. That weapon, key, spyglass just happens to be in their pocket, on the table next to them, always within reach.

Another way some players avoid saying 'yes' or accepting the focus is to keep changing the placement of the scene. They search across the space literally looking for the scene.

'Where is it?'
'I don't know.'
'Maybe it's here?' (running across the space)

Sometimes, players leave the scene to search for people or to search for the scene as if it were lost. Encourage players to bring the scene to them. They do not have to search for it. If they create it, it will be there. This could also be an indication that players need extending skills. They need to know how to develop the ideas they have established rather than continue to search for new ones. [See Program three.]

Encourage players to give the offer full focus by bringing their ideas to the centre of the stage and dealing with them there. Sometimes the scene appears to become physically off balance. Rather than playing in the centre of the playing space, players wander to the side. Sometimes they turn upstage and play the scene with their back to the main playing area. This could indicate that the players are running away from the central offer in the scene. They are fearful. They have lost belief in their ideas. Stop the scene. Relocate it in the centre of the space in a position where the focus is accessible to the audience and the other players.

As you can see, a lot happens in the first thirty seconds of a scene. Whether it is a one minute Theatresports game or a long improvisation, there are many choices players can make. The first thirty seconds or so of a scene are critical to the establishment of, and belief in, the place where the scene is set.

While some hilarious scenes result from no place and little belief, the role of the coach is to encourage players to make choices that extend them beyond instant gratification and cheap laughs.

Split focus

Split focus occurs when two offers are given at the same time. This is common, particularly with beginner players who are eager to add their ideas to the scene. A decision must be made in a split second to clear up the confusion. Players are often confused as to which idea to go with. It is natural to want to go with your own idea rather than someone else's. One player must yield immediately and give the other player's idea the focus. There is nothing worse than two players fighting over the ideas in the scene. They compete to be heard. This is blocking.

Robert McFarlane

Heaven Scent sharing an horizon focus — Marko Mustac and Tanya Bulmer

Encourage players to share the scene. Reward players who yield to the focus and give up their ideas for the development of another person's. When two ideas are given at the same time and neither player will yield, the coach makes choices from the offers made in the scene.

Always yield to the stronger offer. The stronger offer is usually vocally louder and physically larger. This will be the offer that has drawn the audience's attention.

Offers should support and extend the current onstage focus before introducing a new focus which will advance the scene.

Split focus also results in a struggle for status. Each player believes their idea to be more important than the other player's idea. Dare players to drop status for the sake of the scene.

Sidecoach: 'Listen to each other.'
'Drop status.'
'Yield.'
'Raise the other person's status.'

•

Tip

Always overaccept the status (be it high or low) of the player/character who holds the focus in any particular moment of the scene.

A moment of adjustment and yielding builds trust between the players, clarifies the scene and wins the hearts of the audience.

The other alternative during split focus is for a third player to enter and yield to the offer they think is the stronger or, on rare occasions, bring on a completely new offer. Quick decision making can clear up the split focus and save the scene.

Moving focus — THE PRESENT GAME

You will recall THE PRESENT GAME from Program one where it served as an aid to giving, receiving and naming offers. Now introduce it to clarify the focus. It helps us to name the first offer, give it focus and move it through space. We then develop the game into longer scenes.

Aims:

- To establish the first offer in the scene
- To establish focus in the scene
- To establish size, weight and shape of the offer
- To name the offer in the scene
- To remain physically active and connected with the scene
- To listen

In a simple short exchange, this game establishes the foundations of a scene and prepares the scene for an extend or advance. Outline the rules of the exercise again, demonstrating with a player from the group or getting two players to demonstrate for the whole group.

How it works again: Player A names player B and offers player B a present. Player B accepts the present, names it, and adds 'and…'.

Player A: 'John, I've got a present for you' (bringing out something imagined and tiny from her pocket).

Player B: 'Gee, thanks Lyn! Wow it's a ring, and it has our initials engraved on it.'

At this point both players share the focus of the imagined ring on player B's hand. The scene continues.

In this short scene both players have yielded to a simple physical offer and shared a focus which is integral to the plot.

The moment of transfer and the turning offer

There is a moment in improvised scenes and Theatresports games that I call the turning offer. It is the moment when the focus is shared by both players and an offer transfers from one player to the another. In a two player scene, it usually occurs within the first ten seconds of playing. It establishes the focus and provides a springboard for the scene.

THE PRESENT GAME demonstrates it perfectly. The moment of transfer in THE PRESENT GAME occurs when the present is handed from one player to the other. It is the moment of simultaneous giving and receiving. In the above scene 'at the beach', it occurs when the second player enters and hands the suntan lotion to the player on the beach. At this moment both players share the same point of focus and are actively engaged in the same scene. If the transfer is steady and well accepted the scene will be off to a good start.

•

Beware

Some players look everywhere except at the present. Their eyes raise to the ceiling as they try to think of what the gift could be. Encourage them to find the focus and yield to the offer, see it, create it, take its weight, adjust their body to accept the weight.

Sidecoach: 'Look at the present.'
'Accept its size.'
'Feel its weight.'

•

Beware

Some players give the gift and hide the information and the focus from their team-mate. They may tell the other player to close their eyes while they bring in the present. This hides the information from the other player. If this occurs in performance all the audience will know more about the size, weight, etc of the gift than one of the players. It could be a huge gift. When the other player opens their eyes not having this information, the result could be hilarious but will not help the improvisation. All players must have the same access to the same information, especially during the early stages of training.

Watch for players who are troubled by what to give their partners. Remind these players that the gift is merely an idea or shape until their partner names the gift.

Some players look at the gift and become fearful of naming it. The terror of not seeing something compounds. Sidecoach these players towards establishing the focus.

Sidecoach: 'Unwrap it.'
'Take it out of the box.'
'There is something in the top right-hand corner, take it out.'
'What is it?'

•

Magic moment

Coach Robyn Butler tells the story of a year seven student who looked at his gift not knowing what it was. As a result of careful sidecoaching towards the focus, he began to visualise the gift quite clearly.

Coach: 'What is it?'
Student: 'A letter.' (unrolling it)
Coach: 'Keep looking at it. What does it say?'
Student: 'It is written in Greek.'
Coach: 'Read it.'
Student: 'It's written in ancient Greek.'
Coach: 'Translate it.'
Student: 'The enemy is about to attack!'

The student, the rest of the class and the coach were all surprised at this spontaneous information. The student read the document imaging the information. Robyn's sidecoaching of the focus empowered the student to freely use his imagination.

Repeat The present game without words. This will alert both players to every nuance in the scene. Player B must use the mimed gift and therefore extend the activity. This gives rise to happy, quiet scenes and clear work.

- Note the energy in the room.
- Watch them watching each other's faces.
- See how they are more inclined to care about each other.
- Watch them enjoy playing.
- See their need to see what their partner makes of or does with the gift.

Continue The present game building longer scenes, developing the focus to incorporate offers of place (where the present-giving is happening), offers of activity (doing something with the present), and by starting a scene with an offer of place and giving the present after the place is established. The present game becomes a starting point for a No-blocking scene.

No-blocking scenes were introduced in Program one. Here they function as an introduction to scene-work and as a Theatresports training and performance game.

NO-BLOCKING SCENES

training game and scene-work
2–32 players
10 minutes
10+ years

performance game
1–2 minutes

Description: Situation, activity, or neither given. Players begin a scene accepting every offer given by the other player.

Resource: A clear space.

Time-out: Absolutely never!

Example of a title: An activity — something to do. Egg sorting; Putting up posters; Making pizza.

Aim: To accept everything said and/or done by the other player.

Degree of difficulty: 2

Skills required: Ability to listen, watch, give, receive and name offers.

Suggested preparation: Warm-up; YES LET'S; THE PRESENT GAME in English, gibberish and mime.

How it works: Two players enter the space. Give players a starting point. For players who need a challenge, ask them to start a scene from nothing. Players accept every idea given by the other person. NO-BLOCKING SCENES can be played with or without talking. When either player blocks the ideas, stop the scene and have another player take their place.

SHARING AURAL FOCUS

training game
4–32 players
5–10 minutes
14+ years

Description: Players form pairs and play two scenes concurrently, yielding to the aural focus.

Resource: A clear space.

Time-out: Players establish their position in the space.

Example of a title: Not applicable.

Aim: To establish and yield to the aural focus.

Degree of difficulty: 3

Skills required: Foundation scene-work skills.

Suggested preparation: THE PRESENT GAME.

How it works: It is easier to see and yield to physical focus than it is to hear and yield to the aural focus. This exercise demonstrates ways of sharing the aural focus. It is an exercise for players with some degree of skill who are ready to deal with more complex issues of focus.

Place four players in the space in two pairs, one pair on each side of the space, with the coach at the front facing both pairs, like the conductor of an orchestra, as both pairs play THE PRESENT GAME at the same time. The coach as conductor indicates when players speak, at what volume and when to freeze, using clear arm signals (with one arm assigned to each pair). They fade one scene out as they bring the other scene in.

Both teams share the aural and visual focus and experience being sensitive to another scene. Neither team looks at the other; each is aware of the other team using their peripheral vision and listening carefully. The coach balances the focus, bringing one team to life as the other one fades to stillness.

When the pairs have become alert to aural and visual focus, the coach steps aside, and the teams balance the two scenes themselves purely by listening. Each pair adjusts its volume to make provision for the other scene. Slowly, players become sensitive to aural focus, and gain the skills to share it.

This is an interesting theatrical device. Players and audience easily accept the convention.

•

Tip

Use this when training to play the Theatresports performance games REMINISCENCE, STATUES, SONG, OPERA, and all the games that rely on clear aural focus.

•

Summary

Write on the board:

focus + agreement + reaction = yield

offer + blocked breath = blocked offer

offer + breathing = yielding

The focus exercises and scenes described to this point have been quiet, relaxed scenes without the mania, over-excitement and speed that we sometimes associate with playing Theatresports games. Players have been encouraged to take their time finding the focus and their function in a scene. The resulting scenes may not have been hilarious and rollicking with zeal. Many scenes may have been more naturalistic than you would have expected. The work has demanded clarity, concentration and accuracy. It is better at this stage of the training to build a solid understanding of the principles of improvisation than to try to entertain an audience. Remember, a pianist practises scales before playing a sonata.

Keep a sense of humour in all of the above. Some funny moments will eventuate from scenes built from truth. When the unexpected arises from a truthful, clearly established moment, it is worth a thousand cheap laughs. Solid scene-building will not only lay foundations for improvising but will clarify and inform acting from a text.

Check

Focus foundation skills

Before players progress to scene-work and the playing of Theatresports performance games, check that they are confident in the following:

- Have they grasped the concept of focus?

- Can they identify and yield to still focus?
- Can they identify and yield to moving focus?
- Can they recognise the seven focus zones?
- Are they able to offer and accept a range of focus zone shifts?
- Can they give and yield to offers of place?
- Can they perform a function serving the focus in a scene?
- Can they develop short scenes from offers of activity and place while supporting the focus established by the first player?

If the answer is yes to these questions for the majority of players, they are ready to proceed to scene-work that leads to playing Theatresports performance games.

To this point the players have worked in pairs, small groups and as a whole group. They have played short scenes or parts of scenes in pairs, threes and fours in front of the whole group. They are now ready to identify and deal with focus in new ways.

part B

TRAINING GAMES

Part A introduced the concepts of still and moving focus. Players identified and clarified the focus of a frozen moment to develop the scene as it had been established.

The games in this section use the focus of a frozen scene as the offer to start a completely new scene. The new scene begins from the frozen moment of the previous scene and is endowed with a new place and activity. It is important that players are confident in the basic skills of offer, yield and focus before they attempt advanced games such as BLIND FREEZE TAG and SPACE JUMP.

FREEZE TAG

training game
3–32 players
10–20 minutes
12+ years

performance game
4 players
2–3 minutes
12+ years

Description: Situation given. Two players begin a scene. At any moment a team member calls 'freeze' and enters the scene tagging one player and taking their exact physical frozen position. The entering player gives an offer that begins a new scene based on the frozen positions.

Resource: A large clear space.

Time-out: Never.

Example of a title: Physical activity, something to do: Painting a wall; Weeding the garden; Making pancakes.

Aim: To find a complementary action for a given focus.

Degree of difficulty: 2.5

Skills required: Ability to identify and yield to an offer of focus.

Suggested preparation: Warm-up; WHERE DO YOU COME FROM?; KNIFE AND FORK; YOU; THANK YOU; STILL FOCUS; MOVING FOCUS.

How it works in training: This game requires players to begin scenes using the focus of a frozen moment. Two players (players A and B) begin a scene from a given activity. Remaining players watch the scene from two lines, one on either side of the space. At any time any player on the outside lines calls 'Freeze'. The pair playing the scene freeze their action holding their positions. The player who called 'Freeze' (player C) taps either player and takes their exact position giving a verbal offer that starts a different scene using the frozen position as the starting point. Player B overaccepts player C's offer. The player who is tapped by player C joins the other players in the lines. Player C and the remaining player play the new scene. Continue the game until all players have played a variety of scenes. Each scene lasts for five to ten seconds.

Finding a complementary action is the key to this work. If on the call of the freeze the frozen players have been milking a cow, with player A holding his hands in front of his body in a frozen milking action and player B holding a bucket, the oncoming player, player C, must decide which position to take. Let's say player C taps the milking player (player A), kneels down and takes up the hands in front position.

Player C's job is to give an offer to the bucket holding player (B) that endows her/him with a new place and activity so both players can start a new scene. Player C gives an offer of place, activity and probably at the same time an offer of status.

For example, player C takes the position with the idea of holding a steering wheel. Now player C must justify the position of player B who is squatting next to them. 'Pass me the road map Jayne and I'll find the street.' With this, player B now knows she is in a car, and that the bucket has become a road map. Jayne passes the road map and the scene continues until another player calls freeze.

In the above example, player C used their own frozen position as the initial impetus to develop the scene. Another way of approaching the scene is to use player B's frozen position as the initial impetus. What does the bucket holder look as if they are doing — vomiting, looking down a mine-shaft, washing their hair? Any of these ideas are good, as are countless others. Now, what would be a complementary action for player C? What do they need? What is between my hands that they could use? 'Here — I've got two picks, let's split that gold nugget.' Both players bring the scene to life.

The tap on the shoulder should be a tap and not a punch. The game should move in fast progression. Scenes should not continue for more than ten seconds. Five second scenes are adequate. Dare players to call freeze and run into the space before they have an idea. This reduces preplanning and maximises their spontaneous impulse. If two players call a freeze simultaneously, each taps a player, takes up a position and continues a new scene.

How it works in performance: This game serves best as a warm-up and training game. Some experienced players perform the game in front of an audience, rotating the four members of their team every ten to twenty seconds and playing the game within a two or three minute time structure. Advancing and extending skills are necessary before attempting FREEZE TAG as a performance game. It can also be played as a warm-up in front of the audience with players from all teams participating.

BLIND FREEZE TAG

training game
10 players
3–10 minutes
14+ years

Description: Situation given. Two players begin a scene. Remaining players form a line behind the scene. The first player in the line (player C) has their back to the scene, the other players face the scene. At any moment, player C calls 'Freeze', turns and enters the scene, tagging one of the players and taking their exact frozen physical position. The next player in line, player D, turns their back to the scene. Player C gives an offer that begins a new scene based on the frozen position.

Resource: A large clear space.

Aim: To find a complementary action for a given focus.

Degree of difficulty: 3.5

Skills required: Ability to identify and yield to an offer of focus.

Suggested preparation: Warm-up; YES LET'S; WHERE DO YOU COME FROM?; YOU; THANK YOU; STILL FOCUS; MOVING FOCUS; FREEZE TAG.

How it works: This is the same as FREEZE TAG but involves fewer players and introduces the blind element for the oncoming player. The game moves in fast rotation. Eight players form a line behind two players (A and B), who play a scene. The player at the start of the line, player C, always turns his/her back on the scene and enters the frozen scene on the call of 'Freeze'. They hear the scene but cannot see it. The player who is tapped returns to the other end of the line. Player D now becomes player C. Ideally, player C calls the freeze.

If the game slows down, an outside player or coach calls the freeze. Player C runs into the scene. The pace of the change-over needs to be very quick. Slowing the pace drops the energy, slows the mind and hinders spontaneity.

The scenes will probably run between five and fifteen seconds.

BLIND FREEZE TAG is an advanced game. It works best when all players understand the mechanics of focus and are ready to be challenged further.

TRAINING FOR SPACE JUMP

Most players who have seen Theatresports want to play SPACE JUMP. Introduce it slowly and clearly, building on the skills covered in Parts A and B of this program before playing the performance game as outlined in Part C. One player enters the space and begins an activity from a given offer of place or activity, eg having a shower. Let's say they have established the water and the soap and begun showering for about twenty seconds. Call a freeze. A second player enters the space and uses the frozen position of the first player to begin a completely new scene. They give offers of place, activity and/or status that let the other player know who, where and what they are. The frozen player overaccepts the offer and they both play the new scene. Call another freeze and a third player enters to use the frozen positions of the two players to begin a completely new scene.

At this point all the detailed focus work will pay off. When players enter the scene and become the focus, or link the two onstage players by literally filling the gap between them, ideas come easily. Encourage players to have something to do in the scene and give clear vocal and physical offers that endow the other players with who, what and where they are.

Encourage players to enter the scene and take up a physical position rather than stand and talk about it from the sidelines. Players cannot use preconceived ideas because they do not know what the frozen positions of the onstage players will be.

Now call a freeze and bring on a fourth player to use the three frozen positions as a starting point for a new scene. Continue building scenes in this way with entering players endowing the still focus. Play a variety of scenes of different lengths.

•

Tip

Encourage players to place the onstage players at a higher status than themselves.

•

Beware

Sometimes the fourth player enters and controls the onstage players rather than allowing them to improvise. Some of the telltale signs are:

Coming into a scene and assuming a dictatorial role — gym instructor, chiropractor, dancing teacher etc. They command the onstage players to do things. This is a common complaint, not only in SPACE JUMP but also in STATUES. Beware the player who starts the scene with 'No, no, no, you're doing it wrong!'

Controlling other players is a symptom of players not yielding to the onstage frozen positions. Encourage players to take their time and to wander through the frozen positions until they find the focus and a function within the new scene.

Some Theatresports players rely on gags such as the old 'I'm having a baby!' scene. They fall to the floor screaming as if in labour. This guarantees a huge laugh but pulls the focus and the status away from other players. It does not necessarily use the shapes of the frozen players but pulls top status. Help this type of player to make alternative choices by trusting the other players and sharing the control of the scene. [See Program three – HE SAID/SHE SAID.]

When players have experienced entering and beginning a new scene from the frozen positions and played short scenes with up to four players in any one scene, go back to the beginning and do it all again with four different players. Establish these skills before going on to the performance game SPACE JUMP, where the times of the scene lengths are strict and the scenes revert in order to the beginning. [See Part C – SPACE JUMP].

•

Summary

To date players have experienced a range of focus shifts. They have spontaneously identified the focus of a frozen moment and endowed it with new ideas. They have yielded to other players' endowments of them. They have worked in quick rotation and developed fragments of short scenes into scenes of 20–30 seconds or longer. Players are now ready to flex their muscles and attempt a variety of Theatresports games that put these focus skills into practice.

part C THEATRESPORTS PERFORMANCE GAMES

Developing scenes into games

Most players quickly absorb information about focus. In the excitement of playing Theatresports games for the first time, particularly in front of an audience, basic skills often fly out the window. Many scenes are lost as a result of dropped offers and a lack of focus on stage.

Many players stand 'offstage', that is, to the right or left of the onstage action. It is then difficult for them to clearly see the focus created by the onstage players.

Problems arise when players enter a scene with their own ideas rather than developing the ideas that are currently in the story and feeding the onstage focus. This is usually a result of panic and not listening or watching. Many players confuse the issue further and ignore the focus completely when they overindulge in the use of props. [See Process – Props.]

Soccer players on the bench prepare to go on the field. They focus their attention on the ball and the onfield action. The same applies to Theatresports players, who need to be in rhythm with the onstage scene, alert and listening to the offers, keeping a keen eye on the focus in case they are needed. Offstage players need to be acutely sensitive to the onstage focus at all times. Encourage players to enter only to serve the scene.

Every Theatresports game requires clearly maintained focus. The following Theatresports games are particularly focus-dependent. They cannot be played unless all players yield to the focus to develop a simple plot and tell a story. To deny the physical focus in these games is to deny their educational value and reduce their potential.

PLAYING SCENES WITH MOVING FOCUS AND NAMING THE OFFERS

SLOW MOTION COMMENTARY

classic

performance game
4 players
1 minute
10+ years

Description: Two team members play a given action in mimed slow motion to a commentary (usually fast) given by two offstage players.

Resource: A clear space.

Time-out: Yes. Decide who moves in slow motion and who commentates.

Example of a title: An activity: The pancake tossing championships; The Olympic window cleaning competition; Lizard polishing.

Titles which suggest a competition work well in this game, as two similar yet independent activities can take place in the same scene at the same time.

Aim: To clarify and name the offers of a moving focus.

Degree of difficulty: 2

Skills required: Ability to move in slow motion and to identify moving focus.

Suggested preparation: Warm-up; WHERE DO YOU COME FROM?; SLOW MOTION RACE.

How it works — Step one: Divide the group into pairs. Name players in each pair A and B. Players A begin a given physical task in extreme slow motion, eg tossing pancakes, washing the car. Players A do not speak but must be able to clearly hear their player B. Players B stand or sit in front of their partners, naming and describing the physical actions aloud, watching every move with care.

Coach the pairs as you wander the room.

Sidecoach: 'Slower; S-L-O-W motion!'
'Yield to the physical offer. Name the action.'
'Yield to the verbal offer. Extend the action described.'
'Advance the focus.'

The slow motion enables the miming player to clearly advance the scene. When tossing pancakes the slow movement of the eyes from the pancake in a pan (focus zone body) to the pancake rising in the air (focus zone epic) provides both players with the opportunity to extend the action and advance it with clarity.

Step two: Sidecoach towards an event and when an event occurs, towards an ending. Short, simple scenes develop as the task is completed.

Step three: Players A and B change roles. Begin a new task, eg glass blowing, carpet laying, fixing an engine.

Step four: When all players have a clear grasp of the skills, introduce the game as it is played in performance. Begin with four players working in front of the whole group. First decide which two are commentating and which two moving in slow motion.

All four players now play the same scene. The two commentators sit in front of the action where they can see all the physical offers made by the two moving players.

Set the task, eg bed making. Ask the slow motion players what they think of when they think of bed making. One may say, 'Tucking in the corners'. The other could say, 'Puffing the pillows'. Ask the rest of the group for their ideas. Answers such as unfolding the sheets, smoothing out wrinkles will be given. All are good answers. No answer is better than another. They are all helpful ideas.

Both moving players begin their activity in slow motion, making their own bed and providing the offstage commentators with two different starting points. It would seem that the focus is split. But the commentary will clarify the focus by naming the actions made by the moving players.

Both commentators describe the actions of both moving players, but it is helpful if each offstage commentator selects one particular player and concentrates on his/her physical offers while using their peripheral vision to see and also commentate on the other moving player. Sidecoach commentators to ensure that neither moving player is overlooked. The commentators do not look at each other; their focus must be on the moving players.

The commentators begin their commentary speaking one at a time. However, as the pace builds to a climax of bed making, both commentators may overlap, each shifting the focus between the two moving players and sharing the commentary between them.

Naming and describing the slow motion strengthens the belief of all four players and builds their confidence in the task at hand.

The commentary must be audible and clear. It should not be shrill and unclear. It can be quite frenzied providing it is vocally clear and not pushed.

While this performance game appears very simple, its structure is quite complex. The communication between the onstage and offstage players relies on clear naming of physical offers. The vocal offers should enhance the onstage playing not direct it. The onstage players need to give large, clear physical moves and facial expressions that advance and extend the action. The offstage players name what they see and describe the details.

Sidecoaching SLOW MOTION COMMENTARY

Tip

Many players forget to move in slow motion, or begin in slow motion and then speed up. Keep both players at the same slow motion pace.

Sidecoach: 'See the other player out of the corner of your eye. Go slower than the other player.'

Continue to sidecoach the scene towards an event.

Now sidecoach the commentators to identify the verbs. This will clarify the activities. Encourage commentators to name the physical offers — smoothing, puffing, folding, etc.

The onstage players need to listen to every word spoken by the commentators. They provide offers which can be yielded to and incorporated in the scene.

The offstage players must keep their eyes on the focus created by the onstage players to save them at all times.

•

Beware

Some commentators talk off the track or to each other rather than watching the onstage action. Remind them to keep their eyes on the moving players at all times.

Make sure each scene has a beginning, a middle and an end. Sidecoach the scene until all four players support the event and bring the scene to a satisfactory conclusion.

The structure of this game is particularly suited to a scene involving a competition. For example, in a bed-making competition, the two onstage players will be in competition with each other to make a bed better than their opponent. Be alert for the turning offer. At some point both players will want to win. The commentators need to name the physical offers particularly clearly at this point and state the rules of the competition. 'It's three points off for a torn sheet and it looks as if Big Bertha is going to win! Oh no! Ralph the Ripper is ripping both sheets and now picking up the pillow and tossing it at Bertha.' They could begin a slow-motion physical fight. This is fine as long as the moment of transfer provides a transition. There must be a change of status. One player will need to yield to the offer and drop status. Both players accept the offer of a fight and overaccept the idea of a winner and a loser. This is a difficult concept for players in early training, who may hang on to the idea that a drop in status is a drop in personal achievement.

Sometimes the commentators speak at the same time. To clarify the aural focus, they should sit close together and be alert to the moment when each will speak. Some players squeeze the other player's hand to signal they are about to speak, or tap the other to indicate they are passing the speaking over. This is a good training tip. Keep sentences short. Comments such as 'What do you think, Brian?' or 'And over to you, Cliff' will give both commentators a chance to have a say and share the commentary.

Variations

Not all Slow motion commentary scenes are played with two onstage players.

Vary the game with one onstage player and two commentators to reduce an overload of physical offers, or two onstage players and one offstage commentator to reduce an overload of vocal offers.

Introduce a slow motion, non-speaking referee who enters and signals the winner, clarifies the rules, indicates fouls, etc, then leaves. This player moves at the same slow motion pace as the onstage players. The single offstage commentator needs to place the physical offers of the referee at top status. 'The referee signals a foul and is deducting two points from Big Bertha.'

Changing the fielding

If too much fighting and competition comes from the physical offers in the scene, vary the structure of the game by changing the fielding of the players. Give the players a different function. [See Basic terms and skills – Fielding.]

SLOW MOTION COMMENTARY scene

Another option for the game is to abolish the concept of competition. Place the onstage players in a situation with a shared activity, eg both making the same pancake or making the same bed.

For example, the robbery. Onstage slow motion robbers commit the robbery while the offstage commentators provide the voices of the neighbours next door watching the crime take place or two police in the squad car watching the robbery and radioing to base.

•

Tip

SLOW MOTION COMMENTARY is usually played as a one minute game. Extend to two and three minutes as SLOW MOTION COMMENTARY scenes develop.

When you see a conclusion in sight:

Sidecoach: 'Find an ending.'

Bring offers to a conclusion as the end of the scene nears. Remind players not to introduce new offers too close to the end of the scene.

•

Magic moment

Team *Here and Now* was given the task 'mowing the lawn'. What a wonderful surprise when Brett Wood, seeing the onstage player pushing a lawnmower, became the blade of grass. It took about fifty-five seconds for Brett to be chewed by the mower and somersault into oblivion. Needless to say Brett received Moment of the match for brilliant yielding.

Corrie Ancore

Geoff Kelso in action, Jenny Lovell timekeeping — Belvoir Street Theatre

•

Magic moment

At the International Tournament Expo '88 Brisbane, we formed 'scratch' teams by mixing players from different teams and selecting the combinations at random; a bit like Russian Roulette Theatresports.

Two Swedes, Helge and Pedr, a Dane called Pia and Aussie Geoff Kelso formed a team. The Swedes and the Dane spoke little English (and less Australian), and the Aussie spoke no Danish or Swedish. All players had been playing in English. Pedr and Pia began a slow motion scene on stage. The two offstage players, Helge and Geoff sat by their microphones ready to commentate.

What a surprise for the audience of 600 when Helge Skoog unexpectedly began commentating in Swedish. Hardly anyone could understand the language. I laughed so much I thought I'd cry when Geoff yielded and continued the commentary as if he understood every word spoken by Helge. The audience fell on the floor laughing. The onstage players continued the slow motion, but only one of them could understand the Swedish and neither could understand the English. Geoff continued to agree with every Swedish comment, 'Yes, and that's right, Helge…' and the two of them brought together a side-splitting commentary that broke every international language and custom barrier. A brilliant moment for Kelso — one of his finest!

STATUES

classic

performance game
usually 4 players
1 minute
10+ years

Description: Team members of one team mould another team into shapes. These shapes form the starting positions for the improvisation. All frozen positions are justified in the scene.

Resource: A clear space.

Time-out: No.

Example of a title: No title given.

Aim: To build a scene from a still focus.

Degree of difficulty: 2

Skills required: Introductory knowledge of focus and endowment.

Suggested preparation: Physical and vocal warm-up; Hospital tag; Thank you; Freeze tag; Blind freeze tag; What are you doing? — build into scenes; Marko's game — then bring the scenes to life.

How it works: This game combines all the still focus skills. Four players are moulded into four positions by the opposing team. Players bring the scene to life and justify their frozen position within the establishing scene. Place players in positions with all other team-mates in sight. If they cannot see all other team-mates, they are allowed to quickly look and then return to their moulded position. One by one they justify their position, unfreezing within the developing scene.

Sometimes it is difficult to know who should make the first offer. Any player who has an idea for the first offer starts the scene by making a vocal or physical offer.

Vocal offers will state the justification. 'Yes, I can see the rabbit down the burrow,' says a player with hand cupped over their face and kneeling on the ground. The first offer establishes the location, situation or characters. All players yield to the situation given or implied by the opening offer. Other players join the scene as it unfolds. Players cannot unfreeze until they can justify their position. Talking is not always

Corrie Ancore

Little Gloria — Jenny Hope (left), Penny Biggins, Felicity Biggins, Kerry Adams unfreezing in STATUES

required. It is perfectly acceptable for a player, unsure of how they fit in, to wait in silence for an idea or for one of the other players to endow them.

•

Beware

Players tend to panic in their excitement to unfreeze. Sometimes they all speak at once not listening to or watching for the offers given by their team-mates. Sidecoach players to yield to the focus and serve the scene.

Players may finish in the same freeze from which they started, but this is not compulsory. When players return to the shapes from which they started, the game is called TABLEAUX. Do not introduce TABLEAUX too early. It can encourage bridging and end-gaining.

Most players talk about themselves in STATUES: 'Oh no, I've got my head stuck in the washing machine…' Encourage players to look at their position in relation to the whole team.

Sidecoach: 'Endow the other player.'
'Find the focus.'
'Make the other player look good.'

Beware players who move from their position without justifying it. Encourage these players to hold the freeze until they can justify their function in the scene. Remind them not to panic. They may be required to hold their position for almost the full minute in silence. Remind players that this is a short game. Too much talking will slow down the story and not allow all players to unfreeze.

Beware players who over-talk the scene. These players talk to control the scene. It is an indication of fear. This game requires economic, relevant offers. Too often players speak to justify their position, then stand around without a physical commitment to the scene.

•

Tip

- If a player talks for more than five seconds, they are probably talking for too long.
- Encourage players to endow other players before talking about themselves.

•

Magic moment

Murray Fahey stood with hands pointed towards a player crouched on the ground. I was placed in a position with one foot raised in the air standing behind the crouched player. Murray, who had the clearest access to the focus of all players endowed us with characters, functions and clarified the focus with one sentence, 'Look out Lynee, I'll kill the cockroach with my gun, you stamp on it to make sure it is dead.' This was a perfect example of selfless playing. Murray not only named the principal offer in the scene — the focus — but endowed two other players with a function. Within three seconds we knew exactly what to do. We were awarded Moment of the match for the death of the cockroach.

SUBTITLES

performance game
4 players
2 minutes
10+ years

Description: Situation given. Two players improvise a given scene in gibberish which is translated by offstage players into English.

Resource: A clear space.

Time-out: Yes. Decide which players speak gibberish, which players translate and who translates for whom.

Example of a title: Sigfried's last wish; Safela crosses the Tiber; The curse of the kimono. The scene usually reads as if it was a foreign film. The title is more helpful if it contains character names and/or the name of a country. The titles above lend themselves to action and epic events. They provide a starting place, a main character and an event. They also provide a style for the gibberish. It is good fun to vary titles to encourage a variety of gibberish — Japanese, French, Slavic, Swahili, German, Latin American, Ancient Greek.

Aim: To name a gibberish focus and translate it into English.

Degree of difficulty: 2.5

Skills required: Ability to bring together vocal and physical offers, gibberish and English.

Suggested preparation: COLOURS; YES LET'S; HERE AND NOW — English and gibberish; Advance and extend exercises in English and gibberish. [See Program three.]

How it works: This game functions similarly to SLOW MOTION COMMENTARY. It is a game involving the clarification of split focus. The onstage players play a scene in gibberish. The offstage players clarify the focus and tell the story, translating the gibberish into English.

The same attention must be given to the onstage offers by the offstage translators as it is in other split focus games. The onstage players in this game do not mime the action — they speak lines in gibberish that are translated. They offer physical and vocal ideas for the scene.

Begin with these simple steps to build skills before playing the game with four people.

Step one: Begin the work as a whole group. Divide the group into pairs of A and B. Players A begin a demonstration, eg baking a cake. Players B sit in front of the A players and concentrate on the focus created by the A players. A players begin the cooking demonstration, physicalising the activity and speaking the directions in gibberish as they move. B players translate from gibberish to English, one-sentence-at-a-time.

Wander through the room and sidecoach according to what you see.

Sidecoach: 'Yield to the vocal inflections of the gibberish speakers.'
'Yield to the physical offers made by the gibberish speakers.'
'Advance the scene.'

Check that gibberish sentences are spoken one at a time and translated immediately as each sentence is concluded.

Sidecoach: 'Complete the task.'
'Action an event.'
'Find a beginning, middle and end.'

As the little scenes develop there will be much laughter in the room. Remember, gibberish releases energy and gives rise to spirited, noisy work.

Step two: Players A and B change roles. Begin a new scene: Performing a brain operation; Changing a tyre.

Step three: When all players have a clear understanding of the function of both roles, introduce the game with four players.

Beware of being bogged down by thinking up funny translations of gibberish instead of playing the scene.

The set-up of the game should be as follows: there are two players on stage (A and B) and two players off stage (players C and D) in a place that allows them to see the entire onstage area. The players have agreed who is translating for whom (say C translates for A, and D translates for B).
A speaks a line, C translates into English.
B speaks a line, D translates into English.

If players do not translate line-by-line, the plot becomes confused. When players are practised in line-by-line translation, they become quite fast. The translation moves as though subtitles were appearing on the screen as the action is played.

•

Tip

If there are two male players and two female players, it is usually clearer for the female player to translate for the female player, and the male for the male. Because male and female voices are pitched differently, it is easier for audience and players alike to identify which translation belongs to which onstage player.

•

Beware

Beware of gratuitous gagging. There are inherent jokes in the game. Some players speak for twenty seconds or more in gibberish and the translation given is only one or two words. While this is a good joke, it will not develop the plot. Its gag value is effective only once.

VOICES OFF

classic

performance game
4 players
2 minutes
10+ years

Description: Situation given. Offstage players provide the voices for onstage players. The onstage players mouth the words and provide physical offers for the players off stage.

Resource: A clear space.

Time-out: Yes. Decide which players will provide the voices and which the actions.

Example of a title: The best titles are those which suggest characters or events: The proposal; On the ski slopes; At the laundromat.

Aim: To bring together the vocal and physical offers in simple scene-playing. To share the responsibility and control of the scene.

Degree of difficulty: 4

Skills required: Concentrated listening and watching.

Suggested preparation: Warm-up; CHAIN TAG; HERE AND NOW; THE MIRROR GAME; SPEAKING IN ONE VOICE.

How it works: This is another game where the split focus is clarified and named by offstage voices. Two onstage players mouth the words of a scene while two offstage players provide their voices.

The players on stage must move their mouths clearly and slowly, overemphasising all their physical offers. If they mouth the word 'No' they should shake their head and use facial expression to communicate their opinion and clarify the offer.

The main offers at the beginning of the scene come from the onstage players. The offstage players overaccept every offer given by the onstage players.

Onstage players are not puppets attempting to mouth the words spoken by the offstage players. The onstage players lead the action. For this reason each offstage player should keep their eyes focused on the player whose voice they provide. Clarity of offers in this game is vital. Eventually all players give and yield to offers simultaneously.

The offstage players must sit in a position where they can see every nuance made by the onstage players. The offstage players must be clearly audible for players and audience.

If there are two male players and two female players, it is usually clearer for the female player to provide the voice for the female player and the male for the male. If you have an uneven number of females and males in the team, eg three women and one man or vice versa, be sure each onstage player is clear about who is providing their voice. All onstage players must be able to distinguish the voice of the player providing their voice.

This is one of the most complex Theatresports performance games, requiring clear communication between all four players. Begin with these simple exercises before approaching the game with four players.

Step one: Begin with the whole group working at the same time, dividing into pairs naming themselves A and B. Player B provides the voice for player A. Player A begins a scene, completing a simple task, eg chopping onions. Player A begins the scene crying and ends the scene laughing. This provides the possibility for a transition in the scene. Player A chops the onion and mouths the crying while player B makes the sound of the crying (and not the sound of chopping the onion!).

Wander the room sidecoaching the pairs.

Sidecoach: 'Fill their mouth with sound.'
'Yield to the focus.'

'Find a reason to stop crying.'
'Find a reason to start laughing.'

Playing the scene is the most important part of the improvisation. A simple transition will develop a simple plot.

Step two: Players A and B change roles. Begin a new scene, eg at the skin specialist, trying on new jeans.

Step three: When all players have a clear understanding of the function of both roles, introduce the game with four players. Player A begins laughing, player B begins crying, while players C and D provide the relevant voices offstage. At the end of the scene player A must be crying and player B must be laughing. This simple exercise sets up the scene and provides a bridge to the end. In the middle of the scene, players find the moment of transition and are changed by the information.

Sidecoach: To onstage players: 'Make eye contact with each other.'
'Find a reason to make a transition.'
'Find an ending to the scene.'

This simple laughing and crying structure lays a solid foundation for a variety of emotions to be expressed during a VOICES OFF scene.

Do not underestimate the complexity of this game. The communication channels between all four players can become quite confused. For this reason all offers need to be clear, deliberate and carefully placed. Players should not give offers too quickly. The onstage players should be open to giving an offer and allow for the possibility that the offer could change half way through should the offstage voices fill their mouths with the unexpected. The mouthers should move their mouths slowly and clearly, and yield to what they hear. This game is not about achieving perfect lip-synch; it is about remaining open to the offer on a thought by thought basis. This game thrives on big commitment to an idea and willingness to throw that idea away if required.

Players should also endow offers with opinions and support them clearly with big facial expressions. This is the ultimate yielding game. Players who are good at this game are continually having ideas and throwing them away mid-thought as they overaccept unexpected new offers.

Variations

North American players have experimented with a number of ways of providing the voices for the onstage players. The best of these is: three players on stage (mouthing); one player on stage travels between them providing the voices for the three different characters (degree of difficulty: 4.5).

REMINISCENCE

performance game
4 players
2–4 minutes
15+ years

Description: Situation, first line or characters given. Two players reminisce. The other two players improvise the moments of the 'memory'.

Resource: A clear space.

Time-out: Yes.

Example of a title: Two trapeze artists; Remember the time we climbed the Eiffel Tower; At the police station.

Aim: To explore an inter-weaving of plot, time and character.

Degree of difficulty: 4

Skills required: Bridging, shelving, characterisation, sensitivity to aural focus; a good working understanding of advancing and extending.

Suggested preparation: Vocal and physical warm-ups; split focus exercises; aural split focus exercises.

How it works: This combines the skills of many focus and storytelling games. Two offstage players tell a story and two onstage players bring the story to life.

Although the two reminiscing players are considered offstage players, they sit on stage to one side of the action. Unlike VOICES OFF and other split focus games, they sit where they can see the onstage players while remaining visible to the audience.

The onstage players represent the characters as remembered by the offstage players, and play the scenes set up by their offstage counterparts. They take on the characteristics of the storytellers, they grow younger and older according to the time frames introduced by the storytellers and they yield to every offer given them.

There should be a 50 per cent sharing of the scene between the two pairs of players, eg the offstage reminiscing players should allow the onstage players to fill out the moments — vocally and physically communicating until the next offer for a jump in time or place is called.

Example

The reminiscence is established by the offstage players. They set the place and introduce the scene.

A: 'Remember the time we climbed the Eiffel Tower?'
B: 'Yes we were in Paris. I remember it well. It was the first day we met.'
A: 'That's right. I was standing at the base of it and looking up when you walked up and spoke to me.'

The onstage players improvise the remembered scene.

C: (Stands looking up at the height of the Eiffel Tower.)
D: (Walking up to C and speaking.) 'Excuse me, do you speak English?'
C: 'Yeah, I'm from Sydney. Don't I recognise you?'
D: 'We used to catch the same bus to Uni.'
C: 'What a coincidence. What are you doing in Paris?'
D: 'I've come to climb the Eiffel Tower. Want to join me?'

C: 'I'd love to.'

The reminiscing players advance the scene.

A: 'That's right. You were so plucky to speak to me like that. You started taking the ropes out of your bag and throwing them up onto the first ledge. You were really showing off.'

Cut to the rope throwing and showing off.

The exchange continues back and forth between the couples.

A and B set up the scene and C and D play out the moments. A and B jump time and place, as they reminisce through their friendship. C and D play out these moments, yielding to the offers given by A and B.

Sometimes A and B disagree:

A: 'Remember the time we climbed the Eiffel Tower?'

B: 'Yes we were in Paris. It was the first day we met.'

A: 'No it wasn't. The first time we met was at a party in Dunedin.'

B: 'I've never been to Dunedin.'

A: 'Yes you have but you were so drunk you don't remember.'

Cut to the party in Dunedin. B is lying on the floor drunk. A trips over B's body on the floor. They begin a conversation.

•

Beware

This disagreement will not block the ideas in the scene if all four players agree to disagree and find the alternative opinion of the remembered event. One of the characters must drop status and overaccept that they are wrong. The onstage players overaccept the new offer and bring the scene to life immediately. The disagreement must advance the plot and tell us more about the characters and their relationship. Too much disagreement will sidetrack and derail the scene. Remember the players must eventually 'climb the Eiffel Tower'.

•

Tip

The characters can disagree on times and events but they do not fight about the fact that it occurred; if they do, nothing will occur! They will not progress the scene.

Saying or expressing 'No' is not blocking if the players have the skills and the maturity to give up their ideas and go with another player's ideas.

This game is a combination of Time warp, Space jump and Typewriter. It involves detailed narrative and provides an opportunity to explore and create a variety of characters. Introduce it to players who crave advanced focus and character and story-building work, and are ready to combine intricate advancing and extending with a variety of focus shifts. It is a challenging, sophisticated and delightful game that promotes beautiful scene-work.

•

Tips for text

Choose the reminiscing characters from a known text; for example, Hamlet and Ophelia. They tell the story of their friendship. Other players enter to play all the other characters. You may need more than four players. Competition in this instance is irrelevant. The game structure encourages a deeper understanding of the text and the characters in it.

SPACE JUMP

classic

performance game
4 players
4 minutes
12+ years

Description: Situation given. The first player plays the scene for thirty seconds until 'Space jump' is called. They freeze their action. A new player enters and begins a completely new scene based on the frozen position as the starting point. Both players play the new scene for thirty seconds until 'Space jump' is called again. They then freeze and a third player enters and makes a new scene from the frozen position of the onstage players. This continues until all four players are on stage. The whole team plays the new scene for sixty seconds. Then each player leaves in reverse order every thirty seconds. The scenes revert one by one until the first player is alone again, playing the initial scene.

Resource: A clear space.

Time-out: No.

Example of a title: Water skiing; Giving up smoking; Taking a midnight swim.

Aim: To build scenes from still focus, establish character and place, and overaccept new physical endowment.

Degree of difficulty: 3

Skills required: Ability to identify still focus, to endow place, time, relationship and status.

Suggested preparation: Vocal and physical warm-up; Hospital tiggy; Where do you come from?; Thank you; Freeze tag; Blind freeze tag; Still focus developed into scenes. [For introductory information, see Part B of this program — Training for Space jump.]

How it works: This game is the ultimate still focus game. All the skills from Still focus come into play. Four players enter the game one at a time every thirty seconds. As they enter they use the still focus position of the onstage player(s) to introduce a completely new scene. It is as if we have four TV channels. At the call of 'Space jump!' we change channels to a new program. We build up the scenes, player by player, changing from channel to channel. The first scene begins with one player, the second scene two players, the third scene three players until we have all four players on stage. Then the players leave the stage one at a time. As they do so, the scenes revert in reverse order. We move back through the TV channels. But on the way back, although we have the same characters, the story has advanced to another moment.

For example, if a character is walking along a ledge in one scene, and on the return 'Space jump' finds herself on the ground, she incorporates the position, advancing the plot by having fallen.

Repeat Still focus and Moving focus games and scene-work from Parts A and B in this program, but this time have the oncoming player change the scene rather than continue in the same scene.

•

Tip

The use of the focus needs to be specific. Encourage players to enter and become the focus rather than talking.

•

Beware

Some players enter taking top status rather than yielding to the focus. These players are taking control rather than improvising. Encourage these players to endow onstage players with a higher status than their own.

Robert McFarlane

Here and Now — Berryn Schwerdt finds the central focus between David Wood (left) and Brett Wood (right)

•

Tip

Encourage entrances from a position where players see the onstage action. Enter with an offer, physical or vocal, that will change the onstage player's time and place.

•

Tips for tots

Children under the age of 12 years enjoy SPACE JUMP. However, most can only play it as it goes forward. They generally have difficulty returning to former scenes and going backwards. For players in this age group play scenes going forward only. It is possible to achieve SPACE JUMP with this age group, but it requires so much intervention from the coach that the spontaneous joy and flow of improvising can be lost.

•

Tips for text

Choose a text and play the game introducing new characters and locations at different parts of the plot, eg *Macbeth*. Macbeth starts the first scene, Lady Macbeth is player B, Duncan is player C, a witch is player D. On the return, Duncan's ghost haunts Macbeth, Lady Macbeth is sleep-walking and finally the tormented Macbeth is dying. Players need to be quite familiar with the chosen text.

•

Magic moment

Sydney team *Once In a Lifetime* took the audience's breath away when they created an inspired space jump. With what seemed to be just three bodies lying on the floor, legs entwined, the fourth player lay on the floor with them and began to rock up and down. Without speaking, they all yielded to become a miraculously operational see-saw. Another 5-5-5. Moment of the match.

Melbourne Theatresports introduced the big 24 person SPACE JUMP, in which all players from the competing six teams join forces to cap off a good night of Theatresports with the 'big one'. The audience goes wild as the 24 players go all the way forward and all the way back.

At the 1986 Australian Theatresports National Finals in the Playhouse, Victorian Arts Centre, 800 audience members noisily reminded the 24 onstage players of the changing scenes when, in the confusion on the way back through the scenes, the players forgot where they were up to.

SPACE JUMP is undoubtedly Australia's and New Zealand's favourite game. It is not unusual to hear audience members call out 'Space jump!' in the hope that teams will choose to play it. I believe SPACE JUMP typifies the Down Under playing style more than any other Theatresports game.

In Calgary they abandoned the game years ago. We play Theatresports in bigger theatres than the North American improvisors, so our style is generally more physical. We tend to use more space and broadly speaking, our style of improvising lends itself to playing big focus shifts and physical games. SPACE JUMP is a celebration of our playing style. When we play SPACE JUMP, we play it big, bold and with abandon. The game is not only a showpiece for individuals but is truly a team game. It requires a balance of physical and vocal offers, wit, spontaneity and craft.

When a 'jump' is good, it is the best game on the board.

REVERSE SPACE JUMP

4 players
4 minutes
15+ years

Description: Situation given. Four players play for thirty seconds until 'Space jump' is called. They freeze their action. One player leaves and the remaining three begin a new scene using the frozen position as the starting point. The three players play the new scene for thirty seconds until 'Space jump' is called. This continues until there is only one player on stage. The single player plays the new scene for sixty seconds. Then each player returns in reverse order every thirty seconds. The scenes revert one by one until the four players are on stage again, in the initial scene.

Resource: A clear space.

Time-out: No.

Example of a title: In the ghost train; Fighting a fire; Santa's sleigh disaster.

Aim: To firmly establish character and place, but yield instantly to new physical endowment of a still focus.

Degree of difficulty: 4.5

Skills required: Ability to identify still focus, to endow place, time, relationship and status.

Suggested preparation: Vocal and physical warm-up; HOSPITAL TIGGY; WHERE DO YOU COME FROM?; THANK YOU; FREEZE TAG; BLIND FREEZE TAG; STILL FOCUS; BACKWARD SCENE; SPACE JUMP.

How it works: The major difference between REVERSE SPACE JUMP and SPACE JUMP is that players are not building on ideas, but taking them away. Players must decide spontaneously who is going to leave the stage rather than who is going to enter. Then the remaining onstage players endow their own frozen moment with all the details required to begin each new scene. This is not a game for the fainthearted. Introduce it on those rare occasions when skilled players are ready for further challenge. I do not recommend it for performance. We began experimenting with it some years ago but abandoned it because we were having more fun solving it than the audience had watching it.

part D FOCUS IN PERFORMANCE

Finding the common focus

So far we have looked at focus from the player's perspective. Now we broaden our concept of focus to include the perception of it by the audience. Their perception will be affected by the shape of the theatre and the arrangement of the seating around the playing space. Audience members will have different perceptions of the focus depending on where they are sitting.

In performance, players need to place the focus of their scenes in a position which enables the audience to clearly see it.

Offstage players need to see the scene from the same perspective as the audience. In some cases, this will require players to move to the front of the action and crouch in front of the audience. Only then will oncoming players have access to the same information as the audience.

How the focus zones work depends on the shape of the theatre. For our purposes, theatres can be divided into three basic shapes, which we will deal with separately.

Theatre — three basic performer/audience formations

End-on or proscenium arch

In this formation the audience sits in a block directly in front of the playing space. Whether sitting in the stalls or in the dress circle, the audience sees the performers straight on. The players have a wall behind them and wings on each side.

The focus of the scene is mostly placed in front of the players. If you are playing a scene in an operating theatre, the surgeons will need to stand behind the patient, facing the audience. Offstage players must watch the action from the same perspective as the audience. You cannot see the whole scene from the wings of a proscenium arch theatre. Poorly placed offstage players will miss key offers, and split the focus. All offstage players should sit at the front of the playing space. The focus zones that work well 'end-on' are body, horizon and epic.

Half-round

In this formation, players have a wall behind them and the audience is seated around the playing space and sees the performance from one of three sides of the action.

Again the focus of the scene is mostly placed in front of the players, but allowances are made for the audience on the sides. For our scene in an operating theatre, the surgeons stand facing the audience with the patient in front of them. Offstage players must sit at the front or the sides of the action where they can see the onstage focus.

All the focus zones work well in the half-round: body, eye contact, earth (if the audience is raked above the playing space), underground (momentarily), horizon, epic and inner landscape.

In the round

In this formation the audience surrounds the playing space. Players have no walls behind them and there is always a part of the audience sitting behind them.

The focus of the scene is placed in the middle of the players. It is possible for players to share eye contact in every scene and game. Placement of games usually played in a straight line (eg Poem, Song, Shared story) needs careful consideration. They can be played with the players spread out and facing each other or facing the audience with their backs to each other. The scene in the operating theatre becomes naturalistic, with the surgeons surrounding the patient as they do in a real operating theatre. The audience looks over the shoulders of the surgeons and shares the common focus. Offstage players sit directly in front of the audience around the edges of the playing space, watching the onstage action from the same perspective as the audience.

The focus zones that work well in the round are body, eye-contact (which is extremely powerful in the round), earth (if the audience is raked above the playing space), underground (momentarily). Both horizon and epic are successful only when players use the full 360 degrees of horizon available to them.

Improvisation 'in the round' is a rare sight. In Sweden and Sydney, Theatresports is played in a boxing ring! At La Boîte Theatre in Brisbane, Theatresports is played in a box. Players enter from the four runways that lead off the centre square. They watch the scenes from the benches that surround the centre square.

The fourth wall

The fourth wall is the imaginary area of belief that separates the player from the audience. The fourth wall is an area of potent focus. When the fourth wall is removed the player speaks openly to the audience as an aside, as demonstrated by some of Shakespeare's characters, and stand-up comics.

When the fourth wall is in place the audience is separated from the action by an invisible screen on which the player paints an extension of the set or location. In *The Cherry Orchard*, for example, the characters look to the fourth wall and 'paint' the orchard. This 'painting' is known as the process of imaging.

Improvisation and Theatresports provide the opportunity to enjoy both theatre styles.

Training for theatre spaces

Training for a variety of theatre spaces begins in the training room, where scenes and games are played in a circle formation for in the round and end-on for proscenium arch, and other variations. Do not limit your work. Experiment with a variety of configurations, adjusting your teaching accordingly. Teaching in the round, for example, can be confusing if you are used to teaching out the front and are not used to a quarter of the class sitting behind you. Stand with the players as they watch the scene-work. Stand as part of the circumference of the circle with them. [See Process – Coaching strategies – Circle.]

When training for a performance, let the teams experience watching other players from the same perspective as the audience and learn to adjust their playing to the specific requirements of the space.

When staging a play, acting, lighting, design and direction all work together to support the focus as agreed during rehearsals. When improvising and playing Theatresports games, these decisions are made on the spot. Crafted improvisors adjust their playing to any theatre shape. Improvised scenes often move so very quickly, agreements are made and decisions reached in an instant. When working in front of an audience, players need to know where to place the scene and the best positions from which to watch and enter.

Advancing and extending the narrative

program 3

Commandment

**Thou shalt not waffle.
When in doubt, break the routine.**

Recounting the day's events to a family member or telling a joke at a party, we have all advanced and extended the narrative. If our audience is hanging on our every word we make the most of their attention. We extend the ideas and develop them further, sometimes out of all proportion. We elaborate, decorate and fill out the information — extending the moment to its full potential.

We sense when our audience becomes bored and stops listening. If we lose their attention we adjust our vocal tone and change the rhythm of our storytelling. We introduce new information and characters and advance to where something happens. Advancing the plot usually regains or maintains the attention of our listeners.

Advancing and extending are key elements of comedy and drama. They affect the timing by controlling the rhythm of the storytelling. A 'thriller' holds our attention, extending the narrative and, when we least expect it, advancing in such a way that we jump out of our skin. We want to be shocked but we do not want to be shocked too often. If the storyteller advances too often and too quickly we could lose our belief in the story.

Similarly, comic moments are built on the timing of the advancing and extending. Comedians decide what to extend and when to advance by gauging the reaction of their audiences. Charlie Chaplin and other great clowns extend and advance non-verbally to create physical comedy. Other comedians advance and extend verbally. The British comedian Ronnie Corbett tells a story by extending and overextending two or three points. The comedy lies in the simplicity of the plot-line, the detail of the extending, the shelving, and the reincorporation of early plot points to tie up the threads of the story.

Our aim is to develop skills to advance and extend:

1. The offer
2. The focus
3. The status

•

Remember

Two powerful ways to advance the narrative are to change the status or the focus.

Prior to all advancing and extending work, warm up with games that develop ideas and encourage listening: GIBBERISH CIRCLE, SOUND BOARD, THE MIRROR GAME and WORD BALL.

Now that players can give and receive ideas and support the focus they have created, they need to know how to develop their ideas further and when to introduce new ones. The following training games and exercises assist players to do just that.

part A FOUNDATION SKILLS

The first step is to clarify the difference between advancing and extending. Up until now we have begun the programs with physical work. In this instance, it is clearer for most players to begin with verbal work.

THE VERBAL OFFER

ADVANCING AND EXTENDING THE VERBAL OFFER

training game
2–32 players
10–15 minutes
8+ years

Description: Title given. One player tells a story, another player tells them what to extend and when to advance.

Resource: This is one of the few training games that can be played while seated.

Time-out: No.

Example of a title: What I did during the holidays; My trip to Paris. The story can be based on fact or fiction.

Aim: To clarify and explore the difference between advancing and extending the verbal offer and the effects of both.

Degree of difficulty: 1.5

Skills required: Ability to listen and overaccept.

Suggested preparation: Warm up; BALL GAMES.

How it works: The whole group works at the same time. Players work in pairs around the room, sitting or standing. First give a clear description and demonstration of verbal advancing and extending.

Extending is dealing with one offer or idea and developing it. It usually involves describing an idea further and exaggerating one point.

Advancing is moving the story on to its next phase. It may involve time shifts, location changes, new characters and new information.

Step one: I usually play this game with one player, asking them for a title of a story. I tell the story and the player tells me what to extend and when to advance. The whole class watches this demonstration.

Example — my trip to Paris:

Player A: 'I went to Paris to visit my boyfriend.'
Player B: 'Extend boyfriend.' (Tell me more about him, elaborate, fill me in, describe him, etc.)
Player A: 'Jean is handsome, drives a Peugeot and lives on the South Bank.'
Player B: 'Advance.' (Move the story forward.)
Player A: 'I was very excited to be going.'
Player B: 'Extend excited.' (Tell me more about your excitement.)
Player A: 'I was so excited, I couldn't sleep the night before I was to leave. My palms were sweaty all day. I had butterflies in my tummy and I couldn't think straight. I was so excited I was waving goodbye to everyone at the airport, I even kissed people I didn't know goodbye, and in my excitement I got on the wrong plane without my passport.'
Player B: 'Advance.'
Player A: 'Anyway we were twenty thousand feet in the air when I heard the captain say we were en route to Saudi Arabia…'

The story continues until there have been enough examples of both advancing and extending to give a general idea. Remind players B to be mindful of their timing. They give the instruction to advance or extend while player A is still talking. The rhythm of player B's interjections should vary and not wait until player A grinds to a halt but support the storytelling. Player B always names the offer they want player A to extend. This exercise allows both players to share the responsibility for and control of the developing narrative.

Step two: Now the group divides into pairs to experience storytelling in this way. The pairs name themselves A and B. Player A tells B a story from a given topic. B tells A when to advance and what to extend. When one story is complete, players change roles.

Most stories advance and extend for long periods. After about three minutes:
Sidecoach: 'Bring the story to its natural conclusion.'

Variations

Vary the content. Ask players to write three lies and three truths about themselves on a piece of paper and then read them to their partner:

- I was born in South Africa.
- I nearly died of heart trouble when I was born.
- My parents divorced when I was eight.
- My family changed our name by deed poll.
- I live in a brick house.
- I have twenty-two cousins.

Player A reads these to player B, who chooses one of the lies or truths as the beginning of player A's story. Player A tells the story, never revealing which statements are lies and which are truths.

This is a joyful exercise. Players of all ages marvel at the possibilities this exercise provides for the developing story. They are 'brimming with good ideas'. Remember, sidecoach the stories towards an ending or they can go on forever.

Written work

An understanding and enjoyment of advancing and extending helps students develop their language and written work. The teacher and the student share a common vocabulary, and in written work the student intuitively seeks adjectives and adverbs when extending and verbs when advancing.

•

Feedback

Bring the group together. Ask them about the stories.

- Were they believable?
- Were they entertaining?
- Did the story lead to an event?
- Did the story go into areas that neither player could predict?
- What was the difference between extending the ideas and advancing them?
- Did they say 'and suddenly' every time they were asked to advance or did they find other ways to advance? If they did, what were they?
- Did the advancing lead to a change of location?
- Did the advancing lead to a change of focus?
- Did the advancing lead to a change of status?
- How did the storyteller vary their vocal pitch, range, volume? Did these have an effect on the story?

The beauty of this exercise is that players cannot think into the future. They are encouraged to improvise! Storytelling in front of the whole group is less confronting when players are confident in the ways of advancing and extending and have experienced a degree of success in pairs.

•

Tips for text

For players 14+: For players who crave more, repeat the exercise in character and/or in the style of Shakespeare or rhyming couplets and so on to explore the language further.

THE PHYSICAL OFFER

Now players have an understanding of the terms and techniques, and have experienced success with the verbal offer, introduce advancing and extending the physical offer. Players complete a simple activity without words, developing the physical narrative, focus shifts, new characters and new information. Begin with the whole group divided into pairs, and conclude with sidecoached scene-work in front of the whole group.

EXTENDING AND OVEREXTENDING THE PHYSICAL OFFER

training game
2–32 players
10–15 minutes
8+ years

Description: Activity given. One player begins a physical activity in silence while the other tells them what to extend.

Resource: A clear space.

Time-out: No.

Example of activity: Give players something to do: Cleaning your teeth; Making the bed.

Aim: To extend and overextend the physical offer.

Degree of difficulty: 1.5

Skills required: Understanding of extending.

Suggested preparation: Advancing and extending the verbal offer.

How it works: We begin the physical extending work in silence, the whole group working in pairs. They name themselves A and B. Player A begins an activity, eg cleaning their teeth, while B watches. Player A begins and extends and overextends every idea and physical action. They do not think about advancing. In this exercise the observing player reminds the player to extend their ideas rather than advance them. When they have worked for three to four minutes, sidecoach the scenes towards an ending. The players change roles.

This exercise emphasises the simplicity of extending. A player begins cleaning their teeth. They pick up the toothpaste and unscrew the top. They extend unscrewing the top rather than advance to removing the top. They twist it, place it between their knees, take out a hanky and wrap it around the top. Finally in desperation they put it in their mouth and twist it between their teeth. They break their tooth. An exciting routine develops. No matter how hard we try to be mundane and ordinary, when we extend one idea and overextend it, it naturally advances. A multitude of ideas spring from that first simple single one. Players are surprised by their own sense of invention. The work is simple and clear. It is similar to building a clown routine. Clowns create and solve problems by extending and advancing. Clowns, like children, extend moments as far as possible. The results are usually very funny.

ADVANCING AND EXTENDING THE PHYSICAL OFFER

training game
2–32 players
10–15 minutes
8+ years

Description: Activity given. In silence one player improvises the scene. The other tells them which physical offers to extend and when to advance.

Resource: A clear space.

Time-out: No.

Example of a title: Task — Plant a tree; Train a pigeon; Fly a kite.

Aim: To advance and extend the physical offer.

Degree of difficulty: 1.5

Suggested preparation: NAMING THE OBVIOUS; HERE AND NOW; all work in this program thus far.

How it works: The players remain in pairs. This time both players move around the room. One player sidecoaches the other. Player A begins the unspoken scene with a task, eg planting trees. Player B moves like a shadow next to or behind player A, telling them which physical offers to extend and when to advance. When the story is complete or when players have played for three to five minutes, sidecoach the scenes towards an ending. Players A and B reverse roles.

Watching this work is fascinating. Calm, centred work with a natural rhythm develops, providing a relief from frenetic improvising when players may lose their timing and panic. It is important to provide players with a balance of fast and slow work. Three minutes of this every day commits the skill to the body and mind.

•

Feedback

Now is a good time to bring the group together to discover what they have experienced. Ask them what happened.

- When did the story move forward?
- When did something happen?
- What is the result of extending/overextending?
- Did the status of the player change when they were involved in the activity?
- Did they run out of ideas or did the ideas flow on?
- What is the difference between advancing and extending?
- What effect did extending have on the focus?
- What effect did advancing have on the focus?
- Were there shifts in the focus zones? When did these occur?

Summary

- Extending usually maintains the scene focus, rhythm and status.
- Overextending eventually results in a natural advance.
- When something happens, it advances the story.
- Advancing is associated with a change in rhythm.
- Two powerful ways to advance are to change the focus or change the status.

Trusting your instincts advancing and extending

Stanislavsky tells us that in performance 90 per cent of the actor is immersed in the life of the character while the remaining ten per cent is saved for the actor's third eye, which directs the performance. This allows the actor to hold moments for timing and deal with the unexpected while letting the character live.

The process for the improvisor is similar. Ten per cent of their attention is saved for the little voice that reminds them of what to extend and when to advance. When we listen to our natural sense of timing, the instinct is rarely wrong. The following training game educates our instinct to yield to the creative impulse in a variety of ways.

Sidecoach this exercise in front of the whole group. A player begins a physical activity, eg fishing. The coach reads every offer given by the player and tells the player what to extend and when to advance. Sidecoach the first physical offer the player makes. Let's say the player sits on a chair and begins wiping their forehead, endowing the scene with heat.

Sidecoach: 'Extend the wiping.'

Tip

Always name the offer that is to be extended. This clarifies and pinpoints the offer and the focus in the scene. It allows the direction to be specific.

Let's say the player wipes their forehead again and exhales audibly.

Extend every offer. Sidecoach the voice onto the breath. The player may want to speak.
Sidecoach: 'Extend the exhalation.'

Perhaps the player allows the sigh to develop into a slow pant.
Sidecoach: 'Extend the heat and the panting.'

The player continues to wipe their forehead. They wipe their hand on their shirt, panting with the heat.
Sidecoach: 'Extend the wiping further.'

The player picks up the tail of their shirt and wipes their brow.
Sidecoach: 'Advance.'

The player reaches for a bottle of water at their feet and drinks. Note the change of focus.
Sidecoach: 'Extend the drinking.'

The player empties the water, turns the bottle upside down, searches for another bottle, finds it and drinks the contents.
Sidecoach: 'Extend the search.'

Continue to sidecoach until the player has exhausted all possibilities, then introduce a new element in the story.
Sidecoach: 'Advance.'

The player picks up a fishing rod and casts the line. At this point the advance shifts the focus and offers a change of pace and mood. The focus has introduced a new focus horizon. The player notices a tug on the rod.
Sidecoach: 'Reel in the fish.'

Sidecoaching assists players to recognise their own good ideas, extend them and develop their potential. Add your ideas only if players need help. Sometimes players introduce a new idea unaware either of its obvious potential or of having introduced it.

Advance the scene when the current offer has been fully extended. The observant coach recognises a hand gesture, a shift of weight, a drumming finger or an almost vocalised thought as evidence of impulses. Name the offer given by the player.
Sidecoach: 'Extend the drumming finger.'

Reinforce every impulse with encouragement. These small physical offers can be sidecoached to develop the physical traits of character.

Building the scene with two characters

We continue the work now with two players in a simple scene in front of the rest of the group. Sidecoach the advancing and extending of almost every offer made in the scene. To encourage the two players to share a focus and to assist the coach in watching the work and sidecoaching it, place the scene in a location with a strong focus, eg in a movie theatre. Place two seats in the centre of the space, next to each other and facing the screen (the fourth wall).

Both players share the same objective — to enter the movie theatre and watch the movie. Keep the players' principal focus on the fourth wall. The players do not speak until they are seated, and then only if they really need to.

Tom and Glenn play the scene in the movie theatre. They enter the theatre.

Sidecoach: 'Both players — extend the sense of the dark.' They peer into the darkness.
'Tom, extend searching for your seat.' Tom begins to look.
'Tom, keep extending.' He looks for the row numbers in the dark until he is on the floor crawling in search of them.
'Tom, advance.'
'Glenn (who is sliding along the row, climbing over people), extend the climbing.' As he does so, he continues to stumble and fall over the imaginary people in the seats.
'Glenn, advance.' He finds a seat and sits down.
'Glenn, extend the settling into the seat.'
'Tom (who is now seated), advance.' Tom begins to eat popcorn.

'Tom, extend chewing the popcorn, extend the sound of the chewing, overextend the sound.'
'Glenn (who is yielding to the offer of the sounds of the chewing next to him), advance the focus.' Glenn turns and looks at Tom.
'Tom, accept the offer.' Tom looks at Glenn.

Continue to sidecoach in this way, making your choices from the physical offers given by each player, and slowly sidecoach the players to make eye contact. Both players are relaxed and have advanced the scene, creating a sense of place and character.

Sidecoach: 'Make eye contact. Speak when you want to.'

The scene now goes to voice. Sidecoach towards an event and to an ending.

Develop all the physical offers given by both players. Extend their ideas and their relationship to their environment. The resulting characters and circumstances produce moments of comedy and drama. The resulting scenes vary in style from naturalistic to absurd.

•

Summary

The players have seen and experienced a range of advancing and extending. They have developed their own and other people's ideas in training games and short scenes.

•

Check

- Do they know the difference between advancing and extending?
- Can they advance and extend verbally and physically?
- Do they understand how and when to advance and extend?

If so, they are ready to use these skills in scene-work and to play the following training and performance games.

part B

SCENE-WORK

Now it is time to bring skills together. You will recall the Yes and… and Yes but… games from Program one. We now endow players as experts (as we experienced in Here and now from Program one) and combine these with physical and verbal advancing and extending skills to build scenes. This promotes chatty, relaxed work.

Introducing the expert

Keith Johnstone developed the concept of introducing the expert to the interview situation. When players are endowed as experts they are less inclined to fear being wrong. They are more inclined to improvise without prejudging their ideas. Whatever a player says is absolutely true. They are an expert!

YES AND EXPERT

training game
performance game
2–32 players
5–10 minutes
8+ years

Description: Interview situation, characters or first line given. One player interviews an expert.

Resource: A clear space. A chair for each player. This can be played sitting on the floor or at desks.

Time-out: No.

Example of a title: Choose subject matter that is unknown to both players, eg Egg sorting; Camel hump riding; Soil classification. When players have built confidence, introduce subjects they know and let them explore the content.

Aim: To explore advancing and extending.

Degree of difficulty: 1.5

Suggested preparation: All exercises already covered in this program.

How it works: First work with the whole group watching one pair in demonstration. This will clarify the exercise. It is a good idea for the coach to be one of the demonstration players, preferably the interviewer.

Two players begin seated. Player A is an expert in a given topic. Player B endows player A as a world expert. Everything player A says is right. Everything player A says is exciting new information. Player B asks questions and makes offers that player A can answer with 'Yes and…'.

Player B: 'Good evening and welcome to our show. Tonight we welcome Dr Rosamund as our guest. So, Dr Rosamund, you are the world expert in soil classification?'

Player A: 'Yes, and I also classify soil on other planets.'

Player B has introduced the topic with a solid offer in their first question. Player A has agreed with the offer and extended it. The 'yes and' has provided player B with a logical, obvious offer for their next statement. It provides the next offer in the scene. Players fearlessly accept one another's ideas.

Player B: 'Do you find a larger variety of soils on planet earth compared to other planets?'

Player A: 'Yes and Australian soils are especially varied and of particular interest to me.'

Player B is not left searching for a following statement or question. Each offer logically builds onto the next. Both players experience a sense of confidence within the structure. Both are listening to each other and extending each other's ideas.

Player B: 'Can you identify all the different soil types found in Australia?'

Sidecoach (to the physical offer): 'Advance the scene and pick up the soil.'

Player A: 'Yes, and I just happen to have three samples with me today.'

Sidecoach (to a shared focus): 'Yield to the focus. Pick up and see the soil.'

Both players now share the focus of the soil. The soil is the gift in the scene. THE PRESENT GAME is now being used as a basis for developing scene-work. 'Yes and…' is encouraging the advancing and extending and all offers are being named. Each of the players is taking fifty per cent of the responsibility and has fifty per cent of the control of the developing scene.

The moment of transfer will occur as the interviewer leans over to touch the soil. Sidecoach the interview towards an event. Something happens and both players deal with the consequences. Bring the scene to a tidy close.

Player B: 'Goodnight doctor, and thank you for coming on our show.'

Divide the group into pairs. One player is the interviewer and the other is the expert. All players begin a new scene with a new given topic. Each player should experience both roles.

As you walk around the room, sidecoach the pairs if they need assistance.

•

Tips for tots

Players under twelve years require more consistent sidecoaching. You may need to become a player coach with each pair. Stand close to them and help them communicate their thoughts by briefly becoming a character in their scene.

YES BUT...

Some players naturally prefer to say 'Yes but...' rather than 'Yes and...'. Rather than wimp out of improvising and watering down the other person's idea, encourage players to include a new offer with the 'yes but'. This usually turns the improvisation on its head! The 'buts' are usually witty and often weird but the other player always has plenty to play with.

Player A: 'Do you like fish?'
Player B: 'Yes but not very much.'

This has watered down the idea and half killed it.

Player A: 'Do you like fish?'
Player B: 'Yes but only the man-eating variety.'

This has accepted the offer and given the other player plenty to work with. When YES BUT... is working well it will not block or wimp on the original idea but advance it.

Extended activities: Watch television interviewers and note their 'Yes and...' and 'Yes but...' techniques. Do they listen to the interviewee, yielding to their answers? Do they use the answer as an offer for the next question? Some block or wimp on the information. They ignore the answer, preferring to consult their clipboard in search of a good idea. Why then did they ask the question if they do not want to hear the answer and develop it? Good interviewing is a skill. Many media interviewers could use 'Yes and...' and 'Yes but...' practice.

Watch interviewees, politicians, sportspeople, those in the public eye being interviewed. Do they say, 'Yes and...'? Are they responsive to questions? What are they hiding or revealing as they answer questions? When do they block or wimp on the answers?

I watched Theatresports fan and comedian Peter Cook being interviewed by Clive James. The dialogue was playful, full of laughter and yielding. Both men listened to each other's questions and answers. Peter Cook played 'Yes and…' and 'Yes but…' throughout the interview. They bantered and joked keeping all the ideas alive. Offers were never dropped.

I tell students that always saying yes is impossible in the real world. Canadian Theatresports teacher Dennis Cahill once said, 'If we'd said yes to everything in our life, we'd either be dead or in gaol years ago.' From the youngest age, we learn to say no. 'No, don't touch that/eat that/cross that road/say that!' etc. Saying no is an important part of our safety and survival. However, when we improvise these dangers do not apply. We can say yes without fear.

It is sometimes more difficult for female players to say yes. Their conditioning has been to say no and not to accept the offer. [See Status, sexism and the politics of gender.] For these reasons, improvising and saying yes is empowering for all players, particularly women.

THAT'S RIGHT

Michael Robinson

training game
performance game
2 players
3 minutes
10+ years

Description: Topic given. Two players are experts. They discuss the topic, prefacing everything they say with, 'That's right…'.

Resource: A clear space, two chairs.

Time-out: No.

Example of a title: The platypus; Malaysian rubber plantations; Granite; Dogs.

Aim: To develop the concept of the expert.

Degree of difficulty: 2

Skills required: Ability to yield.

Suggested preparation: YES AND…; YES BUT…

How it works: Begin with two players in front of the whole group. When players understand how the game works, give a new topic, divide the whole group into pairs and play the new scene, all playing at the same time.

Both players are experts. Both players agree with everything the other says. The first player makes a statement. The second player agrees, 'That's right', and makes an associated statement that is either an extension or an advance. They must follow each other immediately without pausing to think or say, 'um…'. From here on, both players exchange statements, prefacing every statement they make with, 'That's right'. It is best if the players start with simple, ordinary statements about their topic. They may use facts they know. They will quickly exhaust them and be forced to invent. The statements must be logically connected. The game is not about exchanging ludicrous or absurd facts. Both players continue, agreeing with every offer, until they draw it to a close.

Example as played by Michael Gregory and Michael Robinson at Harold Park Hotel, Sydney:

> Title: The platypus
> Robinson: 'The platypus lives in the water.'
> Gregory: 'That's right, the platypus is in fact 97 per cent water.'
> Robinson: 'That's right, the other three per cent being fur and gristle.'

(And so they continued.)

Now would be an opportune time to turn to Part C – EXPERT DOUBLE FIGURES. This is the supreme expert interview game, which works well when all offers are advanced or extended and the physical and verbal yielding are balanced in the storytelling

Robert McFarlane

Michael Gregory as the expert

Developing the narrative

The following training games further develop narrative skills. They are particularly helpful for developing teamwork. They are suitable for two Theatresports teams (each of four players) training together.

TAG SHARED STORY ADVANCE AND EXTEND

training game
8–12 players
4–10 minutes
8+ years

Description: Title given. Players advance and extend the narrative on the call given by another player. Players work as a team, telling the story as a tag relay.

Resource: A clear space.

Time-out: No.

Example of a title: The adventures of Sylvia; My first day at a new school.

Aim: To develop the narrative as a group.

Degree of difficulty: 2

Skills required: Listening, yielding and shelving.

Suggested preparation: The above steps of advancing and extending in pairs; SHARED STORY; DIE GAME (elimination not necessary).

How it works: This is an advanced version of SHARED STORY, which was introduced in Program one. It develops the skills of the training games from Part A of this Program.

Half the group members stand in a line. The other half sit in a line running parallel to and facing them, and pair off with the player standing opposite them. The standing players tell a shared story. Each sitting player calls when to advance and what to extend to their respective partner (who is the player standing directly opposite them). The standing players share the storytelling. They tag the player standing next to them, who continues the same story. Players are advised not to hog the storytelling but to tag the next player after about ten to twenty seconds. It is not necessary to finish the sentence before tagging the next player. It is helpful if the coach calls the tags until players are able to share the responsibility rather than taking control. Players then pass the tag at their own discretion. The tagging passes the duty of calling the advancing and extending on to the next seated partner. All players are responsible for continuing the same story and picking up the narrative from where the previous player left off. The players bring the story to its natural conclusion. This exercise provides an opportunity for shelving, where reincorporation of early offers will make sense of a rambling story.

•

Tip

A great game for hoggers and a true test for good shelvers.

READY GO

Dean Carey

training game
4–8 players
4–10 minutes
12+ years

Description: Title given. The team tells a story, advancing and extending the plot to the call given by a fellow team member.

Resource: A clear space.

Time-out: No.

Example of a title: Give topics and titles that encourage imaging, or imply an event or adventure: The day the rain turned to fire; Flight to doom; The caravan connection.

Aim: To consolidate physical and vocal advancing and extending skills, and to promote imaging.

Degree of difficulty: 2.5

Skills required: Ability to share responsibility for storytelling. This game combines all the skills from the above exercises and games, and is perfect for a team in training.

Suggested preparation: All exercises already covered in this program; Shared Story; Die Game (elimination not necessary).

How it works: Players form a line and tell a shared story on a given topic. Player A takes a step forward and begins to tell and physicalise the story at the same time. When player A has established the first few offers in the scene, player C says 'Ready'. At this, player B steps forward, stands next to player A and shares player A's focus and, using their peripheral vision, copies every move and nuance made by player A as if they were player A. Player B does not mouth player A's words but concentrates on imaging the same pictures and sharing the same physicality. After about five seconds player C says 'Go'. At this, player B picks up the story at the point where player A left off. Player A then goes to the end of the line. The new player C calls 'Ready' and the new player B steps forward to image and physicalise the story with the new player A. The game continues until the story is complete.

Player C's role is to find the moments of advance and extend. 'Ready' is usually the moment of extend and 'Go' is usually the moment of advance. However, this is not a hard and fast rule. All players have the opportunity to be player C and experience this pivotal role.

The game provides a structure for independent training. The role of the coach is built into the game as players coach themselves and make the appropriate sidecoach calls such as:

'Physicalise as you speak.'
'Take a risk.'
'Extend the moment.'
'Develop the narrative.'
'Advance the focus.'
'Find an ending.'

•

Tip

Begin with the coach calling the 'Ready' and 'Go' until players understand the mechanics of the game.

This game is similar to Die game but is a better game for developing group trust and support because it does not split the team with elimination and competition.

SPIT FIRE

training game
2–32 players
2–4 minutes
10+ years

performance game
2 players
2 minutes
15+ years

Description: Title given. Players tell a story incorporating random words called by another player. The incorporation occurs as quickly as possible.

Resource: A clear space. Can be played seated.

Time-out: No.

Example of a title: The ozone layer disaster; The day my car broke down; The day I met Tom Cruise. The story can begin as a factual or fictional account.

Aim: To deal with an overload of offers and incorporate them into a story.

Degree of difficulty: 2.5

Skills required: Ability to listen and shelve.

Suggested preparation: All exercises in this program thus far.

How it works: Players form pairs and name themselves A and B. Player A tells a story from a given title. Player B sits opposite their partner and listens carefully to the story, throwing in unrelated words. The storyteller incorporates these as quickly as possible, justifying their place in the narrative.

The game continues until the story reaches a satisfactory conclusion or the storyteller can no longer deal with the overload of offers — hence 'Spit fire'. Players then exchange roles.

The value of SPIT FIRE for players in early training lies in their overacceptance and incorporation of another person's ideas as quickly as possible. Repeat the game with the storyteller physicalising the actions as they speak.

This is the ultimate offer incorporation game. We called this game FREAK OUT in the 1970s. Play it, and you'll know why.

Example

'I was at the bus-stop one (aeroplane) day when an aeroplane flew (ping pong) over and ping pong balls fell out of its fuselage. This (cat) reminded me of Tiddles my cat, who also (birthday cake) plays tricks with ping pong balls. Tiddles was a birthday present given to me after (door) I blew out the candles on my birthday cake two years ago. He poked his nose around the back door, a tiny (Lithuania) kitten of Lithuanian descent.'

•

Tip

Let them play with the language. The words can be incorporated in any form: eg 'mountain' can be incorporated as mountains, mountaineering, mountainous, mounted, etc. Words can be changed to verbs of any tense, adverbs, adjectives or nouns.

The unrelated words may send the story into the realms of fantasy and free-association, which leads the story far away from the original topic or title. During the early days of training, stories involve rambling free-association without a clear plot. Storytellers tend to say 'and suddenly' to justify the incorporation of the new word.

Stories seldom have endings, and the end rarely associates with the story's beginning or the title. Allow the free-association, and when players are confident encourage them to apply advancing, extending and shelving skills to structure the plot.

As players become more skilled, encourage the narrative to return to the original title. Shelving early offers and reincorporating them later will harness the plot and bring the story to a satisfactory conclusion.

Beware of throwing words in too fast during the beginning of the story. The objective of the game is to complete the story rather than have a ramble of free association.

While SPIT FIRE is mainly concerned with advancing the narrative, extending an offer or moment will aid the story by slowing the pace of the narrative. Extending the offers gives them value, weight and purpose within the story. It is during an extension that the reincorporation of a shelved offer is likely to occur. Skilled and instinctive players will incorporate the unrelated words as both an advance and an extend.

The players giving the unrelated words need to be clearly audible.

Leave some time after both players have experienced the exercise to discuss the story and the difference between the two roles. It is a game that provokes discussion.

The role of player B

As players become familiar with the game, they become aware that the unrelated words are thrown in to support the story at the moment when the plot needs to advance. For this reason SPIT FIRE is a good teacher of timing. Player B should not wait until the story grinds to a halt but give the new unrelated word just prior to the completion of the most recent image. Give the words loudly and clearly a moment before the storyteller needs the next thought.

The role of player B is not as easy as it seems. Some players become so involved listening to the story that they experience difficulty thinking of unrelated words. These players image the story with the storyteller rather than remaining objective.

•

Tips for tots

For players 8–10 years, give words that relate to the story if they find throwing in the unrelated words beyond their reach.

Subjectivity and objectivity

While remaining objective may seem incongruous with the training so far, it is in fact a valuable skill for all improvisors and communicators. The offstage player is both objective and subjective simultaneously. They are subjectively involved in the scene and at the same time objectively aware of its needs.

For these reasons SPIT FIRE is a valuable training game for those who require the skills to listen to information, assess it objectively and relate to it subjectively. It keeps the improvisation exciting and robust.

TAG SPIT FIRE

training game
4–12 players
4–8 minutes
14+ years

Description: Title given. A team of players shares the narration. They incorporate random words as they are called by allocated players sitting opposite them. The storytellers tag their team-mates, passing on the storytelling and the throwing of the random words.

Time-out: No.

Example of a title: Waiting for the last train; My first day on the job.

Degree of difficulty: 3

Skills required: Ability to listen and shelve.

Suggested preparation: SPIT FIRE in pairs.

How it works: Half the group stand in a line. The other half sit in a line running parallel to and facing them. Each player makes a pair with the player opposite. The standing players tell the story. The sitting players throw unrelated words to their corresponding standing player. Only one pair are storytelling at any one time. When ready to pass the narrative on, the storyteller tags the next player, who continues the same story. The storyteller usually tags the next player before the overload occurs, ie before spit fire.

ADVANCING AND EXTENDING IN GIBBERISH

Gibberish is a helpful tool at this point of our advancing and extending skills training. It enables players to connect physical, verbal and emotional impulses and to image and continue a story in ways other than English. A teacher at the Sydney International Grammar School (where the students learn a number of languages at primary and secondary levels: Italian, French, Japanese, etc) plays improvisation games in a variety of languages with her students. This enables players to think on their feet in another language, rather than translating. When they do not know a word, they are sidecoached to speak in gibberish rather than lose their train of thought. This is a unique and creative use of gibberish. The following training game operates on similar principles.

GIBBERISH/ENGLISH ADVANCING AND EXTENDING

training game
2 players
2–4 minutes
10+ years

Description: Title given. One player tells a story in gibberish and English, changing from one language to another on the call of another player.

Resource: A clear space.

Time-out: No.

Example of a title: The day I saved the rainforest.

Aim: To advance and extend ideas physically and verbally, speaking in English and gibberish.

Degree of difficulty: 2.5

Skills required: Ability to speak and image in gibberish, and to construct a story with a beginning, middle and end. Players need all the skills from the advancing and extending work developed thus far.

Suggested preparation: GIBBERISH CIRCLE; advancing and extending storytelling exercises in English.

How it works: Players form pairs and name themselves A and B. Player A starts a story on a given topic in English. Player B sits opposite player A and tells player A when to speak in gibberish and when to speak in English. The two languages interchange until the story reaches an ending.

Player A physicalises the story while speaking in both English and gibberish. The story continues to advance and extend in both languages.

Most players B instinctively call the changes according to the needs of the narrative as the plot advances and extends. The changes are called before player A completes one image in either language. These calls are timed to support the narrative, not at the expense of it or player A's confidence. Both players work together, sharing the same images to develop the narrative and bring the story to a satisfactory conclusion.

•

Tip

When I first started teaching I set the above task for a class of 36 year nine students and called the changes for the whole group. The noise was so deafening the players could not hear me calling the changes from gibberish to English. I hit a garbage can with a broom to signify the language changes but this only added to the cacophony. I then changed my signal to a visual cue — turning the lights on and off. It worked. Another method of signalling the change is to play chords on a piano.

•

Tips for text

Select a piece of dialogue from a play. Players think the meaning of the text but speak in gibberish. They continue to affect each other and listen to each other, contacting the thoughts and emotions of the lines.

Now turn to Part C of Program two and play the Theatresports performance game SUBTITLES.

Refining advancing and extending skills for scene-work

Too much verbal extending complicates scenes and over-emphasises the talking. The following three training and performance games are valuable exercises for refining communication skills. They skill players in advancing and extending economically by reducing the amount of talking and adding value to the verbal content.

INTRODUCING SUBTEXT

The subtext is the unspoken meaning that lies underneath the dialogue. It is conveyed through body language and mood. In reducing the amount of speech, the following games encourage players to communicate and develop subtext. Economy of language is a valuable skill.

ONE WORD SENTENCES

Keith Johnstone

training game
performance game
2–4 players
1–4 minutes
10+ years

Description: Situation given. Players play the scene speaking in sentences of one word.

Resource: A clear space.

Time-out: No.

Example of a title: At home after work/school; Apprehending the car thief.

Aim: To introduce subtext and advance the action with a minimum of words.

Degree of difficulty: 2.5

Skills required: Ability to advance and extend the physical and verbal offer.

Suggested preparation: All verbal and physical advancing and extending games in this program thus far; THE PRESENT GAME; NO-BLOCKING SCENES.

How it works: Two players begin a scene. They accept all the offers and simply play the scene speaking in sentences of one word.

For example:

Player A: 'Coffee?'
Player B: 'Thanks.'
Player A: 'Tired?'
Player B: 'Exhausted.' (Extends tired.)
Player A: 'Why?'
Player B: 'Work.' (Advances scene.)

Note that one word sentences may advance or extend the action. Players are free to move around the space developing physical communication through body language. One word sentences encourage the development of subtext. Players are free to express how they feel or what they really want through vocal inflection, range of pitch, and eye contact. Silence becomes important and physical offers advance and extend the ideas without talking.

Sidecoach: 'Go to two word sentences.'

Player A: 'What happened?'
Player B: 'I'm fired.'
Player A: 'You're kidding?'

Sidecoach: 'Go to three word sentences.'

Introduce three word sentences when players have clarified the narrative and are moving through the space rather than overloading and overtalking the scene.

Player B: 'I stole money.'

Here the players have economically advanced the narrative and arrived at a crucial point in the plot. Now vary the pattern.

Sidecoach: 'Player A use one word sentences, player B use three word sentences.'

Vary these with sentences of any number of words as necessary.

The Theatresports performance game 'N' WORDS (Part C of this program) operates on a similar principle. Players speak in sentences of a given number of words. When played as a performance game this structure holds little educational value if players merely count the words on their fingers in an effort to speak the correct number of words. The game has greater value to the drama, English, language or communication student if it is introduced to solve improvisation problems and develop storytelling skills.

•

Tip

Introduce ONE WORD SENTENCES whenever players overload scenes with too many verbal offers.

•

Tips for text

Select a piece of dialogue from a play, and have the characters speak only one word for each thought in the text. This encourages exploration of the subtext by releasing players from the burden of too many words. From time to time vary the number of words permitted.

CONTACT

training game
performance game
usually 2 players
2–4 minutes
12+ years

Description: Situation given. Players play the scene speaking only when making physical contact with another player.

Resource: A clear space.

Time-out: No.

Example of a title: Set a clear relationship between the characters, eg Dentist and patient/The extraction; Boss and secretary/Giving dictation. [See Status, sexism and the politics of gender for breaking clichéd role models in these types of relationships.]

Aim: To further develop the subtext, relationships and dramatic tension through physical contact with another player.

Degree of difficulty: 3

Skills required: Ability to create and build a scene.

Suggested preparation: Begin with two players in a NO-BLOCKING SCENE.

How it works: Players begin the scene and speak only when they are in physical contact with another player.

•

Beware

Gratuitous hand on arm touching, shoe on shoe touching or meaningless touching of any kind is to be avoided. For example, in a scene played in a dentist's surgery, encourage players to physicalise the scene.

Sidecoach: 'Move around the space and find the scene location.'
'Open the drawers.'
'Take out a file.'
'Read it out loud.'

Player A, the dentist, cannot read the file out loud until she makes physical contact with player B. When player A uses the information she sees on the file to confront player B, she could poke player B repeatedly on the chest and advance the scene.

Sidecoach: 'Take a big risk.'

Player A: 'These results are wrong!'

Player B: (Dropping to knees and grasping player A's feet.) 'I'm sorry, Miss, I confused the files.'

In this example player B has taken a risk that demands a status transition and advances the narrative.

Sidecoach: 'Answer the phone.'

Now player B must find another means of contacting player A in order to speak on the phone.

•

Magic moment

On one occasion I played this game and, after fainting in the arms of the other player and falling to the floor, both of us heard the sidecoach: 'Answer the phone'. We could do nothing but improvise. We could not think ahead. The other player had to drag me along with him as he crossed the room to answer the phone and then justify his actions as he spoke into the receiver.

Sidecoach players to find the silences in the scene. Silences encourage players to remove the physical contact, thereby advancing and extending through the physical action rather than talking. These silent moments hold potential for comedy and drama.

While this game is a marvellous performance game, it is best used in training to clarify the narrative and advance and extend the plot while keeping players physically active. Introduce it when players lack emotional or physical commitment to the scene or each other. This game encourages players to look at each other [see Focus zones – Eye contact] and make physical contact with each other while speaking. Encourage players to continue to make contact when they are not speaking. Both mixed and single sex groups could benefit from this challenge. It promotes huge advances and wonderful extends and creates a unique style of improvising.

CONTACT is at its best when players are listening to each other, sharing the scene and making the other player look good.

ADVANCING AND EXTENDING PHYSICAL OFFERS

These training games are also performance games. They are structured to maximise the physical offer and rid scenes of too much action or too many players on stage.

ENTRANCES AND EXITS

training game
performance game
3–4 players
2–4 minutes
14+ years

Description: Situation or characters given. Two team members begin a scene. Players justify their entrances and exits to keep two players on stage.

Resource: A clear space.

Time-out: No.

Example of a title: In an aeroplane; In a cafeteria. A place where characters play a variety of functions.

Aim: To develop narrative and clarify the function of every character.

Degree of difficulty: 3

Skills required: Ability to establish place and characters and to overaccept other people's ideas.

Suggested preparation: MARKO'S GAME; FREEZE TAG; NO-BLOCKING SCENES.

How it works: Two players begin a given scene. When a third member enters to establish a relationship or function within the same scene, one member immediately leaves the stage, justifying their exit. The scene continues with players entering and exiting. Players can enter and re-enter as the same or different characters.

The game makes for quick advances in the narrative and distribution of stage time between players. Generally the onstage characters extend the story, which is advanced when the new character enters.

The mechanism of the game forces teams to deploy their players, and encourages them to play a clear function in the scene.

•

Tip

Introduce the structure at any time in scene and performance game playing. The mechanics of the game provides a natural stimulus for spontaneity and unpredictability.

Variation for players 15+: Play the scene aiming for only one player on stage at a time. This further reduces the amount of verbal input, and encourages players to physically establish the scene location. Players increase the risk by calling on an offstage player, forcing themselves to exit; or an offstage player announces their entrance, forcing the onstage player to exit.

IN/AUS or IN/OUT

training game
performance game
2–4 players
2–4 minutes
15+ years

Description: Situation or characters given. Each player receives a 'specific' word. Whenever that word is spoken (by themselves or another player) they must enter the scene if they are offstage or exit the scene if they are onstage. These entrances and exits must be justified within the story.

Resource: A clear space.

Time-out: If necessary.

Example of a title: In a submarine; At the Tupperware party. The choice of words is important. Select a full range of common and proper nouns, verbs, etc. For example, choose a proper noun, 'Doris' or 'Venezuela', a common noun, 'car', and a homophone, 'two/to/too'. Words such as 'rung/wrung' and 'iron' which are both nouns and verbs are perfect as they offer a variety of usage and broaden the content. This could stimulate a discussion on language.

Aim: To weave the threads of a substantial plot while justifying all entrances and exits.

Degree of difficulty: 4

Skills required: Ability to listen, develop characters, locations and relationships, and maintain and develop a plot.

Suggested preparation: Freeze tag; Blind freeze tag; Entrances and exits.

How it works: Players are each allocated an entrance/exit word. The words are revealed to all players and the audience.

Players improvise the scene, using these words often while keeping them plausible within the story. Players justify their entrances and exits. On most occasions a player's word is said by another player, but players are permitted to say their own word to give themselves permission to leave.

•

Beware

This could lead to wimping. If so, players are not permitted to say their own word.

In/Aus is a derivative of Entrances and exits. Use it to challenge advanced players. Although it is wordy, it will not foster gratuitous gagging if the clarity found in Entrances and exits is continued.

Background: This game was developed in West Germany and taught to the international players at the Theatresports Summer School Calgary 1990 by Jochen Baum. Four players asked for ordinary, not clever words. The unfolding scene was so funny that we sang the praises of this terrific idea. The game reaches its full potential when all players commit to the scene rather than trying to be clever or funny.

HE SAID/SHE SAID

training game for
TYPEWRITER
performance game
2 players
2–4 minutes
15+ years

Description: Situation or first line given. Two players play the scene. Player A gives a line of dialogue. Player B gives player A a stage direction and follows it with their own line of dialogue. Player A responds by giving player B a stage direction and follows it with their own line of dialogue, etc.

Resource: A clear space.

Time-out: If required.

Example of a title: The proposal; First line: 'I'm leaving'.

Aim: To affect and be affected by another player and share the responsibility and control of the scene.

Degree of difficulty: 3.5

Skills required: Ability to listen, yield, overaccept, develop functional characters in a scene, create location, develop relationships, endow the scene with subtext, yield to focus.

Suggested preparation: Exercises which involve eye contact, scene building, offers of place, and NO-BLOCKING SCENES.

How it works: Begin with two players in front of the whole group. They sit on chairs to put them at ease. Give an opening line of dialogue that will propel the scene into action — 'I'm leaving'. Introduce the pattern and structure of the game: player A says their line of dialogue, player B gives a stage direction for player A followed by their own line of dialogue. Player A, who has carried out the stage direction they have been given, gives a stage direction for player B, and then says a line of dialogue, and so on. Sidecoach players from stage direction to dialogue clearly and slowly until they understand and remember the pattern.

Example

Player A: 'I'm leaving.'

Player B: '(She said going to the wardrobe and packing her clothes.) You can't leave me now I need you.'

Player A: '(He said running to the wardrobe and blocking my path.) Get out of my way!'

Player B: '(She said stamping her foot and flicking her hair with her usual defiance.) You look like your mother when you do that.'

Player A: '(He said with that annoying grin on his face, clicking his heels and strolling over to the cocktail cabinet singing his favourite song.)'

[Player B sings *I've got you under my skin.*]

Player A: 'How dare you sing that? It reminds me of our honeymoon.'

Player B: '(She said running to the window and climbing over the balcony.) Come back, darling, you'll hurt yourself.'

Player A: '(He said...)...'

NB: Each player in the above example says all the text in quotation marks — including the text in round brackets which is their spoken stage direction to their partner.

This example is extremely advanced and players would only achieve this level of complexity after some time improvising. I have included it as an example of the detail and drama that can be achieved in this game.

Corrie Ancore

Lisa Peers (left) and Mark Ferguson — *Film by Paul Cox*

Some players experience frustration and confusion when learning this game. Reassure players that the structure of the game can be confusing. Congratulate them when they master the pattern. Simple dialogue and stage directions can achieve wonderful results if the coach is clear on the following:

1. The players must confront each other and need each other in the scene.

2. The stage directions must be stage directions. They must give the other player something specific to do, rather than emotions to feel or descriptions.
3. Generally, the stage directions advance the action rather than extend it.
4. Stage directions rarely include adverbs. Use adverbs in association with clear stage directions. 'She said walking to the window slowly.'
5. There is more risk associated with moving another player towards you than with moving them away. It is riskier to say 'He said taking me in his arms and kissing me passionately' than it is to say 'He said jumping out the window'.
6. Always refer the stage direction to the first person pronoun — 'He said kissing **me**' rather than the third person pronoun 'He said kissing **her**'. This commits the player emotionally to the scene.
7. Players make no moves other than the stage directions given.
8. The line of dialogue is clearer when it is related to the previous stage direction.

This is one of the most helpful games I have ever played or taught because it encourages players to tell each other what they need in the scene.

•

Tips for text

This game unlocks the text for actors. The actors use the dialogue from the text and give each other stage directions that help them work the scene. When both actors know the objective of each character they direct each other towards achieving it. It is a particularly helpful game for love scenes and fight scenes. Both players communicate the limits of the physical contact; for example, 'He said, grabbing my ponytail and pulling me brutally towards him'. In this example players help one another to choreograph a fight scene. The physical moves develop as a result of the interaction. This exercise empowers actors to make strong choices. Once players have experimented with HE SAID/SHE SAID and moved the text, they dispense with the game structure and keep the moves that were developed to support the dialogue. Then the actors have a personal attachment to the dynamics of the scene.

All moves must be relevant to the objectives implied by the text. All moves must inform the text. See the game as a starting and unlocking point rather than an end result. Introduce the game only when all players have a clear understanding of the scene and the functions and objectives of each character, and use it to further clarify these.

A number of teachers have reported great success with the exercise. Students are able to unlock and move text from Shakespeare to Shaw, and enjoy the sense of play the exercise promotes.

•

Tip

HE SAID/SHE SAID can be performed as a Theatresports performance game but is more beneficial in the early days of training to clarify the narrative and as a training game for TYPEWRITER.

Background: In Sweden they call this game 'He said taking his trousers off'. If we are to use it to have the other player affect us, perhaps we should call it, 'He said taking my trousers off'!

ADVANCING AND EXTENDING VERBAL, PHYSICAL AND STATUS OFFERS

At this point BORIS is a helpful training game. It advances and extends the narrative in three different ways.

BORIS

training game
performance game
2–3 players
2–3 minutes
15+ years

Description: First line or situation given. One team member interrogates another using an invisible hit person — Boris — as a method of persuasion.

Resource: A completely cleared space. The room must be free of all objects which could be harmful if overturned or struck by any player. This is an extremely physical game and must be handled with great care.

Time-out: No.

Example of a title: 'So, Doctor, where were you on the night of June 15th?'

Aim: To advance and extend the narrative in three ways: 1) physical; 2) verbal; and 3) status.

Degree of difficulty: 4

Skills required: An understanding of advancing, extending and basic status.

Suggested preparation: MASTER/SERVANT GAMES [see Program five]; SPIT FIRE; all advancing and extending games in this program thus far.

How it works: BORIS is based on a Commedia dell'arte scenario. The status relationship between the three characters is clear. The interrogator has top status, Boris has second status and the victim has the lowest status.

Player A interrogates player B, bringing an imaginary monster or thug, Boris, into the scene when the information is not forthcoming. Boris is invisible. An optional third player (player C) acts as the interrogator's assistant (Igor).

Player B, the victim, physicalises all the tortures and actions Boris performs on him/her and vocalises the agonies as they occur.

Although Boris is imagined, his presence in the room is extremely clear and always frightening. The victim should establish Boris clearly. Endow Boris with height, size and strength. Imagine him as a two metre incredible hulk. Boris can lift you up with one finger and drop you or throw you against a wall.

Boris is used to develop the story. Boris helps the victim to advance and extend the narrative. Call in Boris when the victim is hedging, wimping, blocking, stalling or giving unnecessarily original offers. Boris literally pummels the scene out of the victim.

Example

Player A: 'So, Doctor, where were you on the night of June 15th?'
Player B: 'I was at home reading.'

Player A: 'I don't think so, Doctor; perhaps Boris could help you remember. Igor, bring in Boris.'
Player C: (Lurches towards the imaginary door and opens it.)
Player B: 'No! No! Please no! Not Boris!' (Face distorts as s/he sees Boris walk through the door. Raises eyes towards the ceiling and cowers in chair.)
Player A: 'Boris, help the good doctor remember.'

Then the physical improvising begins:

Player B: (Screaming, hurls him/herself out of the chair and against the wall, landing on the floor.) 'I was at the laboratory!'
Player A: 'And what did you find at the laboratory?'
Player B: 'Nothing!' (Climbing back onto the chair regaining composure.)
Player A: 'B-O-R-I-S!!!!'
Player B: (Right arm raising up his/her back and twisting violently) 'Stop! Stop! I confess!'
Player A: 'Igor, get the doctor a glass of water.' (Player C does so.)
Player B: (Drinking water, suddenly finds the mimed glass leaves her/his hand and smashes against the wall.)
Player A: (Yielding to the physical offer and focus.) 'Boris thinks you're stalling us.'

While the details of the script vary, the scenarios tend to be similar. The scenes are physically robust as player B advances all the physical action, creating Boris and all his moves.

All players share the same clarity of focus when Boris is created. If they see him, the audience sees him.

Use this game to develop the skill of advancing the narrative through physical action. The extending occurs as a result of the sudden and unexpected physical advances.

This is a highly developed game and I include it for those players who are ready to take the work further.

Advancing and extending the narrative (verbal)

Boris also relies on a detailed interweaving of offers. Players A and B set up a string of events through the process of interrogation. Each question asked by player A must be yielded to and overaccepted by player B and shelved. As player B confesses, the offers string together, justifying the questions and answers. For example:

Player A: 'What about Virginia?'
Player B: 'Virginia has nothing to do with it, she's my wife.'
Player A: 'I thought Suzanne was your wife.'
Player B: (Yielding to both offers.) 'It is true, I was married to both of them.'

The offers of both Virginia and Suzanne are now shelved and can be reincorporated by either player later in the story. Both players reincorporate offers to interweave strains of the narrative and make sense of the rambling plot.

Extending the status

Boris is an invisible servant character. He is a servant to the interrogator and always obeys him/her. Boris will always have second status. He is more important than the victim and is completely under the control of his master/mistress.

Both players accept Boris as the powerful catalyst in the scene and endow Boris accordingly.

The comedy and drama develop as the status relationships are stretched to their limits. Characters advance the action when they challenge the status relationships, usually, however, returning to the original pecking order.

Boris as a performance game

Although Boris is listed as a training game it is also an enjoyable performance game. But it can become quite predictable. For this reason do not play Boris game on game in performance. Boris is best used as a 'one off' game. Playing two Boris scenes in a row is not recommended, especially if the first Boris scene is extremely successful.

To vary the game and reduce the physical violence, change Boris to a small, mean, nose-tweaking, hair-pulling monster who tickles his victim. Although this game is extremely physical, players with physical disabilities can enjoy the benefits of Boris by adjusting his tortures.

ADVANCING AND EXTENDING THE NARRATIVE (PHYSICAL AND VERBAL)

MARY HAD A LITTLE LAMB

advanced
training game
for company work
2–10 players
10–15 minutes
15+ years

This should be saved for older or more experienced players who crave more. It is an exercise to be introduced by experienced coaches who can identify subtle offers and have the skill to determine when the group is ready to attempt the game. The coach must also sense when the game is not working and have the skills to sidecoach offers from breath to voice. It is a helpful training game when introduced at the right time with the right group. Groups need a good working knowledge of each other and the coach. I have included it at this point because it involves 'offer for offer' playing and requires an understanding of advancing and extending.

Resource: A large, clear space.

Time-out: No.

Example of a title: A nursery rhyme, eg *Hickory Dickory Dock*; four lines of Shakespeare; four lines of a popular song.

Aim: To identify and overaccept subtle physical and vocal offers.

Degree of difficulty: 4

Skills required: A high degree of concentration and listening, yielding to physical and vocal offers, advancing and extending.

Suggested preparation: Physical and vocal warm-up; Hospital tiggy; The mirror game; Speaking in one voice; Twenty-one.

How it works: This advanced exercise stretches the skills of teams and small groups who are ready for highly concentrated work. It relies on deep communication and careful yielding to every offer given, including the offer of breath.

The whole group works together throughout the exercise. They begin standing in a circle so that every player has eye contact with every other player. The exercise is akin to The mirror game but here we mirror not only the physical offers but vocal offers as well. Instead of working in pairs, we work as a whole group and have a predetermined objective: to build towards saying one or two lines of verse together. The build is slow and it could take anything up to ten minutes to achieve several lines or a full verse. Although the group is clear about the objective, they do not know how they will arrive at it or how long it will take.

Set the objective before commencing: select a simple rhyme, line of poetry or Shakespeare. A simple nursery rhyme is a good start, eg 'Mary had a little lamb, its fleece was white as snow'. The players work towards saying these lines.

Players stand in a close circle holding hands or shoulder to shoulder. All players keep eyes open, and maintain eye contact with all other players, ready to overaccept all physical and verbal offers. They remain alert and build on every offer given by each other to build towards their objective.

The first offer could simply be a breath. They begin by concentrating on breathing together. The next offer could build from a little movement of the face, hand, leg, etc. Whatever the movement, they repeat it and link the breath and movement, slowly building these towards sound. They yield to every physical and verbal nuance made by other players. They repeat the offer over and over until it develops into the next, concentrating on physicalising the language.

Gradually they build breath onto voice, as vowels and consonants develop. If the group begins with lips closed, the breathing leads to a soft gentle hum, which eventually develops to make the 'M' of the first word 'Mary'.

The movement further informs the vocalisation. This will occur in a variety of ways. A slow rock back and forth could begin. The rocking could develop into an arm swing which throws the mouths open. The hum is repeated until the mouths open and the 'Ma' (of Mary) is sounded. Now they must yield to the offers that will lead them to the 'r' and the 'y'.

The sounds and the movements develop extremely slowly. Sometimes it is not possible to determine which player gives the new offer. Each player becomes so in tune with the group, that the sound and movement cannot be separated from each other and there is no recognised group leader or initiator.

Sometimes as the sounds and movements grow and change from offer to offer, the hand-holding drops and anything eventuates. The players continue to keep eye contact as they explore the space, the movement and the developing sound. Sometimes players spread out over a wide space. The sound varies from very loud to very soft. The group continues building on every offer until at least one or two if not all the lines of the predetermined nursery rhyme, jingle or poem are spoken.

When the group is stuck on a sound or movement:

Sidecoach: 'Extend the current sound and movement, allowing it to grow into the next phase.'

When the group has extended an offer as far as possible, propel them towards an advance:

Sidecoach: 'Take a risk, advance!'

Different levels are explored and various vocal tones and sounds are found.

•

Beware

Pushing the voice is harmful. Support all sound with breath. Remind players to breathe — sometimes they forget.

This exercise is excellent for centring energy before a performance. It unites a team or company in a common objective. The exercise is not to be rushed. A slow build-up of energy will achieve the best results.

Music: This exercise is perfect for introducing live musical accompaniment, ie players playing their own instruments or working with a musician.

Explore the rhythm, pace, onomatopoeia, alliteration and muscularity of language. Taste the vibrations and the movement of the tongue as it moves between the vowels and consonants. A perfect preparation for developing improvised songs.

•

Tips for text

For players 12+: It is helpful for detailed script development work when groups develop plays from improvisations. Use it to find the muscularity of the language of a specific text; for example, replace the nursery rhyme with a line of Shakespeare — players work towards saying, 'If music be the food of love, play on'.

•

Summary

Players have experienced a variety of advancing and extending methods. Their skills should now be solid.

•

Check

- Do players advance scenes by actioning events?
- Do players extend other players' ideas as well as their own?
- Do players sense when the story needs further development?
- Do they develop the story rather than talking about it?
- Do they enter scenes when required and leave when their function is served?
- Do they find scene endings?

If the answer is yes to all the above for the majority of players, they are now ready to further these skills, playing the following Theatresports performance games.

part C

THEATRESPORTS PERFORMANCE GAMES

The following games represent the majority of the Theatresports performance games. They should not be played until players have a grounding in the foundation skills covered in Programs one, two and three.

EXPERT DOUBLE FIGURES

classic

performance game
4 players
usually 2 minutes
8+ years

Description: Interview situation. First line or characters given. Two players provide the arms for the other two players, who are the interviewer and the expert interviewee.

Resource: A clear space. Two chairs.

Time-out: No.

Example of a title: You are renowned for performing your own frontal lobotomy; An Olympic wrestling champion.

Aim: To accept and combine simple physical and verbal offers. To weave all ideas into a simple plot. To create characters.

Degree of difficulty: 2

Skills required: Ability to listen, yield, name and overaccept offers.

Suggested preparation: YES AND...; YES BUT...; THAT'S RIGHT.

How it works: Player A is the interviewer and player B the expert. They stand (or sit) facing the audience with their arms behind their backs. Player C stands (or kneels) behind player A, with their arms extended under the underarms of player A. This creates the illusion that the arms belong to the player in front. Player D does the same for player B.

The players providing the arms yield to the vocal offers, supporting the narrative by extending the moments with physical gestures. The other players make verbal offers, overaccept the offers made by the arms and justify them.

Use the first statement to introduce the expertise of the interviewee. Start or end the interview with a handshake. The interviewer and the expert develop the narrative using 'yes and' and 'yes but' as the principal foundation exercises for this game.

Begin with the expert and interviewer players in front making the verbal offers. Then introduce physical offers provided by the arms and hands of the players behind. Then all four players are yielding to each other. Encourage the hands to make emotional offers such as grabbing the head in confusion or slamming the fist onto the palm in anger. The result is very funny and provides a situation where anything can happen.

Sidecoach the expert to share their operation, experiment or exhibit with the interviewer and include them in the physical offers. The expert might allow the interviewer to hold the scalpel while the incision is being made. As the story develops, it advances and extends with physical and vocal offers, all four players yielding to each other. Sidecoach both speaking players to look at their hands from time to time, see the offers they are making and yield to them.

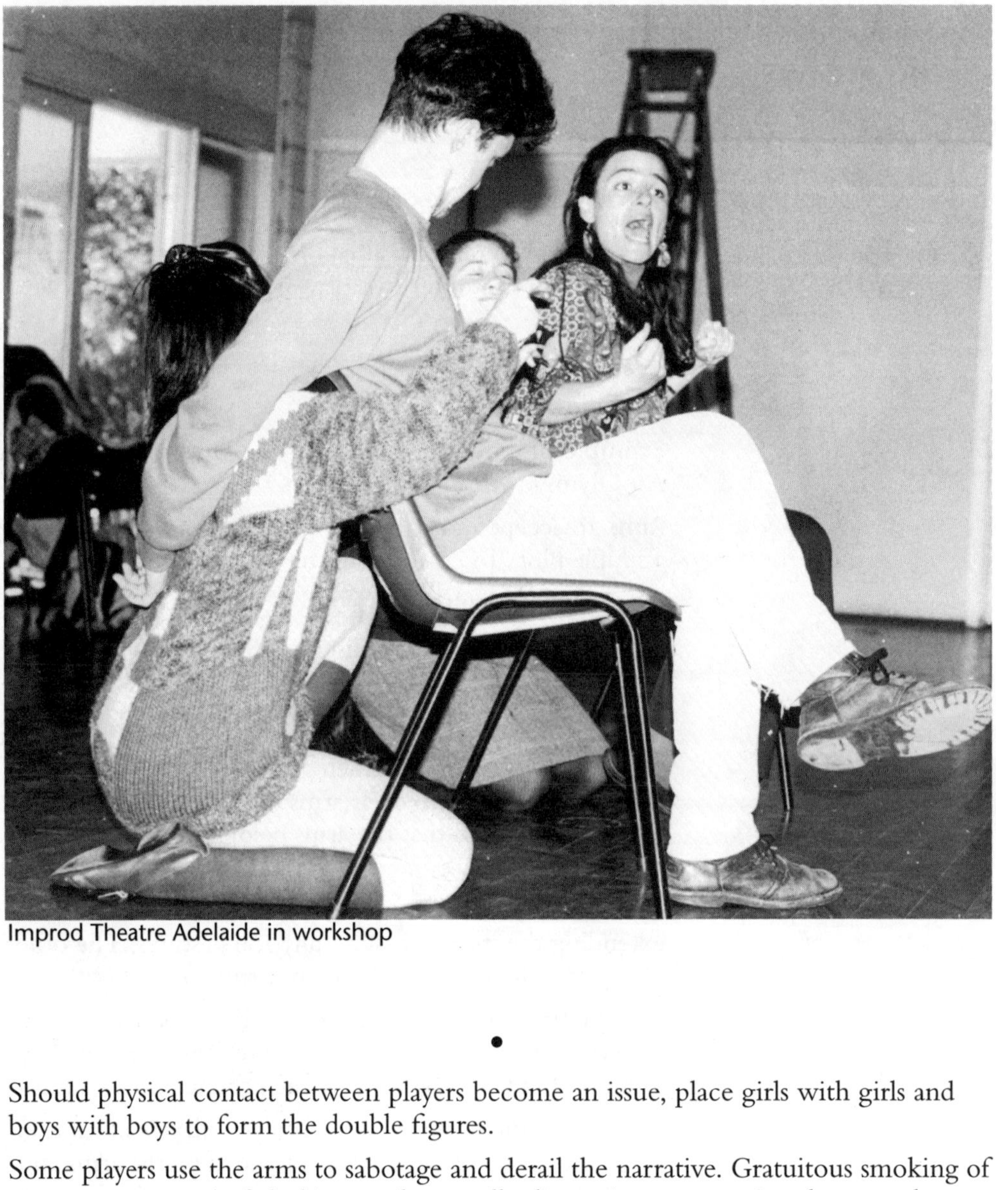

Improd Theatre Adelaide in workshop

•

Beware

Should physical contact between players become an issue, place girls with girls and boys with boys to form the double figures.

Some players use the arms to sabotage and derail the narrative. Gratuitous smoking of cigarettes, removal of clothing, and generally distracting arm-waving do not enhance the improvisation or develop the plot.

•

Tip

Bring something indicative of the expert's skills into the scene. Allow the expert to action their skill rather than talk about it.

Example

Interviewer:	'You are renowned for performing your own frontal lobotomy.'
Expert:	'Yes, and I just happen to have my scalpel here with me.'
Interviewer:	'Perhaps you could demonstrate the operation for us.'
Expert:	'Yes, I'd love to and I'll start by making an incision here.'

•

Global

Remind players all mimed props are available and within their reach.

Background

This is one of Theatresports' most popular games. The double figures structure is not new. It has been used in Vaudeville and is well known as an entertainment in Japan.

•

Tip

EXPERT DOUBLE FIGURES can be used as a handle in association with other games.

•

Magic moment

The funniest EXPERT DOUBLE FIGURES scene I have ever seen was played by *The Funky Chickens* in the Cranston Cup Grand Final 1986. The team used the DOUBLE FIGURES as a handle for a scene called 'The graduation'. The four players managed an assortment of characters by changing roles and positions to create six different characters. They stood, sat,

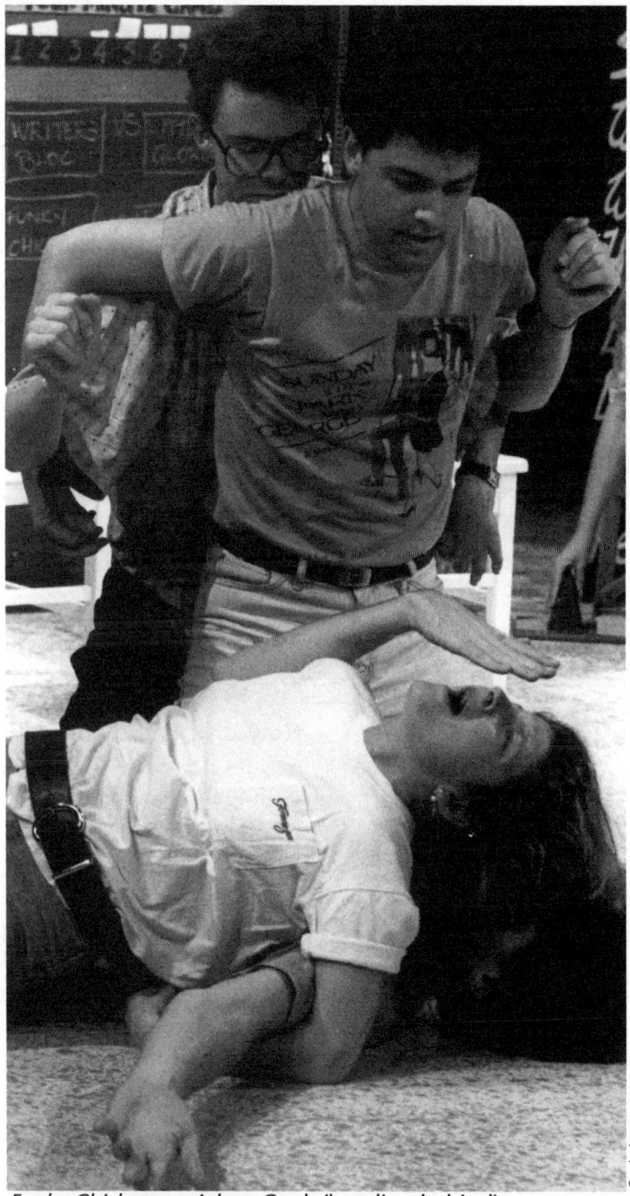

Corrie Ancore

Funky Chickens — Adam Cook (kneeling behind), Michael Turkic (kneeling front), Lisa Kelly, Mark Ferguson moved around the stage and lay on the floor creating organised mayhem with hilarious results.

Variations

Expert double figures (two players) Two players form a double figure and give a lecture demonstration on a given topic. There is no interviewer. The players (as one character) advance and extend the scene, fielding questions from the audience.

Expert double figures (three players) Play as standard Expert double figures. The expert is the only character formed using double figures. The interviewer remains as a single player.

PUPPETS

performance game
3–4 players
usually 2 minutes
10+ years

Description: Situation or characters given. One, two or three members of the team are puppets. The remaining player/s are the puppeteers. The puppets are responsible for the dialogue, but they cannot move unless moved by their puppeteer/s.

Resource: A clear space.

Time-out: If necessary.

Example of a title: Fixing the car; A jockey and trainer.

Aim: To advance the narrative from a specific physical shape and focus.

Degree of difficulty: 2

Skills required: Ability to yield to physical and verbal offers, to identify a range of focus shifts and to overaccept new and unexpected focus shifts.

Suggested preparation: Yes; You; The mirror game; The mirror game as Puppets; No-blocking scene as Puppets.

How it works: Begin with the whole group working in pairs. Players A are puppets, players B are the puppeteers. Set a simple task, eg cooking an omelette. The puppeteers set their puppets in motion. They move the puppets' legs, arms, head, etc. The puppets cannot move unless moved by the puppeteers. The puppets speak. The puppeteers are silent. As the puppets are moved, they accept and justify each position, incorporating them into the plot. Similarly, the puppeteers yield to the verbal offers made by the puppets. Simple moves with single lines of dialogue for every new physical position or focus will clarify and build the narrative. All moves and dialogue advance the story. Players work together to complete the task. Sidecoach towards an event.

•

Beware

Remind players that the puppets are real people. Some puppeteers are too rough when moving players. Gentle turning and tilting of the head is better than fierce pushing. To move players forward, experiment with gentle tapping on the back of the legs rather than moving the legs. The puppets remain flexible to maintain their sense of balance.

Robert McFarlane

Marko Mustac is manipulated by an audience puppeteer

Variations

When playing with four players, two players are puppets and two players are their puppeteers. As skills develop, vary this with one team member puppeteer moving the other three as puppets.

This is a popular audience participation game using audience members as puppeteers. The game holds a few standard gags, the most common being a comment on the puppet not being able to yield to an offer because they can't see or move to the focus until their puppeteer moves them. The most common gag line is, 'Yes I would if I could only see it!' The audience responds with huge laughter. However the audience also recognises the invention in the game. It is a game that holds great improvisation potential.

TYPEWRITER

classic

performance game
2–4 players
usually 3–4 minutes
12+ years

Description: First line given. A team member types a story, speaking aloud. The others improvise the story.

Resource: A clear space. Minimal or no props.

Time-out: Yes. Designate typist.

Example of a title: Choose first lines that are active, descriptive or poetic: Elasto women leapt into action as…; The blood red moon hung ominously in the sky…

Aim: To develop narrative skills and characters to serve the plot.

Degree of difficulty: 3

Skills required: Ability to: listen, yield to, and overaccept offers; develop a plot from beginning through middle to end; deal with an event; develop characters; incorporate stage directions and dialogue.

Suggested preparation: Physical and vocal warm-up; MARKO'S GAME; SHARED STORY; HE SAID/SHE SAID.

How it works: The typist sits to the side of the action and mimes typing a story which s/he narrates as it is typed. S/he has top status. S/he can change their mind, cancel ideas or refine old ones. The other players become the characters created by the typist. All onstage players yield to every offer given by the typist. The characters vocalise and physicalise the scene as written by the typist. The characters may also extend and advance the scene. They do not merely repeat the dialogue the typist writes but take the opportunity to invent their own dialogue when appropriate.

Encourage typists to introduce characters one at a time and to introduce new chapters to advance the narrative. They should beware of overloading scenes with too many characters. Too much embellishing and cleverness will confuse the plot.

•

Tips for tots

For players under 12 years begin with the stories of simple fairy tales or books the class may be reading. Introduce a 'Dear Diary' scene. An offstage player reads from a page in their diary outlining the day's simple events. Another player plays the scene.

•

Magic moment

1986 Festival of Sydney and 1987 Cranston Cup Champions *Writers' Bloc* [see Global network – Sydney] hit the jackpot at a workshop for national players at La Boîte Theatre, Brisbane when Andrew Denton tagged typist Steve Johnston. The team continued to tag-typewrite throughout the story, sharing the narrative as characters and typists.

SCENE WITHOUT QUESTIONS

performance game
2–4 players
2 minutes
12+ years

Description: Situation or characters given. Players are eliminated if they ask a question. They justify their exit when eliminated.

Resource: A clear space.

Time-out: Yes.

Example of a title: Give opening situations and titles that require questions (this ups the stakes): At the dole office; At an immigration interview.

Aim: To name offers in the scene rather than ask questions.

Degree of difficulty: 3

Skills required: Ability to overaccept, make positive offers, establish character, relationship and place.

Suggested preparation: YES AND...; YES BUT...; THE PRESENT GAME; NO-BLOCKING SCENES; ENTRANCES AND EXITS.

How it works: One or two players begin a scene as if they were playing a NO-BLOCKING SCENE. If a player asks a question, that player must leave the scene and justify their exit. New players enter or exit the scene at any time, advance or extend the narrative and serve a function in the scene. The most important elements of this game are scene-playing and storytelling.

Players who have asked questions are not permitted to re-enter the scene. They cannot return as a new character even if the scene requires it. The onstage characters must overaccept the need for a new character and find ways of exiting and entering as the new character. Occasionally this game finishes with a soliloquy given by the sole remaining player, as all other players have been eliminated.

This is an excellent game for teaching advancing. When improvisors ask a question, they could be wimping and passing the responsibility for advancing on to the other player. Making statements encourages the players to share the responsibility for the narrative.

The game reinforces the value of YES AND... and YES BUT... as foundation tools for storytelling. Players are less inclined to ask questions if they employ the strategies of YES AND... and YES BUT...

•

Tip

Deploy your team with care. Do not have too many players on stage. Save players for those times when onstage players ask a question and are forced to leave the stage. When players have asked a question they must justify their exit before leaving. They cannot simply leave the stage.

By the same token, do not be afraid of asking questions. They increase the risk factor. Asking questions advances the scene and allows all players stage time. Do not penalise players for asking questions. Skilled players deal with the unexpected and yield to the sticky moments when they arise.

Magic moment

The best example of this I have ever seen was Scene without questions on a runaway train. One player asked a question and justified their exit by seeing a passing sign, saying, 'That's my station', miming opening a window and jumping out!

Other justifications such as, 'I'll go and get mum,' provide an opportunity to leave the stage and advance the story by introducing another character.

Some players love asking questions. This is terrific, but beware of the player who wimps out of the scene leaving the narrative to the others. All exits must be justified.

The inherent structure of the game forces players to share the responsibility and control of the story-line. The game's value lies in its reinforcement of teamwork, saving and daring to take a risk. Players should be rewarded for making their team-mates look good.

Competition

If this game is played in a Theatresports competition it is important that:

- the judges are aware of the high risk factor of the game and score accordingly;
- the judges do not penalise teams for asking questions but score on the strength of the narrative, the risks taken in developing the scene and the justification of the exits and entrances;
- it is not an appropriate tie breaker in a game on game situation. The pressure such a situation creates on individual players is not conducive to the spirit of healthy competition.

For advanced players: Play a Scene with questions where every line of dialogue is a question.

Soundtrack

performance game
2–4 players
2–4 minutes
12+ years

Description: Situation given. The scene is played to a soundtrack which offers changing musical styles at regular intervals.

Resource: A clear space. A tape of music which changes theme and mood at approximately twenty second intervals, and facilities to play it.

Time-out: No.

Example of a title: In the trenches; The rollerblade king/queen.

Aim: To use music as a stimulus for improvisation and to respond to a variety of musical offers to advance and extend the plot through physicalisation.

Degree of difficulty: 3

Skills required: Ability to characterise and develop plot inspired by musical offers.

Suggested preparation: Physical warm-up; No-blocking scene without words; Mime to music; Advancing and extending the physical offer.

How it works: A soundtrack is played. Teams improvise the scene, directly inspired by the music. The players do not dance to the music. Their movements are informed by the rhythm and the emotional content of the music. Players extend the concept of Mime, playing the scene to music without words. Scenes can be naturalistic or stylised. I recommend that players do not talk or dance during the scene. They tell the story through improvised movement rather than relying on dialogue or dance. It is not a hard and fast rule that the scene be played without words or dance; being heard above electronic music can be difficult and dancing rarely advances the plot. In some circumstances speaking or dancing could work. I simply alert players and coaches to the obvious difficulties.

The musical soundtrack contains a wide variety of musical styles: classical, tribal, muzak, swing, medieval, bossa nova, symphony, reggae, etc. The wider the variety, the greater the source of inspiration. Music with vocals is not recommended. The lyrics usually confuse or interrupt the development of the improvised plot. Preprepared tapes should contain at least one change of music every 20-30 seconds. The music is more beneficial when it suggests a definite mood and rhythm. Soundtrack may be played for varying lengths and as a handle to other games.

Improvised live music is an alternative to taped music. Improvising musicians provide offers which lead the action rather than follow the onstage action. This is contrary to most other scenes, where improvised music adds to the onstage ideas and supports the story rather than leads it.

Each music change advances the story. Entrances for new characters, changes in focus, status, mood or plot turning points are emphasised and very powerful when they occur on the music changes or as a result of them.

•

Tip

- Choose Soundtrack when there has been an overabundance of spoken scenes.
- The Soundtrack scene does not have to last the length of the music. Remind players that the scene can be finished with the usual 'lights down'.

•

Tips for tots

For players of 8-12 years, introduce one theme of music only. Keep the scenes quite short; approximately one minute. Add the musical changes as skills develop.

RADIO PLAY

performance game
1–4 players
2–4 minutes
12+ years

Description: First line or title given. Team tells the story in the style of a radio play.

Resource: A clear space. Optional: a microphone on a stand (could be functional or prop), musical instruments or props to use as sound effects.

Time-out: If necessary.

Example of a title: Hassan awoke with a fright as he heard the creak of the door; Brenda saves the day.

Aim: To develop voice, sound and storytelling skills by exploring the medium of radio.

Degree of difficulty: 3

Skills required: Ability to listen and create location and character through sound and voice; create a story with a beginning, middle and end; make and use sound effects; imaging.

Suggested preparation: ONE-WORD-AT-A-TIME STORY; SHARED STORY; SHARED STORY MIXED GENRE; TYPEWRITER.

How it works: Players stand around a microphone (real or imagined) and tell the story as if performing a radio play. Players image the story to create the reality for listeners.

This game is a close cousin of TYPEWRITER. Many players choose to use a narrator to clarify the plot. Players support the narrator by creating the characters that serve the scene. Experiment with improvised music and sound. Create mood and extend and advance moments with effects to create footsteps, door slams, animal noises, etc. Musical introductions and songs, commercial breaks and the like allow RADIO PLAY to utilise many of the skills learnt in other games. Explore the medium of radio by placing the scene in a modern radio studio or by standing around the microphone as if in a 1940s radio serial.

This is a particularly good game for visually impaired players. The scenes are aurally exciting rather than physically active.

For advanced players try RADIO PLAY in the style of (for example) Brenda's moment of triumph in the style of a gothic horror story, detective serial or children's radio.

For a change, listen to RADIO PLAY with your eyes closed, or play it in the dark.

OPERA

classic

performance game
usually 4 players
4 minutes
12+ years

Description: Title given. Opera sung.

Resource: A clear space with costume and props. If using props, some suggestions are: hats, swords (plastic or foam), chalices, crowns, cloaks. Live improvised musical accompaniment, eg guitar or piano, is a possible lovely addition but not essential.

Time-out: Yes. During time-out, players only need cast the one or two principal characters. Deciding the full scenario reduces spontaneity.

Example of a title: Kevin the counterfeit king — this title offers a central main character who is obviously a baddie.

The rodeo queen — this title offers a central heroine and a place.

Aim: To sing an original opera.

Degree of difficulty: 3.5

Skills required: Ability to build the narrative towards an event; listen and yield to musical offers; and develop rhythm, rhyme and timing.

Suggested preparation: Vocal warm up; Sound board; Sing madrigals; Sing Speaking in one voice; Sing Poem and Rhyming couplets; The present game; Sing The present game; sing No-blocking scene; Inner song (see below): use the caller structure to build sung scenes.

How it works: One or two players introduce the basic element of the plot. They set up the problem, the place, the characters. They begin by simply singing the story in a clear voice. Keep the plot as simple as possible. Sing the whole story or combine big songs with spoken dialogue. Every sung line either advances or extends the narrative. Other players support the story as chorus, furniture, incidental characters, etc.

Teams usually require all four players to perform all the characters required by the plot. Professional teams sometimes fill out their ranks with another team playing the chorus. Extend skills by developing harmonies, duets, trios, solos, and choruses. Any style is permitted — rock opera, modern opera, Gilbert and Sullivan and traditional. The basic key to Opera lies in the epic nature of the storytelling. The emotions are so heightened that players are lifted beyond normal speaking into song. Opera is a Down Under favourite.

•

Beware

Some players talk about themselves too much during an opera: 'I am the king of this land' or 'I am the princess of the forest'. Encourage players to also sing about their feelings for others and to endow other characters as they develop the plot.

•

Tips for tots

For players of 8–12 years, simply sing scenes and dialogue rather than construct an opera. It is a good idea for the coach to narrate the scene or to participate as a singer if required.

For content

Traditional operas include the following themes, characters and ideas:

- Love
- Kings, queens, princes, princesses, nobility, leaders, courtiers
- Priests, archbishops, monks, nuns, devotees
- Wars, battles, knights, heroes, fighting men, armies
- Daggers, spears, bows and arrows, shields, swords
- Miracles, inns, wharves, forests
- Witches, soothsayers fortune-tellers, gypsies, magic
- Servants, bodyguards, maids, ladies-in-waiting, attendants, butlers
- Messengers (most operas predate modern technological communications)
- Arranged marriages, clan feuds, religious feuds, skullduggery, schemes
- Tyranny, tragedy, plottings, ascending thrones, royal lines
- Bastard children, lost heirs, swappings at birth

- Madness (especially due to love)
- Contracts, letters, notes
- Mistaken identities, disguises
- Women playing men (roles formerly played by castrati)
- Feasts, celebrations, banquets, dancing, speeches
- Dying slowly from terrible wounds, illness, wasting diseases, poison
- Shakespeare, literature
- Legends, epic stories, myths, archetypes

•

Remember

Sing an opera about anything, whether it be epic or domestic. Singing raises the story and the characters to epic proportions. For this reason the players' belief must be strong to sustain the size of commitment the style demands.

Robert McFarlane

Heaven Scent sing an opera — Marko Mustac, Tanya Bulmer

About opera

(notes by Peter Fyfe)

Traditionally, opera stories come from legend, literature and Shakespeare. The stories are epic in nature. They span from days to years. While the plots may be fairly thin, the emotions are always deep, rich and real. People's feelings are often expressed in an aria, which is simply a sung soliloquy. Opera characters often tell the audience who they love and why, what they are going to do about something, and how they feel about it. When characters die in operas (and they do it all the time) they nearly always sing on their deathbed.

Most operas have more than one act/scene, and these are often in different locations.

The use of the horizon and epic focus zones is very powerful when playing opera scenes.

Opera is a combination of all art forms. While it is primarily music and drama, dance and visual arts play an important role.

GIBBERISH OPERA

performance game
3–4 players
4 minutes
15+ years

Description: Title given. The team sings an original opera in gibberish and an offstage player narrates the story.

Resource: A clear space with some props and costumes. Optional live, improvised musical accompaniment, eg guitar or piano.

Time-out: Yes.

Example of a title: The curse of kimono; Little red riding hood.

Aim: To tell an epic story with epic characters singing in gibberish.

Degree of difficulty: 3.5

Skills required: The narrator requires skills to lead the storytelling and give offers to the onstage players. The onstage players require the ability to advance and extend the plot, make physical offers while singing in gibberish and develop characters to serve a plot.

Suggested preparation: Warm-up — physical and vocal; THE PRESENT GAME sung in gibberish; HE SAID/SHE SAID sung; TYPEWRITER sung; GIBBERISH/ENGLISH ADVANCING AND EXTENDING.

How it works: This is a derivation of the classic, OPERA. Developed by New York Theatresports, it provides an alternative to game on game OPERA playing. One team chooses to play a classic OPERA while the other performs their OPERA in gibberish, using a narrator to set up the scenes and translate quirky plot points.

The narrator sits to the side of the action and introduces the opera as if they were presenting a television special 'At the Opera'.

> 'Good evening, and welcome to the Sydney Opera House for this glorious rendition of *The curse of the kimono*. We open with act one where we see Noriko in her bathroom, at this point unaware of the kimono curse.'

The narrator guides the opera in the same way as the writer guides the book in TYPEWRITER. S/he advances the plot, introduces new locations and characters, and clarifies the story for the audience.

INNER SONG

training game
for OPERA
performance game
2–4 players
2–4 minutes
12+ years

Description: Characters, situation or title given. Team plays the scene. Characters sing their inner thoughts at the call of an offstage player or timekeeper.

Resource: A clear space, with minimal or no props. Live, improvised musical accompaniment, eg piano or guitar, is a possible lovely addition but not essential.

Time-out: Yes.

Example of a title: The death of a family pet — this title offers a central event and an objective for the scene.

The booze bus — this title offers a variety of characters and opinions to be expressed.

Simple domestic situations that introduce basic events, problems to solve or bring characters and relationships together are perfect for this game.

Aim: To express inner thoughts and subtext through song.

Degree of difficulty: 3

Skills required: Ability to express characters' inner thoughts at the call of an offstage player or coach.

Suggested preparation: Warm-up; SOUNDBOARD. Slowly introduce the sung thoughts into NO-BLOCKING SCENES. Play TRUTH and introduce sung thoughts via a caller.

How it works: Team plays the scene singing their inner thoughts as subtext. These songs describe their inner wants, desires and opinions, and build the characterisation. The songs extend and express how the characters feel about each other and the events that occur in the story.

One or two players begin the scene. An outside caller, usually the coach (until teams are proficient in providing their own caller), takes the offers from the scene and asks players to extend these ideas.

A character might reveal that she is scared of spiders. The offstage caller takes the opportunity to extend this idea by calling, 'She sings of her fear of spiders'. Such a call supports the narrative because the song tells us more about the character and her fear. The player breaks into a short song about her fear of spiders and when she has finished, the spoken scene continues from where it left off. The other character continues as if they have not heard the song but the other player can use the information gathered to advance the plot. It is likely now that she will meet a spider. Her reaction to it will be justified in terms of what she has sung.

If there is a lack of offers in the scene, the outside caller advances the action by freezing the scene and offering something totally unexpected that will aid the development of the narrative.

Sometimes characters sing together when the caller pulls the characters together into a duet.

Sidecoach: 'The spider and the girl sing of their new-found friendship.'

•

Tip

Songs need not be long. Short sung sentences can be strung together. Complex rhythms and rhymes are not necessary.

SING ABOUT IT

training game
performance game
2–4 players
2–4 minutes
12+ years

Description: Title given. One, two or three players play a scene, and when an offstage player calls 'Sing about it' the onstage players burst into song.

Resource: A clear space, with minimal or no props or costume. Live, improvised musical accompaniment, eg piano or guitar, is a possible lovely addition but not essential.

Time-out: Yes. Decide singing players and calling player.

Example of a title: Trouble at Timezone; First day on the job; Visiting Nana. Titles that provide a setting for a scene or introduce one or two characters and offer a range of locations and emotions are best. Titles are scene starters not song titles. They do not include song styles.

Aim: To play a scene in sung and spoken narrative.

Degree of difficulty: 3

Skills required: Ability to advance and extend a narrative speaking and singing, to yield spontaneously to offstage calls and develop plot and characters.

Suggested preparation: Vocal and physical warm-up, NO-BLOCKING SCENES, NO-BLOCKING SCENES sung, advancing and extending exercises, SPIT FIRE sung, TYPEWRITER, TYPEWRITER sung.

How it works: One or two players begin a scene. The narrative is spoken until the offstage player calls 'Sing about it'. Then the player who was speaking spontaneously bursts into a song specifically about the current offer. If the player simply said, 'Hello mum' when 'Sing about it' was called, they would sing about their mum or about saying hello to their mum. They sing, extending the idea, and when they are ready they stop singing and continue the spoken narrative.

The singing can be as long or short as the player wishes and the style of singing can be as simple as singing on the same note or as elaborate as a song with rhyme and a specific style. The singing ability and confidence of the player will determine this. Players can sing solo, as separate characters, independent storytellers, a duo, or sing as a chorus. The offstage caller or coach can call 'Sing about it' at any time, or as often as the narrative requires.

In INNER SONG, the offstage caller makes a specfic song choice which guides the players and the content of the scene, eg 'She sings the song of the lonely locksmith'. Players accept and incorporate the new information of emotion and profession. In SING ABOUT IT no new information is given by the caller, but the call may come at the most unexpected time on the least likely offer. This promotes spontaneity and sparks the thrill of playing and watching the game. The singing players are best advised to relax and simply enjoy this roulette style of improvising. This is a popular performance game and a helpful training game for players at all levels.

For advanced players 15+ who crave more: In Tokyo we experimented with different styles in which to SING ABOUT IT. From time to time an offstage player or coach may call, 'Rap about it', 'Rock about it', 'Croon about it' and so on. The team continues the scene singing in the designated style. We had so much fun developing this that many styles were employed including jazz, scat, chanson, tango and mambo. Imagine my surprise when I called, 'Kabuki about it' and they did, drums, chant and all!

KARAOKE VIDEO

performance game
2–4 players
2–4 minutes
12+ years

Description: Title given. One or two players sing an original song. The other players provide the characters and improvise the video clip of the song.

Resource: A clear space, with minimal or no props or costume. Live, improvised musical accompaniment, eg piano or guitar, is a possible lovely addition but not essential. Video camera and screen if appropriate.

Time-out: Yes. Decide singing players and moving players.

Example of a title: Holiday time; Friends forever; Every day; Race to the top; Zoo crazy. Titles that suggest a variety of interpretation, up to three characters and offer a range of locations and emotions are best. Titles may suggest specific song styles, eg pop, ballad, rock, blues.

Aim: To tell a story in song and movement and incorporate and extend knowledge of film and video with improvisation.

Degree of difficulty: 3.5

Skills required: Ability to develop plot and characters, tell a story in song and movement, and yield to a combination of musical, sung and physical offers.

Suggested preparation: Vocal and physical warm-up, NO-BLOCKING SCENES, NO-BLOCKING SCENES sung, SONG, TYPEWRITER, TYPEWRITER sung. Some discussion of the concept of Karaoke and the styles and characteristics of video clips and how they are made is helpful. This includes acting style, use of camera angles and such details as camera shots, eg close up, mid shot, two shot, long shot.

How it works: One or two players begin to sing a story at one side of the playing space. They face the audience but include the playing space in their focus. They sing solo, as a duo or as separate characters. They give offers for the moving players who become the characters in an improvised video clip in the centre of the playing space. The moving players physicalise the story in mime, listening carefully to the sung offers. They are silent and do not mouthe the words of the song. For the most part the singers initiate the offers for the video players who overaccept the ideas and extend them, developing the narrative further whenever they can.

Background: This game was created in Tokyo where players naturally extended the idea of song to incorporate the popular Japanese pastime Karaoke.

Japanese from all walks of life are familiar with and have participated in Karaoke in bars, restaurants and Karaoke parlours. Karaoke provides social entertainment for friends, classmates, business colleagues and families. The most unlikely individual, the shyest personality, and the person you least expect to reveal themselves as an extrovert, will quietly select a song, grasp a microphone, follow the lyrics on the screen and in full view of a restaurant, perform a ballad, rock song or a tender Japanese love song. The Karaoke bar affords anyone the opportunity to experience Andy Warhol's 15 minutes of fame.

The game was an immediate success in Japan. We divided the stage into two distinct areas defined by lighting. Players had great fun experimenting with bringing the video concept to life; creating staged visual effects to satirise the genre, such as moving scenery to create the illusion of travelling in a car and imitating the mosaic screen effect used to censor X-rated moments. This is created by players flickering their fingers in front of the offending focus.

Extended activities: With older players and students of film and media, it could be fun to incorporate a video camera and screen. While the game is in progress the camera operator could video the moving players and the improvised video clip could be performed live and simultaneously appear on a screen for the audience.

THE GUIDE

classic

performance game
3–4 players
4 minutes
14+ years

Description: A movie description is given. The players base their scene on the description.

Resource: A clear space, a film guide (book, newspaper or magazine), minimal costumes and props.

Time-out: Yes. Determining who will play the central character may be helpful.

Example of a title: '*My Life as a Dog* — an irrepressible mischievous 12-year-old Swedish boy in the 1950s lives with his dog, elder brother and an ailing mother until he is shipped off to live with relatives in a small village.'

Choose content carefully. Good film scenarios can be found in TV magazines, newspaper TV liftouts and publications such as *Halliwell's Film Guide*.

Choose from a variety of channels and styles. Some film descriptions are useless because they provide no pegs for the narrative. Choose those with a basic outline of the plot or alter the plot to suit your needs.

Aim: To weave the threads of a substantial plot to create characters and a unique story.

Degree of difficulty: 3

Skills required: Ability to create characters that serve a specific function in a predetermined plot outline. Ability to improvise, bridge, advance and extend with dexterity.

Suggested preparation: THE PRESENT GAME; NO-BLOCKING SCENES; build GUIDE characters from MIRROR BODIES and MIRROR FACES. [See Program seven.]

Corrie Ancore

Writers' Bloc — Anthony Ackroyd (left), David Witt (front), Steve Johnston, Andrew Denton (right)

How it works: This game is usually played for the full four minutes. Players weave a story from the threads of a basic plot outline. This is an exciting and challenging game. It is also great fun. Players love creating film characters. THE GUIDE allows all players to lay their ham on the line. Crazy impersonations of actors and the era and film style are fun to create and to watch. But good GUIDES do not rest on gags alone. All this fun must be supported with listening and story-building. The challenge is to juggle all the aspects of the story. Players must introduce characters to serve a function in the story.

•

Beware

Movie descriptions that review the film and emphasise the actors rather than the characters are not helpful. It is more important that players explore their own version of the character rather than mimicking the actor in performance. Players should be Rambo, not Sylvester Stallone.

While there is fun in pretending to be Sylvester Stallone or Arnold Schwarzenegger, there is more educational mileage in exploring the style and plot of a film that players have never seen. Choose a variety of relationships, plots and styles deriving from the movies of all decades this century. For example, 1960s beach parties, 1950s science fiction, 1920s Keystone Cops. A lot of fun can be found when you choose a variety of styles.

•

Tip

Reduce the amount of violence that could occur in car chases, show-downs, etc. Encourage players to direct their energies towards the story-telling rather than overemphasising the physical violence. [See Process – Coaching strategies – Dealing with physical violence.]

PLAY IN THE STYLE OF

classic

performance game
3–4 players
4 minutes
14+ years

Description: Title given. The team chooses from three styles in which to tell the story.

Resource: A clear space, props and costumes available.

Time-out: Yes.

Example of a title: *Little red riding hood* in the style of Shakespeare/Kung Fu film/TV game show; *Romeo and Juliet* in the style of a western/news report/fairytale. Have a brief synopsis of the story outlined for the players to clarify plot points.

Aim: To tell a story within a genre.

Degree of difficulty: 3.5

Skills required: Ability to action and deal with events, understand genre, establish location and character, play function in a scene, and to develop a story with a clear beginning, middle and end.

Suggested preparation: No-blocking scenes; Shared story; Shared story mixed genre; Entrances and exits.

How it works: The team is given the title and a choice of three styles. The players then nominate one style in which to tell the story. Vary the content according to the age and skills of the players. The above example would be relevant to a wide range of players from 14 years. Choose more challenging titles for more advanced players, eg *Romeo and Juliet* in the style of film noir/a documentary/a Kung Fu movie. Encourage the team to satisfy the plot by dealing with the main characters and events. Use the style to give the story a new perspective. [See Appendix B – Styles/genres.]

Vary the three choices of styles — do not offer three similar styles of television shows. Allow for a range of literary/cinematic/theatrical/television styles.

Competition: This game is only fair in competition when all team members are familiar with the given stories and styles. If some players know the story/style and others don't, explain. A brief outline of the story read by the coach (in training) or compere (in performance) will clarify the plot.

For experienced players: When team members are familiar with all of the playing styles given, they may ask the audience to choose one.

Players looking for a further challenge may choose to improvise the story using all three given styles. They begin the scene in one of the given styles and, at the call of an offstage team member or the timekeeper, they continue the scene in the style called. They may choose to play each style once or, if time permits, several times.

•

Tip

IN THE STYLE OF is perfect to use as a handle. If using it as a handle, be careful not to overload scenes with too much information or too many devices.

•

Tips for text

Use the game to explore novels, plays, films, and other areas of the curriculum.

•

Magic moment

Many Theatresports players have a favourite IN THE STYLE OF story. There's *The Sound of Music* in the style of *World Championship Wrestling*, when Melbourne player Kate Herbert endowed the audience as Austrians and they spontaneously sang *Edelweiss*! But Melbourne Theatresports will never forget one of the first scenes played at St Martin's Theatre, when the team *Lost On Stage* played the legendary *Goldilocks and the Three Bears* in the style of *The Young Ones*. Colleen Burke (Rick), Michael Blair (Neil), Sam Brown (Mike) and Russell Fletcher (Vyvyan) received one of the first 5-5-5 ever from the judges. The scene was a riot and the packed audience nearly went through the roof when Russell Fletcher, who incidentally has red hair, capped the scene by disappearing around the back of the stage and re-entering from the audience screaming, 'Well this must be the forest!' while making rude signs and generally doing some splendid 'Vyvyan' acting.

BALLET

performance game
usually 4 players
2–4 minutes
10+ years

Description: Title given. Team dances a ballet. Offstage narration is optional.

Resource: A clear space; some costume and props. You may wish to use live, improvised musical accompaniment, eg piano or guitar, but it is not essential.

Time-out: Yes.

Example of a title: Winning Lotto — this title offers a strong event that will have an effect on the characters in the story. The Wedding — this title offers two central characters and an event.

Aim: To explore improvisation through dance and to dance an original ballet.

Degree of difficulty: 4

Skills required: Ability to advance and extend physical offers and characterise through movement.

Suggested preparation: Warm up — physical; The mirror game; Thank you; Mime; Soundtrack.

How it works: The narrator sits to the side of the action and introduces the ballet as if they were presenting a television special, 'At the Ballet'.

> 'Good evening, and welcome to the Sydney Opera House for this glorious rendition of *Winning Lotto*. We open with act one where we see Mrs Fulton at the sink washing the dishes. Little does she know who is waiting to knock on the door…'

The narrator guides the ballet in the same way as the writer guides the book action in Typewriter or the narrator guides the plot in Gibberish opera. The narrator guides the story, accepting offers from the players and giving offers when necessary. Players build characters, dancing their emotions and the actions of the plot. The narrator advances the action and accepts offers from the ballet. The players (dancers) yield to the narrator's offers.

•

Tip

Ballet can be performed in a number of styles, including jazz, classical, modern, rap, disco, primitive, etc.

•

Tips for tots

For players under twelve who do not have extensive storytelling skills, the coach narrates the story. Choose stories appropriate to their age and skills, eg fairytales.

•

Magic moment

This has always been a popular game and well played in New Zealand. The Auckland team *Four Play* danced *The Taniwha* (native New Zealand lizard) and the *Kotuku* (heron) at the New Zealand national finals 1988. It was a sensation. There was none of the usual hilarity of leaping and catching which always brings huge laughs. Instead, the James Hay Theatre audience of 1000 was treated to an improvised classical ballet. You could hear a pin drop as we sat in awe of Juliette Monaghan's dancing, the depth and clarity of characterisations and the simplicity of the storytelling.

IN A... WITH A... WHILE A...

classic

performance game
3–4 players
4 minutes
15+ years

Description: Situation given. Team plays the scene combining these elements.

Resource: A clear space. Minimal props and costumes.

Time-out: Yes.

Example of a title: In a classroom, with a teacher, while an examination takes place. In a jungle, with a toothbrush, while a thunderstorm occurs.

Aim: To play a scene within the framework of the given circumstances.

in a = place
with a = character or object
while a = given circumstances (weather/historical period/event...)

Degree of difficulty: 4

Skills required: Introduce the game slowly to players who have already mastered the skills of:

- Setting location
- Playing an objective
- Developing character
- Dealing with the given circumstances
- Advancing and extending the narrative

Suggested preparation: MARKO'S GAME; NO-BLOCKING SCENES set in a variety of locations.

How it works: Players begin a scene, first establishing the place. They add the other elements as the narrative develops. Players enter the scene to perform specific functions that develop the narrative to support the title.

•

Tips for text

When used to bring the basic principles of scene playing and improvisation together, this game is not only valuable for Theatresports but for improvising the given circumstances of a text. In the study of the play *Romeo and Juliet,* players could extend their knowledge of the text by using IN A... WITH A... WHILE A... to bring the text to life: In a tomb, with a vial of poison, while a spouse lies dead at your feet.

Match the content of IN A... WITH A... WHILE A... to the skills of the players to help them to achieve success in bringing together the elements of the given plot. For example, the following is appropriate for beginner players: In a laundromat, with detergent, while an electrical fault occurs. For more skilled players: In a poolroom, with a cabbage, while an earthquake occurs.

Include the game in a Theatresports performance only when players fully understand its mechanics; it's harder than you think. Skilled professional players enjoy the game. It frees them to play wild and marvellous scenes and gives them an opportunity to experiment with a variety of theatre styles: absurd, fantasy, science fiction, naturalism, realism, etc.

Background: I have some doubt as to the educational value of this game. The Canadians abandoned the structure long ago. I believe this occurred when the set-up for the scene was gathered from the audience members, who gave totally impossible examples and situations which did not foster good storytelling. While professional players can weave the circumstances together in a *My word* type of storytelling mode, unskilled players cannot be expected to do so.

STUNT DOUBLES

performance game
4 players
2–3 minutes
14+ years

Description: Situation given. Two players play the scene as if they were actors in a film. They call their 'stunt doubles' to stand in for them.

Resource: A clear space.

Time-out: If necessary. Decide who plays the actors and who plays the stunt doubles.

Example of a title: Rocket ship to Venus; Renovating the house.

Aim: To overaccept an idea and extend it until it reaches a natural advance or conclusion. To explore the role of the stunt person.

Degree of difficulty: 3

Skills required: Ability to recognise focus, create characters, events and place, and to extend an idea as far as possible before advancing it.

Suggested preparation: Physical and vocal warm-up; CIRCLE TAG; THANK YOU; FREEZE TAG in fast and slow motion.

How It works: Four players play a scene: two are actors portraying a story, two are their stunt doubles. The actors begin the scene, playing the characters truthfully. They set up tasks and before they embark upon them, they freeze and call for their stunt doubles to take over the action. The stunt doubles tag the first players and take their exact positions at which the first players move off stage. The stunt doubles extend the action, usually in slow motion, until it reaches its climax or advances to a new action. Slow motion is effective because it emphasises the physicality while minimising danger. When the action is complete and the stunt doubles have reached their new position, they freeze and call 'first players'. The first players tag the stunt doubles and continue the scene from the new positions. These exchanges occur as often as required. First players call 'stunt doubles' when the task is dangerous, exciting, could tire them or is below their status to enact.

•

Magic moment

Sydney Cranston Cup Season '89 team *The Shorts* — Michael Gregory, Brad Hall, Felicity Biggins and Kerry Adams — played a story from the audience scene as a STUNT DOUBLE. On the ten second bell one of the first players said 'Kiss me… stunt doubles'. The lights slowly faded as the stunt doubles slow motioned a kiss. The audience went wild. A perfect Moment of the match.

FIRST AND LAST

performance game
2–4 players
2–4 minutes
15+ years

Description: The first and last lines of the scene are given.

Resource: A clear space.

Time-out: If necessary.

Example of a title: First line: 'We'll catch the first train at dawn'. Last line: 'Not with my mink you don't'.

Aim: To explore bridging and build the narrative from a given beginning towards a given end.

Degree of difficulty: 3

Skills required: Ability to develop a plot.

Suggested preparation: Warm-up; YES LET'S; SHARED STORY; DIE GAME.

How it works: Players are given the start and finish. They invent the middle of the scene. Players begin the scene with the first line and develop the characters and location. The players develop the scene towards the last line, which usually becomes the punch line.

Give players the lines on a piece of paper or write them on the blackboard. In the excitement of playing the scene it is easy to forget the final line.

Beware of a fixed time limit. Sometimes a time limit can panic the players rather than allow them to fully explore the narrative.

FIRST AND LAST effectively builds bridging skills. However use it sparingly. It is generally more important for players to improvise freely towards an unknown end.

POSITION VACANT

Writers' Bloc

performance game
2–4 players
2–4 minutes
12+ years

Description: Job given. Interview situation. One or more team members are interviewed for a job. Their objective is to convince the panel of their expertise.

Resource: A clear space; a number of chairs.

Time-out: If necessary.

Example of a title: Hurley twister (invented job); Snake vet.

Aim: To advance and extend on an unknown topic. To develop job interview skills. To introduce basic status.

Degree of difficulty: 3

Skills required: Ability to advance and extend with confidence and clarity. Ability to create character and endow other players with status.

Suggested preparation: MASTER/SERVANT [see Program five]; ADVANCING AND EXTENDING THE VERBAL OFFER as experts; YES AND...; YES BUT...

How it works: One or two players form an interview panel. One, two, or three players are interviewed for the job (separately or together). At the end of the interview, the panel decides the successful applicant.

Background: This was developed from the Expert and interview scenes by the Sydney team *Writer's Bloc* — Andrew Denton, Steve Johnston, David Polterak and David Witt.

It is an exciting performance game, exploring wit and language, and is most valuable in the classroom.

'N' WORDS

performance game
2–4 players
2–4 minutes
12+ years

Description: Situation given. The team is given the number of words to be used in each sentence.

Resource: A clear space.

Time-out: If necessary.

Example of a title: At the laundromat; Bringing home an injured animal.

Aim: To advance and extend using language economically.

Degree of difficulty: 3

Skills required: Ability to listen; count; endow; vary vocal range; use silence; establish a place, relationships and functional characters; and to advance the scene.

Suggested preparation: One-word-at-a-time story; The present game; The present game with 'n' words; No-blocking scene with 'n' words; One word sentences (also play two and three word sentences as scenes).

How It works: The scene is played using only sentences consisting of the specified number of words. The number of words used can be consistent throughout the scene, eg 5; or it can change through the scene as signalled by an offstage player, eg 1, 3, 2, 6, 10, 1.

This game is a derivative of the training game One word sentences. This performance game has been developed from the training game and is of little educational worth if simply played for its gag value. Players will simply count the words on their fingers. While this is very funny, the gag soon becomes boring. Use this game to challenge players after they have experienced One-word sentences in training.

The role of the number-caller is very important. Callers need to be aware that generally small numbers encourage physical advances and big numbers encourage verbal extensions. Numbers over ten should be used very sparingly. Players must be accurate but not too obvious in their counting.

Performance: This game is particularly effective when teams wish to clarify their thoughts, separate offers and play a simple narrative scene without becoming too verbal.

ALPHABET GAME

training game
performance game
usually 2 players
2–4 minutes
14+ years

Description: Situation given. Players play the scene beginning each new line of dialogue with the next letter of the alphabet.

Resource: A clear space.

Time-out: Not necessary.

Example of a title: Waking up late; Collecting for the Salvation Army; White water rafting.

Aim: To develop a plot and the characters that serve it while speaking each new piece of dialogue with the next consecutive letter of the alphabet.

Degree of difficulty: 4

Skills required: Ability to overaccept; listen; justify characters and dialogue within a developing plot; establish location, endowment and relationship; and to know the alphabet well.

Suggested preparation: THE PRESENT GAME; SPIT FIRE; NO-BLOCKING SCENES; then add the alphabet.

How it works: Players begin a scene from the given situation. One begins his/her line with an 'A', the next with a 'B' etc.

> Player A: 'All this money and nowhere to stash it.'
> Player B: 'Be careful with that gun, you'll hurt someone.'
> Player A: 'Can you tell if it's loaded?'
> Player B: 'Don't point it at (drops to the floor shot)…' etc.

This is a good brain tester. It is a real test of advancing and extending, with each new idea moving the plot forward as players search for the next letter of the alphabet. It is not as easy as it seems. It is a useful handle to add to games or scene-work as it eliminates superfluous talk. It is easier for players to start with the letter 'A' and end with 'Z'.

The audience loves this game. They think through the scene with the players struggling to find the next letters and are disappointed when the alphabet is lost and overjoyed when it is refound.

•

Tip

Remind players to keep their sentences short and to beware of overload. This is one time when 'less is more'.

ACCENT ROLLER-COASTER

performance game
2–4 players
2–4 minutes
16+ years

Description: Situation given. One or more players begin a scene and change the accent of their dialogue as called by an offstage team member or timekeeper.

Resource: A clear space and a list of accents (for example: French, Italian, New Zealand, Cockney, Scottish, South African, New York, Texan, U.S. West Coast, Swedish, Aussie, Far North Queensland, Japanese, Polish, etc.)

Time-out: Decide which player will call the accents.

Example of title: Purchasing a new sound system; Clearing out the garage; A school reunion.

Aim: To speak in a range of accents and dialects, and to use language with confidence.

Degree of difficulty: 4

Skills required: Ability to overaccept, listen, develop story-line and characters.

Suggested preparation: Practise a variety of accents and dialects.

How it works: One or more players begin a scene. They speak in their usual accent until an offstage caller or timekeeper announces a new accent. The players continue the same scene in the given accent. Great fun can be had with this game as players flex their language skills tripping around the accent world. Beware players do not simply gag or send up cultures and races. The real skill lies in finding accuracy in speaking in a variety of accents and dialects. The offstage player should not change the accent too often but wait for a time when the scene needs to advance and the energy needs to shift. A change in accent will always change the energy level.

A helpful way to begin accent preparation is for players to stand in a circle and, one at a time, say a word or phrase in a particular accent accompanied by a movement. The accent is given by the coach. The movement is motivated by the energy of the word or phrase spoken and reflects the accent used. All players then simultaneously imitate the phrase and movement. For example:

Coach: 'French.'
Player A: 'Croissant.' (Said in French accent while twirling handlebar moustache.)
All players: 'Croissant.' (Said with same accent and movement.)
Player B: 'Storm le Bastille!' (Said in French accent, raising triumphant fist in air.)
All players: 'Storm le Bastille!' (Said with same accent and movement.)

PLAYBOOK

Michael Robinson and Brent Applegath

performance game
2–4 players
2–4 minutes
14+ years

AKA: ACTORS' NIGHTMARE

Description: Situation given. Players play the scene while one player speaks only lines from a given text, eg *Macbeth*. Other players justify the offers made from the text.

Resource: A clear space, a text (a play is usually better than a novel).

Time-out: Not necessary.

Example of a title: The driving lesson. It is also possible to start from a line given from the playbook, eg 'Tomorrow and tomorrow and tomorrow'.

Aim: To develop a plot and the characters that serve it while yielding to offers and incorporating them within the developing story-line.

Degree of difficulty: 4

Skills required: Ability to overaccept; listen; justify characters and dialogue within a developing plot; establish location, endowment and relationship.

Suggested preparation: Familiarise players with a text. Character developing games: Mirror bodies; Mirror faces; The present game; Spit fire.

How it works: Players begin a scene from the given situation. Player A, the playbook player, holds the text, eg *Macbeth, Death of a Salesman* or *Away*. This player yields to all the offers but speaks only dialogue from the given text. S/he can read any character's lines, selecting at random. The other players overaccept the offers made by the playbook player. These ideas are justified immediately in the scene. All players play the scene as if there is nothing unusual about a line such as 'Is this a dagger I see before me?' appearing in the middle of a scene such as 'The driving lesson'. Player B can overaccept and extend from the offer given by the Shakespeare text and say, 'I'm sorry, my father's a butcher and he always leaves his tools lying around'. Or advance from the line, 'Yes, it is a dagger. To protect us. I've been carrying it since receiving the anonymous letters'.

The playbook player plays the scene, keeping their head out of the book and only reading to speak a line. The style of the improvisation is often determined by the content and style of the text.

This is a helpful game for exploring the possibilities of a text. The game allows us to hear and speak a range of language and styles juxtaposed with colloquial speech. Vary the text according to the age and reading ability of the players.

Sidecoach players to actively deal with the events that arise from the scene.
Sidecoach: 'Pick up the dagger and do something with it.'

•

Beware

Some players drop offers. Offers are as important as the gift in The present game. A danger is that the players block the playbook player, making their lines incongruous by gagging, ie sending them up. This can be funny but will not allow an interesting story to develop.

Performance: Give the audience the choice of a few texts and allow them to decide from which text and page number the scene will be played.

PAPERS

performance game
2–4 players
2–4 minutes
14+ years

AKA: Line in a bucket (In this case, papers are placed in a bucket rather than scattered across the floor.)

Description: Situation given. Lines of dialogue are written on pieces of paper and scattered across the floor. Players begin a scene, and from time to time pick up a piece of paper and incorporate the line into the scene.

Resource: A clear space. A number of single lines written on pieces of paper.

Time-out: No.

Example of a title: In a cold storeroom; Collecting shells; In a nuclear power plant; In a cable car.

Example of lines: These aren't my socks; Oh no I just killed the cat!; Where did you put the marmalade?; There's a great show on Channel 9; Dad will be home at four.

Aim: To incorporate seemingly incongruous offers immediately into a plot and justify them in the story.

Degree of difficulty: 3

Skills required: Ability to: overaccept; shelve; and create simple plot, character and location.

Suggested preparation: Spit fire; Tag spit fire; Advancing and extending the physical offer; Extending and overextending the verbal offer.

How it works: Players begin the scene with the given situation. At any time and at their own discretion they pick up a piece of paper from the floor, immediately read this line aloud and justify it within the plot.

This is a good fun game but should be used sparingly as it relies more on the device within the game than skill building. Vary the content of the lines from the sublime through the sensible to the ridiculous. Beware of saying a line from a piece of paper, justifying it and dropping it as an offer. It is better to use the line to advance the story into unexpected areas than simply rest on the gag.

It is helpful if players screw up the piece of paper and throw it out of the playing space when they have used the line. Remind players to announce the line when they read it. The audience should be aware of the exact dialogue written on the piece of paper. I believe Papers is more beneficial than Line in a bucket because it keeps all players physically active in the scene rather than breaking the scene reality when they move to the bucket.

Papers is a very funny game and players experience a feeling of achievement even if the narrative is not well structured. However, it is sensational when all the lines are justified.

Performance: Do not play Papers game on game. It is a novelty game and can only be played once in a performance.

SIDEWAYS SCENE

performance game
2–4 players
2–3 minutes
12+ years

Description: Situation or activity given. Players play the scene where the floor is the wall.

Resource: An extremely clear space. If using props or chairs, be very careful.

Time-out: If necessary.

Example of a title: Window cleaning.

Aim: To encourage lateral thinking and explore the physical offer on a variety of levels.

Degree of difficulty: 4

Skills required: Ability to build scenes, character and location and to create a scene environment.

Suggested preparation: Physical warm-up, eg HOSPITAL TAG; WHERE DO YOU COME FROM?; YES LET'S; THANK YOU sideways.

How it works: One or two players begin the scene using the floor as the wall with their feet facing the audience. There is great physical fun rolling on the floor, creating doors, making coffee, weeding the garden, while dealing with the world turned sideways. Experiment with this game but do not use it too often as it encourages gags and being clever. Push players past gags such as the fly stuck to the wall, etc. These are very funny when they are born of ingenuity but if you play the game too often, some players tend to repeat the gag rather than make new discoveries.

Performance: Do not play this game on game. It is a novelty game. Choose as part of a physical challenge.

BACKWARDS SCENE

performance game
usually 2 players
2–4 minutes
14+ years

Description: A line is given which is the last line of a scene. Players start with this line and play the scene backwards from the end to the beginning.

Resource: A clear space. Minimal props.

Time-out: If necessary.

Example of a title: I think we're lost.

Aim: To encourage lateral thinking and experiment with the structure of language and narrative.

Degree of difficulty: 5

Skills required: Sophisticated language skills.

Suggested preparation: Warm-up — very fast tag game; Freeze tag; Blind freeze tag; One-word-at-a-time in pairs — one word ball per pair; Shared story; Die game; Scenes in English/gibberish.

How it works: In a backwards scene it is the story that goes backwards from end to beginning, not the individual words of dialogue. Instead of having a natural reaction to an offer, players justify their partner's last line and movement by supplying the line that motivated and preceded it. They provide the reaction before the action. When played well, the backwards scene looks like a film running in reverse, even though each sentence is spoken forwards.

> For example, player B backs out of the room, saying 'Hi, good to see you', and slams the door.
> Player A, left alone, says the line that preceded player B's action: 'I think I hear someone at the door'.
> Player B knocks at the door.
> Player A: 'Max should be here any minute.'

The narrative tends to go forward for a few lines, then backs up before it goes forward again.

If players are thinking too much and becoming bogged down, play the game in gibberish. This will free the emotions and physicality. Players will use tone and pitch to imply their actions and reactions.

Even experienced veteran players find Backwards scene scary. They say they just look at each other and go for it. This is high-risk playing. A good backwards scene is rare.

A popular way of playing a Backwards scene is to play it as a Backwards expert interview scene (as they play it in Seattle) with first and last lines given: The scene always begins with, 'Good night, and thanks for being on our show', and always ends with 'Hi, and welcome to the show'. The interviewee's answers precede the interviewer's questions.

While this game is rife with gags and tags, at its best it exposes the structure of language. When we move backwards through language, we learn much more about it.

•

Tip

Play the game in foreign language class.

Some players will thrive on this one, while others will find it difficult.

Performance: Don't make this game obligatory — allow players to choose it as part of a physical or narrative challenge. Do not play it game on game.

SIT, STAND, KNEEL AND LIE

performance game
4 players
2–3 minutes
14+ years

Description: Situation or activity given. At any time there must be one player sitting, one standing, one kneeling and one lying.

Resource: A clear space and a chair.

Time-out: If necessary.

Example of a title: Washing the dishes.

Aim: To advance and extend the narrative, explore a variety of spaces and levels and justify physical offers.

Degree of difficulty: 3.5

Skills required: Ability to make quick physical movements and tell a story while moving at speed.

Suggested preparation: CIRCLE TAG; FREEZE TAG; BLIND FREEZE TAG; HE SAID/SHE SAID.

How it works: This is a very silly game but a lot of fun and a good energy raiser. Encourage players to use all moves to advance or extend the plot. Introduce it when

4 x 4's — John Thompson (sitting), Ian Shrives (standing), Kate Herbert (kneeling), Carole Patullo (lying)

players have a grasp of advancing and extending and would benefit from risking more and playing a fast physical game.

Characters serve the plot and play a function. At any one time there must be one player sitting, one standing, one kneeling and one lying. Encourage players to take risks, change positions, and justify the change.

The game produces fast, physical scenes as players readjust their positions to yield to the ever changing physical advances.

Performance: Play as a physical challenge. The game is great fun but rarely works game on game.

TIME WARP

performance game
3–4 players
2–4 minutes
15+ years

Description: Situation or first line given. Players start the scene and at the timekeeper's discretion a whistle is blown, the action freezes and a change of time and/or place is given. Players resume the story in the new time frame or place and utilise their frozen positions to start the new scene.

Resource: A clear space. Some props and costumes. A microphone for the caller or timekeeper is optional in performance.

Time-out: If necessary.

Example of a title: The wedding; The bikies' annual picnic. For example, a ritual or event that brings characters together.

Aim: To tell a story weaving characters through a series of scenes where the elements of time and location change.

Degree of difficulty: 4

Skills required: Ability to deal with detailed shelving; create characters, relationships and locations; and respond to the events and changing circumstances of the plot as it unfolds.

Suggested preparation: Warm-up: FREEZE TAG; NO-BLOCKING SCENES — developing characters from MIRROR BODIES and MIRROR FACES; ENTRANCES AND EXITS.

How it works: This game developed as an extension of TYPEWRITER. It combines the skills of TYPEWRITER, REMINISCENCE and SPACE JUMP. Skilled teams successfully manage to combine the mechanics of the game with good storytelling. A good timekeeper calls the jumps from the offers given in the story. These jumps advance the story and develop the characters. Call a TIME WARP when a scene is losing momentum, when a change in focus has occurred, or when a particularly interesting physical position arises.

For example, 'The Wedding' — the bride and groom are at the altar, the minister begins the ceremony miming a prayer book. The bride and groom kneel; the timekeeper blows the whistle (signifying 'Freeze') and calls, 'Time Warp! — The day the bride and groom first met'. The players begin the new scene from this position, eg gardening, looking for a contact lens, stamping cans at the supermarket. The minister can exit the scene and return as another character, or remain in the new scene, either as the same character (the minister) or as a different character.

Time warps introduce jumps which clarify relationships between characters. A scene might begin at a reunion; the timekeeper calls, 'The first time they met ten years ago'. In jumping time and place, players reveal new information about their past and future. Scenes are clearer when the characterisation is bold and believable. Characters age, get married, die, and are born in any order given at the timekeeper's discretion.

•

Tip

There are inherent gags in the game. Beware the overuse of time calls that do not advance the scene. The most common of these is, 'Three hours later,' and the players hold the same position as if they had been doing the same action for three hours. This will gather a good laugh but can become a cheap device if repeated too often.

Performance: In training the time warps are called by the coach. In performance the time warps are called by the timekeeper or a team member. The development of the plot rests on the time warp caller as much as the players. Clear whistle blowing and audible time warp calls are helpful to the smooth playing of this game. In performance a microphone will aid the clarity of the calls. Timekeepers find calling the time warps difficult if the players do not give clear narrative offers on which to base the changes.

GIBBERISH INTERPRETER

performance game
3 players
2–3 minutes
12+ years

Description: Interview situation with topic given. One player speaks only gibberish, one only English, and one player speaks both.

Resource: A clear space. Minimal props and costumes.

Time-out: If necessary.

Example of a title: In an airport lounge with a prima ballerina; Marriage proposal in a restaurant kitchen.

Aim: To tell a story, advancing and extending, with an interpreter translating from gibberish to English and vice versa.

Degree of difficulty: 3.5

Skills required: Ability to speak in gibberish, play basic status relationships, advance and extend offers in gibberish and English and play a character.

Suggested preparation: GIBBERISH CIRCLE, GIBBERISH/ENGLISH ADVANCING AND EXTENDING, MASTER/SERVANT in gibberish and with an interpreter. [See Program five.]

How it works: Three players play the scene. One speaks only English, one speaks only gibberish and one (the interpreter) speaks both. Begin an interview situation with a high status international guest who speaks only gibberish, a reporter who speaks only English (bottom status) who relies on the interpreter (second status) to translate the questions and answers.

Sometimes GIBBERISH INTERPRETER is played with the expert understanding English but not speaking it. At other times, the expert does not understand English. I suggest the second approach. The role of the interpreter is particularly challenging. They are the pivotal point of the advancing and extending. They take the English question from the reporter, translate it into gibberish for the expert then translate the answer into English for the reporter. It is best if the interpreter passes the questions on instantly and economically. They also incorporate the physical offers of the expert.

This is a potentially exciting game. It has all the obvious gags of any gibberish game but the scene value should be fully explored. The gibberish interpreter structure is an exciting addition to scene-work.

GIBBERISH JOKE

training game
performance game
2 players
2–4 minutes
15+ years

Description: First line given. Players tell a joke in gibberish, or English and gibberish, interrupting each other as they disagree on how the joke should be told.

Resource: A clear space.

Time-out: If necessary.

Example of a title: Did you hear the one about the artichoke and the policeman?

Aim: To improvise a story sharing the advancing and extending with another player.

Degree of difficulty: 4

Skills required: Ability to name and shelve offers; to overaccept all offers even when the offer would seem to be a block.

Suggested preparation: YES AND…; YES BUT…; THE PRESENT GAME in gibberish; GIBBERISH ADVANCING AND EXTENDING exercises; EXPERT in gibberish.

How it works: This is an age-old joke structure. Two players are both endowed with being world expert joke tellers. They both know all the jokes. Whatever joke you ask them to tell, they are not only familiar with it but probably made it up. There are two ways of playing this game. The first is that both players speak in gibberish throughout the story; the second is that both players change from gibberish to English and back again at their own discretion or on the call of an outside player. Either way the set-up is the same.

One joke teller begins the joke, the other player interrupts the joke disagreeing with a minute detail. The first player yields to the modification and continues telling the joke. Too much argument about the modifications will not advance the story. Someone must yield.

Performance: The game rarely works in performance. It is one of those games that work better in training. Play it to sharpen skills.

If playing GIBBERISH JOKE in performance, do not play it game on game. The scenario format will probably not interest an audience more than once. Make it a players' choice game. Players could elect to play it in a gibberish challenge.

Do not be discouraged if players cannot make sense of the game. It is an advanced game for skilled players and skilled coaches. One day you will teach someone who instinctively knows how to play it. It requires specific timing skills. There are no gags to lean on in this one. It is a game that demands pure craft and instinct. When somebody plays it well, you'll know!

Endowment

program 4

Commandment

Thou shalt not shine above thy team-mates.

When we improvise we invest our belief in the ideas we create. We call this investment — endowment. Endowment is a natural process. We endow people, places and things every day of our lives. As children we endow our toys. We talk to our teddy bear and because we believe he can talk, he does. The scruffiest doll we endow with great beauty, the smallest hidey hole we endow as being our secret fortress.

Endowment is a vital skill for improvisors. We can endow another player with high or low status, the place with being indoors or outdoors, the occasion with being trivial or important. Every time we are on stage we can endow the audience, props, costume — everything — and create a new world, simply by saying 'What if…?'.

Endowment allows players to make offers and yield to ideas on a sophisticated level. It requires players to think about other players and their environment rather than thinking about themselves. Players endow each other with:

1. Physical and emotional qualities and characteristics
2. Relationships
3. Status

The power of endowment and the value it has as an improvisation and acting tool lies in how we give it and how we yield to it. Our aim is to develop the skills to:

1. Endow an offer
2. Recognise an endowed offer
3. Yield to an endowed offer
4. Overaccept an endowed offer

part A FOUNDATION SKILLS

ENDOWING THE OFFER AND THE OTHER PLAYER

From the first training sessions most players instinctively endow offers and other players. For example, during THE PRESENT GAME players introduce simple endowments when yielding to the shape, weight and size of the gifts. They create these physically when giving and receiving gifts. The endowments tell us about the gift.

Now that players are skilled in making and receiving offers, yielding to focus, extending their ideas and advancing the narrative, introduce endowment as a means of further enriching the ideas. Introduce endowment to develop the physical and emotional qualities of characters. Use it to create atmosphere and to reveal the subtext of the scene.

We can isolate endowment as a skill by playing endowment games in which the quality being endowed is unknown to the receiver (the endowee). To maximise the problem solving and the communication through a variety of ways other than 'telling' the endowment, many of the training and performance games are played in gibberish.

Using gibberish

Step one: Before commencing endowment games, warm up with gibberish exercises. Begin with GIBBERISH CIRCLE to build gibberish confidence. Gibberish releases the voice and connects the impulse to the emotion. The exercise becomes very loud; the results are energetic and provide a great release of emotion. Remember that players love to shout but take care that they do not strain their voices.

On the other hand, amid the din some players are very frightened of making strange sounds. Dare them to be liberated by it. Encourage a wide range of vocal tones, pitches and accents.

If the energy is down, warm up with games that involve agreement and raise and channel energy: ALL THOSE PEOPLE WHO and WHERE DO YOU COME FROM? These are not played in gibberish. [See Warm-up games.]

When smiles turn into laughter, players begin to relax. They start to have fun. As the sense of fun increases, so does the quality of the improvisation. The work could become extremely noisy. Give them permission to play.

Step two: When the gibberish is flowing, repeat THE PRESENT GAME — this time in gibberish. Tell players to sing the present-giving scenes in gibberish.

Step three: Review GIBBERISH ADVANCING AND EXTENDING. [See Program three.]

Gibberish endowment games

It is important that the following three training games are learned and played in the order as listed. While it would seem easier to endow another player with a physical endowment than an occupational or emotional endowment, teach the occupational, then the emotional, then the physical. This prepares players for the performance game ENDOWMENTS, when they will bring the three elements together. Their scenes will be clearer if they first establish the scene location. The occupation endowment is more likely to establish the location than either of the other two. In these endowment games, the audience is privy to the secret endowment, which is unknown to the endowee.

Notes for the following games

The following three training exercises are played with two people while the rest of the group watches as audience. All players are 'on the bench' waiting to play when required. This can be exhausting work for many players. Save players who need support. Send in a third player to clarify and assist rather than overload the scenes with new ideas. Rotate players often.

The following descriptions do not even begin to convey the joy, life and thrill of this work in action. Be prepared for exuberance. When energetic and played at high risk, the following scenes can be uproarious. Watching players think laterally and solve the problems together is exceptionally exciting.

Under no circumstances should they play charades. They play the scene as realistically as possible. The scene ends when the endowee clearly plays the occupation, expresses the emotion or manifests the physicality which has been endowed. Repeat the exercise with new players until all players have experienced playing the roles of both endower and endowee. These skills take time to learn. While they may be frustrating for some players at first, continue to challenge them to grasp the skills; they are fundamental and must not be overlooked.

The role of the endower is active. They are the initial offer-giver in the scene. The endowee receives the information and yields to the endowed offer. They overaccept the information and immediately give an offer back as to what occupation/emotion/physicality they perceive themselves to be or have. The passing of offers back and forth resembles a game of tennis. If either player stops playing or gives offers that do not respond directly to the offers given by the other player, the game is not being played correctly.

Sidecoach (to endowee): 'Overaccept the offers.'
Sidecoach (to endower): 'Give the offers clearly.'

OCCUPATION ENDOWMENT

training game
2 players
no set time
12+ years

Description: One player endows another with an occupation. Both players speak in gibberish.

Resource: A clear space.

Time-out: No.

Example of a title: Choose simple, well known occupations such as doctor, teacher, butcher, hairdresser, ambulance driver, then advance to more unusual examples (such as accountant, baton twirler or undercover detective) when skills develop.

Aim: To introduce basic endowment skills. To offer, and yield to, occupation endowment.

Degree of difficulty: 2

Skills required: Ability to offer, yield, overaccept and communicate in gibberish.

Suggested preparation: GIBBERISH CIRCLE; THE PRESENT GAME in gibberish.

How it works: Player A (endowee) leaves the room. In player A's absence, player B (endower) is told an occupation by the coach. The spectators hear the endowment. Player B then endows player A with the occupation on their return, treating player A as if they had the chosen occupation. The endower creates the place and the given circumstances that are obvious for the endowee's occupation. If the occupation is a doctor, the endower may become the most obvious thing a doctor needs — a patient, holding their stomach and groaning as if in pain or on an operating table. Send in extra endowers if required. The scene ends when the endowee actively portrays the occupation endowed.

EMOTIONAL ENDOWMENT

training game
2 players
no set time
12+ years

Description: One player endows another with an emotion. Both players speak in gibberish.

Resource: A clear space.

Time-out: No.

Example of a title: Choose simple, well known emotions: love, hate, happiness, sadness, embarrassment, greed, etc.

Aim: To introduce basic endowment skills. To offer and yield to emotional endowment.

Degree of difficulty: 2

Skills required: Ability to offer, yield and overaccept, and communicate in gibberish.

Suggested preparation: GIBBERISH CIRCLE; THE PRESENT GAME in gibberish; OCCUPATION ENDOWMENT.

How it works: Player A (endowee) leaves the room. In player A's absence, player B (endower) is told an emotion by the coach. The spectators hear the endowment. Player B then endows player A with the emotion on their return, treating player A as if they were expressing the emotion given. To achieve this the endower can do one of two things: they can cause the emotion and set it in action or they can respond to the endowee as if they were expressing that emotion.

To cause the emotion, the endower sets up the given circumstances which would cause the emotion. If the emotion were terror, they might terrorise the endowee by jumping out at them and scaring them until the endowee reacts with terror.

The alternative method is to respond to the endowee as if they were expressing the emotion. To do this the endower acts on the endowee, treating them as if they were terrorised. They attempt to calm them down, speak to them in soothing tones, etc.

The role of the endower is active. They are the initial offer-giver in the scene. The endowee receives the information and yields to the endowment offer. They overaccept the information and immediately react with the emotion they perceive themselves to be experiencing.

Sidecoach (to endowee): 'Overaccept the offers.'
(to endower): 'Give the offers clearly.'
(to both): 'Use the gibberish language.'

The endower cannot show the emotion to the endowee — they cannot be terrorised themselves. The endowee should not copy the emotion the endower is giving. Some discussion of the causes and effects of a variety of emotions will be helpful. Some emotions are more clearly endowed when they are caused: embarrassment, love, jealousy, happiness. Others are more clearly responded to: sadness, paranoia, anger. There is much fun in trying a variety of emotions both ways and discovering the skills of affecting the other player. Send in extra endowers if required. The scene ends when the endowee clearly reacts with the emotion endowed.

PHYSICAL ENDOWMENT

training game
2 players
no set time
12+ years

Description: One player endows another with a physical characteristic. Both players speak in gibberish.

Resource: A clear space.

Time-out: No.

Example of a title: At first choose simple, easily identifiable physical characteristics: bad breath, tallness or shortness, etc. Then play with the more obscure characteristics: levitates, breathes fire, etc. Be sensitive when choosing physical disabilities. [See Appendix B – Endowments.]

Aim: To introduce basic endowment skills. To offer and yield to physical endowment.

Degree of difficulty: 2

Skills required: Ability to offer, yield and overaccept, and communicate in gibberish.

Suggested preparation: Gibberish circle; The present game in gibberish; Occupation endowment; Emotion endowment.

How it works: Player A (endowee) leaves the room. In player A's absence, player B (endower) is told a physical characteristic by the coach. The spectators hear the endowment. Player B then endows player A with the physical characteristic on their return, treating player A as if they had the physical characteristic given. If the characteristic is bad breath, the endower is affected by the smell of the breath and repelled every time the endowee opens their mouth.

The role of the endower is active. They are the initial offer-giver in the scene. The endowee receives the information and yields to the endowment offer. They overaccept the information and immediately give a physical offer in return for the characteristic they perceive to be their endowment.

Sidecoach (to endowee): 'Overaccept the offers.'
(to endower): 'Give the offers clearly.'
(to both): 'Use the gibberish language.'

If the endowment is a wooden leg, the endower cannot show the leg by simply screwing one onto the leg of the endowee. This type of demonstrating is charading rather than endowing. Send in extra endowers if required. The scene ends when the endowee takes on the physical endowment.

Summary

Endowment foundation skills

All players have now experienced thinking in gibberish, and yielding to and overaccepting endowments in gibberish.

Check

- Do endowee players overaccept their endowment and yield to the offers given by the endower(s)?
- Do endower players place the endowee at the focus of the scene, giving them top status?
- Do all players extend the offers in the scene?
- Do players vocalise in gibberish, supporting the sound with breath and a range of pitches and tones?

If the answer is yes for the majority of players, now put all three endowments together. Play with three onstage players endowing a fourth player with three endowments: an occupation, an emotion and a physical characteristic. Turn to Part C and play the Theatresports performance game Endowments (p 270). Play the game without a time limit at first, then introduce the time limits.

part B

SCENE-WORK

We owe much to Viola Spolin for her work on endowment. For further endowment exercises, see her book, *Improvisation for the Theatre.*

I have chosen the following exercises for scene-work endowment because, more than any other, they illustrate the power of endowment. They are played in English and are a complete contrast to the gibberish games in Part A. They tend to promote naturalistic scenes that relate to identifiable, real life situations and offer a balance to energetic work, giving players an opportunity to explore calm, subtle scene-work. They remind us that when we endow other people, we help make them who they are. While the scenes are not always physically and vocally energetic, the endowments are active and drive the scenes.

PARTY ENDOWMENTS

Keith Johnstone

training game
4 players
4–8 minutes
14+ years

Description: Scene and occasion given. Three players leave the room, to return as guests. The fourth establishes the party. S/he is the host. All players endow every other player with an attribute. The guests enter one at a time and join the party.

Resource: A real door, tables and chairs to establish the environment. Props and costumes are of no value when first playing the game but could be useful if developing the game and the characters in further scene-work.

Time-out: Some time spent with players discussing the general appearance of their environment, eg preparing the room, its furniture, etc.

Example of a title: A 21st birthday party — endowments: attractive/boring/funny;
A going-away party — endowments: charismatic/clumsy/attractive;
A school reunion — endowments: tasteless/intelligent/attractive.
Balance the endowments. Make one or two very positive. Too many negative endowments will send characters away from each other rather than bring them together.

Aim: To invest other characters with a variety of endowments.

Degree of difficulty: 4

Skills required: Ability to endow players with qualities that affect the scene.

Suggested preparation: SOUND BOARD; FREEZE TAG; ENDOWMENTS; Open scenes (improvised scenes not played in game structures); Open scenes with objectives and character endowments, eg great, beautiful, smelly, brilliant, charismatic, boring, sickly, frail.

How it works: This scene is played in English. Three endowments are chosen and told to all players and the audience. Then the host is chosen and the environment is clearly established. All players have a clear idea of the layout of the apartment, beach house, loft, or wherever the party is taking place. Spend time arranging the space and clarifying what is on the fourth wall, eg glass window overlooking the harbour,

French doors to the beach, a fireplace. This detail gives the players a clear idea of their environment.

Each player secretly chooses one endowment for each other player from the given list of three. Their choice is private. Players do not choose an endowment for themselves. For example, player A decides player B is attractive, player C is boring, player D is funny. Player B could decide player A is funny, player C is attractive and player D is boring. Players do not tell anybody what they have decided. The three guests leave the room.

The scene begins. The host prepares for the party. One by one, at random intervals, the guests arrive.

1. A guest knocks at the door.
2. S/he does not enter until the host opens the door, greets him/her and closes it behind them.
3. Only the host answers the door.
4. Players endow each other from the first moment they see each other. The endowment should become immediately obvious.
5. The rules of etiquette prevail. Players are not rude to each other but play their endowments truthfully.
6. The endowments are never spoken of. They are actively portrayed, and continue for the whole scene. For example, players do not say 'Gee you're funny'. Instead they laugh when the other player speaks.

The attitude of each player to each of the others should be obvious from their first interaction. All dialogue is rich with subtext as the opinions of all players are revealed. The scenes are usually naturalistic. When more than one conversation occurs at the same time, sidecoach players to freeze to clarify the split focus. When all the endowments are obvious, the scene needs advancing. Up the stakes by coaching the players to go for what they want. Most players single out one endowment and associate that endowment with their main objective.

Sidecoach: 'Go for your main objective.'

The endowments allow players to have an opinion about every other player and their environment. If a player finds the host tasteless, they will probably find the environment tasteless. Every player has something to think about and something active to do. All dialogue has purpose and springs from an opinion.

After each scene, discuss the status in the scene. How did the endowments affect the status and the focus?

The random nature of the endowments generates a wide range of possibilities for scenes, including comedy, pathos and drama.

•

Tips for text

For players 14+: This game provides one of the most helpful links between improvisation and acting. In creating it, Keith Johnstone bridges the gap between the skills required for acting from a written text and the skills required for improvising.

Take the endowments given in a text and play a scene with characters endowing each other from the knowledge provided by the writer. In particular Chekhov,

Shakespeare and Williamson plays lend themselves to this set up. All characters have attitudes to and opinions of the other characters.

Reserve this work for players 14+ who are mature enough to benefit from the skills the game has to offer and use the discoveries to take the work as far as possible. What I have outlined above merely scratches the surface of the possibilities.

•

Tips for tots

Endowment games are difficult for players under 12 years. In my experience endowment is a concept beyond the skills and maturity of these players.

ENDOWMENT SCENES

training game
2–24 players
60–100 minutes
16+ years

Description: Situation and endowments given. Pairs of players repeat a short scene, each time with a different endowment.

Resource: A clear space with enough area for each pair to work apart from the others; a board to record the group's responses; a video camera is helpful if available.

Time out: No.

Aim: To introduce acting skills, create belief, play an objective and motive, and deal with subtext and obstacles.

Degree of difficulty: 3

Skills required: Ability to listen to and yield to the offers given by another player, image a place and a physical endowment and to sustain belief with sensitivity and maturity.

Suggested preparation: NAMING THE OBVIOUS, NAMING THINGS AS THEY ARE NOT, PRESENT GAME, NO-BLOCKING SCENES and other preparation for scene work.

How it works: Players divide into pairs. If there is an odd number, groups of three can be accommodated. Players name themselves A and B or A, B and C. The group is given a scene which they play six times, each time with a different endowment. They remain with the same partner throughout. The whole group spreads out across the playing space and plays scenes at the same time; the coach is the only observer. Players are encouraged to relax and 'live' the scenes rather than 'play act' the scenes. After each endowment is played, the group comes together to discuss their experiences.

The following scene is described to players and becomes the basis on which all excercises are built. The coach should elaborate on this basic outline to give players a rich picture of the scene, but should not tell players what to expect.

Player A is renting a two bedroom house for $200 a week. They can no longer afford to live alone and have advertised for a flatmate in the newspaper. They must find someone to take the spare room today for $100 as the rent is due immediately. Player B can no longer stay at their current accommodation and needs to find somewhere to live or they will be sleeping in the car.

Perhaps they have had an argument with their family or had to relocate because of work. They can afford $100 and have it with them. Both player A and player B are desperate to achieve their objectives. This morning player B rang player A in response to the advertisement. They made an appointment for player B to inspect the house. The scene starts when the door bell rings.

To maximise the improvisation, in all the following endowments refrain from describing to players what they could experience. Simply outline the bare bones of the information as above, and direct them to play their objective and clarify their endowment for the other player. Don't tell them what to expect, just what to do. All endowments except the last two are announced to the whole group. If players ask too many questions before they start, assure them that the answers will become clear when they play the scene. The scene should run for about three minutes. Give the players a half-way call and a 30 second call as a reminder to find an ending.

Endowment one

The players meet, introduce themselves and inspect the dwelling in detail. Player A shows the prospective housemate all the rooms, describing the idiosyncrasies of the bathroom, laundry, car space, backyard, balcony etc. There are no obstacles to achieving their objectives. As if by magic, the players' needs are complementary. If player B has a car, player A happens to have a garage; if player A has a video recorder, player B has a television.

Remind players to endow the other player as a stranger. If players are too familiar at the commencement of the scene, stop the work and clarify this endowment. Also remind players that in this first scene there is no obstacle to their objective. Players should not assume characteristics such as accents, limps, addictions or secrets that are not relevant to the simple needs of the scene.

•

Feedback

At the end of the scene bring the players together and ask them the following:

- Is there a player A who did not receive the $100?
- Is there a player B who did not agree to move in?
- Describe in three words the character you just met.
- What did you see? What textures and colours were in the house? Find three words to describe the place you just saw.
- Did one character have higher status than the other or were they even?
- Write examples of this feedback on the board.

Players will usually experience a happy interaction with their partner and describe each other as easy going, cheerful, friendly, happy and open. The house will usually be described in a positive light. It is often open, bright, interesting, clean and has a good view.

Endowment two

Players return to their partner and play the second scene as if the first had not occurred. The players' objectives and situation are the same as they were earlier, however now the players give each other physical endowments. When the door bell rings player A meets a stranger who is the most attractive looking person they have ever seen. Player B has a magnificent face, healthy skin, sparkling eyes, perfectly proportioned body, and luxurious hair, and player A finds they cannot keep from looking at them. It is not necessary that player A is physically attracted to player B (and this may not be appropriate with some groups of players who find this endowment confronting).

Player B endows player A very differently. They see a person with the worst flaky dandruff problem in the world. Player A has dandruff in their eyebrows, on their shoulders and when they move dandruff flies off their scalp. The entire space is covered: it is in the hall, the bathroom and the kitchen looks as if a sugar truck has overturned.

It is imperative to remind players that they do not act their own endowment. Player B does not assume a sexy way of walking, nor does player A begin scratching their head and doing dandruff acting. In fact both players are simply themselves as they were in the first scene, but are now endowed by the other player. It is also important to remind players that it is not necessary to discuss the endowments, however if mentioned both players deal honestly with the dandruff. They are simply present in the scene and will affect the interactions between players and possibly the outcome. Player B may eventually decide that the dandruff is too disturbing and they cannot live in the house. But players cannot make these decisions at the beginning of the scene: the decision arises from the experience. At the start of the scene they must be committed to their original objective and if that objective is changed, it is for specific reasons.

•

Feedback

At the end of the scene bring the players together and ask them the following.

- Is there a player A who did not receive the $100?
- Is there a player B who did not agree to move in?
- Did player B say they were moving in but actually lie?
- Describe in three words the character you just met.
- Find three words to describe the place you just saw.
- Write examples of these on the board.
- Was the issue of the dandruff discussed?
- How did the endowments affect their opinion of the other character?
- Did their partner treat them differently this time? If so, how?
- Was their partner's physicality different? Did they stand closer or further away this time?
- How did this affect the other player?
- How did this affect the scene?

Some players will experience definite physical reactions to their partner's endowment. Player B may hold their breath in the dandruff filled house or feel discomfort due to the stares and interest of player A. Some players describe player A as desperate, lonely and emotionally needy. Player A may experience vagueness, giggles, an inability to find rooms in the house or they become tongue tied. One girl imagined player B to be so good looking that she did not want him to move in because she felt inferior by comparison.

Both players often describe the space as dark and shabby when it had previously been light, airy and spacious. Players also report that the focus of the scene has changed. Player B is conscious of the space while player A is focussed on player B.

Whatever their responses, we find that the physical endowments have affected status and relationship, introduced a subtext and possibly become an obstacle to achieving the scene objective.

Endowment three

Player B speaks English and player A speaks only gibberish. Neither player can understand the other. The objective of both players is the same as in the earlier scenes.

•

Feedback

Ask the group the usual questions regarding which objectives were achieved and how they saw the other character and the house. This scene often reveals hidden prejudices about non-English speakers. It can also lead to very funny scenes. Some players are excited by the prospect of living with someone from another culture. Others say the smells in the house, the different food and decor were too much of a change from what they are used to.

Endowment four

This endowment is optional and requires a particularly mature group. Up until now all the information has been given to the whole group. Announce that player A will play the scene as they did in endowment one. Now gather all players B and give them their endowment in secret. They endow the house with a personal history and strong memories. After they arrive they slowly realise that this is a house from their past. They have either lived in it or visited it as a child. Although parts of the house may have changed over the years, enough fragments remain to jolt their memory. The smell, carpet or view from a window spark memories that return during the scene. Advise players it is important they do not have an extreme emotional response. They are happy rather than traumatic memories. They can share them with player A during the scene if they wish.

•

Feedback

Many times the memories are so vivid they affect the objectives of both players. Were the objectives achieved? Has the endowment become an obstacle to their objective? What affect did the endowment have on players' opinion of each other and the space?

Endowment five

Player A endows player B as a member of a religious group. Player A sees a person in complete brown Buddhist robes, a Salvation army uniform, priest's collar, nun's habit, or Hare Krishna robes and adornments.

Remind players that player B has the money to pay. This is not a request for charity accommodation and the money is not an issue. The important factor is the endowment of player B's beliefs and spiritual ideals. Player B should not overact their religion. They are simply people who live their belief. If players are ready for a challenge, allow player A to decide the religion of player B when the door is opened.

Player A (opening door): 'Thanks I gave at work.' (Quickly closes door.)

Player B (not knowing their endowment but pursuing their objective): 'Hello I rang earlier about the room.'

Player A (opening door again): 'Oh I'm sorry, I thought you were collecting for the Salvation Army.'

If players are not ready for this challenge allow them to briefly decide the religion before the scene commences. This is not a discussion and requires but a few words.

•

Feedback

Ask the usual questions at the end of the scene.

I have seen player A attempting to dissuade player B from moving in. But player B is usually a very positive person and cannot be deterred too easily. Sometimes player B's sense of self is so strong they are endowed with great status by player A. Sometimes player B completely takes over the environment planning to change rooms, knock out walls, and make prayer and meeting rooms. On the other hand I have seen scenes where player B is so humble that they require nothing more than a mat in a small room.

Endowment six

Both players are given secret endowments. It is important to make clear to players that at the end of this scene they do not discuss these endowments. Gather all players A and explain that they have a relative, mate, or friend who is a thief and stores stolen goods at their house. Everything in their house has a serial number that can be traced as a stolen property and they have to be extremely careful. They use the stereo equipment, kitchen goods and furniture which they need and store in an area which they keep locked. They do not allow anyone to enter the locked area.

Gather all players B for their secret endowment. For the first time player B is given a different objective in this scene. They have no intention of moving into new accommodation and are casing the house with the intention of returning and robbing it of all its valuables. They need to determine the movements of player A. Is there a time when player A is not at home? They need to check access and security of the building. If it is higher than the first floor, how will they remove the goods? Where can they park the van? Are there window bars, security doors, or alarms? Player A must never suspect and can be given the $100 if necessary. Player B must be very discreet. Can they leave with a key?

•

Feedback

Ask players to describe the other character in three words. Secretive, fishy, guarded, nosy, beady-eyed and suspicious are words that are often given.

Did player B look different in this scene compared to endowment two when they were good looking? Ask players to describe the difference.

I asked one player B to describe the physical characteristics of player A in endowment six and he said he would not recognise her on the street. He was amazed to find he had not made eye contact with her or looked at her face for longer than a brief glance throughout the scene. His focus had been completely absorbed by the space and the goods and solving the problem of removing the goods at a later date.

- Ask them to describe the house.
- Did they exchange the $100?
- Did player B manage to procure a key?
- Is player A going to allow B to move in? Why?
- What do players think is their partner's motive?

At the end tell them the objectives and motive of their partner. Player A is often completely charmed by their partner and quite shocked at having been so easily deceived.

Three player groups

The third player can be accommodated in the following ways. In endowment one, they are a stranger to both other characters, they arrive after player B, and have an identical objective. Player A has two rooms to rent at $100 each. In endowment two, player C is endowed with being very wise. Even the most mundane statement is accepted as words of wisdom by the other players. In endowment three, player C comes to rent the third room and can speak both English and gibberish. They interpret for players A and B. In endowment four, player C is a friend of and arrives with player B. Player C is also religious and looking for accommodation. In endowment five, they are a stranger to both players, come to rent the third room but are not endowed with any memories. In the final endowment, they are in league with player B but pretend to be a stranger. They have also come to rent the third room. An alternative to this last endowment is to give player C the secret endowment of being an undercover police officer posing as a prospective flatmate.

•

Feedback

Ask the players to consider the power of the endowment process. In discussing this remind them they have experienced a range of scenes that include physical, language, and culture endowments which have allowed them to explore issues such as prejudice, morality, customs, culture, beliefs and spirituality. Describe to them what you saw watching each scene. Convey the difference in the physicality of players during the scenes. Report the changes in vocal dynamics and vocal energy and tone in the room while the different scenes were in progress. Replay for them the video of their work.

•

Tips for text

The power of endowment is undeniable. It is the key to rich relationships and active acting. One actor endowing another is interesting to watch. Their mind is active. They create subtext. In defining another character they further define and develop their own. Find the endowments given in a text. Find the opinions character have of each other and their environment. Discover when these change and the reasons for change. [See Party endowments.]

Summary

Endowment scene-work skills

Players have now experienced a wide range of endowment skills. They have experienced giving and receiving endowments in gibberish and English. Use the following as a guide to assess their skills development. When playing the above scenes and training games:

- Do players endow their environment and other players?
- Do they overaccept their endowment as given by other players? Are they aVected and changed by it?
- Can they sustain the endowment for the length of the scene? Is their endowment consistent?
- Do they allow the endowment to inform the scene rather than talk about it?
- Do they allow the endowment to inform how they speak as well as what they say, and how they move as well as what they do?

The following Theatresports performance games further support these skills.

part C

THEATRESPORTS PERFORMANCE GAMES

GIBBERISH ENDOWMENT PERFORMANCE GAMES

ENDOWMENTS

classic

performance game
3–4 players
usually 2 minutes
12+ years

AKA: STANDARD ENDOWMENTS; GIBBERISH ENDOWMENTS

Description: One team member leaves the stage. The remaining team members are given three attributes (one occupational, one emotional, one physical) with which to endow the offstage team member on their return. The team endows these attributes using only gibberish and without resorting to charades.

Resource: A clear space.

Time-out: If required, but only after the endowee has left the stage.

Example of a title: A butcher/with a tattoo/sad.
Nurse/with her face on the back of her head/happy.
Teacher/with bad breath/embarrassed.

Aim: To communicate an endowment in gibberish.

Degree of difficulty: 3

Skills required: Ability to speak gibberish with a range of tone and pitch. Ability to overaccept and advance and extend offers.

Suggested preparation: THANK YOU; FREEZE TAG; SOUND BOARD; GIBBERISH CIRCLE; ADVANCING AND EXTENDING THE VERBAL OFFER in gibberish; GIBBERISH/ENGLISH ADVANCING AND EXTENDING; OCCUPATION ENDOWMENTS; PHYSICAL ENDOWMENTS; EMOTIONAL ENDOWMENTS.

How it works: One team member leaves the room or theatre stage accompanied by another class member (in training) or timekeeper (in performance). If unable to leave the room, players create a cone of silence by putting their hands over their ears and singing aloud to themselves. They won't hear a thing! The remaining players receive the three attributes with which to endow their team-mate on his/her return. The team fields its endowers according to the needs of the scene. In some cases all players will be required on stage to help with the three endowments. In other cases, perhaps only one player endows all three traits.

The coach (in training) or the timekeeper (in performance) signals the out-of-earshot endowee that play is about to commence. On their return a whistle is blown. From this moment the only language spoken is gibberish.

The unfolding scene consists of the endeavours of the team to give the offers that will allow the endowee to yield in a way that will lead him/her to their endowed profession, physical state or problem, and prevailing emotion.

Utter Codswallop — (left to right) Robyn Butler, Murray Fahey, Ewan Campbell

In most cases, endow in this order: 1) occupation/place; 2) physical quality; 3) emotional state. Establish the occupation by creating the workplace. Give the endowee the focus and the status in the scene. The endowing players perform a function in the workplace and become the people the endowee requires to fulfil their occupation. If the occupation is teacher, the other players become the students. To endow the teacher with top status, they stand when the teacher enters. When the endowee yields and becomes the teacher, the players interact with the teacher, they endow the bad breath, then they create an event which causes the teacher's embarrassment. Endowing in this order is not a hard and fast rule but it is usually the clearest method.

Sidecoach (endowee): 'Overaccept the offers. Make offers.'
(endower): 'Give the offers clearly.'
(both): 'Use the gibberish language. Be active in the scene.'

When the endowee knows their occupation,
Sidecoach (the endowers): 'Advance the scene.'

The endowment is usually clearer when it is vocalised. Keep each player connected to his/her voice. The endower uses a range of pitches, inflections and vocal tones to convey the endowment.

•

Beware

Endowers tend to overload the endowees with too many offers.
Sidecoach (endower): 'Give him/her focus.'
'Give her/him status.'
'Let them know where they are.'
'Give one offer at a time.'

•

Tip

Five second ENDOWMENTS: Brisbane team *Carnival Knowledge* (Andrew Buchanan, Annie Burbrook, Adam Couper and Michael Golledge) trained and succeeded in yielding to the occupational endowment within five seconds. They began with ordinary occupations and graduated to some not so ordinary: a urologist, an actuary and a homeopath — all within their five second ENDOWMENTS training game. To achieve this they always gave the endowee top status and gave them the complete focus. It worked.

Competition and performance: In Australia, the judges usually score the scene immediately after it is played. We ask the endowee what they thought their three attributes were after the score is given. This places the emphasis on the scene-work rather than the correct answer. Some North American Theatresports companies ask the endowee to name the three attributes as soon as the scene is finished. The judges then score the scene. Both methods are perfectly acceptable for professional adult players. To emphasise the process and scene-work rather than the product and end result, use the Australian method when coaching school teams and non-professional players.

•

Magic moment

At the Australian National Final '86 at the Playhouse Theatre in Melbourne, the winning team, *Gutless Wonders*, played the clearest endowment game I have ever seen. The joy of this scene came not only from watching the skill of players Christine Keogh, Doug McLeod and Ross Williams endow Glenn Robbins as a good looking journalist who was suicidal, but also from Glenn's overaccepting all the offers and extending the scene to the fullest. It took about ninety seconds for Glenn to receive all the endowments. The team spent the next thirty seconds preventing the suicidal journalist from jumping off the stage while the Playhouse capacity audience yelled, 'Jump!'

ENGLISH ENDOWMENT PERFORMANCE GAMES

PROPS
classic

performance game
1–4 players
2–4 minutes
10+ years

Description: Situation given. The team is given four props with which to begin a scene. These are endowed in a variety of ways as required by the story.

Resource: Four separate props, eg a doll, a ball, a telephone, a photo frame.

Time-out: If necessary.

Example of a title: Cooking Italian; Racing in the Grand Prix.

Aim: To use props laterally and endow them as required in the developing scene.

Degree of difficulty: 3

Skills required: Ability to think laterally and accept an overload of offers, incorporating them in a story.

Suggested preparation: SAVING [see Warm-up games].

How it works: The team is given four props with which to begin a scene. These props are endowed to become anything the scene requires, and change as often as the scene suggests.

Give every player a prop (all the same or different), and players individually or in pairs use the prop in as many different ways as possible, naming each offer as they claim it. The pace of this is determined by the individual players. Most coaches begin by passing one object around a circle, each player using it as something different. For example, a doll may be used as a telephone, stethoscope, cricket bat, telescope, etc. Usually, players think ahead of their turn and preplan how they will use the prop. This is not conducive to improvising. It is slow and some players experience the pressure of being clever and funny.

Props circuit

As an alternative, set up a props circuit. Begin by choosing a number of props and placing them evenly around a circle on the floor. For example, a chair, ball, feather duster, fan, softball glove, telephone, bucket and wig could all be used. You need the same number of props as you have players. Each player stands by one prop and at a given signal (eg the blowing of a whistle) players pick up their prop and use it in as many different ways as possible, naming it as they do so. For instance, a player may pick up a feather duster, play it like a flute and say 'flute'. Then they use it as a telephone receiver and either say 'telephone' or 'hello'. They use the items in as many different ways as possible, as quickly as possible. At the sound of a second whistle, players stop, put down their props and move to the next prop around the circle. Keep intervals between whistles to about 30 seconds. All players work at the same time; the value of working this way is that players cannot preplan ideas, or be critical of their own or others' ideas. Be aware that this exercise becomes very noisy, but is the best props warm-up I have found.

Beware

Don't use props which could be dangerous. [See Process – Props and costumes.]

WHAT IF

performance game
3–4 players
2–4 minutes
12+ years

Description: Situation given. The team plays the scene.

Resource: A clear space.

Time-out: Yes.

Example of a title: What if the moon were made of cheese?; What if cars ran on water?; What if the hand that rocked the cradle ruled the world?

Aim: To explore and justify a hypothetical situation and deal with the effects of a range of given circumstances.

Degree of difficulty: 3

Skills required: Ability to endow an environment, play a scene within it and solve problems.

Suggested preparation: Warm-up games; THANK YOU; WHAT ARE YOU DOING? into collage scenes; FREEZE TAG; NO-BLOCKING SCENES.

How it works: The team plays the scene in which the hypothetical situation is a reality. They invent the possibilities and characters that could live in the created world and satisfy as much of their curiosity about the new world as they can.

Background: This game found its Down Under beginnings in Hobart, where it became a team and audience favourite. They understood how the game works and played it regularly with great success. It had been played in Canada but few other Australian Theatresports centres chose to play it.

I think it is a particularly helpful game for student players. It demands lateral thinking and specific endowment skills. It challenges players to create situations, invent characters specific to a created environment and justify their choices.

SCENE WITH/WITHOUT

performance game
3–4 players
usually 2 minutes
14+ years

Description: Situation given. Team plays the scene with or without a given circumstance.

Resource: A clear space.

Time-out: Yes.

Example of a title: Scene with or without fire/sun/ozone/Cleopatra.

Aim: To establish the given circumstances and play the scene endowing it as necessary.

Degree of difficulty: 3

Skills required: Ability to create and sustain an environment.

Suggested preparation: Warm up; use MARKO'S GAME as a starting point for spoken and/or moved scenes; NO-BLOCKING SCENES from MARKO'S GAME; SAVING; PROPS.

How it works: The team decides to play the scene with or without the given circumstance before they are given the title. They play the scene.

This is a marvellous game for creative problem solving and scene playing. I highly recommend it. It develops valuable skills for wider improvisation, drama and text work.

MURDER ENDOWMENTS

classic

performance game
4 players
4 minutes
14+ years

Description: The audience chooses a murderer from the team members. This player leaves the stage and enters the cone of silence. The audience then chooses a victim from the remaining onstage players. The place of death and the murder weapon are given by the compere. On the murderer's return, s/he must kill the victim in the correct location with the correct weapon. The scene is played in English.

Resource: A clear space and minimal props and costumes.

Time-out: Yes. Establish clarity of place.

Example of a title: In a library with a lawnmower; In a submarine with a shoe box. The weapon is unrelated to the place of death.

Aim: To explore motive, characterisation and subplot while playing an objective.

Degree of difficulty: 4

Skills required: Ability to create characters, weave a plot, endow place and endow another player with motive.

Suggested preparation: YES; YOU; YES LET'S; NO-BLOCKING SCENES; SCENES WITH AN OBJECTIVE; PARTY ENDOWMENTS.

How it works: The onstage players endow the location and the murderer's role within it. If the murder is to take place in the library, the returning player could be told to 'Shhhhh!' while other players create the shelves, the photocopier, the front desk, mimed book reading, etc. The clear endowment of place from the outset is most important to the development of the scene.

The murderer must overaccept all the offers, yield to the place as soon as possible and kill the correct victim with the correct weapon. Under no circumstances is the weapon named or charaded by the endowers.

Finding the victim takes time and the murderer must give and receive offers to solve this problem. In Melbourne, players developed the game using a motive. The victim endows the murderer with a motive — they give the murderer a reason to kill them.

For example, in the library, the victim may be rude to the murderer; they stamp his hand and not the book. They anger the murderer or annoy them. This makes for interesting characters and plot development. It allows the scene to develop before the murder takes place. It is imperative that the murderer continue to be active and make offers rather than passively waiting for information. Players have difficulty providing the motive if the murderer remains passive and unyielding.

The murderer must then be endowed with the correct weapon. As it cannot be named, the players work hard setting up the need for the weapon (a lawn mower) in the scene location (a library). This takes skill. All offers must be made clearly and extended. Players could complain that the carpet on the library floor is too long. Overaccepting the offer, the murderer finds ways of cutting the carpet, killing the victim with the correct weapon as they do so.

In Sydney, the game has developed a more 'Russian roulette' style of endowment. Rather than look for a motive, the murderer first tends to seek the weapon and attempts to kill everyone with books, paper clips, chairs, anything in sight. The other players work hard endowing the need for the correct weapon and justifying the failed murder attempts.

When finally the correct weapon has been endowed, all murder attempts on the wrong victims must be justified. For example, if the lawn mower is mown over the toes of a player who was not selected as the victim, the player must justify not dying with a response — 'Oh, thanks, I needed my toenails trimmed'. The murderer continues to search for the correct victim. This method of playing doesn't always work. However, when this is played clearly and offers are not dropped, the scenes can be quite bizarre and very funny. I recommend a combination of both styles.

Beware the 'talking head' syndrome in MURDER ENDOWMENTS. It is not a guessing game. The scene must be moved and played.

This is a game for skilled players. It sorts the blockers from the yielders. It is a very useful game for understanding subplot, subtext, and function of character. This is a real teamwork game.

PERSONALITY ENDOWMENTS

performance game
3–4 players
usually 4 minutes
14+ years

Description: Situation given. One player leaves the stage and enters the cone of silence. On their return, they are endowed as a famous person. The scene is played in English.

Resource: A clear space, props and costumes.

Time-out: Yes.

Example of a title: Mick Jagger in a caravan park; Mother Teresa in Woolworths.

Aim: To create characters that serve a function in a scene.

Degree of difficulty: 3

Skills required: Ability to create character and play a function in a scene. Select this game only when players are proficient in the previous endowment games.

How it works: This scene is played in English. The endowers and audience know the secret endowment. Endowers create the environment and treat the endowee as if they are the famous personality. The endowers first establish the place. They then endow the player as the famous personality. They never use the personality's name. They complement the scene, becoming the characters the famous personality needs. In the case of Mick Jagger, they become photographers, fans, Jerry Hall, other musicians, etc. In the case of Mother Teresa, they become other nuns, starving people, God. They endow the player with status and place them at the focus of the scene.

When the endowee knows they are Mick Jagger or Mother Teresa, they yield and become them. Ideally the scene continues in the endowed place, developing a full plot with an event.

PERSONALITY MURDERER ENDOWMENTS

performance game
3–4 players
usually 4 minutes
14+ years

Description: The audience chooses a murderer from the team members. This player leaves the stage and enters the cone of silence. The audience chooses a victim. The place of death, the murder weapon and the famous personality are given. On their return, the murderer is endowed as the famous person and must kill the victim with the correct weapon. The scene is played in English.

Resource: A clear space. Props and costumes.

Time-out: Yes.

Example of a title: Napoleon, in Turkish Bath, with a toothpick.

Aim: To explore motive, characterisation and subplot while playing an objective.

Degree of difficulty: 4

Skills required: Ability to play and endow detailed characterisation and status, and to develop a detailed plot.

How it works: This game is an example of a combination of two other games, MURDER ENDOWMENTS and PERSONALITY ENDOWMENTS. Select this game to stimulate and challenge advanced players who are eager for more endowment skills.

Status

program 5

Commandment

Thou shalt always be changed by what is said to you.

Most of us have experienced a sense of feeling important. We recall moments when we were praised and given positive attention that made us feel good. We felt as though we had high status. We also recall times when we felt very unimportant. Perhaps we were mocked, scolded, bullied or ignored. We experienced a sense of low status. When we endow other people with being more or less important than ourselves, or when they endow us with being more or less important than them, we establish a status relationship.

The status between one individual and another creates a pecking order. It decides rank and hierarchy. This is a natural process. Whether in our family, at work or in the schoolyard, we create and experience status relationships every day. How we win status, lose it, keep it, regain it, or give it to another person, determines our relationships with other people and our place in the scheme of things.

Status is determined by many factors: wealth, birthright, religion, education, size, race, beauty, knowledge, wisdom, and the value these have within the specific pecking order. In some societies, status structures create a class or caste system.

The theatre roots of status lie in the Commedia dell'arte, where families of masked characters performed scenario-based improvisations from master/servant relationships. There is enormous comic and dramatic potential in the reversal or change of status relationships: in today's terms, this is when the worker stooges the boss or when the roadrunner stooges the coyote; the interplay between and reversal of top dog and under dog. Today, these same elements and characteristics are as familiar to us — and as comic or tragic — as they were to audiences 400 years ago.

Study of the Commedia dell'arte and its characters further informs an understanding of status and the history of improvisation as an art form.

We owe so much to Keith Johnstone for his work on the exploration of status and status relationships. The Status chapter in *Improvisation and the Theatre* is the foundation statement from which this work springs.

A skilled improvisor:
- Gives clear offers of both high and low status
- Recognises, yields to and accepts offers of both high and low status
- Makes transitions between high and low status

part A FOUNDATION SKILLS

Recognising status when it is still

The first step in understanding status and how it works is to recognise the status signals created through body language. We begin by identifying still status.

STILL STATUS

training game
2 players
10–20 minutes
12+ years

Description: Two players take up positions, each sitting on a chair. The class discusses the status of each player.

Resource: Two chairs in a clear space.

Time-out: No.

Example of a title: Not applicable.

Aim: To establish characteristics of high and low status.

Degree of difficulty: 2

Skills required: Ability to concentrate and discuss as a group.

Suggested preparation: YES LET'S; YOU.

How it works: This exercise is conducted with players working in front of the whole group. Two players enter the space and take up a position, each on a separate chair. They freeze their position in a relaxed pose. They keep their eyes fixed and still. They remain silent throughout the exercise. The group decides:

- Which player looks more important
- Who has the higher status
- Who has the focus

- Who looks as if s/he will speak first

Throughout the discussion the onstage players remain in their frozen positions keeping a consistent eye focus.

From time to time, when asked by the coach, one of the two players readjusts their position. They stay on or move off the chairs to become more important than the other player (raise their status) or become less important than the other player (lower their status). They readjust their position to give the other player focus and to endow them with status. They also readjust their position to take the focus and the status from the other player.

High status people tend to	**Low status people tend to**
Take up a lot of space	Take up very little space
Breathe deep breaths	Breathe short shallow breaths
Stay quite still	Fidget a lot
Keep consistent eye focus	Look around excitedly/nervously/often
Own their space	Be guests or servants in the space
Have no need to block	Not want to block
Stretch out their arms	Fold their arms across their chests
Sit with their legs astride	Cross their legs
Keep a straight back	Hunch over
Hold their heads high	Bow their heads
Not show white of eye	Be wide-eyed a lot of the time
Speak in a clear voice	Mumble

There are exceptions to these, but for the most part they hold true.
Sidecoach players to readjust their positions to consider a variety of still status positions. Sidecoach players one at a time to:

- Be higher status than the other
- Be lower status than the other
- Be the same status as the other
- Give the focus and the status to the other player
- Give the focus to the other player but keep the status

Finding the status when it is moving

Status is active. It shifts and changes. As characters win, lose, give and receive status, dramatic and comic potential is created.

MOVING STATUS

training game
2 players
8–15 minutes
12+ years

Description: Players make physical and verbal offers that raise and lower the status of the other player.

Resource: A clear space. Two chairs.

Time-out: Not applicable.

Example of a title: Not applicable. Provide a place where two strangers could meet, eg a park or a bus stop.

Aim: To recognise and yield to offers of status in short scenes.

Degree of difficulty: 2

Skills required: Ability to offer and yield, and an understanding of still status.

Suggested preparation: YES LET'S; YOU; STILL STATUS.

How it works: This exercise is conducted with two players working in front of the whole group. Begin with a STILL STATUS freeze. The group decides which character it believes will speak first. The players on the chairs bring their short scenes to life from the frozen moments. As the conversation unfolds, freeze the scene from time to time to ask the group which player has the higher or lower status. Use the content gathered in the scene and the body language of the players to make your assessments. Work with different combinations of players.

Sidecoach changes of status carefully. Both players must yield to all offers. All offers must be named. Both players must take the risk and speak. Some players are afraid of losing status. They see it as a loss of personal power. This could cause them to block or railroad the scene. To keep the scenes positive, introduce the concept of happy high status.

part B SCENE-WORK

HAPPY HIGH STATUS

Keith Johnstone

training game
scene-work
2 players
usually 4 minutes
12+ years

Description: Situation and characters given.

Resource: A clear space and two chairs or one bench.

Time-out: No.

Example of set-up: Describe a park, the weather, the time of day — eg a pleasant sunny day at lunch time, on a bench in a mid-city park.

Aim: To experience happy high status.

Degree of difficulty: 2

Skills required: Ability to create location, character and status.

Suggested preparation: YES; YOU; STILL STATUS; MOVING STATUS.

How it works: This exercise is conducted with players working in front of the whole group. Two players take up a position of high status on a park bench. Their objective is to stay extremely high status. They take up a lot of room, breathe deep breaths, keep quite still and express all the physical characteristics of high status people. They begin a conversation, attempting to be of higher status than each other while remaining happy, charming and nice to be with.

Sometimes high status characters become mean. They challenge each other to hurtful one-upping matches. To combat the type of blocking that often results, introduce two happy high status characters.

Happy high status characters are pleased to speak to other people. They have no fear. They happily give offers and receive them. They are not mean. They give their money and time away. They do not insult other people but use their generosity to help others. They give offers and they yield to them. They laugh. Continue to sidecoach towards a happy high status scene.

HAPPY LOW STATUS

Keith Johnstone

training game
scene-work
2 players
usually 4 minutes
12+ years

Description: Situation and characters given.

Resource: A clear space and two chairs or one bench.

Time-out: No.

Example of set-up: Describe a park, the weather, the time of day — eg a pleasant sunny day at lunch time, on a bench in a mid city park.

Aim: To experience happy low status.

Degree of difficulty: 2

Skills required: Ability to create location, status and character.

Suggested preparation: YES; YOU; STILL STATUS; MOVING STATUS; HAPPY HIGH STATUS.

How it works: This exercise takes place with two players working in front of the whole group. Two players take their places on a park bench. Their objective is to remain extremely low status. They sit in a hunched position on the edge of their seats with their knees and toes turned in. They touch their faces, fidget and make short quick movements. They look down and, when they dare, glance at one another and make eye contact. They then look away quickly and giggle. They begin a conversation, each attempting to remain lower status than the other while remaining happy, charming and nice to be with.

Sometimes low status characters whine and complain a lot. They get on our nerves. As they try to go lower than each other, they physically grovel on the ground. Their scenes do not advance.

Happy low status characters are charming. They simply raise the status of the other character. They smile while they do so. They are cheerful and delightful. The audience loves them — so does the other character.

Allow the players to make these discoveries. Do not instruct or script them, although you may guide them gently by sidecoaching.

Endowing the other player with an offer of status

When players can identify the difference between high and low status and have experienced the above, bring the highest and the lowest of the pecking order together in a simple master/servant relationship.

Note: I have decided to follow tradition and call the high status role 'master' for the sake of simplicity. Of course, both males and females play the roles of both master and servant.

MASTER/SERVANT(S)

training game
2–32 players
3–5 minutes
12+ years

Description: Two players name themselves the master and the servant. They play the scene.

Resource: A very clear space. Bopper of rolled up newspaper (roll three sheets of newspaper into a long, tight cylinder).

Time-out: Not applicable.

Example of a title: Not necessary. Players choose their own situations.

Aim: To experience the difference between high status and low status in the master/servant status relationship.

Degree of difficulty: I

Skills required: Ability to give an offer of status and receive an offer of status.

Suggested preparation: Vocal and physical warm-up; any group game; TWENTY-ONE; STILL AND MOVING STATUS.

How it works: The whole group works at the same time. Players form pairs. Player A is the master, player B is the servant. They endow each other with the appropriate status. The servant's objective is to please their master and to keep out of trouble. The master's objective is to have their servant serve them.

The master always has higher status than their servant. They carry a rolled up newspaper (a bopper) with which they hit the floor firmly as a reminder of their status when the servant displeases them. At this the servant immediately drops to their knees, lowers their head and says, 'I'm sorry, I'm sorry!'

The ensuing scenes are energetic, noisy and usually very funny.

Repeat the game with players exchanging roles.

•

Beware

Players must **never** hit another player. They only hit the floor. Make this clear from the outset. If players cannot refrain from hitting each other, do not go any further with this exercise. Go immediately to CAR STATUS.

Summary

Introductory status skills

When all players have experienced being the master and the servant, bring the group together and summarise the status endowment work thus far. Discuss the following:

Of the master role:	**Of the servant role:**
Did they enjoy being the master?	Did they enjoy being the servant?
Was their partner a good servant?	Was their partner a good master?
Was the servant obliging and dutiful?	Was the master mean and cruel?
Did the servant work hard?	Did the master overwork them?
Was the servant rude and overbearing?	Was the master kind and gentle?
Was the servant easy to listen to?	Did the master raise their voice?
Was the servant respectful?	Did they respect their master?
Did the servant protect their master?	Did they feel protected?

Some players prefer playing one status position to the other. The crafted improvisor has the skills to play both roles. Give all players the opportunity to develop skills to play both status roles.

Developing the pecking order

Now that players have experienced both high and low status in pairs, it is time to develop the pecking order by creating a third position. Bring together three players. Give a master one bopper and two servants.

ONE MASTER — TWO SERVANTS

training game
3 players
about 4 minutes
12+ years

Description: Situation described in detail and given. Two players play servants to one master. Each servant attempts to be higher status than the other.

Resource: A clear space, one bopper.

Time-out: Not applicable.

Example of set-up: Establish the master's boudoir. Establish the bed, the length of the back wall, wardrobe, etc. Establish and describe the place, with the players and the class hearing all the information. Allow the master to make many of these decisions. Guide them towards good use of the fourth wall. [See Program two part D.]

Aim: To explore the pecking order of three status positions.

Degree of difficulty: 3

Skills required: Ability to give and overaccept offers of status. Ability to change status.

Suggested preparation: Vocal and physical warm-up; any group game; TWENTY-ONE; MASTER/SERVANT.

How it works: This scene is based on a classic Commedia dell'arte pecking order scenario. Three players work in front of the whole group. One master has two servants. The scene develops from a simple scenario. The master is leaving in a matter of hours for Paris and requires one of the servants as a travelling companion and servant on the trip.

Each player has an objective. The master's objective is to choose the perfect servant for a trip to Paris. Each servant's objective is to please the master better than the other servant and to be chosen to go to Paris.

Each player has a task. The master's task is to ensure the packing is completed. Each servant's task is to better please the master with packing.

The servants establish the scene. They are in the boudoir packing their master's things for the trip. The master enters to 'break the routine' and advance the scene. Allow the master to make the choice of when to enter. Be ready to sidecoach should they enter too soon or too late. By the end of the scene the master will have decided which servant travels to Paris.

Accurate sidecoaching will allow players to bring a short scenario to a satisfactory conclusion.

Sidecoach servants: 'Get each other into trouble.'
'Keep packing.'
'Flatter your master.'

Sidecoach master: 'Find out which is the best servant.'
'Make them run your bath.'
'Stop their arguing'
'Test their loyalty.'
'Hit the floor.'
'Make your decision.'

The structure of this scene causes the servants to vie for the second status position. The results are hilarious and foster exciting, unpredictable improvisation. The permutations and combinations of three-way scenes such as this are a constant delight. Much of our comedy and drama is based on similar set-ups.

MISTAKEN APOLOGY

training game
2 players
usually 4 minutes
15+ years

Description: Situation, characters or first line given. A servant confesses all to their master.

Resource: A clear space, a bopper and a chair.

Time-out: No.

Example of set-up: First line given (master's line): 'Tillie, come in here immediately.'

Aim: To extend, overextend and advance offers of status.

Degree of difficulty: 3

Skills required: Ability to advance and extend.

Suggested preparation: Warm-up; any group game; TWENTY-ONE; MASTER/SERVANT in pairs; ONE MASTER/TWO SERVANTS.

How it works: The servant is called in to the master because they have done something wrong. The servant confesses to a multitude of wrongs, but not to the specific deed their master has in mind. The master never has the opportunity to state their original complaint because the servant is so busy apologising for other wrongdoings. The scene usually runs at a rapid pace.

Sidecoach master: 'Be changed by the information.'

The master endows all the servant's offers with importance:

Master: 'Tillie, come in here immediately.'
Tillie: 'Oh, madam, I'm sorry, I know you're angry with me.'
Master: 'Yes, I am.' (Bangs bopper.) 'I want to talk to you about...'
Tillie: (On knees.) 'I'm sorry, I'm sorry. I'll tell you everything about the rose garden.'
Master: 'The rose garden? Not my prized roses!'

This follows a Commedia dell'arte routine where, traditionally, Arlecchino (the servant) stooges his way from one misadventure to another. Here the servant confesses to all sorts of wrongs. She names them and surprises the master and herself by these confessions which she admits and describes in great detail.

Tillie: 'Well, only half are totally destroyed, the rest will be fine with replanting.'
(Master bangs bopper.)
Tillie: (On knees.) 'I couldn't help it madam. The poodle dug her way into the rose garden and I...'
Master: 'The poodle!' (Names the new offer.) 'Not Fifi?'
Tillie: 'Yes madam.'
Master: 'Where's Fifi?'
Tillie: 'Well madam, dead.'
(The master faints. Tillie revives her and the scene continues.)

Generally speaking, the narrative is developed as the master invites the advances, but the servant names the offer and extends it. Both characters actively overaccept all the offers, advance, extend and where appropriate shelve the important ones to bring the scene to its conclusion.

This game will be of more benefit in a workshop and training situation than in performance.

KING/QUEEN

training game
scene-work
2–32 players
usually 5–20 minutes
12+ years

Description: King or queen selected. Other players enter as servants to please their majesty and stay alive. At any time, for any reason the king/queen can click their fingers and say, 'Die!' At this, the servant falls to the floor, dead!

Resource: A clear space and a chair.

Time-out: No.

Example of a title: Not applicable.

Aim: To explore the master/servant relationship.

Degree of difficulty: 2

Skills required: Ability to endow.

Suggested preparation: Yes; You; Still status; Moving status; Master/servant.

How it works: The king or the queen is chosen. They are placed on their throne in a clear space. The other players are servants, who enter singly, in pairs, or small groups. They must at all times strive to please the king or queen. If they fail, they will die.

They bow and dare to bring on news. 'Madam, I bring a letter from the emperor.' 'Your Majesty, I'm the new chef. Would you care to select from the menu?'

At any time, sometimes for reasons known only to themselves, the king/queen can click their fingers and say, 'Die'. At this, the servant falls to the floor, dead! The king/queen do not kill those who please them, only those who displease them.

Each player attempts to please the throne in their own way, bringing on their own character and circumstance.

Dead bodies leave the scene after about five seconds. These players can return as different characters. For safety, do not allow the bodies to be dragged or removed.

Do not play this game in performance. It is a workshop gem.

•

Good idea

Give a player who rarely experiences high status the opportunity to sit on the throne. The shy, underestimated, overlooked person often reveals remarkable changes in their physical presence and may relish the high status experience.

•

Tips for text

Explore status relationships on text. Put an actor playing Macbeth into the role of king. The other players playing Lady Macbeth, Banquo, Macduff, etc, enter to serve their king.

Then, place low status characters from a text on the throne, giving them power beyond the experience of the text.

CAR STATUS

training game
scene-work
4 players
usually 4 minutes
15+ years

Description: Situation established and explained. Characters and status order given. Players speak only to the status directly above or below them.

Resource: A clear space and four chairs.

Time-out: No.

Example of a title: Four friends travelling across the Nullarbor to a wedding; Four nuns travelling to a retreat in the mountains; Madonna, her agent, her hairdresser and her lead guitarist travelling to the Grammies.

Aim: To explore a consistent pecking order.

Degree of difficulty: 3

Skills required: Ability to play status and a function.

Suggested preparation: Warm-up; any group game; TWENTY-ONE; MASTER/SERVANT in pairs; ONE MASTER/TWO SERVANTS.

How it works: The four players take their seats on the chairs positioned as a car, two in front and two behind. Designate the four players – Status 1, 2, 3, 4. It does not matter which status position is the driver.

Players speak only to the player of status immediately above or below them. Status 1 only speaks down to status 2. Status 2 speaks up to 1 and down to 3. Status 3 speaks up to 2 and down to 4. Status 4 only speaks up to 3. Although players do not speak to every other player, they hear every offer. Offers from all players must be dealt with. Status 4 offers are as important as status 1 offers. If status 4 needs to stop the car, all players deal with this offer. They stop the car. They may drive off and leave him/her there. They may disagree about what to do but they do something.

So far we have dealt with pecking orders of two or three. The pecking order is now extended to four places. While status 1 and 4 can't actually speak directly to each other, they have a relationship. For example, status 1 may be disrespectful of their hen-pecked father, status 4, but critical of others' disrespect for him. Status 1 may shield 4 but never speak to him.

As a result status 2 is given an order by status 1 which is passed down the line to status 3 and then to 4. Hence status 2 and 3 are caught in the crossfire between status 1 and 4. While it seems that status 4 would be the underdog, the positions of 2 and 3 are dangerous because they bear the brunt of the blame and provide the link between status 1 and 4. So we have the birth of middle management!

The comedy and drama are generated by all the status positions as they argue and pass the blame, all the while remaining respectful of the status above them and using the status below them as a scapegoat.

Designate the set-up, the characters and their status clearly. Do not rush the coaching of this game. Develop foundation skills to sophisticated scene-work. Not being able to speak with all characters, players find alternative means of communicating. These scenes are often extremely funny as characters develop unusual interactions and relationships.

Performance

This game rarely works in performance. It is more of a workshop and training session gem. Never play this 'game on game' in performance.

UP AND DOWN

training game
3–20 players
usually 20 minutes
14+ years

Description: Player A leaves the room. Situation and status pecking order given. On their return, player A determines who they are, the status pecking order, and where the scene is located. All players speak only to the player whose status position is immediately above or below them.

Resource: A big space.

Time-out: No, but the whole group should take time to establish the location and consider their status position while player A is out of the room.

Example of set-up: In the dining car on the Indian Pacific/the Ghan/the Orient Express; At a birthday party.

Aim: To explore pecking orders.

Degree of difficulty: 3

Skills required: Ability to give and receive offers of status and work as a group.

Suggested preparation: YES; STILL STATUS; MOVING STATUS; MASTER/SERVANT; CAR STATUS.

How it works: Player A waits out of earshot. The remainder of the group establish a full pecking order — in a class of twenty, from one to twenty. A status position number is kept for player A. Players speak only to the status position immediately above or below themselves. All players must acknowledge the offers made by player A (the endowee) even if they cannot speak to him/her directly.

Groups of players decide on their relationships and roles. For example, in a scene in the dining car on the Indian Pacific, status 1 – the Prime Minister; status 2 – the Minister for Transport; status 3 – train conductor; status 4 – ticket collector; status 5 – chef; status 6 – head waiter; status 7 – player A/kitchenhand; status 8 – dishwasher; status 9 – model; status 10 – photographer; etc. The coach and group make these decisions together.

On player A's return, the other players endow player A with his/her status position and role, eg status 7/kitchen-hand. Although status positions 6 and 8 are the only players to speak directly to player A, player A continually gives offers to determine the status positions of all twenty players. Player A is always actively involved in the scene.

The scene is finished when player A tells the coach that they believe they know each player's status position. Player A then lines up all the players, including her/himself, in order of status. Then player A names their own occupation and as many of the others as they can.

Ask players to give offers to clarify the pecking order for player A. If player A does not complete the full status order of all players, set the scene in motion again. The scene is complete when player A states all status positions and roles of all characters.

•

Tip

This is a good scene for the coach to play with the group.

Check

Status foundation skills

Players have now experienced giving and receiving a range of status endowment offers and developed characters in simple and complex pecking orders. Use the following as a guide to assess their skills development.

When playing the above scenes and training games, do players:

- Yield to sidecoaching of their status?
- Understand the difference between high and low status?
- Play a range of high and low status?
- Cheerfully and easily drop status?
- Enjoy changing status and endowing other players with status?
- Actively endow other players truthfully?
- Action events in the developing scene?

If most of the group answers yes to the above questions, players are ready to expand their skills and play a status transition.

MAKING A STATUS TRANSITION

Now that players clearly endow status, they are ready to advance the plot and make status transitions.

Remember

A status change is one of the most theatrically powerful ways to advance a scene. A change in status is thrilling to watch. Some players find it difficult to do, especially when they associate dropping status with losing personal power.

When players express their emotions and play their status they deepen their commitment to the ideas. This raises the stakes. When the audience identifies clear pecking orders and truthful emotional expression, it deepens their understanding of the characters and their interest in the plot.

The moment of transition and the turning offer

From Program one we know that an event is something that happens; an important offer that provides a moment of transition between one part of the story and the next.

Players usually spend ten to thirty seconds establishing the place or activity, setting up a routine. The routine is broken when something new occurs to interrupt the activity. In most instances the new information provides a turning offer. It sets the scene for a moment of transition when something will happen and the scene will advance.

We know from Program two that the turning offer is the moment when the focus is shared between two players and an offer transfers from one player to the other. The turning offer also provides a moment for a status transition.

Status hat games

Hat games are exciting and provide a clear demonstration of status, how it is endowed and how it is lost and gained. They teach status transitions effectively because they are active and immediate. Status hat games are many and varied. I learned the following status hat games from David Lander.

Rules for hat games

Players don hats that represent status positions. There is one hat fewer than there are players. The bottom status player wears no hat. Players attempt to raise their status by grabbing the hat that represents the highest status. Although they change hats and status, players remain the same character throughout the scene.

Players cannot defend their hat by physically blocking a grab or holding on to their hat. The hatted player, however, can grab their own hat off their own head, but only when the opposing player is making a grab for it.

If the opposing player attempts to grab the hat and fails, the hatted player removes their hat and uses it as a bopper hitting it on the floor, verbally berating the opposing player, who must drop to the floor and say, 'I'm sorry, I'm sorry!' The hatted player replaces their hat and the scene continues.

When playing with two hats and three players (eg see below, THREE WAY HATS) and a player with the second status hat acquires the top status hat, s/he throws the second status hat to the ground and the other two players vie for it.

Remember

- Players **never** talk about the hat!
- Players are encouraged to risk losing their hat and change status as often as possible in order to serve the scene.
- In an endeavour to guard their hat some players walk out of the scene or leave the given playing area. Remind these players that the main objective is to play the scene and risk losing the hat.

Beware

Never use peaked caps. These are dangerous because they can cause eye injury when players grab for the peak. Do not use stiff or delicate hats because they will be destroyed. Always use only wide-brimmed, soft, floppy hats or stetsons. These are easily removed, durable and cannot cause injury.

HAT GAME

training game
2–32 players
usually 5–10 minutes
12+ years

Description: Player A wears a hat. Player B enters and endows player A with top status. Player B attempts to get the hat and gain top status.

Resource: A clear space and a floppy-brimmed or stetson hat.

Time-out: Not applicable.

Example of a title: Not applicable.

Aim: To play an objective. To explore high and low status, and experience a status change.

Degree of difficulty: 2

Skills required: Ability to make and yield to status offers.

Suggested preparation: Vocal warm-up; physical warm-up, any group game; TWENTY-ONE.

How it works — Step one: Begin with the whole group standing in a circle. One hatted player enters the circle. A player without a hat joins them to endow the player with high status, play the scene and 'get the hat'. As each hatted player loses the hat they leave the scene, being replaced by the new hatted player and another player from the circle enters to 'get the hat'.

> Player B: 'Excuse me, Madam, but I seem to have lost my way. Could you tell me the way to the Town Hall please?'

Player A must yield to this offer and give the directions. By yielding to the focus (pointing to the Town Hall), player A is accepting the offer, risking the hat and playing the scene. Encourage all players to yield to offers and the new focus. These are moments when the transitions occur. Player B attempts to grab the hat, and with it the top status, at any time throughout the scene.

If player B is successful, player B dons the hat and becomes the new high status player and a new low status player enters the ring. The new low status player now endows the hatted player with high status and introduces a new location and a new scene.

Whether played in a circle or as scene-work (two players out front and the rest of the group as benched players, waiting to enter), the same conditions apply. The coach encourages all players to participate actively. It is important that each departing low status player is replaced immediately with another player to keep the energy level high. The game continues with a swift turnover of players.

When a player is particularly agile and 'keeps' the hat, send in a third player to help the second. Both try to 'get the hat', challenge the top status and extend the pecking order.

Step two: Encourage the scenes to last longer so that players experience more than one status transition. When the lower status character (player B) gets the hat, continue the scene. Player B has top status and player A attempts to regain the hat and the status.

Player B: 'Excuse me, Madam, but I seem to have lost my way. Could you tell me the way to the Town Hall please?'

Player A: (Directing player B.) 'Any fool knows where the Town Hall is. Down to the right of...' (Loses hat and changes vocal tone.) '...the post office. See even an idiot like me knows where it is. Perhaps I can escort you there.'

Player B: (Hitting floor with hat.) 'Yes carry me there.'

Player A: (Lifts player B, carries her to the Town Hall, puts her down and grabs hat.) 'You've crumpled my jacket.' (Hits hat on floor.)

Player B: (Grovelling.) 'I'm sorry. Here, allow me to have it dry-cleaned and pressed for you.' (Grabs hat.)

Player A: (Yielding and endowing.) 'Oh my God, you're Cynthia Roberts the concert violinist. I'm coming to your recital this evening.' (Grovelling.) 'Can I have your autograph?'

THREE WAY HATS

training game
scene-work
3 players
usually 4 minutes
12+ years

Description: Situation, occupations and hats given. Three players vie for two hats. The hats determine the status positions. Player A wears the top status hat. Player B wears second status hat. Player C wears no hat and is at bottom status. Player C attempts to get either hat. Player B attempts to get player A's hat. Player A attempts to retain top status but risks losing the hat. As players win and lose hats they change status but do not change character.

Resource: A clear space and two hats.

Time-out: No.

Example of a title: The set-up is always clearly task associated. Characters serve the appropriate roles and functions — Building a wall: apprentice, brickie, contractor; Making a wedding cake: pastry chef, apprentice chef, reception manager.

Aim: To explore the status transition.

Degree of difficulty: 3

Skills required: Ability to change status.

Suggested preparation: Vocal and physical warm-up; any group game; TWENTY-ONE; HAT GAME.

How it works: The set-up is always similar regardless of the characters or their tasks. The second status hat (the brickie) begins the scene. The lowest status no hat (first-day apprentice) arrives late, full of apologies. The brickie teaches the apprentice how to lay bricks. During the scene the apprentice repeatedly attempts to get the hat. If s/he succeeds, s/he becomes higher status than the brickie but remains the apprentice.

Scenes usually develop more clearly if the status 2 and 3 characters (the bricklayer and apprentice) play together at the beginning of the scene for at least one minute. This gives both characters an opportunity to explore their status relationship and acquire the hat and status at least three times.

Carefully sidecoach the moment after the hat transition. Encourage the characters to deal with the transition using the focus and offer currently in play. For example:

Apprentice: 'There's a hole in this wall.' (Names offer and identifies focus.)
Brickie: 'What do you mean, hole? Idiot.' (Removes hat, hits floor, replaces hat, yields to focus, risks hat, lowers body, and looks through hole.)
Apprentice: 'See, I can see light.'
Brickie: (Peering through, now at the same height as apprentice.) 'That's not a hole, you fool, it's a drainpipe.'
(Apprentice takes hat from brickie and puts it on.)
Brickie: 'You're right, it's a drainpipe with a hole. Sit down, have a cuppa tea and I'll fix it for you.'
Apprentice: 'Yes, get me a cup of tea.'
Brickie: 'Certainly.' (Grabs hat from apprentice's head.)
Apprentice: (Grovelling on ground.) 'I'll get you a cuppa.'
Brickie: (Banging hat on floor.) 'Stop all this talk about tea. Just fix the hole.'

The status transition has been dealt with 'in the moment'. Too often players introduce new subject matter after a status transition. Encourage players to deal with the focus and ideas in play, and extend them before introducing too many new ideas and a new focus.

When the players have established the scene and their relationship, the third, top status hat (contractor) enters to advance the scene.

The timing of the third player's entrance is important. Leave the decision to the player but sidecoach them if necessary. You might need to keep them off, you may have to bring them on. The contractor's arrival ups the stakes. The pecking order broadens.

To explore the relationship between the contractor and the bricklayer, sidecoach the apprentice to leave the stage. The apprentice later returns and the three characters vie to win status and hats. Amid the physical and verbal excitement, all characters attempt to complete building the wall.

Sidecoach players: 'Go for the hat.'
Sidecoach hatted players: 'Risk your hat.'

The objective of all players is to get and keep the hat of highest status. The task of all players is to build the wall.

This set-up typifies the thrill of the status change. All players can be encouraged to win and lose status with grace and confidence. No other game teaches the comic moment so clearly. Every status change becomes an advance in the scene.

•

Tip

It is important that the energy levels remain high throughout this game. For advanced players who crave more, from time to time add the handle of ENTRANCES AND EXITS or CONTACT to build narrative and increase spontaneity.

TOP DOG / UNDER DOG

training game
always 3 players
1–2 minutes
12+ years

Description: Place, activity or situation given. One player experiences status changes as a result of the offers made by their inner voices provided by two offstage players. The voices express the onstage player's rises and falls in confidence and sense of personal status as the scene progresses.

Resource: A clear space.

Time-out: Yes. Determine who is to play the central character, and who is to play their top dog and under dog.

Example of a title: Dressing for your first date; Waiting for the job interview. A place or situation where the character can talk to themselves alone and experience both self-doubt, self-confidence and indecision.

Aim: To experience a status transition.

Degree of difficulty: 2

Skills required: Ability to give and receive offers. Ability to play high and low status.

Suggested preparation: Warm up; STILL STATUS; MOVING STATUS; HAPPY HIGH STATUS; HAPPY LOW STATUS.

How it works: This game taps a character's sense of personal status. It also further develops focus and endowment skills and deepens an awareness of character building. It allows for emotional and status transitions that advance the plot. To ensure clarity of focus, always play with three players.

The onstage character does not speak. They initiate the physical offers. They establish the location and mood. In the scene, 'Dressing for your first date', they open the wardrobe, look through the clothes and sing softly. Then the inner voices speak.

Opposite her/him, in a position where they can see every facial expression and physical offer made by the onstage player, sit the two players who are the onstage player's inner voices. One is the top dog, one the bottom dog. Top dog is the character's positive inner voice. The top dog cheers the character, encouraging, flattering and generally raising her/his status by making them feel positive. Top dog solves problems. The bottom dog is the character's negative voice. They deflate the character, strip them of confidence, find problems and negate their ideas.

When the character goes to the wardrobe to select a shirt, the voices begin.

> Top dog: 'Now which one will I wear? The red always looks terrific and the weather is perfect for it. Yes I'll be a smash hit in this.'

Character selects the shirt and puts it on.

Bottom dog allows the positive action to extend and, mindful of timing and being careful not to overload the scene, waits for the moment to advance. As the character is admiring herself/himself in the mirror and top dog is flattering her/him, bottom dog strikes:

> Bottom dog: 'Oh no, there's a stain right across the front. I can't go in this!'

The onstage character overaccepts this offer. S/he makes the emotional transition from confident happiness to disappointed alarm. The onstage character advances the physical and extends the drop in status as far as possible. Just before s/he reaches despair scrubbing the stain frantically or throwing clothes out of the wardrobe looking for an alternative, top dog saves her/him with a good idea.

> Top dog: 'No need to panic. The black one will be fine. Now for my hair.'

These transitions continue throughout the developing scene. Both top and bottom dogs yield to the physical offers made by the onstage character extending and advancing as necessary. The onstage player takes responsibility for giving the offstage voices ideas and clearly expressing a variety of emotions. The three players work together to conclude the unfolding scene, which can be comic and/or dramatic.

Check

Status transition skills

At this point in training, players call on skills they have covered in all the programs thus far. They play complex scenes and build detailed plots. They make status transitions. Address the following skills list before progressing to the performance games.

- Can they play high and low status?
- Can they give the status offer principal focus in the scene?
- Do they enjoy dropping status rather than begrudge losing status?
- Do they extend offers of status?
- Do they recognise a status transition as an advance in the narrative?
- Do they enjoy making or effecting transitions?
- Do they experience an internal response to an offer of status and express their reaction physically and/or vocally?
- Do they allow other players to give the principal status offer in the scene rather than controlling the status choices and the power base in the scene?
- Can they extend offers of status and convey them through body and voice?
- Are they changed by, and do they react to, the status of other players?
- Do they respond to sidecoaching?
- Do they recognise and convey the difference between a variety of status positions?

• Can they recognise and yield to status transitions made by themselves or other players?

If the answer is 'yes' to the above for most players, introduce the Theatresports status performance games.

part C THEATRESPORTS PERFORMANCE GAMES

FAMILY STATUS

classic

training game
performance game
3–4 players
usually 4 minutes
13+ years

Description: Situation, characters and status pecking order given.

Resource: A clear space. Costumes and props, two boppers (optional).

Time-out: No.

Example of set-up: Kitchen, Saturday morning, grandma – status 1, mum – status 2, 16 year old – status 3, dad – status 4. Backyard, Sunday afternoon, 5 year old – status 1, pop – status 2, 12 year old – status 3, mum – status 4. Make the point that the status pecking order need not be the stereotypical choice.

Aim: To explore status relationships in the family and develop a consistent pecking order.

Degree of difficulty: 4

Skills required: Ability to make and yield to status offers. Ability to play character.

Suggested preparation: Yes; You; Master/servant; Still status; Moving status; Hat game; Three way hat game; Top dog/under dog.

How it works: This scene-work puts into practice all the skills explored in Parts A and B of this program. Some scenes are as exaggerated and as physical as Master/Servant and Hat Game. Other scenes are quiet and subtle.

Establish the environment with the players. All characters speak to every other character. Clarify the scene by giving some of the characters objectives. For example, mum (status 2) and dad (status 4) ask grandma (status 1) for a loan of $10 000 for the 16-year-old's (status 3) education. Simple objectives enrich the playing by driving the scene. Encourage players to yield to every status offer.

To build relationships and clarify the plot, find opportunities for two of the characters to interact rather than overcrowding the scene with too many players. Not all characters are required in the scene at the same time.

•

Beware

Some players enjoy playing family animals (eg dog or cockatoo) as a status position. These are great fun but beware the focus they pull. They are richer and more effective when the animal-playing player is sensitive to the needs of the scene. If necessary sidecoach the animal to sleep or to leave the stage and to return only if required.

STATUS

scene-work
performance game
3 players
usually 4 minutes
13+ years

Description: Situation, characters and status pecking order given.

Resource: A clear space, costumes and props.

Time-out: No.

Example of set-up: A plastic surgeon, a nurse and the patient; The principal, teacher and student.

Aim: To experience and explore a consistent pecking order.

Degree of difficulty: 4

Skills required: Ability to make and yield to status offers and to play character.

Suggested preparation: Yes; You; Master/servant; Still status; Moving status; Hat game; Three way hat game; Top dog/under dog.

How it works: Give players their characters and their status. It is more interesting to give atypical status positions to the characters; eg student – top status; teacher – second status; principal – lowest status. Players play the scene exploring the relationships. Players develop a narrative around a pecking order. All skills from Parts A and B of this program are required. As audience we enjoy seeing the opposite status to what we would expect, eg low status mugger, high status victim.

STATUS TRANSITION

training game
performance game
2 players
2–4 minutes
14+ years

Description: Situation, characters and pecking order given. Characters undergo a change of status as a result of the scene events.

Resource: A clear space, minimal set, minimal costumes.

Time-out: No.

Example of a title: The job interview; The retrenchment; A pilot and a hijacker.

Aim: To explore a change of status.

Degree of difficulty: 3

Skills required: Ability to endow status, overaccept offers, and make clear transitions.

Suggested preparation: Warm-up; MASTER/SERVANT GAME; STILL STATUS; MOVING STATUS; HAT GAME; HAPPY HIGH STATUS; HAPPY LOW STATUS.

How it works: Two players begin with opposing status. The relationship between a job applicant and prospective employer is explored through the gulf between these status positions. Each endows the other with the relevant status. As a result of the information in the scene a transition occurs. At the end of the scene, both players have changed status positions. The characters remain the same, only their status changes. The lower status character (applicant) finishes at higher status, the higher status character (employer) finishes at lower status.

It is sometimes helpful if players begin in frozen positions that depict their status. The interviewer sits behind a desk, leaning back, hands behind head, taking up a lot of space in a high status position, while the interviewee stands, head bent, at the door in a position of low status. By the end of the scene, players have exchanged status and finish in the physical position from which the other player started: the interviewee sits behind the desk and the interviewer is cowering in the doorway. Changing positions helps players to physicalise the status. They keep the scene moving rather than talking too much. This allows for a clearer transition. Remember they change status positions not characters.

Some players tend to block a change of status. In this scene the transition is the major objective of both players. They must listen carefully to the offers given by the other player and use all the information to make the transition. The transition is gradual and develops from the narrative. It cannot be pushed or imposed by either player. Encourage players to yield to every offer in order to make the transition. Sidecoach the moment of transition carefully. Sidecoach players to identify the moment and overaccept it.

Performance: Play as part of a STATUS CHALLENGE rather than 'game on game'.

part D

STATUS, SEXISM AND THE POLITICS OF GENDER

September 1990 — Intermediate Training, Heffron Hall, Darlinghurst, Sydney

I called a NO-BLOCKING SCENE. *Activity — defusing a bomb.*

Margaret sets the scene. She is the bomb disposal expert. She establishes the activity. She is defusing a bomb. Her offers are clear and precise. She is in control.

He enters unannounced, uncalled for, and not required. Margaret yields to the entrance, endows him as Sergeant.

'We've got a live one here, Sergeant,' she says referring to the focus of the scene — the bomb.

What does he do?

'Right, Private,' he says, 'I'll fix that!' He physically takes the imagined bomb out of her hands.

In one single movement he demotes her, steals the focus, places himself at top status, then actually, physically takes the scene away from her. He robs her of the scene.

It is a delicate task to balance the sexual pendulum in theatre improvisation, Theatresports on stage and in the classroom.

While Theatresports is one of the few sporting activities that men and women can enjoy together, socially and professionally, it is still a tentative hotbed for the same gender discrimination that men and women encounter in everyday life.

If a player's instinctive reaction to an impulse is a clichéd, sexist reaction, the improvisation is likely to insult at least 50 per cent of the players and audience.

October 1986 — Belvoir Street Theatre performance, Sydney

Situation — DEATH IN A MINUTE — *in a hospital*

A female player ran to the performance area beginning the scene, making an intuitive physical offer to establish an operating theatre. She held her hands creating the surgical gloves and made a perfect offer with her right hand: 'Scalpel!'

It was an obvious intuitive reaction to the suggestion; a clichéd doctor's request. Seeing that offer, a male player entered the space. He took the imagined scalpel out of her hand and said, 'Thanks nurse'.

The audience hissed and booed. She graciously continued the scene playing the nurse, allowing him to play the doctor. I don't think he even realised what had happened.

Australian women in Theatresports

Despite a few hurdles such as these, Australian women have held their own in Theatresports. For the most part, traditional theatre and the entertainment industry are weighted towards male performers. It is exciting to see a theatre activity where men and women can enjoy the benefits of balance. It is keeping the balance that is challenging.

The ratio of women to men players in Australia has generally been equal. This is probably because, since its inception, Belvoir Street Theatre has nurtured 'women in theatre'. The first full-time Theatresports administrator appointed by Chris Westwood, the foundation General Manager of Belvoir Street Theatre, was Deb Collins. Deb encouraged women players, women stage managers and teachers. This no doubt had a direct effect on other Theatresports centres in Australia and New Zealand. Positive discrimination and gender balance has been continued as a matter of artistic policy by Theatresports Inc management.

In 1987 Deb Collins organised a two day Women in Theatresports Workshop. All the women obviously enjoyed the opportunity of being free to play all the status roles in a way that they had not previously experienced. Lone male Murray Fahey shared the teaching with me. It was the playing the women needed to do alone. The issue of the male teacher was never raised.

In 1988 a female player suggested the idea of an all-women Theatresports night — women players, compere, timekeeper, musician, judges, etc. The following Sunday after the game, the players discussed the notion. I was surprised by the response. The women did not feel they needed singling out and special treatment. The male players stated that they wanted the women to play with them. It was agreed both men and women enjoyed playing together, even if not in the same teams. They wanted to be in the same production at the same time.

In 1990 in Sydney the onstage sexism resurfaced in a new guise. We noticed a new pattern in the playing. Men and women began to play a different style of improvisation and Theatresports. Sometimes when men and women played together in the same team in front of an audience (mixed playing), we noticed women players tended to function differently in a scene from the men. Broadly speaking, in more cases than not, women became more inclined to play a reactive role in their improvising and men took an active role. That is, the men tended to do the scene, make the announcements and the women tended to field the scene and deal with the consequences. It was not that the women could not make announcements and advance scenes, but that some men bulldozed women players on stage.

Robert McFarlane

The Indestructibles — (left to right) Madeline Aroney, Julia Zemiro, Josie O'Reilly, Robyn Butler

We noticed the men's first offers were more easily recognisable to the audience and drew fast laughs. Their style was physical and more often than not wild and wacky. Their ideas were packaged and slick. Men were inclined to make sound effects for onstage objects — creating car doors, opening cans etc. The men plugged into the popular culture, playing scenes and characters that the audience immediately identified.

We noticed the women frequently made emotional and relationship-based offers to establish a scene. They established the place and their own position in the scheme of things. They established status. The women's playing rhythm seemed slower than the men's. They wanted to tell their stories differently. The women tended to extend the moments creating a different style of narrative. They were funny, but the scenes took longer to get a laugh — not that playing for laughs is important. The audience may be moved rather than amused by what they see.

While all players shared the responsibility for the narrative, men played in the immediate moment and women tended to work towards the end result of the scene. When women tried to play their scenes in the immediate moment some men pushed them out of the scene. The result was that women were forced to play a faster, more aggressive style of improvisation in order to compete with men for stage time and status.

The old clichés had found their way back to the stage. Nothing as blatant as the 'doctor/nurse' incident resurfaced but gender-based stereotyping continued. It wasn't just the men who reinforced the gender cliché. The women found they were stereotyping themselves. Player Robyn Butler confesses to washing a lot of dishes on stage and I have done my fair share of ironing and filing!

Offstage, women had held positions such as artistic director, national coach, lighting and production manager, competition coordinator, compere, timekeeper, coach and team captain. Yet they found they were being railroaded by the men on stage. It seemed to occur more blatantly in front of an audience in performance than in training. The predominant Theatresports style had become fast, zany and male dominated. Women would go on to establish a scene and be removed by a funnier offer made by a male player. The original offer given by the female was destroyed. The women concluded that they could not compete. It was time for another workshop.

In October 1990, Robyn Butler, Jenny Lovell, Julie Dunsmore and I planned a second 'Women in Theatresports' workshop. The difference between this training session and the first all-women workshop in 1987 was that both men and women, beginner, intermediate and veteran players were welcome to train together. Our aim was to promote the idea that players, irrespective of their sex, should strive to serve a scene function as a priority, whether it be high or low status; and that women are as capable of playing and as entitled to play top status as are men.

To avoid future clichéd stereotyping, in this workshop men were asked to endow women at all times with top status. Women were encouraged to take top status. We listed top status professions that recur in improvised scenes. We decided that the women would play the top status and/or stereotypically male profession — eg the doctor instead of the nurse, the firefighter rather than the distressed victim.

Occupations

Surgeon	Managing Director
Doctor	Scientist
Astronaut	Truck driver
Psychologist	Chef
Prime Minister	Journalist
Firefighter	Bank manager
Judge/lawyer	Psychiatrist
Teacher	Horticulturalist
Major/General/Colonel	Professor

The following lesson plan was made. We agreed not to talk about sexism or any issue until after the three hour session. The other rule was that men and women were welcome to play in any scene at any time but all scenes had at least 50 per cent female players.

Plan: MEETING AND GREETING, warm-up — physical and vocal, NO-BLOCKING SCENE beginning with an occupation from the list. Two players set the scene, yielding to the first offer of place, occupation and status in the scene. They play without blocking. QUEEN (KING/QUEEN, played as QUEEN only); PARTY ENDOWMENT.

What eventuated here was astounding.

October 1990 — Heffron Hall, Sydney

I called, 'No-blocking scene. At the psychiatrist! Two people up.'

Maria, who is a counsellor and was a beginner player, started the scene.

Maria yielded to her first intuitive response. She lay on the couch. This placed David Wood in high status as 'the doctor'. He immediately dropped his status and fell to the floor. He lay on his back on the ground and said 'Well doctor it all started…'

We couldn't believe it! Maria couldn't believe it. They played a short scene. I stopped them. The look on Maria's face was one of amazement. 'I'm a counsellor,' she kept saying. 'I do this for a living and I perform a stereotype. Why didn't I play the psychiatrist from the beginning of the scene?'

Later, on reflection, Maria wrote, 'I left my life experience at the door instead of bringing it into the room.'

I couldn't help wondering if she had not left her life experience at the door but had in fact brought it into the room.

Since that time we have held several successful all-women Theatresports performances. These shows have found their own pace and momentum, creating rich textured scenes enjoyed by the audience and players. We strive to do less 'cleaning' on stage than we used to and continue to redress the self-demoting and stereotyping wherever possible.

Coaching without sexism

The first place to redress the imbalance is the training room. Here it is important to avoid sexist sidecoaching. Whenever possible and appropriate, place girls in high status positions. Place girls and boys in non-stereotypical roles. If they fall into stereotypical roles, discuss it with the class. Analysis can result in valuable discoveries.

By the same token place players, whatever their gender, in status positions which challenge them. Encourage them to experience an alternative status position to the one they normally hold within that group (whether it be high or low status). Offer them alternative ways to perceive themselves and each other.

Theatresports and improvisation not only provide us with the opportunity to recognise the clichéd responses that surface in us all from time to time, but also give us the opportunity to challenge and break them. As coaches we are continually called upon to examine and redress these inequalities.

Making a transition

program 6

Commandment

Thou shalt always be changed by what is said to you.

The ability to change and be affected by conditions, other characters and events are the necessary skills for the actor and the improvisor. We call these changes transitions.

There are two major transitions we encounter with text and improvisation:

- Emotional transitions
- Status transitions

An emotional transition occurs when a character moves from one emotional state to another. A status transition occurs when a character experiences a change in their position in the pecking order. Both usually result in a change of focus. Whether comic or tragic, a transition advances the plot.

Transitions occur when characters receive and are changed by new information. Sometimes they are changed by what is said by another character, at other times they experience changes in private moments. These are expressed in a number of ways including soliloquy, a shared moment with the audience, a song or through a reaction made in silence.

When we improvise, transitions occur spontaneously. Improvisors write, direct and play the scene on the spot for the first time without preplanning. Special effects and staging such as lighting and music are also improvised. Therefore improvisors must be alert to every offer and remain available to make a transition at any time.

Our aim is to develop skills to:

1. Overaccept other players' offers
2. Recognise the value and potential of a transition
3. Yield and enjoy making transitions even when they demand a drop in status
4. Enjoy giving offers that result in transitions made by other players
5. Yield to the new focus the transition demands
6. Deal with the effects of the transition

part A FOUNDATION SKILLS

GIVING AN OFFER OF EMOTION

EMOTIONAL FACES

training game for fledging or shy players
2–32 players
10–20 minutes
8+ years

Description: Players make faces at each other in response to an offer of emotion.

Resource: A space where players can sit close together in a circle or in a group on the floor, in seats or at desks. Allow for a wider space as the exercise develops.

Time-out: No.

Aim: To introduce emotions and provoke a spontaneous physical response to an offer of emotion and to express it facially.

Degree of difficulty: 0.5

Skills to be developed: Ability to express an emotional offer and physicalise an emotional response.

Suggested preparation: You.

How it works: This is a particularly useful exercise for fledgling or shy players. It works in a similar way to Knife and fork.

Step one: All players work at the same time in pairs, naming themselves A and B. The coach names an emotion. Each player A makes a face expressing the emotion and gives it to their partner. 'Give your partner a scary face/happy face/sad face', etc.

Repeat with each player B sending a face to their partner. Some players naturally include their arms, hands and other body parts when expressing the emotion.

Step two: The coach names an emotion. Players A send a face expressing that emotion to players B, who express their reaction — eg players A send a scary face, players B react with a frightened face. The pairs freeze briefly after the action and the reaction have been made. From time to time choose one frozen pair. Point out the features of their frozen moment. Look at the focus and status relationships. Describe the eyes, mouth, etc of the players as they make and yield to the different emotions.

Step three: Discuss emotions. What are they? Why do we feel emotions? What makes us happy, scared, etc?

Step four: Players sit or stand in a circle. One player makes a face from a suggested emotion, eg excitement, and then passes the face around the circle. Each player copies the face and passes it on to the next player and so on. Begin a new emotion sent from another player.

Step five: Develop step four sending a sound with the face around the circle.

Now that players have begun to express emotions, they build from facial to physical expressions in the following games and exercises.

EMOTIONAL TABLEAUX

training game
2–32 players
10–20 minutes
10+ years

Description: Players form tableaux based on offers of emotion.

Resource: A large clear space with room for players to swing their arms and lie on the floor without touching another person or thing.

Aim: To provoke a spontaneous physical response to an offer of emotion.

Degree of difficulty: I

Skills to be developed: Ability to physicalise an emotional response. Ability to make an emotional offer, yield to an emotional offer and give the offer focus.

Suggested preparation: Vocal and physical warm up; YES LET'S; NAMING THE OBVIOUS in English and gibberish; EMOTIONAL FACES.

How it works — step one: We build on the skills developed in KNIFE AND FORK in Program one. The players work in pairs. They physicalise an immediate response to a series of emotions and states called in quick succession by the coach. The pairs respond without talking or signing to each other. They make shapes together that depict the emotions and hold the simple freeze until the next emotion is called. The calling is clear and emotions are given in rapid succession, as were the offers in KNIFE AND FORK.

Emotions and states of being to call: Love, hate, fear, embarrassment, remorse, regret, suspicion, passion, bliss, greed, grief, anger, bewilderment, loneliness, insecurity, confidence, abandonment, bitterness, betrayal, bravery, victory, alienation, desire, charm, awe, surrender, inadequacy, shame, guilt, solemnity, sorrow, exasperation, hostility, excitement, goodness, domination, restlessness, greatness, rejection, acceptance, fear, intimidation, laziness, gladness, foolishness, freedom, liberation, doubt, kindness, panic, temptation.

This list is by no means complete. [See Appendix B – Topics and titles.] Not all the emotions/feelings will be applicable to players under 15 years. Choose those that are appropriate and relate to the players' age group and experience.

Step two — discussion points: Bring the group together to discuss emotions: what they are and how they affect us.

Each player experiences emotions and images and expresses them with a personal response. Players describe emotions in a variety of ways. None of their responses is wrong or better than another. All are encouraged and heard.

Begin with a range of strong emotions which have been expressed in the tableaux eg happiness/sadness/guilt/love/hate/anger/hope/fear/joy. Discuss one emotion and then a contrasting emotion, using the following as starting points.

Where do particular emotions live in our body? Where do we experience them? Shakespeare houses them in our spleen, heart, etc. Can we describe how they feel? Is the feeling enjoyable?

- If they were a colour, what colour would they be?
- If they were a taste, how would they taste?
- If they were one of the four elements, which one would they be: earth/water/fire/air? Are they a combination of these?

When we express them, which focus zone do we use? The focus zone for grief would be the ground if we are mourning the dead at a graveside.

Step three: Bring the group together sitting looking at a clear space, as if for scene-work. Build on the responses from the discussion. The coach calls the emotions, and players voluntarily enter one at a time to build three dimensional tableaux that depict emotions in frozen moments.

Use the focus zones to clarify each frozen emotion. Each tableau of emotion has a place, a reason, a cause and effect. The players enter one at a time, yielding to the focus created by the previous player's frozen position. This work proceeds in a similar fashion to the STILL FOCUS and STILL STATUS exercises. The group discusses the focus and the needs of each tableau as it is built. The work is not hurried. There is no sense of panic. Some tableaux are complete with one or two players; others require four or five players.

Sidecoach (entering players to): 'Yield to the focus.'
'Use different levels.'

Step four: Bring the above frozen tableaux to life with movement and speech in short simple scenes.

Step five: Players build tableaux that express cause and effect.

In Program four, we looked at the emotional offer in EMOTION ENDOWMENT. We discussed that to have an effect, most emotions need a cause. For example, the emotion embarrassment needs a cause or a reason. Now is a good time to review this information. Bring this knowledge to the physical offers when making the tableaux.

Many tableaux will depict the essence of the emotion more clearly if they express cause and effect in their physicality.

•

Summary

Recap on the emotional endowment work:

offer + yield = action + reaction

action + reaction = cause + effect

Related activities

This work can stimulate a range of written, music, dance or art activities. Use the tableaux as starting points for creative writing. Introduce musical instruments to enhance the mood of the tableaux.

Receiving an offer of emotion

Players have experienced making emotional offers in freezes and have brought them to life. Now develop the skills to receive an offer of emotion, be changed by the offer and make a transition. Like the status transition, the emotional transition reveals players' ability to yield.

Most players yield instinctively. But for many players this work is confronting. Some players want to be the giver and the controller of the ideas. Rather than remain open to be changed, they want to control the emotional life of the scene. Making a transition is the most vulnerable moment for an improvisor. It is the moment when they experience a reaction.

A change of emotional state is usually related to a change in status. When we are sad, we feel downcast; our body position expresses low status body language. When we make the transition to being happy, our body language reveals a higher status. [See Program five.] Some players mistakenly believe that yielding to an emotional offer necessitates a drop in personal status. Encourage these players to make transitions and to trust that a transition provides an important advance in the scene and develops new dimensions in character. Transitions are theatrically powerful. They are exciting to watch and thrilling to do.

BEING AFFECTED BY AND EFFECTING AN EMOTIONAL CHANGE

SLOW MOTION ABUSE HURLING

training game
2 players
1–2 minutes
14+ years

Description: Two players enter the space. They keep a distance of at least two metres between them. They move in slow motion miming and mouthing gibberish words which they 'hurl' at each other in abuse. Both players are physically affected by the insults.

Resource: A very large clear space.

Aim: To affect and be affected by the other player.

Degree of difficulty: 2.5

Skills required: Ability to give and receive offers. Ability to mouth gibberish.

Suggested preparation: Vocal and physical warm-up; Hospital tiggy; Sound board; Gibberish circle; Slow motion race; The mirror game.

How it works: Players stand opposite each other and hurl silent, mouthed abuse at each other in gibberish, moving and mouthing in slow motion. They send abusive blows which travel across the space and land on the other player's body. Both players give and receive the mimed abuse as if they were physical blows. They overaccept the size, severity and power of the abuse as it lands on a specific part of their body. Each player is affected by the other player's abuse. They drop to the ground, reel back or spin around the space as if being struck by a boxer's blows. It is easy to see players who are reluctant to receive and be affected by other players' offers. Encourage them to accept the offers.

Sidecoach: 'Keep the distance.'
'Send it to your partner's leg/head/chest/chin.'
'Allow the abuse to land.'
'Look at your partner.'
'Be changed by its effect on you.'
'Slow motion.'

•

Remember

The abuse is not graphic because the words mimed are in gibberish. They are not 'swear words' in English.

Remind players that giving and receiving will involve changes in status. At the end of this exercise one player will need to yield as if defeated and allow the other player to win.

This exercise is similar to the Slow motion commentary performance game. The slow motion allows the offers to be seen clearly, and easily accepted, extended and advanced.

For variation when players are enjoying the exercise, add two fast commentators. The commentators do not translate the abuse but call the scene as if it were a competition.

Beware

Vocal expression of emotion

It is important with all emotional work that coaches are sensitive to players' vocal needs. When players express emotion, especially when they become excited or angry, breath can become shallow and trapped and voices strained, pushed and harsh. At other times voices may become breathy, too quiet and difficult to hear. For these reasons emotion and status transition work require breath and vocal support. Young voices can be severely damaged if players express their emotions and push their physical resources too far! Support all emotion work with a solid vocal warm-up.

part B

SCENE-WORK

In preparation for making transitions, warm up with games that encourage giving and receiving: Hospital tiggy; Sound board; The present game; It's Tuesday.

It's Tuesday

At this point, introduce It's Tuesday, as described in Keith Johnstones's *Improvisation and the Theatre*. It is of value to the rest of the work. In playing this game we learn to overaccept and express a range of emotional reactions to mundane offers. I will refer to it in the games below.

The moment of transition and the turning offer

In Program five we saw that the turning offer sometimes also involves a change of status. In this program we deal with an emotional transition as part of the turning offer. This transition usually advances the scene.

We return to training games from previous programs. We now play these games emphasising the emotional content of the scenes.

PRESENT GAME EMOTIONAL ENDOWMENT

training game
scene-work
2 players
1–2 minutes
12+ years

Description: One player gives the other player a present, endowing it with an offer of emotion. [See Programs one and two – The present game.]

Resource: A large clear space.

Aim: To make, receive and overaccept an offer of emotion and develop the subtext in the scene.

Degree of difficulty: 1.5

Skills required: Ability to give and receive offers and be affected by another player.

Suggested preparation: The present game.

How it works: Return to The present game, endowing the gift with an emotional offer. The receiving player yields and names the gift, being sensitive to and building on the offer of emotion with which the gift is given. Both players build the emotional subtext as they develop the scene.

Player A endows the gift with an emotion. S/he may not know exactly what is being given as it has not yet been named, but endowing the gift with the emotion of love, fear, hatred, anger or embarrassment will give an emotional commitment to the scene.

Player B must be aware of how the offer is being given. It will give him/her an emotional connection to the scene. It will tell him/her more about the other player and their relationship. How did player A enter the scene? How did player A look at the gift? From where did player A take the gift?

A gift given with a smile, a bowed head and lowered eyes will be a very different gift from the one given aggressively at a fast pace. Both players share an emotional commitment to the scene before a word has been spoken.

To avoid overtalking, play the scene in gibberish or in silence.

No-blocking emotions

training game
scene-work
2 players
1–2 minutes
12+ years

Description: Two players begin a No-blocking scene, each overaccepting the emotional content of every offer.

Resource: A very large clear space.

Aim: To identify and respond to an offer of emotion and be changed by the offer given by the other player.

Degree of difficulty: 1.5

Skills required: Ability to give and receive offers and be affected by another player.

Suggested preparation: Vocal and physical warm-up; Yes let's; Sound board; The present game; Emotional endowment; It's Tuesday.

How it works: This is a derivative of It's Tuesday. It combines No-blocking scenes and the above Present game emotional endowment. Two players begin No-blocking scenes. Each player overaccepts every emotional offer. Each yields with an emotional response which, in turn, is overaccepted by the other player. They are sensitive to the way the offer is given. They yield to the vocal tone and the physicality of the other player.

Encourage players not to overtalk the scene. Good results can be achieved without words or with sounds and limited words or in gibberish. Players are encouraged to be super-sensitive to the emotional content and developing subtext in the scene.

Remind players that emotions are expressed through body language, eye contact or lack of eye contact and vocal tone. Encourage players to relate to each other rather than simply demonstrating their emotions or playing their emotions in a vacuum.

•

Summary

At this point of the training, players call on all the skills they have covered in the programs thus far. They are playing complex scenes and building detailed plots. They are making emotional and status transitions. Address the following skills list before progressing to the performance games.

Check

Emotion transition skills

- Do they endow offers with emotion and give them clearly, voiced and unvoiced?
- Do they recognise and yield to offers of emotion made by other players?
- Can they give and respond to a variety of emotional offers?
- Do they allow other players to give the principal emotional offer rather than controlling the emotional choices and the emotional climate of the scene?
- Can they extend offers of emotion and convey them through their body and voice?
- Are they changed by, and do they react to, the emotional state of another player?
- Do they overaccept that a status transition is often linked to an emotional transition?
- Do they respond to sidecoaching?
- Do they recognise and convey the difference between similar emotions, eg sadness/grief; love/fondness; shock/horror; fear/terror?
- Can they deal with the emotional content of a scene without sending it up?
- Can they give the emotional offer principal focus in the scene?
- Can they recognise and yield to an emotional transition made by them or another player?

If the answer is yes to the above for most of the players, the group is ready to play transition performance games.

part C

THEATRESPORTS PERFORMANCE GAMES

It is true to say that most good scenes involve transitions. These games in particular rely on clear transitions and require an event that causes the change.

EMOTIONS

classic

performance game
usually 2 players
2 minutes
12+ years

Description: Situation given. Players are given two opposing emotions with which to start the scene. They start with the same or opposing emotions. During the scene a transition occurs.

Resource: A clear space.

Time-out: Yes. Designate emotions for players. Establish place.

Example of a title: In the maternity waiting room — hope/despair; At a slumber party — love/hate; In the cockpit — ecstasy/fear.

Aim: To effect an emotional transition as the result of an event.

Degree of difficulty: 3

Skills required: Ability to recognise and yield to a turning offer. Ability to extend and advance.

Suggested preparation: Vocal and physical warm-up; Yes let's; Emotional tableaux; Present game emotional endowment; No-blocking emotions with an objective; It's Tuesday.

How it works: This game can begin in two ways. Usually two players begin with opposing emotions. They establish the scene and create a need to interact. As a result, their prevailing emotional states are exchanged. The alternative is that both players begin with the same emotion and both change to the other.

Players must listen to each other and be changed as a result of the offers in the scene rather than talking about themselves or emoting. If players are talking about the emotion rather than playing the scene, play the scene without words or in gibberish.

•

Tip

- Sidecoach players to overaccept the offers given by the other player.
- Sidecoach players to establish the environment.
- Most emotional transitions involve a change in status.
- Players cannot be directed to feel. They can only be directed to do.

•

Beware

Avoid unnecessary players on stage. A third and fourth player can be of great value to the story if, for example, they precipitate the event and allow the emotional transition to take place rather than interrupt it.

When scenes are simple and not overloaded, the resulting transitions spring from the interaction of the characters.

•

Tips for text

Take a piece of text and map the emotional transitions. How do these affect the characters, the plot, etc? Which event precipitates the transition? Play the text and explore the transitions. Repeat without words, in gibberish, in slow motion, in as many ways as possible.

EMOTIONAL REPLAY

performance game
3–4 players
2–3 minutes
14+ years

Description: Situation and emotions given. A simple scene is played. It is then replayed three times, each time being affected by the different emotion called by an offstage team member.

Resource: A clear space. A pen and paper to record the emotions.

Time-out: Determine which player will present and call the scenes.

Example of a title: Putting down the family pet — guilt/happiness/misery; Buying a train ticket — disgust/panic/calm.

Aim: To endow the same scene with a variety of emotional subtexts and experience a variety of emotional transitions.

Degree of difficulty: 3

Skills required: Ability to field players, express emotional subtext, and end scenes.

Suggested preparation: Warm-up physical and vocal; YES LET'S; IT'S TUESDAY; EMOTION TABLEAUX; EMOTIONS.

How it works: A scene is played four times. Players begin with a simple 'open' scene played without a prevailing emotion. The same scene is repeated, changed by a different emotion each time it is replayed.

One player acts as the presenter of the scenes and takes the list of emotions, ordering them as they wish. The presenter introduces each scene to the audience before it is played and brings the lights down at the end of each scene if required.

Choose a variety of emotions that are not too similar. It is then important to order the emotions. A good order will energise the improvisors and keep the scene progressing. If the scene is 'buying a train ticket' with emotions of disgust, calm and panic, play the 'calm' emotion first, then 'disgust' and finally with 'panic'. This provides an opportunity for development. The presenter establishes the scene, reveals a new emotion and caps it off at the end.

The player who introduces the scenes steps to the centre or side of the playing area and speaks very clearly before each little scene is played.

> 'Buying a train ticket.' The team plays the scene.
> 'Buying a train ticket — calm.' The team plays the scene.
> 'Buying a train ticket — disgust.' The team plays the scene.
> 'Buying a train ticket — panic.' The team plays the scene.

It is as if we are watching a replay of the same event from different emotional perspectives.

Some scenes need as few as one or two players. Do not overload the scenes.

Keep the scenes short, simple and to the point. They may last less than ten seconds.

Keep the dialogue and the physical activity as simple as possible. Remember, the scenes have to be repeated. For the most part keep the dialogue and the physicality of each scene as similar as possible. This avoids confusion and allows some licence in the final scene, where players may want to 'cap it off' by finding a peak or tag in the final moment.

•

Tip

- When training, play the game without words to clarify offers and avoid confusion and talking heads.
- Play the game in gibberish to find the emotional content, raise the energy and free the players of words.

SCENE WITH EMOTIONS

performance game
3–4 players
2–3 minutes
14+ years

AKA: Emotional roller-coaster

Description: Situation given. Players play a scene adopting emotions that are called from the side by an offstage team member.

Resource: A clear space. Paper and pen to write a list of emotions. A microphone is sometimes used in performance.

Time-out: If necessary.

Example of a title: Christmas morning; At the pet shop; On a blind date.

Aim: To yield to a range of emotional offers and play a scene with a variety of emotional transitions.

Degree of difficulty: 3

Skills required: Ability to overaccept emotional offers and incorporate them in a scene.

Suggested preparation: Physical and vocal warm-up; Yes let's; It's Tuesday; Emotional tableaux; Emotions; Emotional replay.

How it works: One player is given a list of emotions or gathers them from the audience and lists them on paper. The other players begin an open scene played without a prevailing emotion. At intervals of about ten to twenty seconds, or at a time when the scene is ready to advance and undergo a transition, the offstage player calls the new prevailing emotion (into the microphone, if one is available for performance). At this all the players in the scene experience a transition from the previous emotion to the new emotion called.

As with Emotional replay the order of the emotions should enhance the theatricality of the scene and help develop the plot, extending the current ideas and advancing the scene when necessary. The offstage player can also then be responsible for bringing down the lights.

•

Beware

Changing emotions can be very funny. However, encourage players to find the scene that operates at a deeper level and make clear, justified transitions rather than making gratuitous changes from one emotion to another. Do not play the game simply emphasising the gag value.

Performance: Play this game as part of an emotion challenge rather than 'game on game'.

Comment: This is a close relative of a game called 'Hitch-hiker' I saw played in Vancouver. Players driving in a car pick up two or three hitch-hikers, each of whom brings a different emotion to the scene. Other players in the car yield to and play the new emotion. At times this is very funny but can become vacuous and gaggy. Sidecoach players towards truthful, justified emotional transitions rather than emotional states that appear without reason and do not inform the scene.

EMOTIONAL BODY PARTS

performance game
2–3 players
2–3 minutes
14+ years

Description: Situation given. Each team member endows a part of their own body with a given emotion.

Resource: A clear space. Props and set if required.

Time-out: If necessary.

Example of a title: In a doctor's waiting room: player A – leg/anger; player B – hands/excitement. At the kitchen table: player A – lips/greed; player B – eyebrow/sad.

Aim: To explore the physicality of emotional conditions and states.

Degree of difficulty: 3

Skills required: Ability to extend the named emotion and manifest it physically.

Suggested preparation: Physical and vocal warm-up; Hospital tiggy; It's Tuesday; No-blocking scenes; Emotional tableaux; Emotional replay.

How it works: Players extend the named emotion into their given body part and allow it to stimulate and inform character as they interact with other characters and deal with the developing scene.

These scenes develop bizarre situations and characters as the players overextend their physicality. Beware of players who tend to become introspective and play on their own. Sidecoach towards their awareness of others and to deal with the developing scene. Beware of split focus and overcrowding. The game rarely requires more than two players.

This game is closely related to the character based games Wild kingdom, Mirror bodies and Mirror faces. [See Program seven.]

•

Tip

Emotional body parts is an excellent teaching tool for character development when improvising and acting from a text. It may be more valuable in training than in performance.

Performance: Play as part of an emotional challenge rather than 'game on game'.

FOUR-SQUARE EMOTIONS

classic

performance game
4 players
4 minutes
14+ years

Description: Situation given. The stage is divided into quadrants. A different emotion is assigned to each area. Players are changed by the emotions as they move from area to area throughout the scene.

Resource: A clear space; chalk or two pieces of rope to mark the areas on the floor; card or paper on which to write the emotions. Some set (eg chairs and tables) could be helpful to establish locations.

Time-out: Yes. Establish place.

Example of a title: At a barbecue — jealousy/bliss/greed/lust; In a restaurant — regret/paranoia/empathy/joy. Give a variety of emotions to stimulate a balance of mood and energy.

Aim: To explore a range of emotions and have them inform a scene.

Degree of difficulty: 4

Skills required: Ability to establish location, characters and relationships. Ability to deal with an overload of offers and make transitions.

Suggested preparation: Solid vocal warm-up; Emotions; Entrances and exits; It's Tuesday; Sit, stand, kneel and lie.

How it works: In this game the emotional transitions take place as a result of where the players move in the space. Divide the floor of the playing space into four equal square parts. Place the four cards, each with a different emotion written on it, on the floor, one in each square. These must be clearly visible to the players and it is best if playing to an audience that they can see them too. Players enter and establish the location and begin the scene. As they move across the floor they are immediately affected by the prevailing emotion of each section.

Players can remain in one area for some time then move to another area or they can move quickly through the whole space. Players overaccept, extend and overextend the dominant emotion of the section. The emotions are often portrayed as obsessions. They are manifested physically and vocally.

•

Tip

- Moving quickly through the space is more likely to advance the scene and precipitate an event.
- Use a variety of levels. Rather than just standing, encourage characters to sit, lie, kneel, and use the whole space. Play SIT, STAND, KNEEL AND LIE.
- More than one character can be in one square at the same time.
- To avoid the talking heads syndrome, introduce activities. Characters inform the activity with their prevailing emotion rather than talk about the emotion.
- One part of the body can be in one square expressing one emotion while another part or the rest of the body is in another square expressing something else. For example, a player can be lying on the floor with legs in the happy quadrant, torso in the sad one.
- Sidecoach players away from all talking at once.

•

Remember

Emotions can be expressed without talking. In this game silence is golden.

When this game is good everyone wants to be in it. This may cause overcrowding and too many people talking at once which muddles clarity and splits the focus. Sidecoach players to leave the stage. They return to a different square when the scene needs advancing.

This game usually leads to energetic, excitable scene-work. Sometimes players become so over-excited they forget to listen to other players. They work on their own, hogging the scene, especially if they are on a roll and receiving a positive response from the audience. The game can encourage gagging and being clever. Nevertheless, the skills involved in making a good one work are worth striving for. The game is challenging for even the most skilled players.

This is high energy scene-work and players usually take their physicality and their vocal capacity to the extreme. For this reason a thorough vocal warm-up is essential.

Background: The idea is not new. Early Christian players marked the stage to represent the opposing areas of good and evil. Research into this could stimulate a variety of scene-work styles.

Tip

For experienced players 15+ who crave more

An exciting addition to boost the epic quality of the game and raise the energy level of the scene-work is to 'sing' the scene or play it 'in the style of Shakespeare'. Introduced too early, this will overload the scene. Introduce to skilled players only.

•

Tips for text

Take a piece of text familiar to players. Find a scene where an emotional transition or an emotional subtext is apparent. Experiment with the scene using the floor plan of FOUR-SQUARE EMOTIONS to play the scene. Coach the emotional changes to occur on the lines of the text. Express the changes through voice and movement.

Competition: Judges should be aware of the risk and skill it takes to make a scene in this structure work. They should also be open to rewarding quiet, subtle play that is not as flashy and robust as the work this game often produces. FOUR-SQUARE EMOTIONS will work best 'game on game' if the two titles offer very different locations and a diversity of emotions.

Performance: When it works, this game is a sensation. It is worth persevering with till you crack it. It is one of those games we don't play often. It is risky and often loud, but the audience loves it.

•

Magic moment

One of the first times this game was played in training, Sydney player Mark Owen-Taylor of the *Southern Cross All Stars* revealed its potential. In a virtuoso performance as a waiter, Mark stunned us all when he entered to take the orders and circled the table three times, changing his emotion and attitude to each diner every time he stepped over the line into another emotional zone. He repeated the cycle when serving the food and while removing the plates. With each entrance he further extended his attitude to each character.

TRUTH

classic

performance game
2–4 players
2 minutes
12+ years

Description: Situation, characters or first line given. The scene is played as truthfully as possible, without gagging.

Resource: A clear space, some set, eg chairs.

Time-out: Establish place and perhaps relationships.

Example of a title: Situation: Introducing the new boyfriend to your parents; Telling your parents you are moving out. Characters: Two gravediggers; Two old fighter pilots. First line: 'Mathews, you're fired'; 'You're reading my diary'.

In early training introduce titles that name offers. A first line such as 'You always do that!' is not a great help to fledgling players. It could encourage hedging the issue and wimping out on naming and dealing with the first offer. 'You always use all the hot water,' is a more helpful first line, as it names the conflict from the outset.

Aim: To explore a situation and deal with an event as truthfully as possible.

Degree of difficulty: 3

Skills required: Ability to play character and deal with an event.

Suggested preparation: Circle tag; You; Twenty-one; The present game; It's Tuesday; No-blocking scenes with an objective.

How it works: While it is true to say that all scenes and games are best played from a sense of truth, in this game players deal specifically with scene content, solving its problems as truthfully as possible. The improvisors play the 'truth' of the situation without sending it up. The scene is usually played in real time, ie players do not usually jump periods of time or locations.

Truth scenes are not boring scenes in which little is dealt with and nothing happens. Encourage players to deal with the conflict within the situation and action an event. Something must happen. Someone must be changed. Playing a truthful reaction provides an opportunity for the characters to undergo transitions and be changed by the events in the scene. It is also an opportunity to enjoy good acting. In this game players cannot rely on wacky reactions and zany plot developments. For the most part, the characters are true to life, and their situations mirror reality. However, Truth scenes are not always naturalistic. Truth is, as we know, often stranger than fiction. When scenes are played truthfully, the characters and the situations are often very funny or dramatic. Of all the games, Truth is one of the most valuable teaching tools for acting students because it challanges them to deal with issues. Its educational value and function cannot be underestimated.

Sidecoach players to:

- Confront conflicts
- Deal with issues
- Overaccept the offers given by other players
- Name the offer rather than wimp out
- Be changed by the events

•

Tip

A good Truth scene is compelling theatre. It provides a balance to zany work. Play it when the players need a rest from highly energised improvising and the audience needs a rest from laughing.

Competition: While the degree of difficulty in playing the game is quite low, judges must be aware that teams take a huge risk playing the game in competition. The scenes are not usually funny; consequently scores tend to be low if the skill of the scene-work is not recognised. For these reasons teams are to be commended for taking the risk of playing Truth.

Comment: Individual styles for playing Truth have developed in a number of Theatresports centres. The game was immediately popular with Melbourne and Brisbane players and audiences. Players addressed solid issues and dealt with the content as truthfully as possible. The audience respected the work and the judges' scores reflected the level of risk and acting skills.

In Sydney we experimented for an eternity to find the balance between naturalism, boredom and soap opera. We played scenes truthfully but nothing seemed to happen. What we failed to do was action an event.

Magic moment

We were training at Deck Chair Theatre in Perth when veteran player Phil Thompson played the funniest Truth I have ever seen. Rather than choosing naturalistic situations, he chose situations that were bizarre and played them as truthfully as possible. It worked! In the situation 'An aardvark in a shoe shop', the shopkeeper dealt with the aardvark without panic and continued to serve it, fitting it with shoes. We played the truth in the extreme. No player sent up the situation. The resulting scene was absurdist in style, not unlike Ionesco's *Rhinoceros*. Players find all sorts of delights in such experimentation.

SEDUCTION

classic

performance game
usually 2 players
2 minutes
12+ years

Description: Situation or characters given. By the end of the scene at least one character is seduced by another.

Resource: A clear space.

Time-out: Yes. Establish place.

Example of a title: In a fruit shop; At the automatic teller machine; At the polling booth.

Aim: To affect and change another character.

Degree of difficulty: 3

Skills required: Ability to overaccept offers, action an objective, play character and change status.

Suggested preparation: All those people who; Sound board; Slow motion abuse hurling; Hat game; Three way hats; No-blocking scenes with an objective.

How it works: Characters establish the location. During a scene at least one character is seduced by another. It is preferable not to predetermine who will be the seducer and who will be seduced. The seduction is not always romantic or sexual; a character may be seduced to change their vote, to buy a product or to change their religious or moral convictions. Players remain open to offers which may precipitate an event and the transition. Choose titles which evoke obvious situations for change. Keep the seduction simple.

Seduction rarely involves more than two characters. Too many players will overload the scene. Deploy team members carefully.

Beware

Some players think into the future, searching and planning for the seduction rather than listening for the transitional offer.

DEATH IN A MINUTE
classic

performance game
2–4 players
1 minute
12+ years

Description: Situation given. At the end of the scene at least one character must be dead.

Resource: A clear space.

Time-out: Yes. Establish place.

Example of a title: In a laundromat; On the golf course; In the pit stop; At the darts championship; In a pig pen; Baking bread. Always give offers of place or activity. Never give a weapon or a victim.

Aim: To action an event and deal with a plot transition.

Brisbane team, *The Bastard Squad,* plays DEATH IN A MINUTE —
(left to right) Tom Dunstan, Roger Beames, Doug Bayne, Bridgette Cooper (standing)

Degree of difficulty: 3

Skills required: Ability to deal with a change of focus and status and advance a scene.

Suggested preparation: CIRCLE TAG; WHAT ARE YOU DOING?

How it works: A short scene is played. At the end of one minute at least one of the characters is dead. The death occurs as a result of the scene action. When a character dies, the remaining players deal with the death and take the plot-line forward.

One of the most powerful plot developments involving status and emotional change is the transition that occurs as a result of the death of a character. Death is an important event. It changes the character who dies and the lives of the remaining characters. Death results in a change of focus. It advances the scene, and changes the status of the remaining characters. It initiates transitions.

Players do not gain the full benefit of the game if they decide before the scene has commenced on the mode of death and who will die. This is called 'bridging'. When players know the end result they build a bridge from the beginning of the scene to the end. While this makes for clear narrative, it does not always encourage improvising. In making these decisions before the scene commences, players simply write sketches rather than improvise scenes.

In bridged scenes the death usually occurs at the end of the minute. No new information is revealed as a result of the death. No allowance is made for changes that could occur as a result of the developing scene. The scene does not reach its full potential. It is not spontaneous.

The more beneficial way of playing DEATH IN A MINUTE is not to decide on the victim or mode of death before the scene, but for players to allow the death to occur unexpectedly at the beginning or the middle of the scene. This encourages them to improvise. Coach players to deal with each offer as it comes rather than to think into the future.

The Moose speaks

'Don't use the 55 seconds to justify the scene. Have the death occur within the first 15 seconds, then deal with the death within the situation. When you have a point in the future it is normal to bridge to it. Bridging is justification rather than doing it.'

•

Tip

Remind players not to preplan too much in their time-out, as this limits the potential of the developing scene. An interesting offer that arises during the improvisation may be blocked or dropped if players keep to preplanned decisions.

•

Remember

Enjoy dying: Death is a moment of top status, but it lasts only a moment. It demands a moment of focus and then the scene advances. Life and the scene go on. When a character dies, s/he relinquishes the control of the scene. For a brief moment they are the centre of attention. Encourage players to yield to the offer, enjoy a clear, clean, brief, uncluttered death, enjoy the transition and allow the other player/s to deal with the death and play the remainder of the scene. Dying is a sign of a selfless improvisor who completes their function in the scene and then allows the scene to advance without them.

When introducing DEATH IN A MINUTE, begin with two players and a place but no time-out. Set up the scene without panic. Both players shake hands and say, 'I dare you to die before me'. Now both players want to die. They share a commitment to the event in the scene. Dying early demands giving up the control of the scene and leaving it to the other player. This is difficult for players who want to remain on stage and control the scene. They take a long time to die, or die and then come back to life. Encourage players to instigate the death, die quickly and stay dead.

Give a clear scene location and characters: an office, a boss and a secretary. The boss calls the secretary in. The secretary enters with something, a coffee cup, a pile of papers, a staple gun. Both players overaccept the status.

> Boss: 'Perkins, come into my office.'
> Perkins comes to the door, opens it, slips on the mat and dies.

> Two more players.
> Boss: 'Marjorie, come into my office.'
> Marjorie enters, comes to the desk apologising, 'I'm sorry it's late, Miss Watson, here's your morning coffee.'
> Miss Watson takes the coffee, drinks and dies.

In both examples the scenes are simple but rich with offers:

- The status is clear
- The location is apparent
- The dialogue is short
- The offers are overaccepted
- Players do not know which offer will lead to the death
- The death is unexpected
- A death has occurred within the first ten seconds of the scene

Watching the remaining player's shock at receiving the unexpected death is thrilling. Now the remaining player/s must deal with the death. This is the moment when the improvising really begins. The moment of not knowing what to do or what happens next is confronting for the remaining player/s. In the panic of the moment the remaining player could:

- Stand in the space and look out at the coach in surprise feeling helpless
- Stand in the space and call 'Help!'
- Go to the telephone and dial for help
- Drag the body to hide it, remove it or bury it
- Question the dead player, 'What's wrong? Are you dead?'
- Try to revive the dead character

The above will not allow the living player to deal with the event — the death — or advance the scene. They are signs that the living player is panicking, losing their belief and feeling helpless.

Coach the remaining player to stay in the scene, keep the reality and belief of the scene and to be powerful rather than helpless in the scene.

The Moose speaks

'Say: "Good! I know what to do," and do it!'

Encourage the remaining player to accept the death, believe it and take the scene forward.

Sidecoach: 'Stay in the scene. Look at the body. Say "Good. I know what to do." Do it!'

When the remaining player says, 'Good, I know what to do,' they are empowered to believe they have an idea. This statement activates a scene transition and advances the plot. It provides a status transition.

> Marjorie (looking at Miss Watson's body): 'Good, I know what to do!' She goes to the safe and begins to dial the code.
> Player C is only encouraged to enter to advance the scene.
> Another player appears in the doorway. 'Hold it right there, Marjorie!'
> In shock Marjorie turns, sees she is caught, has a heart attack and drops to the floor dead. The third player is now left with the scene.
> The third player responds, 'Good I know what to do!' and goes to the telephone and calls the police.

Continue these death scenes until all players have experienced the joy of relinquishing the scene and experiencing dealing with the death of another character.

Disposing of the body

As a general rule, do not remove or drag the body of the other player. Dragging the body off or around the stage is potentially dangerous. It can be embarrassing for players if their underwear is unexpectedly revealed. It is also time-wasting and does not advance the scene. Deal with the death, not the body.

Entering players

Players who enter after the death of another character are to be encouraged to bring on new information and deal with the death rather than stall the scene by asking unnecessary questions about the death. 'What happened? Is she dead?' This is no help at all. They need to advance the scene.

Dealing with the scene focus

Encourage players to clearly establish the scene location and play the activity associated with the place. If the scene is at the golf course, the players play golf rather than talk about playing golf. Sidecoach players to make obvious choices and not to be too clever. Simple choices will lead to simple unexpected deaths.

Begin with as few players as possible. One player selects a golf club, lines up and takes a swing. We now have three main focus zones for the scene: the ground (the tee), the body (behind the golf player as they swing) and the horizon (as we follow the ball into the distance after it has been hit). Encourage oncoming players to recognise and support the focus. Sidecoach them to use the focus as a possible offer of death. As player A swings the golf club, player B yields, stands behind as caddy and is knocked over by the swinging club. Player A swings and player C stands in the new horizon focus and is knocked over by the flying ball. Within ten seconds two unexpected and spontaneous deaths have occurred simply as a result of playing an activity and yielding to the focus.

•

Magic moment

The funniest DEATH IN A MINUTE I've seen was in a workshop in Hobart when Nigel Curtain-Smith and Gary McCaffrie played DEATH IN A MINUTE in a casino. They set up the scene over the roulette wheel, Nigel calling, 'Place your bets, place your bets'.

A third player entered, and the three watched the roulette wheel spin. On the third round, Nigel and Gary simultaneously watched the ball fly out of the wheel towards the third player, who overaccepted the focus and dropped to the floor dead, killed by the flying roulette ball.

Tips for tots

For players 8–12 years: FAINTING IN A MINUTE

The game and concept of DEATH IN A MINUTE is not usually applicable to players 8–12 years. One teacher pushed to play the game by a class of eight-year-olds was confronted with a problem. Some children were confused and upset by the concept of death and disturbed by the game. However, others in the class were not affected and played the game quite happily. To overcome the problem the teacher substituted a faint for the death and played FAINTING IN A MINUTE. The faint is the death substitute in every way, and the game and its coaching are the same. The faint allows players to come back to life at the end of the scene without confusion.

Dimming the lights

Dimming the lights in training during the last 10–15 seconds of the scene reminds players to action an event and draw the scene to a close. This is particularly helpful if players are stalling the death. It is a useful theatrical device.

Tragic deaths

Not all DEATH IN A MINUTE scenes are funny. The moment of realisation when the remaining player is confronted with the death of the other character can be tragic and highly dramatic. Encourage players who are ready to do so to overaccept moments of deep emotion: grief, rage, glee — the full gamut. Characters may advance the scene by expressing revenge and despair. These scenes are moving and allow players to develop a range of emotional responses.

•

Tips for text

Like the improvisor, a crafted actor does not bridge to the end but steps from moment to moment being changed by what is said to them. To achieve this, actors try not to think into the future. This is not easy for the young actor who has rehearsed and performed the same play many times.

In the play *Romeo and Juliet* for example, Juliet's transition from the hopeful young wife to the grief-stricken widow will be more compelling if she wakes in the tomb with hope, expecting Romeo to be alive. The greater her hope at finding him alive, the deeper the tragedy when she finds him and discovers that he is dead.

I remember an incident in a student production of *Romeo and Juliet* at NIDA where I saw the improvised moment meet and inform the written text.

Juliet awoke in the tomb. The scene was not compelling. It was well rehearsed, good, careful acting. I believe the actress was expecting Romeo to be dead rather than believing him to be alive. My mind wandered. I stopped listening. The stage seemed quite dark and I found myself looking at her costume rather than listening to the words.

Suddenly the stage seemed to be drenched in light. The scene came alive. The unexpected happened. My eyes were glued to the stage. Juliet could not find the dagger. The actor's worst nightmare had occurred. Romeo had forgotten to bring it on. Juliet became alive. The audience moved forward in their seats. The electricity pumped. None of us knew what would happen next, but we all knew that somehow she had to die.

Juliet kissed Romeo, begged him to come back to life, ran her hands up and down his body, searched his pockets for a sign of hope. How would she kill herself? No dagger! The stage was bare save for a casket. At last she leapt up. We watched her resignation, 'Good, I know what to do'. She searched for a means to die.

Of all the theatre I have seen, nothing can compare with the thirty seconds that must have seemed an eternity to Helen Buday as she ran like lightning once around the stage, twice around the stage. For the first time the tomb became real, her costume took on a different shape, her body was totally engaged in the business of seeking a means to die.

At the end of the third run she leapt up onto the casket, and pounding and pounding, she beat her head against the casket until dead. The audience sat in shock. We had seen a most compelling moment of believable theatre.

I do not suggest for a minute that adrenalin at this level is a prerequisite for good theatre. But there is something to be said for live theatre when the audience witnesses unexpected and crafted change. An electricity between stage and audience develops and the audience thrills at the possibility of what will happen next. This is the risk an improvisation audience wants to see and the thrill crafted improvisors and actors give them.

Carl Reiner: 'A brilliant mind in panic is a wonderful thing to see.'

Developing a character

program 7

Commandment

S/he that tries to be clever, is not;
while s/he that is clever, doesn't try.

The process of offer and yield and the study of status, endowment and transition work establish valuable foundation skills for the development of character. Theatresports provides the opportunity for players to develop these skills and use the games to explore and inform characterisation working on text and through improvisation.

A major function of characterisation in the drama classroom is to give players an opportunity to express attitudes and beliefs within their own life experience. Players are also encouraged to listen and respond to a variety of opinions and to understand how the world is perceived by people of different sexes, races, status positions and cultures.

Players of eight years and younger recognise the obvious differences between characters that are old and young, male and female, mean and nice, good and evil, and find ways of depicting and playing them. In their personal play children role play recognised character types: mothers and fathers, children and adults. They mimic characters based on occupations: truck drivers, nurses, teachers, models, shop keepers, office workers. Their interpretations are naturally insightful and often surprisingly accurate.

Yet of all the areas of Theatresports, characterisation is the least developed and usually the most overlooked. Too often Theatresports characterisations are clichéd and two dimensional. Butchers are played as big and fat; police are portrayed as red-necked and unintelligent.

While these choices can be very funny and present an opportunity for satire and parody, it is valuable for players also to endeavour to make wider choices and develop richer characters based on a sense of truth.

part A

FOUNDATION SKILLS

There are many ways to stimulate the impulse to develop character. Players respond to a variety of stimuli. A player reads an article about a bag lady in the newspaper which triggers an emotional response. The photo next to the article gives the player a visual stimulus. They see the shape of the face and use the image of it as a simple mask to stimulate the first layer of the characterisation.

Another player reads a speech from Shakespeare. The rhythm of the words, the images they convey, the metre of the lines and the physicality of the language trigger a response and give them ideas for characterisation.

Building on the offer and yield process from Program one, introduce the following simple exercises to stimulate character development. The characterisations begin when players yield to and overaccept their responses, and extend them. After working on their own they meet up with other characters, endow them with qualities and develop a status structure, building the interactions into scene-work. Develop this work into role play situations, text work, and then into playing Theatresports games.

WALKS

training game
2–32 players
10–20 minutes
8+ years

Description: Players experience a variety of walks from which they build characters.

Resource: A clear space; a tambourine, drum or taped music.

Time-out: Some description and modelling (ie a clear demonstration as an example) may be required but no time-out for preparation.

Example of a title: Not applicable.

Aim: To stimulate a variety of physical responses from which to develop characters.

Degree of difficulty: I

Skills required: Ability to use space, listen and respond to vocal commands, and work as an individual.

Suggested preparation: Physical and vocal warm-up; CIRCLE TAG; HERE AND NOW; THE MIRROR GAME; and other slow motion work could be helpful to harness physical energy.

How it works: Build on the physical and freeze work from previous programs, in particular, Knife and fork, Emotional Tableaux and Mirror exercises. The group work as individuals spread out over the space, working from a standing position.

Step one: Each player imagines a string leading them from a specific part of their body. The string pulls them along, exaggerating their movement, encouraging them to walk in a new way.

A string pulls players:

- Up from the top of their heads, centre of the crown, pulling them up onto their toes
- Out from their nose, pulling the neck and upper back forward and causing the top half of the body to lead the lower half
- Out of the upper chest and breast bone, propelling neck and chest forward
- By the lower stomach, tilting the pelvis forward, curving the lower spine inward
- By the bottom, causing the lower back to become concave
- By the knees, causing the legs to bend slightly

Begin each new walk slowly. Imagine the string as if it were real. Take hold of it and pull it to make a slow, slight adjustment. Players make the necessary changes as their bodies yield to the new adjustments.

Step two: After a short time experiencing each walk, bring the group together to discuss and consider the following:

How does each adjustment affect the breath? Where is the breath now held? Where and how does the body compensate for these adjustments? How does this walk affect other parts of the body: legs, arms, head, face, stomach, etc? Is it uncomfortable? If so, where?

What sort of a person walks like this: old, young, important, tough, scared, lonely, popular, sick, etc? Many answers and ideas will arise. All are correct.

Have you seen a person who walks like this? If so, where? Who? What were they wearing? Where were they going? Describe them.

Step three: Set off again with the same or a different walk. Stop and meet another person (who walks the same way or differently). Introduce yourself to another character by name and occupation. Have a simple conversation about the weather. Tell each other where you are going.

Step four: Players choose a walk they wish to explore further. The objective of this exercise is to give players a variety of experiences, tasks, obstacles and situations during which they make simple choices as their character. Players begin the work in silence, spread out across the space, each working as an individual. Give all characters an objective — eg to catch a train to the city. Have the characters begin from home. Narrate a simple scenario as they walk. Give them the impetus to move quickly, slowly, to stop and look at something, to be distracted, to pick something up off the ground, to think they are lost, to ask directions of another character. After they have reached their destination, have them return home.

Step five: Without the imaginary string, players develop characters based on different walks: with toes and feet turned out; with toes and feet turned in; on the heels; on the toes.

Bring the group together to discuss the effects of these adjustments.

Rudolf Laban

The processes and teaching of Rudolf Laban are complementary to the above exercises. Laban's 'eight efforts' of movement allow us to further explore characterisation. Use the 'efforts' as a basis for developing character movements to inform the above exercises. [See Appendix C.]

•

Tip

For all the above exercises: Sometimes free work of this nature is a breeding ground for chaos and could become physically dangerous when thirty players are given free rein of a space. For younger players and groups that require strong direction, structure the work with a tambourine or drum. To keep control of the work within a tight structure, build freeze points into the movement work. At the sound of the drum, players freeze. From these freezes build in runs, walks, interactions and conversations between players across the space.

When the group has explored a variety of characters, bring two together for scene-work. Explore additions of costume to develop the characters further. [See part B this program — Scene-work.]

Masks

The development of mask work and its role in improvisation is a study well beyond the scope of this book. However, there is value in introducing simple mask techniques to explore and develop character. Visual stimulus is a powerful tool. When players wearing a nose or a mask respond to their reflection in a mirror and yield to and overaccept what they see, deep impulses are released and interesting characters develop.

In the work below which stimulates similar responses, when I refer to facial masks I mean the mask made by the muscles of the face — not an external mask worn over the nose, face or head. Players create facial masks

Flying Pig

Melbourne players Mark Neal and Andrew Goodone (masked)

with their own faces and use them as a starting point to create characters. For more advanced external mask and trance work, see Keith Johnstone's *Improvisation and the Theatre.*

MAKING FACES

training game
2–32 players
10–20 minutes
8+ years

Description: Players pass the same and different facial expressions to each other around a circle. These become a stimulus from which to build a character.

Resource: A clear space.

Time-out: Not applicable.

Example of a title: Not applicable.

Aim: To explore the movement of facial muscles and the expressions they create as a stimulus for building a character.

Degree of difficulty: 1

Skills required: Ability to accept and extend physical offers. Ability to make eye contact with another player.

Suggested preparation: Physical and vocal warm-up; YOU; YES; THE MIRROR GAME to harness group energy.

How it works — step one — passing a clap: Begin with players standing in a circle. One player looks at the player next to him/her in the circle, makes eye contact and sends a clap in his/her direction. The clap is passed carefully and slowly from player to player, each making eye contact with the next. Build the speed of the clap around the circle, keeping the clarity of eye to eye contact until the clap flies around the circumference. Change direction, moving the clap first around the circumference then across the circle. Build a vocal sound into the clapping, passing both to the next player.

Step two — passing a face: Sitting or standing in a circle, one member of the group passes a face (a facial expression) to the next player who in turn passes the same face on to the next. Receiving players accept the face and send it on to the next player in the circle.

Players make eye contact with each other as they give and receive the facial offer. Begin slowly. As accuracy and concentration increase, pass the faces more quickly. As the face is passed, allow the breath to release. Players send the breath with the face as part of the offer. Allow the release of breath to develop into sound, and eventually into a word, phrase and sentence. All these are developments, not predetermined responses. As the faces inevitably grow and change, encourage players to allow their bodies to respond. The work will develop further if the same face travels more than once around the circle.

Step three: Working individually in the space, players experiment with a range of facial expressions. They recall those they experienced in the circle and develop new ones. Using the facial mask as the initial impetus, they adjust their body to build characters that move around the space. They interact with other characters, introduce themselves, develop conversations, and experiment by making a variety of choices.

DRAWING FACES

training game
1–32 players
20–60 minutes
8+ years

Description: Players draw simple faces on paper and use them as starting points for creating a character.

Resource: A clear space, paper, crayons, textas.

Time-out: Take time to look at the picture, making the appropriate facial and other physical adjustments as required — but no other preparation time is necessary.

Example of a title: An activity and/or a place of work and a function: At the supermarket stacking shelves; At the railway station collecting tickets.

Aim: To accept and explore a visual offer as a starting point for creating a character.

Degree of difficulty: 2

Skills required: Ability to overaccept a visual stimulus and maintain the physical and vocal adjustment.

Suggested preparation: Physical and vocal warm-up; YOU; MAKING FACES.

How it works — step one: Begin with the whole group working together. Each player draws a simple face with crayons or textas on paper. These are not designed to be works of art but simple drawings that reveal basic facial features: eyes, mouth, ears, hair, glasses; and express simple emotions — happiness, fear, sadness and so on work best. Players give the characters names which they write at the bottom of the pictures: Flossy, Joe, Pinhead, Boof, etc.

Step two: Choose one player and a drawing. Players work with their own drawing or another player's drawing. Hold the drawing up to the player and ask them to adjust their face to recreate the face that is drawn. The player makes the facial and physical adjustments. Now the coach talks to the new character, calling them by name. Ask them questions as if meeting a new friend for the first time.

Coach: 'Hello, what's your name?'
Character: 'Flossie.'
Coach: 'Hello, Flossie. You look very worried. What's the matter?'
Character: 'I lost my bus ticket.'

Sidecoach as if it was a scene. Read the offers given by the player. Try not to put ideas into their head. Help them to learn more about their character by extending their own ideas.

•

Good idea

Sometimes it is a good idea for the coach to mirror the player's facial adjustments and speech. This gives the player the confidence to trust their choice and keep it active.

Step three: Players now work individually. They choose a drawing and work with it, making the facial, physical and vocal adjustments suggested to them by the drawing. They move around the space finding the appropriate walk of the new character, introduce themselves to other characters and have short, simple conversations.

The drawings stimulate similar impulses to those stimulated by traditional face masks. But here the player's face is revealed rather than covered. Most players find they need to return to their drawing at regular intervals for further information and inspiration to maintain the initial energy of the character. To support this process keep the drawings visible to the players at all time. When working with a player, hold their drawing up to their sight line. Players working alone keep their drawing pinned on the wall or placed on a chair and return to it as often as necessary.

Observation

Observation is the natural key to characterisation. Observing people and imagining details about them and their lives gives the actor and the improvisor information to bring to improvised and text-based work. Seeing a character in the street and bringing the observed information into the classroom is exciting. It is more valuable to use first-hand experience of a living character than to copy characters seen on film or television.

Truth is stranger than fiction, and real life holds a store of choices to be observed. Our immediate environments: school, shopping centre, family, street, local picture theatre, church, park — are all places rich with characters of different ages, sizes and shapes, from different backgrounds, and with a variety of ambitions, lifestyles, occupations, speech patterns and idiosyncrasies. All these can be explored in the training and rehearsal room with dignity and respect for the human condition and spirit.

•

Beware

It is not necessary or always appropriate that players go to the extreme of watching strangers in public for long periods. In some situations observation is potentially dangerous. Do not encourage long observation periods on the street or in public places; these could endanger students.

Don't send players under 18 years unsupervised into public places as 'characters'. Players are placed in potentially dangerous situations if they are in role out of the safety of a rehearsal environment. This work is generally more appropriate for adult players in professional vocational training.

PEOPLE OBSERVATION

1–32 players
10–40 minutes
8+ years

Description: Players observe people in the community and bring their observations into the training room, where they develop them into characterisations.

Resource: A clear space and some costume. A note pad and pen.

Time-out: Time in observation usually 3–20 minutes.

Example of a title: Old man in the fruit shop; Bag lady in the park; Punk in the laundrette; Model at the races.

Aim: To develop an awareness of physical and vocal characterisation.

Degree of difficulty: 3

Skills required: Ability to observe a real person and make the appropriate physical, vocal and internal adjustments to bring a representation of the character to life. Ability to maintain and extend the choices made and make detailed physical and vocal adjustments.

Suggested preparation: Some detailed discussion as to the nature and purpose of observation of characters is necessary. Physical and vocal warm-up and preparation; MAKING FACES; WALKS; DRAWING FACES; and extended characterisation work derived from these activities. Scene-work where characters from these activities are brought together is also essential. [See this Program — Scene-work.]

How it works: Building on the interest and skills sparked from the above exercises, players look to real life characters and make the physical, vocal and internal adjustments to 'become' them.

This exercise can be as detailed as the maturity and ability of the players permit. Players of 8–12 years develop detailed characterisations based on observations of simple walks, faces and shapes of the spines of characters they see in everyday life. Older players develop more complex characterisations. [See Tips for text below.]

Some players find jotting down notes and drawing the shape of the spine, facial expression and noting descriptions or what they heard the character say helpful reminders of the details.

The preparation is brought into the classroom, where individuals work in the space and bring their characters to life. Characters introduce themselves to each other and have an informal conversation as experienced in the above exercises.

Selected individuals bring their characters to life in front of the whole group. They are interviewed by the coach, who sidecoaches to make further adjustments if necessary. The coach's role at this point is to sense what is missing from the characterisation and ask the character questions that will answer and clarify details. From what part of the body does the character move? If they had a string leading them, from where is it pulling?

Remember, work from what they know and fill in the details through questions. Stimulate their imagination further: 'Have a think about what Miko's hobbies would be. What is his favourite food? Describe where he lives. What type of books does he read? Can he read? Did he go to school?'

Such questions explore the unknown territory of a character. Beware of making moral or other judgments about characters.

After each characterisation, the coach, the player and the rest of the group discuss the background and the finer details of the character. The player is given feedback about the strengths of the characterisation.

•

Tip

Ensure that none of the characterisations is based on people known to the group if the characterisation could be hurtful to the person concerned.

A day in the life

Some groups require detailed stimulation from the coach to make choices and experience a deep sense of belief. Players in character are talked through a complete day in the life of their character. They live this as it is narrated by the coach. Begin with each player working at the same time, as a character in their own space in the room. They are asleep in their house, on their park bench, etc (each player/character making their own choice). Take them through a journey, waking up, having breakfast, dressing, preparing to go outside, out in the street, achieving an objective, moving in a hurry, moving slowly, waiting, making a phone call, asking for directions, returning home, preparing an evening meal, etc.

Use the information to develop the character further. Detailed discussion regarding the information found in this exercise is a good idea.

•

Tips for text

Players over 15 years develop extremely detailed characterisations involving personal histories and life objectives, and may develop scripted monologues and performance pieces. The list of questions to ask of characters is endless. Here are some ideas to enhance characterisation:

- Who am I?
- Where am I?
- What am I doing?
- What is my name?
- How old am I?
- Where was I born?
- Where do I live?
- Who are the members of my family?
- What are my social, financial, political circumstances and beliefs?
- If I were an animal what would I be?
- If I were an element, what would I be: fire/water/air/earth?
- What are my physical characteristics?
- What are my likes and dislikes?
- What opinions do I hold dear?
- What do I do to achieve these?

- What do I do each day?
- What are my hobbies?
- What am I wearing? Why?
- What is in my bag or pockets?
- What are two extreme points of my personality?
- What is my life objective?
- What is my status relationship to other people?
- What are the three most important events that have occurred in my life?

This list is by no means exhaustive. Its purpose is to spark further questions.

•

Tips for text

Ask the above questions of a scripted character when working from a text. Read and make a list of what every other character says about the specific character to avoid making unsubstantiated judgments. Characteristics may be drawn from observation but must coincide with the information given by the writer.

ANIMAL OBSERVATION

training game
1–32 players
10–14 minutes
15+ years

Description: Players observe animals and bring their observations into the training room, where they develop their observations into characterisations.

Resource: A clear space, a note pad and pen, animals to observe.

Time-out: Some preparation time is required for the animal observation. This can be as short as 10-20 minutes or it can take place over a number of weeks, according to the maturity of the players and the purpose of the exercise.

Example of a title: Not applicable.

Aim: To develop observation skills and explore the physical rhythms, habits and idiosyncrasies of animals and develop these into human characterisations.

Degree of difficulty: 4

Skills required: Ability to observe an animal and to bring a representation of the animal and its characteristics to life. Ability to maintain and extend the choices and make detailed physical, vocal and internal adjustments to portray the character.

Suggested preparation: Some detailed discussion as to the nature and purpose of observation of the animals is necessary. Physical and vocal warm-up and preparation; MAKING FACES; WALKS; DRAWING FACES; and extended characterisation work derived from these activities. Develop into scene-work where characters from these activities are brought together. [See this Program — Scene-work.]

How it works: Building on the above introductory character work, players look to animals (domestic and/or zoo) with the intention of making the necessary physical, vocal and internal adjustments required to represent and 'become' them.

This exercise can be as detailed as the maturity and ability of the players permits. Capitalise on the interest and skills sparked from the above exercises.

Step one — observing the animal: Observation ranges from detailed long-term study at the zoo to simply watching a domestic pet. Players should consider the following in their observation:

- How does the animal move? From which part of its body does it move?
- Where is its body most developed? Why?
- Where does it live? What is its natural habitat? Is it in it?
- What does it eat?
- How does it eat?
- How does it react: to other animals/at feeding time/with its young/when it sleeps?
- Does it express emotions? If so, how, which ones and in what circumstances?
- What are its rhythms (fast, slow, repetitive, erratic)?
- How do these manifest?
- How does it communicate with other animals and humans?
- What does it do when it is still?

This list is by no means exhaustive but is intended as a guide and a stimulus for further questions and discovery.

Step two — recreating the animal: Players work as a whole group across the space at the same time. Then individuals explore their work in front of the whole group. They develop detailed characterisations based on observations of simple animal movements and characteristics. Players recreate the animal from their observation, depicting the animal in a number of circumstances and moods: sleeping, eating, playing, still, moving, etc.

Step three: Two or three animals come together for short periods to interact, rather than play a scene. Players explore the animals' modes of communication and their status relationships.

Step four — making transitions from animals to people 15+: The following exercise is best with players over 15 who have the ability to make detailed observations of animals and can use their imagination to transfer these traits to human behaviour.

The characteristics and rhythms of the grumpy, tired, snarly old dog could make a transition to a grumpy, slow moving shopkeeper; the quick-rhythmed, swooping seagull to the efficient nurse in a ward of noisy children; the strutting peacock to the high status guy at the night-club parading himself on the dance floor, and so on.

Players begin as their chosen animal living in its environment for one to two minutes, then make the transition from the animal to the human. They place their human character in the relevant environment — place of work, bus stop, etc — and give them a task and an objective. They create a scenario that lasts one or two minutes (increase times as appropriate). After the whole group has worked at the same time, individual players may wish to perform their character transitions for the group.

•

Tips for text

Some texts present perfect opportunities to develop characters from animal observations. I remember a student production of Brecht's *The Threepenny Opera* in which the gang characters were based on observations of different animals: rat, squirrel, fox, giraffe, etc. Each character had an individual rhythm, a personality and an inner and outer life, regardless of the size of the part and the number of lines.

•

Beware

In all the above character exercises, WALKS, MAKING FACES, DRAWING FACES, ANIMAL OBSERVATIONS and PEOPLE OBSERVATIONS, some players experience marked physical and vocal changes. They become taller, shorter, bigger, smaller. They experience changes in their way of walking and in the adjustment of their spine. The pitch and range of their voices change. For some, the change in vocal inflection is so marked that their accents change. Players are vulnerable to physical and vocal strain if they are not prepared with a thorough warm-up. Pay close attention to these adjustments and sidecoach players to release physical and vocal tension should it arise.

Props, hats and costume

Introduce hats, props and costume to further inform choices made in the above exercises. However, remember that it is more valuable to spend time exploring the physical and vocal traits of characters than it is to rely on funny hats and silly costume to bring characters to life. Encourage players to select costume and props suggested by an idea that results from exploration of the character, rather than spending time on external accessories as the first step. Encourage minimal use of props, hats and costume. More can be revealed through one hat or a pair of shoes than through too many bits and pieces.

Too much time spent on costume and props may defeat the purpose of the exercises and interrupt the spontaneous impulse. By the same token, other players experience marked and inspired character changes when dressed in full costume. The costume should inspire characterisation rather than swamp the processes achieved in the above exercises.

part B

SCENE-WORK

When players are confident and have experienced a sense of achievement in the above foundation exercises, bring two characters from any of the exercises together in front of the whole group to play a short scene. Place the characters in a shared environment. Keep the characters physically active. Set a task within the environment, eg stacking the shelves and ringing up the cash register at the supermarket, making pizza in a restaurant, sorting letters at the post office. Keep the scenes short to medium in length (two to three minutes). The characters interact, find their status relationship and complete their task. As skills progress give characters scene objectives: to ask the other character out on a date, to tell them 'I love you', to teach them a new part of the job, etc.

Character endowment

Remember the importance of endowment work during characterisations. Endowment is an important key to truthful performance. It enriches and deepens our investment in all the ideas and characters. Characters' treatment of each other clarifies our understanding of the characters and their relationship/s.

Further enrich the scene-work by giving the characters an attitude to their circumstances, job, environment, the other character/s. When a character endows their occupation with being important, for example, they are energised in the scene. When they endow the other character with being charismatic, important, funny, and so on, they have an opinion of the other character. This strengthens their own character. It also provides a stimulus giving them something active to do and something to think about as they work towards completing their task and achieving their scene objective.

Remind players to be changed by the information in the scene and to make status and emotional transitions as a result of information and events in the scene.

Role play and long improvisations

When players are confident in their coach and trust their peer group, the characterisations can become quite deep and continue for some time.

With harmonious groups who have developed skills to this point, it is possible to bring all the players together into a long role play. Introduce a common theme or goal to bring all the characters together — for example, at a school reunion or as citizens coming together to solve a common problem such as a traffic issue or a housing shortage in their shared community.

Long role play requires careful structuring. In preparation, players need to discuss the objectives for these gatherings. The coach best serves the scene by playing the role of facilitator of the event, such as the host for the reunion or the convener of the meeting. The coach's objectives are to keep the belief of all players at a maximum, keep the scene advancing and to stimulate the players to make choices, solve problems and interact with other characters. The coach needs a persona with a name and would probably benefit from, say, one piece of costume.

Longer improvisations such as these last for twenty to forty minutes or more. Players will have a richer experience if they have spent some time developing characters by having made clear choices about the life and history of their persona and chosen some articles of costume.

Players should leave the space and re-enter the environment in character, endowing it with being the community welfare centre, council chambers, police station, etc.

At the close of the scene, players leave the space as the character and return out of costume as themselves. Take time after longer improvisations for players to derole and discuss what occurred and what they experienced. Deroling involves removal of costume and a return from the character's physical and vocal traits to the player's own. [See Process Training sessions – Wind-downs, deroling and centring.] Make time at the end of the session for this. It is very important.

part C

THEATRESPORTS PERFORMANCE GAMES

The following Theatresports games are for the specific purpose of developing character. While these are performance games, their role in the rehearsal and training room cannot be overlooked. They are useful as a stimulus to developing characters when building a play, devising a text or acting from a text, and offer stimuli to creating instant characters. All these games should be considered as a part of the character-building process and used as a stimulus for further work. They build on the skills developed in Parts A and B of this program.

WILD KINGDOM

performance game
usually 4 players
2–4 minutes
10+ years

Description: Situation and animals given. Players develop characters based on their given animal.

Resource: A clear space.

Time-out: Yes — to determine each player's animal.

Example of a title: Lion, penguin, rat and snake in a fast food restaurant; Vulture, koala, kangaroo and mouse at the blood bank.

Aim: To explore a variety of rhythms and characteristics from which to develop characters.

Degree of difficulty: 3

Skills required: Ability to extend physical and vocal impulses and make character choices.

Suggested preparation: Physical and vocal warm-up; HOSPITAL TIGGY; SOUND BOARD; all character exercises from Parts A and B of this program; WALKS, MAKING FACES; ANIMAL OBSERVATION; NO-BLOCKING SCENES with two characters.

How it works: Players usually enter as animals and metamorphose within the first twenty to thirty seconds (called by coach in training, timekeeper in performance, or at the players' discretion). Players develop characters based on the physical and vocal characteristics of their animal. They play the scene interacting with other characters.

•

Beware

Players take care not to pull focus. This is difficult, as the animals are often hilarious. Players enter one at a time and carefully share the focus.

•

Tip

Characters support the scene by finding their function in it. For example, in a restaurant: the penguin — the waiter, the koala — the sleeping drunk in the corner.

Animal observation develops valuable acting skills. Choose animals that will challenge players. If a player is naturally high voiced with a fast rhythm, give them a hippopotamus to slow them down and deepen the vocal range. There is a wealth of work to be developed from this game.

•

Tips for text

Develop text characters from animal observation. Individualise chorus characters by basing each on a different animal.

MIRROR FACES

performance game
usually 4 players
2–4 minutes
10+ years

Description: Situation given. Players are given facial expressions by members of the opposing team. These are used as a basis for characters.

Resource: A clear space.

Time-out: No.

Example of a title: At the hairdresser's.

Aim: To explore character through the facial mask and vocalisation.

Degree of difficulty: 3

Skills required: Ability to respond to visual stimuli and extend physical and vocal range.

Suggested preparation: Physical and vocal warm-up; HOSPITAL TIGGY; YES; YOU; SOUND BOARD; MAKING FACES; DRAWING FACES. Bring these characters together in simple NO-BLOCKING SCENES with an objective and simple endowment of both place and the other character.

How it works: Players form two teams of four players. Players from team A and players from team B line up facing each other. Each team A player makes a different facial expression, which the team B player opposite them mirrors. Team A players leave the stage. Immediately sidecoach each team B player to give voice to their facial expression with a sound and encourage it into a word or phrase. Some will automatically begin to speak in character. Team B players then start the scene with their given facial expressions and starting situation. During the scene they develop their character based on the face as a character stimulus. Players are not required to remain in this shape all the time. It is, however, their prevailing mask — the base from which the character works and to which they periodically return.

Not all the characters are active in the scene at the same time. Not all characters are required to speak. At the end of the scene team B players give different faces to team A players. Team A plays its scene.

•

Beware

Vocal work can become strained and cause restriction if breath becomes strangled. Sidecoach the breathing and relieve players of over-contorting facial and other muscles.

MIRROR BODIES

performance game
usually 4 players
2–4 minutes
10+ years

Description: Situation given. Players are given body shapes by members of the opposing team. These are used as a basis for characters.

Resource: A clear space.

Time-out: No.

Example of a title: In a doctor's waiting room. A place where characters meet.

Aim: To explore character developed from a physical stimulus.

Degree of difficulty: 3

Skills required: Ability to respond to physical stimulus and extend physical and vocal range.

Suggested preparation: Physical and vocal warm-up; Hospital tiggy; Yes; You; Sound board; Walks; Making faces; Drawing faces; observing animals and people. Bring these characters together in simple No-blocking scenes with objectives and simple endowment of place and the other character.

How it works: Four players from team A and four players from team B line up facing each other. Each team A player makes a different physical shape, which the team B player opposite them mirrors. Team A players leave the stage. Immediately sidecoach each team B player to give voice and action to their physical shape. Some will automatically begin to speak and move in character. Team B players then start the scene with their given physical shapes and starting situation. During the scene they develop their characters using the physicality as a stimulus. Players do not have to remain in this shape all the time. It is, however, the base from which the character works and to which s/he returns periodically.

Not all the characters have to be active in the scene at the same time. Not all characters have to speak. At the end of the scene team B players give different physical shapes to team A players. Team A plays its scene.

•

Beware

Vocal work can become strained if the body is uncomfortable and the breath becomes trapped. Sidecoach the breathing and relieve players of over-contorting facial and other muscles.

section 4

warm-up games

Warm-up games

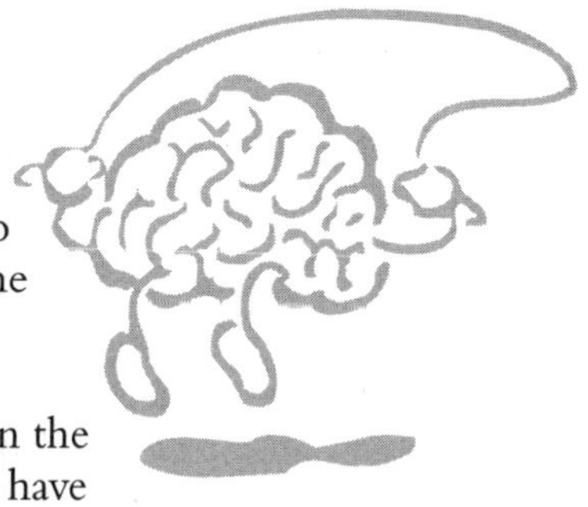

Begin each training session with a physical and vocal warm-up and at least one warm-up game to support your session plan and harness the energy of the group. A good warm-up includes the whole group. Choose games that do not eliminate players or have winners or losers. Games which have a winner early in the session split and deflate the energy of the players who have dropped out.

Assess the energy of the group and choose a warm-up that channels the energy and supports the skill you'll be developing in the session. Players of all ages will benefit from spending at least a fifth of the session warming up. I recommend a warm-up of three to ten minutes at the beginning of a thirty to fifty minute drama lesson or training session.

Note: The success of each game varies from group to group. For example, some groups take an instant liking and respond well to the ball games, while other groups do not like them or lack the concentration span to gain the full potential from them. For this reason I have not included a 'degree of difficulty' assessment in the following warm-up games. It is not important that each group play every warm-up game. Experiment and adjust the warm-up as appropriate to the personality of each group. Many of these suggestions serve the same skills. They develop peripheral vision, eye contact and group trust and encourage the spontaneous impulse.

•

Tips for tots

Many training and performance games are well beyond the skills and maturity of younger players. In the primary drama or improvisation session, warm-up games take longer and often constitute whole sessions. Sometimes groups work for thirty to forty minutes in the hall. Other times a game is played for fifteen minutes in the classroom between one part of the day's work and the next. Choose the games and the length of time you wish to play them according to the needs and concentration span of the group.

MEETING AND GREETING

up to 32 players
10–15 minutes
8+ years

This game was taught to me by Heather Robb

Description: Players introduce themselves to every other player.

Resource: A clear space.

Aim: To make physical and eye contact with other players and to learn the first name of every player.

How it works: Group stands in a circle. Player A (the coach) enters the circle and shakes hands with the player to their left. Player A says their own name first as they shake hands. Player B says their own name. Player A repeats player B's name and player B repeats player A's name.

Player A: 'Lyn.'
Player B: 'Penelope.'
Player A: 'Penelope.'
Player B: 'Lyn.'

Player A then moves on to the next player on their left. When player A has met two or three players around the circle, player B follows, and so on. All players meet and greet every other player twice, once as they move around the circle, and once when they are in their original circle position and standing still. The last person to move is the player who was standing to the right of player A at the commencement of the game. After the last player has completed their circuit, the whole group says all the names together in order around the circle.

This is a most effective name game because each player makes hand to hand and eye to eye contact while speaking to each other player. The status of all players is kept even.

•

Tip

Keep strictly to the exchange of names and hand shakes only.

•

Tips for text

Play the game in character from the play the group is rehearsing. Characters introduce themselves and endow each other with the status and the relationship informed by the text. Players bow or curtsy to other characters of higher status etc.

NAME GAME

4–32 players
3–5 minutes
8+ years

Description: Players say the names of other players.

Resource: A clear space.

Aim: To reinforce the knowledge of the names of all the players in the group.

How it works: Name games are many and varied. This is the most common, and involves sitting in a circle and saying names to rhythmic beats.

The group establishes a simple four beat rhythm. Beat one is slapping the thighs, beat two is clapping, beat three is clicking the fingers of the right hand and beat four is clicking the fingers of the left hand. When the rhythm has been established (not too fast), the first player says their name on the third beat (as they click the fingers on their right hand) and then says the name of another player on the fourth beat (as they click the fingers on their left hand). The new player named continues the sequence. And so on.

For example: slap clap Arnum Linden, slap clap Linden Ari, slap clap Ari Tessa, etc.

Players keep the beat constant. This is good fun and excellent for rhythm development. The game relies on all players having preknowledge of each other's names.

WHERE DO YOU COME FROM?

training game for TIME-OUT
4–32 players
5–10 minutes
12+ years

Description: Players form teams and mime occupations which are guessed by the opposing team.

Resource: An extremely large, clear space.

Aim: To yield to the first idea, develop quick decision making for 'time-out', to introduce mime.

Skills to be developed: Listening; teamwork; mime; fast decision making; making, accepting and naming the first offer.

How it works: The group divides into two. The halves stand at opposite ends of a large space in two parallel lines facing each other, with the largest part of the room between them. Each team has a 'home base', eg a wall or behind a line.

Group A then counts to ten out loud while group B forms a huddle and quickly decides on an occupation and a place to come from — say a window cleaner from Oodnadatta.

At the completion of the count, group A moves forward all together towards group B in one line, taking four steps as they speak together, 'Where do you come from?' then stops.

On hearing the 'Where do you come from?', group B reforms their straight line, parallel with group A, and moves together towards group A, staying in their line, taking four steps as they speak together, 'We come from Oodnadatta.' They stop.

Group A moves forward taking four paces in one long line saying 'What's your occupation?'

Group B moves forward taking four paces in the long line and saying, 'Something beginning with W. C.' (the initials of the occupation). Group B begin miming their occupation, window cleaning. At this point both groups are in two straight lines standing directly opposite each other. Members of group A must guess the occupation from the mime. They call their guesses out loud.

As soon as a group A member calls the correct occupation, group B members turn and make a run for their home base. This is the cue for members of group A to chase and attempt to tag group B members before they reach home base. Any group B members who are tagged become part of group A.

Group A returns to their home base. The remaining members of group B line up along their wall, and immediately start counting to ten. The game is played again (ie group A members huddle and choose a place and occupation, etc).

Continue the game until:

- There are no members left on one team; or
- there is one person left on one team who is the winner; or
- the game has achieved unity, excitement and the goal of fast thinking.

Tip

- If the noise level is too high, continue the game whispering.
- Introduce gibberish, keeping the rhythm alive but keeping the initials of the occupation, the geographic location and the guesses in English.
- Encourage a wide range of geographic locations and variety of real and imagined occupations, eg Sphinx polishers from Egypt, Silk rug weavers from China, Perfect pearl polishers from Acapulco, etc.
- Introduce the accent of the geographic locations — Australian, Greek, Scottish, American, South American, Swedish, German, New Zealand, etc.
- Sing the words.
- Introduce emotions to the occupations — Happy jugglers from Queenstown; Angry carpet cleaners from Christchurch, etc.
- To ensure quick responses and a fast-moving game, encourage speedy movement between the chasing and the beginning of the next counting.
- Encourage the groups to accept the first offer they hear in their ten seconds time-out and yield to the suggestions.
- Make sure the miming group actively mimes the occupation. They work as a whole group, in pairs or individuals when miming the occupation.
- Sidecoach the more difficult and involved mimes.

Sidecoach: 'Make the place clearer.'
'Be specific.'

•

Tips for tots

The motor coordination skills required to play this game are generally too complex for players under eleven years. The chasing is often overwhelming and the game becomes too rough.

•

Beware

The game requires a lot of space and tends to become extremely noisy. Clear the space of all breakables.

CIRCLE TAG

10–32 players
5 minutes
8+ years

Description: Individuals flee the chaser ('it') seeking safety in predetermined positions inside the inner circle.

Resource: A large clear space. Be sure the room is clear and all players have good safe footwear or are all barefoot.

Aim: To raise group energy, encourage lively physical reactions and concentration on the moving focus.

How it works: Give these instructions:

1. Find a partner.
2. Name yourselves A and B.
3. Players A form a circle.
4. Players B stand behind your partner.

The group has now formed two concentric circles. Each pair should be approximately one metre from the pairs next to them. The players forming each pair stand very close to each other.

Choose one pair and place player A outside the circle and player B inside the circle.

Player A chases player B. They can run anywhere in the room, inside and outside the circle, but not between the two members of any pair.

If player A tags player B, player B can tag player A back immediately. This tagging can continue back and forth.

The player being chased can become free and safe by standing in front of any of the pairs. When this happens, the player on the outer circle of the pair chosen is now the target of the chase. The person who had been their partner moves into their position, and the original chased player rests as an A player. The chasing player chases the player who was on the outside of the circle and the game continues.

Players must be ready to save the person being chased. The player on the inside circle welcomes the chased player with open arms, saving them from the chasing player.

Keep the pace moving to ensure a quick turnover of players.

Sidecoach the warm-up as if it were a scene. Stand on a chair if you need to see the action. Keep the rhythm at a consistent pace.

Sidecoach: 'Brian is now chasing Betty.'
'Betty is safe. Brian is chasing Angelo.'

This game should move at a furious pace. It isn't a game of cat and mouse; the aim is not to dodge the chaser for a long time. Players don't have to be good runners. They do have to follow the focus and move with the game. When players are slowing down the action by not risking being caught or not running to safety:

Sidecoach: 'Take a risk, Angelo.'

Keep the energy moving when players slow down rather than run and chase.

Sidecoach: 'Advance the scene.'

If there is an uneven number of players, the coach can play too or players form one trio instead of a pair.

Continue the game until all have had a good run, spirits are high, energy is focused and excess energy has been vented.

COLOURS

2–32 players
5 minutes
8+ years

Description: Individuals flee the chaser seeking refuge in colour spots.

Resource: A clear space.

Aim: To stimulate spontaneous reactions and enliven group energy.

How it works: Players form a circle with one player in the middle. Designate a part of the body, eg left hand, right leg, nose. Players skip, walk, run, jump, hop (on the coach's instruction) around the player in the middle, all moving in the same direction, while the player in the middle counts to ten. On ten all players freeze. The player in the middle names a colour out loud, eg 'Red'. The colour must be visible in the room. All players run to something coloured red and place their left hand (or the designated body part) on it. It could be another player's clothing, the furniture, the carpet — anything coloured red. Players can share the same red object; for example, five players may have their hand on the same red chair.

The aim of the player in the middle is to tag another player before the other player touches something red. The tagged player becomes the player in the middle counting to ten. They name a new colour.

This game is great fun, especially when the body part is something other than the hand, eg the nose, left big toe, back of the right knee.

•

Tips for tots

For players of 8–12 years play as above, and from time to time introduce music to replace the player in the middle counting. The game then works in a similar way to musical chairs. When the music stops, players freeze. The player in the middle then names the colour.

Variation: In South Australia they call this game 'Red elbow'. The player in the middle names a colour and a body part, eg red elbow. The rest of the game is the same, except the body part changes as well as the colour each time.

HOSPITAL TIGGY

2–32 players
5 minutes
8+ years

AKA: HOSPITAL TAG; IMITATION TIGGY; IMITATION TAG

Description: Individuals flee the chaser, mimicking his/her sound and movement.

Resource: A clear space.

Aim: To provoke a physical and vocal response and raise group energy.

Skills to be developed: Physical and verbal offering and yielding, action and reaction.

How it works: One player is 'it' and moves around the space, chasing other players to tag one of them. The other players imitate the way 'it' moves, running, hopping, jumping, etc in the space, and repeat the sounds 'it' makes. This continues until 'it' tags another player who becomes the new 'it'.

The new 'it' usually clutches the part of their body where they were tagged, and makes a sound as a reaction to having been tagged. Usually the part of the body that is tagged becomes the focus of the sound and movement made by the new 'it'. For example, players may be holding their arm or back where they were tagged and calling 'Ouch! Ouch! Ouch!' repeatedly. The other players copy the new movement and sound made by 'it'. The holding of the limbs or bending over of the body plus the sounds 'it' makes is likened to 'it' being injured, thus the name 'Hospital tiggy'.

•

Tip

The coach names each new 'it' clearly and loudly.
Sidecoach: 'Jane's it!'

The whole group then has access to the new information. This game moves very quickly and sometimes becomes extremely loud.

CHAIN TAG

6–32 players
5 minutes
8+ years

AKA: Monster tag

Description: A monster chaser is formed as it forms a chain around its victims.

Resource: An extremely clear space.

Aim: To raise group energy.

How it works: One person is 'it'. Their objective is to chase and catch another player. The other player then holds the chaser's hand and they become a two person 'it'. 'It' begins to grow into a chain that twists and turns to devour those remaining until the group is in a long chain chasing one last player.

YES LET'S

2–32 players
5 minutes
8+ years

Description: Players make suggestions which the group enacts immediately.

Resource: A clear space.

Aim: To yield to and overaccept offers and raise group energy.

Skills to be developed: Offering, yielding, overaccepting, listening, teamwork.

How it works: The group works together, accepting the offer made by one player. The offer can be made by any player at any time. The offer is always prefaced with 'Let's…' and agreed to by the whole group with 'Yes, let's'.

For example, one player:	'Let's run and touch each wall.'
The rest of the group:	'Yes, let's.' (They run and touch each wall.)
Another player:	'Let's hop like kangaroos.'
The rest of the group:	'Yes, let's.' (They hop like kangaroos.)
A third player:	'Let's ride our Harley-Davidsons.'
The rest of the group:	'Yes, let's.' (They vroom around the room.)

When an offer is made the whole group accepts it, calling in unison — 'Yes, let's!' They then mime the activity, making sounds as appropriate. The group continues the activity until another offer is made.

The game has its own momentum and framework. It will run itself until the coach or a player says, 'Let's play another game'. 'Yes, let's.'

It is a lively energy lifter with a built-in mechanism that keeps the status of all players even.

If an activity becomes too exhausting, someone is bound to say, 'Let's lie on the floor and take a rest' or 'Let's sit in a line and rub each other's shoulders'.

•

Tip

A great game to play before going on stage.

Robert McFarlane

Grand final teams warm up with YES LET'S — NSW Conservatorium's Verbrugghen Hall 1990

ALL THOSE PEOPLE WHO

8–32 players
5–15 minutes
8+ years

Description: All players except one are seated on chairs in a circle. The player without a chair stands in the centre of the circle, and calls, 'All those people who…', and seated players to whom this applies must change seats. The centre player's objective is to get one of the vacated seats, leaving another player in the centre.

Resource: A large clear space. Place the chairs in a large circle. There is one less chair than the number of players: for twenty players, nineteen chairs. If the coach is playing there is a chair for every player, but not a chair for the coach. The chairs must be durable and safe, preferably without arms. They are plastic rather than wooden or steel and will not topple over.

Aim: To yield to an initial response. To raise group energy.

Skills to be developed: Making offers, overaccepting, yielding, enjoying saying 'yes'.

How it works: This is like musical chairs except players are not disqualified at any time. Place the chairs in a large circle. Each player except one sits on a chair.

The unseated player stands in the middle of the circle to make the first offer, which always begins with, 'All those people who…'. The unseated player then adds their condition, eg 'All those people who… have shoes on (or) blue eyes (or) forgot to have breakfast (or) watched television before school (or) have brothers and sisters'.

Seated player/s who fit the category immediately stand and run to another chair; they cannot move to the chair on either side of them or return to their own seat for that round. The player remaining without a chair starts the game again. No player is disqualified, no chair is removed.

Players who do not fit the specified category stay in their seats for that round.

If players in the centre cannot think of a new set-up, encourage them to think of an idea based on the last one, eg 'All those people who don't have brothers and sisters'. This is good training for extending and shelving.

In the excitement of running, players yield without judging their response.

This is a wonderful game. It promotes energy and spirit.

•

Beware

Over-enthusiasm can lead to falls and bumps. Remind players to take care of each other.

WHAT ARE YOU DOING?

2–32 players
5–20 minutes
8+ years

Description: A player mimes an activity but names a different activity for the next player to mime.

Aim: To name offers, overaccept ideas and image offers of place.

Resource: A large clear space.

Skills to be developed: Listening, concentration, commitment to the activity, staying in the moment.

How it works: This game can be played at various speeds. Begin slowly, increase to a comfortable pace, then speed up as skills develop.

It can be played in a circle or in pairs. A circle allows the whole group to participate. Begin with a circle and branch into pairs as skills develop.

Step one: Players form a circle.
Player A goes into the centre of the circle miming an activity, eg cleaning teeth.
Player B enters the circle, names player A and asks, 'What are you doing?'
Player A names any action except 'Cleaning my teeth'. For example, 'Flying a kite'.
Player A leaves the circle.
Player B begins the activity of flying the kite.
Player C enters and asks, 'What are you doing?' etc.

Example:

Evdokia: (Riding a motorbike.)
Yiannis: 'Evdokia, what are you doing?'
Evdokia: (Riding a motorbike.) 'Eating toast.'
Yiannis: (Eats toast.)
George: 'Yiannis, what are you doing?'
Yiannis: (Eating toast.) 'Hang-gliding.'

The exercise continues until all group members have been involved at least once.

•

Beware

Do not play in order around the circle, as it promotes preplanned responses and being clever. Players enter at will. If you receive suggestions such as 'Going to the toilet' or 'Having a baby', talk to the players about the in-built safety clause — 'I promise to save you'.

•

Remember

Improvisation is the art of making another player look good.

Increase the potential of the game by adding the following developments.

Step two — developing collage and scene-work: Now build the activities into scenes involving more than two players.

The first activity could be in motion for twenty seconds before player B asks 'What are you doing?' This will reduce panic and allow for spontaneous responses.

Player A enters and clips his or her toenails.
Player B: 'What are you doing?'
Player A: 'Singing Verdi.' (Exits.)
(Player B sings Verdi.)

Other players enter the circle building up offers of place which endow player B. They become the music stand, the orchestra, the audience, the musical notes leaving his/her mouth etc. These players always yield to player B as top status and give them focus.

Player C: (Enters after the scene has lived for at least twenty to thirty seconds.) 'What are you doing?'
Player B: 'Shopping at the supermarket.'

The orchestra and musical instruments leave. Players prepare to become shopping trolleys, stacked cans, check-out operator, etc, as the needs of player C become apparent.

•

Tip

This collage scene building provides a valuable link from the warm-up game into skills and scene-work. Slow the exercise down if the work is too fast. No player is in the centre unless they are serving the focus of an offer, physical or vocal, made by the centre player. If a player is brushing her hair, the others follow her eyeline to create the mirror, or put their hand in hers to become the brush. They do not enter with their own ideas to become furniture or monsters that leap out of the cupboard. They serve the scene and the player, not overload them. Players not required in the scene wait for the time to ask, 'What are you doing?' They intuitively judge the moment, asking when the scene needs changing and/or when the game needs advancing.

Step three — for skilled players: Repeat the game, quickening the pace. Players are removed from the centre of the circle and replaced by another player if they stall, do not mime their activity, repeat an activity that has already been named or say an activity close to the one they are miming; for example, if a player is miming brushing their teeth and says 'Brushing my hair', they must go out of the centre.

Step four — for skilled players 14+: Two players enter the circle, continuing back and forth until one falters; another player then takes their place. Faltering players move back into the circle. These players are not disqualified, just out for that particular turn.

•

Tip

This exercise is a terrific preshow warm-up. It lifts the energy and pace. A great game for accepting the first idea that comes into your head. No one wins or loses this game. The game will always be the winner.

PERFORMANCE GAME

2–32 players
5 minutes
8+ years

Description: Individuals and groups enact spontaneous feats, encouraged by the group.

Resource: A clear space. Played in a circle, on a stage or performance area any size or shape but with all players on the same level.

Aim: To build energy, detailed focus, spontaneity, and company support.

Skills to be developed: Yielding, risking, clarity of offers.

How it works: Player A enters the space. The other players applaud with great enthusiasm. Player A performs an unrehearsed, impromptu act which lasts no longer than five to ten seconds and is usually oversized and played in slow motion. The act may be as simple as placing the finger on the nose, walking an imagined tightrope etc. Anything is permissible. At the conclusion of 'the act' the audience applauds wildly as the player bows.

Encourage players not to pre-empt their act. To assist this, the last player to leave the performance arena may make a gesture to introduce another performer to the audience (ie the players in the circle). The exercise works well in mime. To raise the element of risk in the act, encourage 'Ooohs' and 'Aaahs' from the players in the circle.

Players then perform in impromptu pairs, trios, fours and larger groups.

•

Tip

This is a good company preshow warm-up, energy raiser and confidence booster. I highly recommend it before performing.

SLOW MOTION RACE

2–32 players
5–10 minutes
8+ years

Description: Players compete to move more slowly than each other.

Resource: A large clear space.

Aim: To move in the slowest motion possible.

How it works: All players line up at a position designated as the starting line. They race to the area designated as the finish line. They move as slowly as possible. The winner is the last person to cross the finish line. Make sure all players are continually moving. Cheating players (ie players who are not moving) are sidecoached to take a step forward.

THE MIRROR GAME

2–32 players
5–20 minutes
8+ years

A valuable drama teaching tool, relevant to the teaching of all Theatresports exercises, scenes and games.

Description: Players mirror the actions of another player.

Resource: A clear space. Lyrical slow-paced light music, eg pan flute or new age meditation music, cassette player.

Example of starting points: Starting points give players something specific to do. Every suggestion contains a verb, eg scrubbing the floor. This is more active than 'trying to scrub the floor'.

Aim: To play short scenes making, giving and yielding to one-offer-at-a-time. To develop the physical offer. To introduce the task, ie something to complete.

Skills to be developed: Observation and acceptance of subtle offers.

Suggested preparation CIRCLE TAG; YOU; SLOW MOTION RACE.

How it works — step one: The group forms pairs which name themselves A and B. Nominate one as leader and one as follower. In silence, pairs move in slow motion, one player leading the movement and the other following as closely as possible, as if they are a mirrored reflection of their partner. Movement is likened to the 'Laban Glide'. It is sustained, light and direct. [See Appendix C.]

Concentration during this exercise tends to come and go. Play light sustained music to harness concentration and keep the movement steady.

Sidecoach: 'Move as slowly as possible.'

Even the status by changing the leader at regular intervals.

Step two: Then introduce a no-leader sequence, when both players share the responsibility of leading and following simultaneously.

•

Beware

Some players fail to respond to THE MIRROR GAME. They lack commitment to it. If laughter and giggles occur, allow it but continue to sidecoach concentration on the work. A sense of joy is positive when it is related to the work. If it is disruptive, change the exercise.

Step three: Continue THE MIRROR GAME in pairs with both players sharing the leadership. Give each pair a task. Continue in slow motion. Some examples: feeding a dog, planting a tree, changing a tyre, bungee jumping, catching a fish.

Players follow one idea through from the beginning through the middle to the end without speaking. Suggest they begin and end with a slow motion handshake. On commencement, this initiates a sense of teamwork, trust and commitment to the task. The handshake on completion gives a sense of achievement and provides the little scene with an ending.

•

Tip

THE MIRROR GAME is ideal on a hot day, leading to lovely, slow, legato work. It is less effective on a cold day, as it tends to slow the players down. Don't do it for too long when it's cold.

YES

4–32 players
4–7 minutes
14+ years

Description: Players communicate with other players by making eye contact.

Resource: A clear space.

Aim: To find simple focus through eye contact. To maintain concentration and keep all players in the 'same moment'.

How it works — step one: Players form a circle. Each stands in a neutral position (weight balanced equally over both feet, arms hanging by their sides — not across their bodies). No player leans against a wall. All players should be able to see every other player in the circle. The coach nominates player A, who begins by making eye contact with another player in the circle. This new player recognises the eye contact and says 'Yes'. This player then looks to a third player who says 'Yes'. This pattern of making eye contact continues as smoothly and quickly as possible.

Ask the group: 'Where is the focus?'
Answer: The focus is on the player to whom the designated player looks.
Ask the group: 'Where is the moment?'
Answer: The moment is travelling between both players who are making eye contact.
Ask the group: 'Where should everybody in the circle be looking?'
Answer: At the player who has just said 'yes'.
Ask the group: 'Why should everybody be looking at this player?'
Answer: Because the focus is about to shift and as it does any player in the circle could become the next focus.
Ask the group: 'What is the function of every player in the circle?'
Answer: To save the player who has just said 'yes' by being ready to make eye contact with them. To stay in the same moment as every other player in the circle and support the focus.

Step two: Continue the game until the group is making genuine, even eye contact without too much forehead tension or extraneous eye movement. Check facial muscles are relaxed and there is a consistent buoyant rhythm as the focus changes.

Then add the following:

The designated player (player A) looks across the circle to another player (player B) who says 'Yes'. This is an invitation to player A to occupy player B's space in the circle. By the time player A reaches player B, player B must have vacated his/her place. S/he does this by looking across the circle to another player (player C) and receiving a 'yes'. S/he then moves towards player C, who looks to another player, and so on.

No player may move until they have made eye contact and received a 'yes' from another player. Be prepared for the game to stop and start frequently in its early stages. If it is too rushed, players tend to move before they have said 'yes' or before they make eye contact with another player. Slow the game down until the mechanics of it are refined.

Step three: Replace 'yes' with stream of consciousness word association. Player A looks to player B, who says 'sausages'; player C says 'chops'; player D says 'onions' and so on.

Step four: Replace 'yes' with phrases, sentences, lines from a set text (the play you are rehearsing or a poem you have been studying).

You

4–32 players
4–7 minutes
8+ years

Description: Players communicate with each other by making eye contact.

Resource: A clear space.

Aim: To find simple focus through eye contact. To maintain concentration and keep all players in the same moment.

How it works: This game derives from Yes, and its preparation and set-up are the same. Players form a circle taking a neutral stance. Player A points across the circle to another player (player B), saying 'you' as they point. Player A runs to player B's position. Player B quickly turns and points to another player (player C), says 'you', and runs to player C's position. The game begins very slowly, and when the focus becomes clear and players' reactions speed up, it becomes quite fast and continues to move at a rattling pace.

Yes and You are good warm-up games, particularly before a performance. For many players, making eye contact is a confronting experience. The pressure of 'being in the moment' can cause physical and vocal tension. Panic can cause some players to stop looking and listening. Some players do not register that they are being looked at. They look to players on either side of them in the hope that the eye contact is not being made with them. In the challenge of mastering the progression of making eye contact, speaking and then moving, valuable social skills are acquired.

TWENTY-ONE

4–16 players
5–10 minutes
12+ years

Description: Players count to 21 as a group.

Resource: A clear space.

Aim: To find simple focus through eye contact. To maintain concentration and keep all players in the same moment.

How it works: Players form a close circle, each in a neutral stance. All players should be able to see every other player in the circle. The objective of the game is for the group to count from one to 21. Individuals randomly say the next consecutive number without preplanning and without counting in order around the circle. In the event that two players speak at the same time, the count returns to one. The game finishes when the group has reached 21. This is a perfect game to draw a group together, harness collective energy, and centre all individuals in a common task. The sense of achievement on reaching 21 is euphoric.

•

Magic moment

I was in Brisbane to judge the Theatresports grand final at La Boîte Theatre in 1990 when I first saw this game. Four teams were playing for the Burbrook Cup. Amid the fervour backstage, I suggested to someone that maybe they could have a warm-up. They nodded and at the top of their voice screamed '21'.

At this, 16 players, one timekeeper, one scorekeeper, the compere, the musician, the sound and lighting operators and two other judges arrived in the green room. The average age of this company was about 19. They formed a circle, looked each other in the eye and started to slowly count. It took about three minutes for the company to find its timing, breathing, sense of humour, daring, and whatever it is that Theatresports players have in common. I couldn't believe my eyes. The 24 counted to 21 first time! Then they turned and calmly walked to their posts. The lights went down, the audience roared with the music, then all the players ran on stage and improvised. It works!

BALL GAMES

8–16 players (optimum)
20 minutes
8+ years

Ball games are many and varied. Introduce them to develop focus skills and storytelling techniques. Endeavour always to end ball games on a moment of group achievement. I learnt most of the following games from David Lander.

Description: Players throw and catch balls, building patterns and rhythms.

Resource: A large clear space with room for players to throw and catch a number of balls with comfort without breaking windows, lights etc.

Balls: You will need twelve balls. Six should be exactly the same, and six different. I suggest six yellow tennis balls and six rubber balls the same size but different colours. The important thing is that they are of a weight that allows them to be thrown and caught easily. Do not use ping pong balls or medicine balls.

One additional light basketball-sized ball can be useful, especially in 'silent ball', or to be used as the ball that is passed around the circumference of the circle.

Aim: To have a spontaneous response and build focus as a team.

Skills: Focus awareness, peripheral vision, motor skills, eye/hand coordination, listening and teamwork.

Instructions for all ball games: Begin all ball games in a circle. The ball is always thrown underarm (except for players of 8–12; see below). The ball is always thrown so it can be caught. If a ball is dropped, all players allow the player chasing the dropped ball time to retrieve it and return to the circle. Set up a throw-catch rhythm in the circle before introducing sound or speech. When making sound or speech, players 'speak as they throw'. The sound travels with the ball and continues until the ball is caught. Players inhale as their arm swings back prior to throwing, and exhale on the throw.

•

Tips for tots

Players of 8–12 years start by sitting on the floor in a circle and rolling the ball to each other. One kindergarten teacher and her class of 25 players under six years managed to roll five balls at one time. As eye-hand coordination and motor skills develop, younger players could eventually play the game standing and throwing the ball to each other underarm.

•

Beware

Some players have natural ball skills. Others dislike throwing and catching because they fear they have failed if they drop the ball. These games are not about competition — throwing harder, faster, etc. Introduce ball games gradually, concentrating on the fun and skills to be gained. Minimise attention given to players who may drop the ball more often than others. When the game works well, dropped balls are easily retrieved. If there is laughter, it is shared laughter. The player returns to their place, throws the ball and the game continues. There is no stigma attached to having dropped the ball. It is vital to encourage trust and supportiveness during this work.

However, with some groups, if there are players who have particular problems with their motor skills, you may have to stop ball games altogether. It can be unfair and frustrating for them and the group. There are other games that build focus skills just as effectively.

Be sensitive to the possibility that some players may be colour blind (a surprisingly high number of males are).

In the following exercises the ball symbolises the moment. It provides a focus and discipline for the exercise. Ball games encourage a variety of rhythms to be explored.

BALL GAMES — MAINTAINING A PATTERN

8–16 players (optimum)
20 minutes
8+ years

Resource: For these games you will need six balls of different colours.

Step one: Establish a consistent order in which the balls will be passed in the following steps. Every player has their place in the order. No player is left out or receives or catches the ball more often than anybody else. Each player knows who they will receive the ball from, and who they will throw the ball to. This order never changes (except in REVERSE BALL). Players need to look at only two people in the circle: the person they receive the ball from and the person they throw to. Have them point to the person they will throw to… the person they will receive from…. For example, Cliff throws to Irma, Irma throws to Susan, Susan throws to Andrew, Andrew throws to Ruth, etc. Throwing and catching continues in this order until the coach stops the game, so the last person in the order throws to the first one, etc. Players should throw across the circle, not to players next to them. This pattern does not change for the duration of the following exercises.

Step two — name ball: Choose a particular coloured ball, eg red, to be the 'name ball'. Set the 'name ball' in motion. On the throw of the ball, players say the name of the person to whom they throw. They say the name as the ball travels across the space. They finish saying the name when the ball is caught. Throw the 'name ball' until players are confident.

Step three — hah ball: Choose a different coloured ball, eg blue, to be the 'hah ball'. Set the 'hah ball' in motion. Players say 'Hah' as they throw this ball. When players are confident with 'hah ball', add the 'name ball'. Now two balls are in motion.

Step four — hey up ball: Choose a different coloured ball, eg green, to be the 'hey up ball'. Set the 'hey up ball' in motion. Players say 'Hey up' as they throw this ball. When players are confident with 'hey up ball', add the 'name ball' and the 'hah ball'. Now three balls are in motion.

Step five — silent ball: Choose a different coloured ball, eg purple, to be the 'silent ball'. Set the 'silent ball' in motion. Players say nothing as they throw this ball. When players are confident with 'silent ball', add the three ball games from above. Now four balls are in motion.

Step six — forward and reverse ball: Continue throwing the above four balls, but now all in silence (without miming). At any time the coach calls 'Reverse'. At this the players reverse the pattern — ie they throw to the person they usually receive from and catch from the person they usually throw to. Then the coach calls 'Forward' and the pattern returns to its original order. Continue this until players are confident and can change at regular intervals.

Step seven — line ball: Now you need to use the balls of the same colour (eg yellow). Each player chooses a line from a poem or text, eg a line of Shakespeare, a popular song. To begin, each player says their individual line out loud in order around the circle. Then set the first of the yellow balls in motion, following the same pattern as before. As each player throws the ball, they say their own line. As confidence increases, one by one add another yellow ball until at least four balls are in motion.

Step eight — combination balls: One by one, set any or all of the above balls in motion. Continue until the group reaches a sense of achievement.

•

Tip

Some groups achieve the above almost immediately. For others, five minutes of ball games per session over a number of weeks may be more suitable. Modify the number of balls and the rate of additional balls according to the needs and skills of the group.

Stop the throwing and catching when a ball is dropped. Remind players not to panic. If a ball is dropped, the player retrieves it, and returns to their place in the circle before throwing it again. The excitement of throwing and catching nine or ten balls in a group of about sixteen players is exhilarating.

•

Beware

The following problems could occur:

- A pattern of dropping or jolted catching in a particular part of the circle could indicate that a player's fear of missing the ball is causing them to do so.
- If a player consistently throws the ball too far or too short, this could indicate that the player is projecting their thoughts too far or too short of the receiving player. [See 'Beware' in BALL GAMES, above.]

Sidecoach: 'Make eye contact with the person you receive from and the person to whom you throw.'

If balls are thrown too hard or in a destructive or careless way:
Sidecoach: 'Throw the ball so it can be caught.'

BALL GAMES WITHOUT A PATTERN

8–16 players (optimum)
20 minutes
8+ years

The following games are played in a circle. Players throw the ball to other players without setting a predetermined pattern. The following five ball games are independent of each other.

Name ball: Players form a circle standing in a position that allows them to make eye contact with every other player in the circle. One ball is placed in motion. Players throw to any player across the circle at random. They do not throw to adjacent players.

Players throw and catch the ball in regular rhythm naming the person to whom they throw. Remember the sound travels with the ball and stops when the ball is caught by the named player.

Word ball: As above. Players make eye contact with the player to whom they throw before they throw the ball. As each player throws the ball s/he says one word, building an association of images. Example: cat, mouse, trap, bear, forest.

Word at a time: As above. Players make eye contact with another player before they throw the ball to them.

Players throw the ball building a story from player to player, each speaking one-word-at-a-time. Set a title for the story before the ball is set in motion. Begin with: Once [upon] a [time]. Continue to throw the ball until short sentences develop into simple narrative.

Silent ball: When players have enjoyed the rhythm and achieved satisfying story structures from the above exercises, place a second ball in motion. This ball is a silent ball. Players do not speak as they pass this ball.

The second ball is passed in strict rotation around the circumference of the circle. This ball always travels in the same direction and never misses a player.

The silent ball does not hold a verbal offer. It must be of a different colour and shape from the word ball so that players can distinguish it as the silent ball. It is a good idea if this ball is bigger than the other ball.

Centre word ball: One player stands in the centre of the circle and throws a ball to players in the circumference of the circle, saying a word as they throw. The circumference players always return the ball to the centre player as they say their word. All players tell a story one-word-at-a-time. The player in the centre therefore says every second word, throwing the ball to each player in strict rotation around the circle.

When players are familiar with this rhythm, the centre player throws the ball to any player in the circumference of the circle at random, making eye contact with the person to whom they are throwing. All players continue to build a one-word-at-a-time story as they throw the ball.

Change the player in the centre after every story is complete. Add a silent ball to the circumference of this circle as skills develop.

•

Summary

These exercises develop right and left brain coordination. There are limitless combinations. Invent your own patterns and ideas as the skills of the group develop. One group I coached managed two separate stories in a circle simultaneously with a consistent circumference silent ball for almost two minutes.

SOCK GAME

2–32 players
10 minutes
8+ years

Description: Without looking, players retrieve any object sensing its whereabouts.

Resource: A clear space. One small, soft object (eg a pair of socks folded into a ball, a small bean bag, a blackboard duster) for each pair of players. It is important that the thrown object makes no sound as it lands, but is weighty enough to land; a handkerchief is probably too light. Optional: blindfold per pair of players.

Aim: To develop concentration and spacial awareness.

Skills to be developed: Concentration, personal focus, spatial awareness, trust.

How it works: Players form pairs. Player A acts as a safeguard for player B. Player B closes their eyes (or puts on a blindfold) and gently throws the socks some small distance away from their body — no further than a metre. Player B then moves at a pace with which they feel comfortable towards the point where they imagine their pair of socks to be. Remaining with eyes closed or blindfolded, player B bends down to pick up the socks.

Only one attempt at finding the socks is permitted for each throw. Player B then opens their eyes to see how close they are to the socks. Player B continues to throw and find the socks for five or six turns. Players reverse roles after player B has achieved some degree of success and reached the socks. Should they reach the socks within the first couple of throws, player B extends themselves by throwing the socks a little further each time.

The function of player A is vital. They ensure their partner does not bump into objects or other players and is perfectly safe at all times giving them confidence while their eyes are closed.

This is a quiet, gentle game and perfect for developing concentration before going on stage.

GROUNDING

1–32 players
5 minutes
8+ years

Description: Players image themselves in the greater environment.

Resource: A clear space.

Aim: To centre the breathing and to ground players with a sense of strength, purpose and calm in preparation for work.

How it works: Players stand individually scattered around the room with eyes closed. They keep their spine long and their breathing deep. They imagine a silver thread enters the crown of their head and image it clearly as it passes through the centre of their body between their legs, between their feet, passing through the surface of the floor, through the foundations of the building, to the soil, passing through the layers of soil, to the bedrock, down to the core of the planet. With eyes still closed they continue to release breath and pass the image all the way back up through the various layers, through the top of their heads and out into the atmosphere, until they are ready to open their eyes and begin work.

The coach guides all players through this exercise in a clear voice. Players will not be skilled enough to take themselves through the exercise until they have experienced it and its positive effects many times. It could take time before some players are mature enough to 'ground' themselves. Other players, however, achieve this immediately.

'Grounding' refers to a sense of being 'on the ground'. It prepares players for work. It provides them with a sense of being 'available'. Therefore players should not become sleepy during this exercise. Its aim is to place them in the 'now' rather than in a dreamy state of relaxation. It is a preparation exercise that places players 'in the moment' ready to improvise.

•

Tip

This is a sensational exercise for a cast of players about to go on stage. It is also good preparation for pressure situations such as job interviews, exams, and all those situations which require a clarity of internal focus and concentration.

GIBBERISH CIRCLE

2–32 players
10 minutes
8+ years

Description: In a circle players build a gibberish language.

Resource: A clear space.

Aim: To build confidence and a variety of sounds that develop a vocabulary of gibberish.

How it works: Players form a circle. Player A (the coach) says a one or two syllable gibberish word. The next player in the circle repeats players A's sound and adds another sound. The sounds are passed around the circle until all players make a gibberish addition to the growing words.

If the words become unmanageable and too long, the coach indicates that the next player begins again or chooses part of the last word as a starting place for the new word. Then the game concentrates on building gibberish skills rather than becoming a memory test.

Player A: 'Oona'
Player B: 'Oonapata'
Player C: 'Oonapatabolti'
Player D: 'Oonapataboltisha'

Player E: 'Sha'
Player F: 'Shanooka'

Encourage players to draw on the tones of the other languages they speak and hear, developing a variety of Asian, Eastern, Slavic and European sounds and experimenting with a range of vocal pitches.

Extended activities: Player A makes eye contact with a player in another part of the circle. They give a gibberish offer of any length. They endow the gibberish offer in a variety of ways, eg as top secret information, gossip, orders, outlining scientific or factual information, telling a joke. Player B responds to player A in gibberish. A brief gibberish dialogue may evolve. Sidecoach as necessary. This information may then be passed from one player to another in gibberish. Players may leave their place in the circle and walk to the player to whom they give the gibberish message, warning, instructions, etc. Or they may shout it, call it or whisper it from where they are. The possibilities are endless.

SOUND BOARD

4–32 players
5 minutes
8+ years

Description: Players send sounds to each other across a circle.

Resource: A clear space.

Aim: To provoke a spontaneous offer and yield through sound and movement.

How it works: There are two ways to play this game. The second is developed from the first.

Sound board one: Players form a circle. Player A sends a sound and a movement across the circle to another player. They use any part of their body to send the sound — hands, shoulders, head, back, feet. When it arrives, player B repeats the sound and movement exactly as it was given. They then send a different sound and movement to another player, who repeats player B's sound and movement and then sends their own and so on.

Sound board two: Player A sends a sound and movement to another player in the circle. They send it to a specific part of player B's body. Player B receives the sound and movement on their body. They do not repeat player A's sound and movement but begin the new sound and movement based on their response to receiving player A's sound and movement as it lands.

Receiving the sound and movement is important. Players are affected when they receive the offer. They reel back, making a sound as they do so, or catch the sound and movement on their body. The receiving is the impetus and starting point for their next offer, which they pass on to player C, who in turn receives the sound and movement, responds and sends accordingly.

•

Beware

Some players use their hands too often when giving and receiving. They externalise the offers rather than allowing them to land on their body. They catch them and throw them as if they were a ball. If this continues:

Sidecoach: 'No hands. Use another part of your body to send and receive the sound.'

Direct players to be specific rather than general in their sending. Encourage them to make eye contact and send the offer directly to their chosen player.

If the offer lands on two players rather than one, both players receive the offer simultaneously. If it lands on their chests, both receive it making their sounds together as if playing SPEAKING IN ONE VOICE. They keep eye contact and move together, extending the sound and movement, and together move it on to another part of the circle. This collective sending and receiving has no limit. Groups of three, four, six, eight players can receive offers, yield, extend and send them on to other groups of players.

SAVING

2–32 players
10–15 minutes
15+ years

Saving other players is inherent in all the work. It is more important that players enjoy themselves, feel part of a group and experience a sense of group support than experience a sense of winning or being better than another player. This game is a narrative development game and is often played too fast without a sense of saving.

The game relies on developed narrative skills. Introduce it to older players who are skilled and are ready for 'saving' work.

Aim: To develop a sense of 'saving'.

Resource: One or two props, eg scarf, plastic bucket, plastic spade.

How it works: The group sits in a circle. Each member tells a story using one or both of the props in the narrative. The props become anything they wish them to be and are used as such. The story is told in short sentences and phrases and passed on to the next player, who picks it up and uses all that has gone before to develop a story. The story is fictitious.

Example: Player A (sitting with a bucket in one hand and a spade in the other resting the spade on the bucket): 'I was at home one day when the phone rang. I picked up the receiver and said…' (picking up the spade from the bucket as a receiver and placing it to their ear, then passing both on to the next player).

Player B (holding the spade to their ear and speaking into it): '…"Hello. Yes, I'll be there in ten minutes." It was the call I had been waiting for. I ran to the bathroom, washed my face…' (using the bucket as the wash basin and passing it on).

Player C: 'Combed my hair…' (using the spade as a brush and passing the spade and bucket on).

The story then continues around the circle and the props continue to be passed. If a player stumbles, can't think of an idea, or is grasping at straws with the narrative, the previous player continues to feed the player in need with offers and ideas to stimulate the growth of the narrative.

Let's say that at this point the next player is stuck. The previous player takes the bucket and spade back again and sets up the next action for this player and develops the story.

> Player C: 'I drove straight down to headquarters...' (using the bucket as a steering wheel and the spade as a gear stick, and handing it back to player C, who continues to drive).

If player C is still stuck, the previous player or the coach can save this player by giving them things to do and feeding them ideas.

This helpful, gentle teamwork is important. Too often we become fast, energetic and bulldoze fellow players rather than developing a sense of saving. The pressure to succeed and come up with good ideas occurs too often. Reduce it wherever possible.

BLINDFOLD GAME

4–32 players
10–20 minutes
8+ years

Description: Blindfolded players find and identify sighted players.

Resource: A clear space and a blindfold.

Aim: To develop group trust.

How it works: One player, player A, is blindfolded. Two more players, players B and C, are silently selected so their identity is not revealed to player A. The other players form a circle, either sitting on chairs or standing, around players A, B and C. Player A's objective is to find and identify players B and C. The blindfolded player is free to move anywhere within the circle. Should they reach the circumference, the players forming the circle gently touch the blindfolded player, saying 'Stop', and turn them back towards the centre of the circle.

Players B and C keep their right foot in a fixed position on the floor. They always stay within the circle. They may pivot on their fixed foot and move their bodies up and down, sideways, forward or back. But their right foot must remain on the fixed spot.

Player A claps. Players B and C clap in response. The objective of players B and C is to avoid being caught. They may place their responding clap in a position that will deceive player A; for example, they clap high in the air and then crouch down low. Player A follows the sound until they locate and identify each player.

The identifying is good fun. Blindfolded players identify the player they have found by feeling for distinguishing features. The coach guides this according to the age and needs of the players. 'Are they taller or shorter than you? Do they have long hair or short hair? What type of shoes are they wearing?'

To circumvent any embarrassing touching, be sensitive when guiding this identification process. My experience has been that players of a variety of ages are surprisingly sensitive and respectful of one another when playing this game. I have also been amazed by the acute observations made by the most unlikely players.

You will know if your group is ready for this game.

global network

Global network

At the 10th birthday celebrations for Theatresports Sydney in 1995 many Theatresports centres sent video birthday wishes to be played on a large screen at the party. These included an hilarious EXPERT DOUBLE FIGURES scene and birthday song in German, an impro-cam coverage of the Mixed Doubles performance from Snug Harbour in tropical Queensland, the Japanese Theatresports anthem complete with choreography and harmonies and a full rendition of Happy Birthday sung by players at the three day Theatresports Tournament Palm Springs. It sure is a big family!

Theatresports is now played in more than 10 languages in over 50 cities across 15 countries. Although all companies adhere to similar beliefs and improvisation standards, each has developed a unique playing style reflecting their local culture, climate and geographical location. No other sport reflects its local culture in quite the same way.

Most companies begin with a group of players, an audience and a regular Theatresports season. Eventually they explore non-competitive formats and more open improvisation styles such as Gorilla theatre [see Canada, this section], improvised soap, improvised musicals and formats developed in other countries. Communication between companies continues through international teaching, tournaments and the annual Loose Moose summer school.

Theatresports companies are usually called upon by their communities to develop improvisation performances and workshops for education programs, corporate clients and charity functions. Each company develops according to demand and resources. Many are purely amateur, some semi-professional and for others the demand has resulted in an established theatre company employing professional players and management.

This section was compiled with the invaluable contributions of Theatresports companies around the world.

AUSTRALIA

Sydney

Made by Dennis Watkins and Chris Harriott, the tackiest trophy in town stands more than two metres high and is as coveted as the Brownlow Medal and the Cricket Ashes. Named after Lamont Cranston (Watkins' cabaret persona), the Cranston Cup's shields bear the names of its winning teams: *The Southern Cross All Stars* '85 with Dean Carey, Mark Owen-Taylor, Lyn Pierse (Julie Haseler and Gia Carides also played with this team); *The Funky Chickens* '86 with Adam Cook, Mark Ferguson, Lisa Kelly, Michael Turkic; *Writers' Bloc* '87 with Andrew Denton, Steve Johnston, David Poltorak, David Witt (Anthony Ackroyd also played with this team); *Four Sensitive Guys* '87 with Eric Cambell, Geoff Kelso, Marko Mustac, Richard Mason; *Once in a Lifetime* '88 with Melissa Docker, Murray Fahey, Berryn Schwerdt, Brett Wood; *The Lonely Guys* '89 with Michael Gregory and Marko Mustac; *The Three Guys* '90 with Michael Gregory and Marko Mustac; *Utter Codswallop* '91 with Robyn Butler, Ewan Campbell, Murray Fahey, Brad Hall; *Two Sandwiches Short of a Picnic* '92 and '93 with Ewan Campbell and Murray Fahey; *Dirty Harry's Bathwater* '94 with Andrew (Beef) O'Keefe and Dan Lloyd.

The first Cranston Cup season ran to capacity houses for 22 weeks. Teams came from the Griffin Theatre, the Rocks Players, some players were formed from groups of mates, and others were formed in the foyer half an hour before the show.

More than 30 teams registered for the inaugural Sydney Cranston Cup season. After 18 weeks of heats, teams played three elimination finals before the top teams played off in the first Cranston Cup Grand Final. *The Southern Cross All Stars* played the final round against the *Griffin Gofers* to a house packed to the rafters.

The spectacle included a choreographed entrance staged by Laurel McGowan. Players of eliminated teams danced through hoops and held cards spelling T.H.E.A.T.R.E.S.P.O.R.T.S. in the vein of an Olympic Games opening ceremony. It is said that scalping was rife as tickets sold out weeks in advance.

The Theatresports Cranston Cup season has become one of the consistently largest annual improvisation seasons in the world, if not the largest. Comperes have included Paul Chubb, Andrew Denton, Sister Mary Leonard, Geoff Kelso, Richard Mason, Robyn Butler, Jenny Hope and Penny Biggins. After two years at Belvoir Street Theatre (capacity 320), the grand final moved to bigger venues: the Enmore Theatre (capacity 1800), the Conservatorium's Verbrugghen Hall (capacity 796) and the Sydney Opera House (capacity 2100).

The human scoreboard

The human scoreboard was created in Sydney as a device to relay the judges' scores to the audience seated in the back rows and balcony of large venues. Only days before the sold out Sydney Opera House Grand Final performance (shown on the cover), the promise of a sponsored electronic scoreboard fell through. The problem of how to convey the judges' scores to 2000 people was solved by the first human scoreboard, *Random Numbers*, whose animated interpretations of the judges' decisions were as improvised as the scenes being scored. They skulked across the stage when the scores were low, they marched and strutted when the scores were controversial and they leaped for joy on a 5-5-5. The human scoreboard has added an unexpected dimension that no electronic device could ever have accomplished. It is now a popular and integral part of a big venue production.

Cranston Cup champions 1991 — *Utter Codswallop* — Robyn Butler (left), Ewan Campbell, Murray Fahey, Brad Hall

By 1991 Sydney Theatresports activity had outgrown its position as an umbrella activity of Belvoir Street theatre. The company became an incorporated association, formed a board of directors and took on the responsibility of self government as an independent theatre, education, training and production company. It is the licence holder for Theatresports NSW, ACT and the Northern Terrtory. Belvoir Street Theatre continues as the home of regular Sunday night Theatresports playing, but the company has moved. Its office, training and rehearsal rooms are within walking distance of Belvoir.

The company is active all year round. Classes and workshops are held most evenings. The comprehensive training program offers classes at beginner, intermediate and advanced levels. To serve the needs of the ever-growing number of new players, fledgling improvisors from the classes flex their impro muscles in front of an audience at the Theatresports Gong Show.

The gong

The controversial gong is a loud sounding instrument that is rung by the judges whenever a team is boring. On its sounding the scene stops and the team leaves the stage. Like the 'horn' its chief function is to save the teams from failing and if it is used wisely and is sounded early, will have the audience booing the judges rather than the players. It was first introduced by Dennis Watkins in the early days of Sydney Theatresports. While the audience loved its dramatic, aggressive nature and theatricality, it was disliked by the players, who found it too humiliating and ruthless causing it to be replaced by the subtler, less offensive honking of the 'horn'.

There has been much controversy over the years regarding its re-introduction. It has been argued that its use is inappropriate in most Theatresports seasons but introduced in the right season, under the appropriate circumstances could be most effective, but no one had the nerve to give it another test until recently The gong has finally found its rightful place in Sydney Theatresports and now is featured in a show of its own.

Jenny Hope, director of Sydney Theatresports 'Gong Show', came up with a concept for a try out night for new players and teams at an inner city comedy club. Here the audience sits at tables and eats and drinks while watching new Theatresports players cut their teeth on a small intimate stage before three judges and 'the gong'. In a relaxed atmosphere teams are encouraged to risk dying onstage to the deafening sound of the gong. But instead of instilling the old sense of humiliation and failure, the gong now heralds a time of revelry and celebration. When it is sounded, compere Jenny Hope leads the audience in the song she wrote. Audience and players unite in a resounding chorus with great glee.

You're gonged, you've got to get off,
You're gonged, we've had enough.
You blocked and you wimped and your scene really stinks,
You're gonged, you've got to get off!

Singing the gong song is so much fun that teams and audience look forward to the next time they can sing the gong song. This is a brilliant device, but it is to be used sparingly, in the right atmosphere, with players who can enter the spirit of the gong.

Theatresports Inc continuously produces shows ranging from traditional Sunday night Theatresports to regular theatre seasons, and mid-week shows in venues as diverse as Belvoir Street Theatre, the Enmore Theatre, Sydney's original Comedy Store, The Harold Park Hotel and the Sydney Opera House, which seat anything from 100-2000 people. The shows vary in style from the classic, team-based, competitive Theatresports to completely new impro shows that explore pure scene and character based improvisation.

Recent Theatresports seasons have included Tanya Bulmer's Gothic Theatresports where professional veterans played in teams of two and three but were allotted points as individuals by a tyranical vampire compere (Marko Mustac). On a whim, to the audience's amusement, Count Dracula could allocate hundreds of points for scenes he liked and remove points from those he didn't. Improvised music from Igor Peter Fyfe added to the theme and the season became so popular audience members came to the theatre dressed as 'goths'.

A Mixed Doubles Theatresports season was played concurrently with Wimbelton '94. It was set on a tennis court complete with ball boys and girls, with pairs of players all in white abiding by the strict calls of an onstage court umpire perched high above the action. A courtside television commentator compered, reporting and improvising when the game was stopped for rain.

•

Magic moment

During a gibberish endowment challenge one mixed doubles player was having difficulty endowing his team mate as a pearl diver. A ball boy (Olivier Moreau) crouching courtside saved the day and won Moment of the match when he rolled on his back clutching his tennis ball to become a shell, oyster and pearl.

Seasons of Classic Canadian Theatresports and New York's Stanislavsky Open have found their way to the Belvoir stage. The evergreen Cranston Cup season is played at the end of every year in the Aussie rules six team format. This season contines to draw record crowds at its annual grand final and a constant stream of players in pursuit of the coveted trophy.

Theatresports Inc also produces specialised corporate entertainment tailored to the needs of each client. The performances are audience interactive showcases of the best Theatresports players, games and ideas.

Theatresports Inc has a long established reputation for theatre in education, having successfully toured its Theatresports in Schools Show since 1989. The interactive, partly demonstration shows are of value to teachers and students. The program provides specific workshops for students of various levels, school camps and specialised drama programs. The company is also devising and developing new educational shows which explore current issues such as racism, ethnicity and multiculturalism. Students actively participate in the performance. Occassional weekend workshops for teenagers are popular.

A special school teacher accreditation course has been introduced to keep teaching standards in schools high and to support teachers with skills and refresher courses. Teachers who successfully complete the course are certificated as accredited Theatresports school coaches.

University Theatresports is very popular on NSW campuses, the most established being the University of Sydney. An annual grand final plays to an audience of standing room only cramming the Manning Bar. The playing is wild, daring, and always outrageously funny. Some of the best and more dedicated of these players have graduated to the Theatresports main-stage bringing with them an enthusiastic and devoted Theatresports following.

In 1994 the company brought together players from Australia and New Zealand for the first Theatresports International Superleague played to a capacity crowd at the

Enmore Theatre. Sydney looks forward to more international playing in preparation for the Sydney 2000 Olympics.

Orange, NSW

In Orange NSW, Community Theatre director Jennifer Leslie pioneered the concept of Music Theatresports. After four annual weekend workshops followed by one-off events, Jennifer cast Theatresports players with members of the Orange Symphony Orchestra to form teams for a special performance for the Orange Music Festival.

•

Magic moment

A DEATH IN A MINUTE performed in 1990 by a team of year ten Orange schoolgirls with a tuba not only astounded me with its skill and timing but delighted the other two judges, the Hon. David Simmonds, Federal Junior Minister for the Arts, Tourism and Territories and Julie Owens from the Australia Council Music Board. We awarded it three fives.

Adelaide

In August 1985 Dennis Watkins introduced Theatresports to South Australia, where it was taken up by the 'Workers of the State Theatre Company of South Australia'. Actress Deborah Kennedy was instrumental in the initial organisation. Stephen Ford coordinated the production team and stage managed the events. Geoffrey Rush was compere, and Alan John and later Stephen Rae were Mr Music. The original set was designed by Colin Mitchell, and both set and costumes were financed through the State Theatre Company's Actors' Development Fund.

Performances were held in the 614 seat Playhouse at the Adelaide Festival Centre on Monday nights, the only night the theatre was available. The Adelaide anthem was the theme song from the *Bugs Bunny Show*. The players were drawn from the pool of Adelaide actors from the State Theatre Company, children's television, Theatre In Education, Magpie Theatre and students from the universities and teachers' colleges. The players' theatre experience was diverse, ranging from classical actors to the crazy team of university show-offs, *Get Her.* The audience loved it. They packed the Playhouse every Monday night. The Minties toss was so popular some audience members brought placards with 'lollies' written on them in huge letters in the hope of catching the compere's attention and at least one of the Minties.

Geoffrey Rush's range of skills made him the ideal compere. His complete command of an audience, off-the-cuff comments, perfect timing and sheer madness wove magic in the theatre. He could save any situation and encouraged the audience to barrack for teams in the face of failure. He is famous for supporting a failed moment with the last commandment:

Commandment

It just doesn't matter!

In 1985, at the end of the first season, Adelaide held its first Theatresports grand final on the set of *The Italian Girl in Algiers* at the Opera Theatre to a capacity audience of

1003. This was the biggest Theatresports audience recorded in Australia in the first year of playing. The champion team, *Plastic Max*: Jo England, Isobel Kirk, Glynn Nicholas, and Maureen Sherlock, became the first South Australian champions. Richard Margetson replaced Jo England to play in the first national championships in Sydney.

The most recent surge of Theatresports activity in Adelaide occured in the early '90s when a brave group of actors and drama teachers formed Improd Theatre with a quest to take improvisation into South Australian schools. They developed a program for secondary students which told the history of theatre through improvisation. They also produced Theatresports on Sunday nights in Adelaide.

Melbourne

Within weeks of opening the Sydney and Adelaide seasons, Dennis Watkins introduced his production to the Playbox Theatre, Melbourne. The response was just as positive as it had been in the other two cities. Actors came from all over Melbourne to play, and the curious audience travelled from afar to watch.

The initial workshops were held at St Martins Theatre and were coached by David Lander, who compered the first performance. The first two seasons played to packed houses at St Martins Theatre before moving to the Playhouse at the Victorian Arts Centre, which has a seating capacity of 800.

Melbourne loved its Theatresports so much that the Theatresports seasons paralleled the Australian rules football seasons and the audience swelled to world record numbers. When Theatresports grand finals were held in the Concert Hall, an audience of 2600 crammed the venue. The annual Comedy Festival Celebrity Theatresports has attracted an audience in excess of 2000 at the Dallas Brooks Hall. To conquer these vast spaces, the Melbourne teams of actors, improvisors and stand-up comics developed a verbal and physical boldness which produced a unique, robust improvisation style.

Doug McLeod wrote the Melbourne anthem. These words are loudly sung at the commencement and close of most performances.

Theatresports, Theatresports you're forever in our thoughts,
With your MC
Your judges three
And timer with the Seiko Quartz.
Your teams of extroverts, who give until it hurts
And even then they score three noughts.
You're just like ancient Rome or even Thunderdome
You're just a game, Theatresports,
You're just a game, Theatresports.

John Hargreaves was the first Mr Music. Boris Connolly later shared the position. John Thorn, Greg Murray and Peter Fanon then formed the first Theatresports combo. They did their thing on drums, guitar and keyboard, jamming with the onstage scenes. The strains of their famous play-out, *Another One Bites the Dust* capped the scoring of every scene.

Ian Rolland, as the robed hanging judge, buffered the boos, setting a high standard of play in the first years of Melbourne Theatresports. The audience gave him an umpire's greeting. It was not uncommon to hear, 'Can't you count more than one, Rolland?' from the audience during a performance.

Melbourne compere Simon Rogers

Compere Simon Rogers gave the Melbourne production an echo of Tivoli magic as he danced in bow tie and tails like a music hall showman across the stage. He has the ability to control any size audience and the strongest Minties throwing arm in the universe. Simon has written most of the topics for the games played in Melbourne, reading them out of 'The Book' (Melbourne's version of Sydney's 'Off the Board').

Occasional comperes of Melbourne Theatresports have included Sioban Tuke, Russell Fletcher, John Thompson and Anthony Morgan.

Melbourne Theatresports company Flying Pig developed some original Down Under Theatresports traditions, including the Moment of the match. This prestigious commendation is awarded to a player for courageous yielding.

Another Flying Pig tradition is the Brian McCarthy Memorial Moosehead Award. To perpetuate Brian's work in fringe comedy, two annual fundraising events are held to support the work of comics and improvisors: newcomers, teams, individuals, amateurs or professionals. Melbourne rewards its best and fairest player with an annual Flying Pig Award. Recipients include Ross Williams, Andrew Bayly, Russell Fletcher, Christine Keogh, Geoff Paine and Carole Patullo.

The first Melbourne team to play a national final was *4 x 4's*: Kate Herbert, Carole Patullo, Ian Shrives and John Thompson. In 1986, Melbourne hosted the second national finals and the audience went crazy when the home team *Gutless Wonders*: Christine Keogh, Doug McLeod, Glenn Robbins and Ross Williams took the flag.

Melbourne team *Koyann and Squatzi*, with Michael Blair, Russell Fletcher, Christine Lucas and Brian McCarthy won the third national finals in 1987, played in Brisbane. This team represented Australia at the 1988 Calgary Theatresports Winter Olympics. Brian McCarthy died before representing Australia at Calgary. John Thompson played in his stead. Other Melbourne teams long to be remembered include: *The Natural Normans, Shintaro, Perry-Stroika, Lost On Stage* and bad-boy team *Skinhead Nation,* to name a few.

In recent years Flying Pig has been affiliated with the St Martins Youth Theatre program developing workshops and performances in schools. Special events, such as celebrity Theatresports, can be seen at theatres such as the Universal and Athenaeum particularly during the Melbourne Comedy Festival each April.

Brisbane

Brisbane Theatresports began when Anne Jones raised the idea of Theatresports as a method of promoting community theatre and as a celebration and fundraiser. In May 1986 the first series of workshops was held in Brisbane. The inaugural four week Theatresports season began on 19 September 1986 and was played at 10.30 pm every Friday night at the La Boîte Theatre as a part of the late-night cabaret, *La Bamba*. For the first time in Australia, Theatresports was played 'in the round'. Damien Ledwich's design — set, posters and the notion of an official's uniform, capitalised on the shape of La Boîte, making Theatresports akin to a boxing ring.

The first compere was Lewis Jones. Anne Jones was timekeeper and Mr Music was Michael Roper, who, it is said, held the shows together in the early days.

Theatresports shocked Brisbane on opening night when half an hour before the show the audience queue wound out of the door, down the footpath and around the corner of Hale Street. They could have filled La Boîte twice over.

Brisbane went one step further than Sydney's sin bag. They invented Otto, the sin bin. Cries of 'Otto! Otto!' rocked the theatre as the four wheeled garbage bin was rolled out, lid chomping, anticipating 'eating' the offending audience member or player.

Brisbane adopted the Melbourne anthem and, instead of the compere throwing the lollies, John Morwood invented Trudy Scrumptious, the two metre tall lolly fairy.

Thunderous chants of 'Trudy! Trudy!' kept theatre neighbours awake. Brisbane's hanging judge, David Pyle, was deliciously macabre as the grim reaper. Teams now play for the Burbrook Cup, named after player Annie Burbrook. Other memorable contributors include comperes Brian Cavanaugh and David Fenton. The first champion team, *Mental Floss* (Andrew Buchanan, Adam Couper, Michael Golledge and Judi Patson), represented Brisbane at the second Theatresports national finals in Melbourne in 1986. In 1987 Brisbane hosted the third Australian national finals at City Hall to a capacity audience of 1700.

Theatresports Brisbane is active on many fronts. Performances are held weekly across the city at a number of venues, each season in a different format.

The 'Burbrook Cup' is engraved with the winning teams: *Four Horsemen of the Apocalypse* '90, *The Understudies* '91, *Screaming Wet Jesus* '92, *Skele Dogs* '93, *It Just Doesn't Matter* '94. The 'Suburb of Origin' brings together teams representing the north, south, east and west of Brisbane. The 'Duck Season' is a mid-year event featuring the greatest degree of innovation. Previous Duck Seasons have involved teams from the Youth and University seasons.

'Lightning Doubles' is a professional comedy impro show with six players, an MC and a musician performed in the open bar and grill of Snug Harbour. The audience at three chosen tables each select a two player team for the night. Three or four rounds are played in the first half and the team with the fewest points is dropped. The two players in this team split up and join the remaining teams for the final rounds of longer games. Other similar shows have included: The Love Boat Meets the X-Files (a spoof impro show), The Lightning Doubles All Singing Music Show and The Superbowl (sponsored by the Queensland Fruit and Vegetable Growers Association).

1993 saw the first Theatresports 'Road Trip'— an impro show on wheels. The audience board buses at the theatre bound for unknown destinations. Each bus has its own team for whom the audience become the cheer squad. At severals locations along the trip, the buses stop, all alight and Theatresports is played. On-board bus fun includes competitions, playing eye-spy, and team-mate torture.

The 'Open Season' is played at La Boîte three times a year. It includes veteran players and others who have played for less than a year. It is an innovative season always played with a different format. In 1993 a Beenleigh group began to organise Theatresports shows. Seasons are played at the Beenleigh Art Centre and draw players and audience from Brisbane and the Gold Coast.

To support this variety of activity, the company holds regular workshops for beginner, intermediate and advanced players. Teachers travel to the distant ends of the state where Theatresports is played at Beenleigh, the Gold Coast and far north Queensland. An annual Youth Theatresports Festival involves students who have attended workshops and school demonstrations.

Gold Coast

Gold Coast Theatresports held its first workshop in February 1994 in the foyer of the Roxy Theatre at the theme park Movieworld. The first shows were held at the Stage Door Theatre Restaurant at Broadbeach.

Three seasons later, Gold Coast Theatresports moved house and in May 1995 established the Cove Cup at Sanctuary Cove Village Theatre. The theatre operates as a movie house six nights a week and as the home of Theatresports on Sunday nights.

Wayne Carroll and Bruce Thompson, founders of Gold Coast Theatresports, have incorporated the best of film and live theatre. They video every performance and replay the magic moment at the end of the show on the big screen. Some teams dress in costumes relating to movie themes. Oscars are handed out at the end of the show.

Mackay, Rockhampton and far north Queensland

The Mackay theatre community, led by a group of active drama teachers, encourages the talent of the locals with a thorough three month improvisation and Theatresports training program in preparation for the annual Theatresports season. Adults and children over 15 years train together, form teams and play a season of public performance heats culminating in a grand final. To date grand finals have been played as part of the Mackay Arts Festival. They draw a capacity audience of about 800 and are a talking point in the district for weeks.

The Mackay Festival of Arts continues to be the focus of Theatresports activity for local players and the growing number of devotees from Rockhampton. In 1995 the first Queensland Intercity Challenge was held in Mackay organised through the festival.

Teams from Brisbane and Rockhampton met the Mackay locals for a one night tournament. A Mackay team, *Resort Studs* came in third, *Deep Spud* the Brisbane team second and the victors were the locals, the *Nambypong Dairy Farms Synchronised Swimming Team.* The success and popularity of the event promises future Intercity Challenges.

Hobart

In 1985 local actors in Hobart formed the theatre company Zootango, and Richard Davey, Les Winspear, Iain Lang, Sandy McCutcheon, Helen Haigh and Libby Wherrett held nights of improvised theatre at the Back Space. They improvised open scenes which had no game structures. Martin Brown returned from Belvoir Street Theatre and organised a Theatresports match as he had seen in Sydney. Les Winspear was the first compere and Sandy McCutcheon wrote all the topics. Wal Eastman was the hanging judge and is renowned for organising all the judges and for never having missed a performance.

Hobart loved it. The season attracted an enormous audience. Some people queued for five hours for tickets to the 11.00 pm show. Australia's oldest theatre, Theatre Royal, swelled with a capacity grand final audience of 750. Winning team *Licorice Allsports* (Nigel Curtain-Smith, Catherine Gillard, Gary McCaffrie and David Pidd), confidently headed for the national finals in Melbourne. They were flying by the seat of their pants, truly improvising games they had never seen played.

Later, Robert Jarman arrived in Hobart and explained the game structures and time limits as they were played in Sydney. At the time the Backspace was being administered by the Performing Arts Club. As the group became more involved with their improvisation, they applied for a Theatresports licence. In November 1986 we held the first Theatresports workshops in Hobart. The Tasmanians had been improvising for quite some time and had developed unique ways of playing the games. They had also developed many interesting new games.

The Backspace features a bar in the shape of a question mark right next to the playing area. If the playing lagged, audience and players adjourned to the bar, had a drink and then came back! Legend has it that the playing became so good that beer sales dropped. They replaced the Minties with salted peanuts and beer sales soon sky-rocketed.

Perth

The inaugural Perth game was held at the Hole in the Wall Theatre in 1986 after Dennis Watkins introduced his production and held workshops. The first compere was Damien O'Dougherty and Lucinda Armour was the timekeeper. There was no Mr Music. Later that year Deck Chair Theatre took up the licence and Theatresports was played at the Fly by Night Club. Perth Theatresports is proudly community based. Most teams are formed by community players with a sprinkling of professional actors. There have been various performers at the head of the production, including comperes Phil Thompson, Geoff Kelso and Phil Joseph, and timekeepers Angela Sanderson-Green and Dawn Fitzgerald. The role of Mr Music has been filled by several musicians, including Lee Blundell, who supports the scenes on electric piano and saxophone. Administrator Shane Colquhoun was instrumental in the development of Theatresports in Perth, as were the members of the team *The Zerobusters* (Paul Barker, Eugenio Carroll, Angela Sanderson-Green and Michael Sanderson-Green), who represented Perth at the third Theatresports national final at the 1988 Adelaide Festival of Arts.

Regular teams were *The Fly By Nights*, *The Womrackets, The Fourskinsmen,* and the first Perth champions, *The Suits,* who blitzed the final in 1986 and played on the ABC Television Theatresports program. Other champions were *Zerobusters* '87 and '89, *Fly by Nights* '88, *Bondy's Funeral* '90, *Wormbrackets* '91, *Flying Fibonaches* '92, *Danger Mice* '93, and *Hawaii 555* '94. In 1990 Perth had a record attendance of 800 people at the Octagon Theatre when the two man team Phil Thompson and Geoff Kelso took out the grand final.

Since 1989 Perth Theatresports has operated as an independent body. The company holds workshops for players, school groups and occasionally teachers. Theatresports is played in a variety of venues. Since 1993 it has been played at SWY theatre. Grand finals are usually played at The Octogon or The Hole in the Wall. A 13 week Theatresports season is played during the winter months on Sunday nights.

Workshops are held throughout Western Australia with 1995 being a boom year for country school Theatresports. An artist in residence program has been established in Kimberley schools in the north-west of the state. An accreditation program for school teachers has also been introduced.

Since 1995 senior players have been playing Gorilla theatre [see Canada, this section] during the off season. Theatresports is also played at a variety of community functions including the Farbridge festival, Darlington Arts Festival and at seminars and conferences.

Albany, Western Australia

In 1986 in Albany Western Australia, community Theatresports was so popular that one player walked 12 kilometres into town to the workshop. Onstage players ranged from 12 to over 40 years. Timekeeper and scorekeeper (mothers of two players) sat on stage on wrought iron garden furniture, with a bottle of Ben Ean, a whistle and all the topics in envelopes. A team of mums called the *Big Bad Mamas* were hot favourites.

The judges wore fancy dress, one judge dressed as a pussy cat in fishnets, leotard with tail and stuck on whiskers. When there weren't enough players, compere and teacher Jon Firman volunteered unsuspecting audience members to join teams on stage.

Everyone knew everyone else and community announcements were part of the show. When one ten year old audience member hurled Minties back to the stage, the show stopped, his parents were located and he was placed under adult supervision. All this was achieved from the stage during the show. It was great. There were hundreds of people in the magnificent old Albany theatre, thoroughly enjoying themselves. It was exciting to see Theatresports so much a part of the community.

Teacher Jon Firman went so far as to initiate improvisation and status workshops in the local lock-up, which reportedly had a positive effect on the attitude of the prisoners. In 1987 a brave team from Albany drove to Brisbane for the third national finals played at City Hall Brisbane to a capacity house of 1700.

ACT

In 1987 Fortune Theatre Company staged the first Theatresports season in Canberra at the Childers Street Theatre. The initial weekend workshop was attended by professional and amateur actors, community players and ANU drama students. After a trial night, the first season opened with guest compere Anthony Ackroyd, and David Sanderson as Mr Music. Bernadette 'Boom-boom' Vincent took over as resident compere for the remainder of the first season.

The second season with the Jigsaw Theatre Company was hosted by Michael Fry. Canberra sang Sydney's anthem and played standard classic games in the one, two and four minute categories. Judges were drawn from local celebrities and the available pool of publicity-seeking politicians. Parliament House was a most popular scene location and political satire was rife.

The audience came in droves. At the first grand final, the audience swelled onto the stage leaving about two square metres of playing area for the teams.

The first champions, *Bronte Saw Us* with David Callan, Fiona Carter, Peter Fyfe and Kate Raymond, represented the ACT at the 1987 Brisbane national finals. Other premiership teams include: *The Okey-dokes* '88; *Stay at Home and Tape It* '89 and *The Casual Acquaintances of Buddha* '89. In 1988 *Four Sooths*, with Evan Crocker, Peter Fyfe, Michael Johnstone and Greg Toohey, represented the ACT at the third national finals at the Adelaide Festival.

NEW ZEALAND

Auckland

At the Performing Arts Centre, Auckland, Maggie Eyre gathered some of New Zealand's finest actors to participate in the initial Theatresports workshops. Director John Givins from Television New Zealand filmed the workshops and Theatresports was introduced to the country on the documentary arts program *Kaleidoscope*. Auckland's inaugural game was played at the Pump House Theatre with John Gibson as Mr Music on grand piano, Mark Ferguson as timekeeper and Sister Mary Leonard as compere. Celebrity judges Jennifer Ward-Leyland, Sam Pilsbury and Kate Harcourt scored the event. The audience marvelled at their favourite actors risking all. The Kiwis loved the Aussie Theatresports production. The Minties throw became an integral part of the New Zealand Theatresports ritual. The Kiwis wrote their own Theatresports anthem and were pleased to keep the ten commandments. After the success of the inaugural Pump House performance, the first full season moved to the Maidment Theatre.

Palmerston North

At Centrepoint Theatre in Palmerston North, Artistic Director Alison Quigan staggered main-stage rehearsals so Theatresports could be introduced to the theatre company members as a two day skills training workshop. Again the standard of playing was outstanding. The first season played for four weeks in the theatre restaurant. The original compere was the late Audrey Green, well-known as an announcer on radio 2ZA. Professional and amateurs players formed teams. Players of the team *Over the Top*: a computer programmer, a journalist, a copy-writer and a radio announcer were surprised to become the Palmerston North champions. With no previous stage experience other than Theatresports, they appeared on stage and national television competing with professional actors at the New Zealand national finals, and played one of the finest SPACE JUMPS I have ever seen.

Dunedin

Dunedin Theatresports started at the Fortune Theatre, where Lisa Warrington's University drama students and local community players took the plunge with the professional Fortune Theatre actors. The first season was held in the winter and met with such heavy snow falls that on opening night eight players were stranded and did not arrive at the theatre. In true improvised fashion, teams played in twos and threes and players formed new team combinations. The first compere was Barry Dorking, the timekeeper was Phil Grieve, and Doug Hood was Mr Music.

Martin Phelan, the first player to be honked off in New Zealand, remembers the first game well. He played in the very first scene, TRUTH — first line — ' I'm sorry I was snoring'. He lay down and began to snore. It was a good idea but unfortunately his team-mates did not come on stage. He kept snoring and nothing happened. Eventually after about 20 seconds the first scene in Dunedin was zeroed off.

The second week they changed the performance time to a matinee to combat the weather and the season played for two more weeks. The season champions were *Bats*

Need Friends. The second season saw a team of puppets *Club Bozo* (two players, Richard Huber and Martin Phelan, bringing to life four puppet characters who played all the games) just beaten by *Blue Fondue*, who went on to represent Dunedin in Christchurch at the national finals.

Traditionally Dunedin fields feisty teams who more than hold their own at the national championships. Dunedin Theatresports players have represented their country all over the world at Expo Brisbane, Edmonton Canada, New York and Orlando Florida.

Wellington

At the Down Stage Theatre Wellington, a small company of actors, including Grant Tilly, teacher at the New Zealand Acting School, became the first workshop participants. Four performances were held at the Down Stage Theatre. Lloyd Scott and Danny Mulheron were the first comperes. That year Wellington's Christmas Theatresports Special featured Jennifer Ward-Leyland as the Christmas Fairy and Mark Wright as the pixie. The following year, inspired players Liz Mullane and Annie Ruth, determined that Wellington be represented at the first New Zealand national championships, teamed up with Mark Wright and Ian Rae to form the Wellington team *Markvue and the Chardons.* This reinspired Wellington, and Theatresports played another season the following year at the James Cabaret to packed houses.

Christchurch

Court Theatre Christchurch director, Elric Hooper, put the entire company into Theatresports training. As well as a fine company of actors and teachers, the marketing manager, the stage manager and the administrator took part in the workshop. It is true to say that Christchurch went Theatresports crazy. Everyone was playing Theatresports. Bryan Aitkin took the reins as timekeeper and Judi Douglass organised the teams and wrote the New Zealand Theatresports anthem. The teams were formed from professional actors, university students and school students. The whole community gathered at the theatre on Sunday nights for the event. The Court Theatre began the first New Zealand outreach school and community teaching program with Nelson and Blenheim fielding teams.

New Zealand national network and first national final

The teams playing at the first New Zealand national final were:

Auckland:	*The Von Trapp Family*, with Mari Adams, Bruce Hopkins, Jay Laga'aia and Michael Mizrahi.
	Four Play, with Juliet Monaghan, Richard Smith, David Stott and Sarah Wilson.
Wellington:	*Markvue and the Chardons*, with Liz Mullane, Ian Rae, Annie Ruth and Mark Wright.
Dunedin:	*Blue Fondue*, with Peter Beardsley, Susan Brady, Patrick Davies and Stacy Taylor.

Christchurch: *The Handy Andies*, with Craig Cooper, Guy Grant, Simon Peacock and Tim Rainey.
Puawai, with Serene Butt, Guy Ockenden, Simon Small and Michael Thompson.

Palmerston North: *Over the Top*, with Nigel Corbett, David Hackman, John Haylock and Brett Marquet.

The first New Zealand champion team: *The Von Trapp Family*.

CANADA

Calgary

Calgary is the home of Theatresports at the beloved Loose Moose Theatre. For nearly two decades Sunday nights at the 'Moose' is Theatresports night. The converted livestock auction rooms on McKnight Boulevard are a perfect improvisation theatre. The 180 degree, semicircular, slightly raised stage comes complete with the perfect judges' pit, natural acoustics and intimate stage audience relationship for 260 people. It has been the home for the work of Keith Johnstone, his associate director Dennis Cahill and other founding players since Theatresports began at the University of Calgary in the late 1970s.

Loose Moose is the birthplace of the first games, the concept of judges, teams, challenges and many elements of the competitive improvisation performance phenomenon we call Theatresports.

Calgary is known for its two team format, open challenges and scenes not played to time limits which we call 'Calgary rules'. A typical Theatresports evening will begin with a 10 minute rookie round followed by a 'free impro' round and a Danish game (the audience decides which team wins by calling out very loudly). After interval two teams of seasoned players play a long match scored by judges. Winners of each challenge are awarded six minutes stage time to play a scene of their choice. If they are 'called for boring' (honked off) the opposing team is given the remaining time to play a new scene.

Part of the magic of Loose Moose is that it is a theatre fully equipped and mainly used for improvisation. Stability of tenure has enabled improvisors to incorporate all elements of lighting, sound and scenography within the improvised scene. Lighting operators make offers as well as yield to those given by players.

Calgary is famous in Theatresports circles for the unique sound of the one and only Vanessa Valdes. With direct vision to the stage, sitting in a dark sound booth and surrounded with shelves holding up to three hundred prerecorded tapes and CDs, she made choices with astonishing accuracy. With one ear on the players and the other in head phones, she gave offers for the scenes, adapting furiously to the unexpected narrative twists. This was all achieved with the accuracy of precomposed film score or soundscape.

Scenography

In scripted theatre, set changes usually occur in the darkness or half light at the beginning or end of a scene. At Loose Moose, players have developed the fine art of improvised scenography. One or two scenographers wearing tuxedos appear and provide simple scenery: chairs, tables and even a bed on casters rolled onto a lit stage in full view of the unsuspecting players and audience.

•

Magic moment

One night at Loose Moose Calgary, I saw Dennis Cahill play a very funny scene when a scenographer yielded to an offer and wheeled a life-size two seat rowing boat onto the stage. Another scenographer carried on two oars and delicately handed them to the stunned players. The players climbed into the boat and were immediately on a lake. With spectacular overaccepting Vanessa provided romantic music and sounds of night and nature while the lighting improvisor completed the picture with a full moon.

•

Beware

Some gagging players fall into the trap of hamming up the arrival of the scenery. Some over-enthusiastic scenographers smother scenes with too much interruption which can block the narrative rather than support it.

Balance and listening for offers will aid these inevitable teething problems. Remember that the scenographer is another player in every scene. Remind scenographers that many great scenes are played with nothing. Scenography works best when used sparingly and when, despite the hilarity of the arrival of scenery, the scene continues to develop good narrative, strong characters and other such delights.

Hell judges

Other Loose Moose experiments and inventions have included 'hell judges'. Secret judges sit in the audience armed with boredom buttons connected to lights visible only to the official judges. If the scene becomes boring or goes past its ending, the hell judges signal that the audience is bored and the scene needs to end.

But Theatresports is only one component of Loose Moose activity. The theatre is a laboratory for improvisation, comedy, plays, theatre productions and theatre for children. Loose Moose also performs and develops many open improvisation formats such as Gorilla theatre. Gorilla theatre incorporates the elements of sidecoaching, audience suggestions, challenges and team playing with a winner at the end.

Gorilla theatre is led by an onstage director/sidecoach who stops the scene, rewinds it, asks players to take a different offer or make a different choice, disqualifies or replaces players, and generally directs them through the scene, calling it as it plays. Players take turns performing this function throughout the performance.

One exciting element of Gorilla theatre is 'theme and forfeit' (no longer played at Loose Moose). A theme is chosen for the performance, for example: life and death, love and hate, crime and punishment, etc. Players form two teams who challenge each other to play scenes incorporating the theme. The audience decides if the improvised scene was truthful to the theme. If it was, the players receive a banana. If not, players choose a forfeit from a hat. The player with the most bananas wins the night. Some hilarious forfeits have included an improvised performance art piece or players being asked to leave the theatre and return with a pizza. At the end of show the winner makes a grand exit with a gorilla.

Loose Moose summer school

One important date on the Loose Moose calendar is the annual summer school which brings together players from all parts of the world to work with Keith Johnstone and his associates. For one luxurious week the pilgrims talk, think, eat and dream impro. They trade ideas, formats, teaching methods, styles, exchange improvisation culture, play in a variety of languages and swap Theatresports myths and legends while they create new ones. For every attendant there is great pride in playing Sunday night Theatresports at the legendary Loose Moose.

USA

New York

FREESTYLE REPERTORY THEATRE

home of THEATRESPORTS NEW YORK

New York Theatresports began in 1983. It has played at a variety of venues but is best known at the John Houseman Studio Theatre on 42nd St.

Today Freestyle Repertory Theatre is a company of 20 members and offers a number of improvisation formats which are performed in repertory. Season lengths are determined by the weather: fall season six weeks, spring season eight weeks. Seasons are short because New York theatre rents are extremely high.

Performers undergo an intensive training period which tends to emphasise a more theatrical style of improvisation rather than a stand-up style. The company concentrates on training with a heavy emphasis on narrative.

The best players are selected for the active school program performed in government schools. The program includes children as young as eight years. Programs are developed for children with specific needs from gifted children to those who need language support in English as a second language.

Workshops include skills such as improvised writing, play writing and performing, acting, directing, art, language and oracy skills. School teachers have noted marked improvements in children's language and writing skills through the improvisation classes.

Every year the company hosts a Theatresports tournament called the Stanislavsky Open for anyone who wants to participate.

Theatresports competition varies tremendously with two, three and four team formats, usually comprising of three or four players each. Captains challenge whatever they wish — open challenges, timed scenes, etc. Scenery is minimal: black wooden cubes become whatever the scene requires.

The company is well known for its offshoot developments which include shows such as: 'Spontaneous Broadway' a two act improvised musical backers audition where the audience provides song titles and situations and the players sing the show. Then there is the improvised 'Real Life' at Sardi's Belasco Room where a well known guest tells their life and times which inspires the company to improvise the memories and moments.

Other programs include player training and some business and corporate training performances and workshops.

Palm Springs

The focus of Palm Springs Theatresports is teaching and family counseling. It aims to go beyond basic acting and improvisation to teach skills necessary to enhance the 'quality of life'.

There is a strong youth element and focus. Any person thirteen years or older residing in Caochella Valley is eligible to participate in the Theatresports program which serves students at middle school, high school and college. An annual summer camp program is being planned as well as a Theatresports scholarship and specialised programs for adults and families.

Theatresports Palm Springs was founded by Robert and Carol Teitelbaum in 1993, and today consists of about 40 members and players. Regular training sessions on Tuesday and Thursday nights support the weekly Saturday evening performances which run all year round. Performances consist mostly of open challenges with an emphasis on story.

San Francisco

Bay Area Theatresports (BATS) has been evolving since Rebecca Stockley taught a weekend workshop in 1986. Performances began on the first Monday of each month and a series of workshops was introduced to keep techniques fresh and bring in new players. The regular venue is the Bayfront Theatre located at the Fort Mason Centre, a converted army post with a beautiful view of the Golden Gate Bridge and San Francisco Bay. The theatre seats 200.

Performances usually consist of the 'king-of-the-hill' style: an opening ten minute mini-match from players who have been attending workshops is followed by a main event of two teams from the performance company. Teams comprise three or four players who choose to play together. Each night's winning team faces a new challenger the following week. A typical run includes six weeks of regular competition followed by the four teams, with the highest scene average in any one night, playing off in the semi-finals. The two top teams go head for head in the championship finals.

BATS school's adult education program runs year round with training for beginner, intermediate and advanced levels. Players are often interested audience members who graduate after careful coaching in the training program. Occasionally the company stages short runs of other formats including long form musicals, movie genre and the popular Australian Rules night. The company regularly invites teams from Seattle, Los Angeles and Washington to play. Every other year they stage an international or national tournament. At one of these the mayor of San Francisco declared a Bay Area Theatresports Improvisation Day. In 1996 the company celebrates its tenth year.

Seattle

Unexpected Productions is Seattle's longest running and most successful improvisation theatre company. The foundations for the company were laid and the first Theatresports performance held in 1982 when Keith Johnstone taught a workshop.

In 1983 Seattle Theatresports began performing on Monday nights at Swannie's Comedy Underground. From there, with a small but loyal audience, the troupe moved and added shows at Pioneer Square Theatre, Scoundrel's Lair, and The Group Theatre, where the audience numbers increased.

In 1988 Unexpected Productions was founded as a non-profit company and moved from the Group to the Intiman Playhouse. In May 1991 they moved into their own home at the Market Theatre in the Pike Place Market.

Theatresports here is played with two teams of three. They play a full 90 minute match with one interval. The show begins with a freeze tag, followed by the MC toss up, usually something like STORY STORY DIE. The team that wins the toss up plays the first Judges' Challenge. The judges issue two challenges, one which is more open to developing narrative, and the other which encourages a particular improvisation skill. After these are played the lower scoring team issues the first team challenge which they play first. The challenges are open rather than specific games and continue until the end of the match. Sometimes there will be a group scene to end the show.

In addition to regular performances of Theatresports, and 'Cream of Wit' (a long format improvisation show), the company has produced a variety of shows which push the players' skills to new areas and give the audience a wider improvisation experience. These have included sketch impro 'Nerds Descending a Staircase', the all woman impro review 'Shampoo, Rinse and Repeat', the annual improvised 'A Christmas Carol' and the continuing storyline of 'For Instance', and 'Vault of Horror' to name a few.

Unexpected Productions has a mission to integrate improvisation in school education curriculum development. It holds workshops in schools including the 'Picture This', a program about myth for middle school.

The educational program has developed from a few in-house workshops each year to a year round school that offers classes from beginner to advanced levels and has an active outreach program. The company believes that through improvisation each individual has the opportunity to express thoughts and feelings without reference to right or wrong, good or bad. Improvisation is about making a 'strong' choice rather than a 'right' choice.

Eureka

Theatresports Humboldt Redwoods was founded locally by Bobby Klesper who trained with Keith Johnstone in Calgary. The only Theatresports company in California is located in Eureka about 300 miles north of San Francisco on the coast in a beautiful setting of redwood trees, coastal mountains and ocean vistas.

During the first year, Humboldt became a non-profit program of a local theatre company, North Coast Repertory Theatre, in Eureka. The group performs there on a regular basis, especially in summer. Humboldt has also worked closely with AIDS Education in performance, radio and telephone support, and has performed benefits for the tobacco education coalition and the local police association.

Currently there are six players, a musician and a supportive photographer. The company plays both competitive Theatresports and Keith Johnstone's Gorilla theatre.

When playing competitively players form two teams of two or three, use audience suggestions and play a variety of games including verbal restriction, time-limits and musical games. There is a referee and usually three judges scoring zero to five on technical, narrative and entertainment criteria.

The company performs at the 150 seat North Coast Repertory Theatre and occasionally at local clubs and events such as the world famous Dell'arte school of Physical Theatre's Mad River Festival.

Ventura

Ventura Area Theatresports came into existence as a result of a workshop in 1989 conducted by Barbara Scott of Bay Area Theatresports. The company now offers workshops once a week for beginners. Classes have also been held at youth centres and for older citizens at the Elder Hostel and organisations such as the state hospital.

The company has a strong group of about 20 experienced players who perform on the first and third Saturdays of each month at the Performance Studio, a multi-disciplined arts centre which once housed horses.

The 90 or so capacity audience range from about 20 to 60 years of age and enjoy the classic challenge match and occasionally Gorilla theatre. Teams usually comprise four players. Games are occasionally timed, but players prefer a more open style to support stronger narrative.

GERMANY

Dortmund

The first German company began playing Theatresports in Dortmund on the neck-breakingly thin floor of the impro boards in 1988. The company holds training workshops for new players, and for teachers and students in schools; it also travels to teach in other areas.

Theatresports is played once a month in Dortmund and the company travels to perform about 60 shows a year in other towns. About eight times a year other groups travel to Dortmund to play to an audience of 100–300. So far, teams from Heidelberg, Munster, Mannheim, Denmark and Holland have travelled to Dortmund to play. Most performances are held in little 'off-theatres'. In summer, the audience numbers increase as open-air performances are very popular.

Teams comprise of four players who play challenges and sometimes play to time limits. There is one 'conferencier' (compere who also acts as an impartial judge), a musician and three judges; one specifically judges technique, the second content and

Emscherblut

Emscherblut, Dortmund

story, and the third is an audience member who judges entertainment. Each judge scores out of three points.

Two teams improvise scenes based on specific themes such as film titles and emotions, and categories such as pantomime and operetta. All these are given by the audience. Scenes are played according to the audience's wishes and it is the audience who becomes the 'true referee' — they assess every game through applause. Should a foul occur, eg a scene fails or there is an illegal number of players, the impartial, incorruptible conferencier or the musician interrupt and the offending player must leave the stage.

The company has also developed a children's improvisation theatre and there is a special women's group which performs shows specifically for the women's movement.

Tübingen

Harlekin

Volker Quandt established Tübingen Theatresports, the first in Germany. It began as part of the Children and Youth theatre program, but was so popular that Harlequin was founded in 1992 exclusively as a Theatresports and improvisation company. The group of 10 professional actors began an intensive seven week training program and have been playing Theatresports ever since.

They play Danish style Theatresports in two teams of three improvisors. Each scene is judged by the audience who calls out the name of the team they believe played better and answered the challenge. Since December 1993 they have performed in the foyer of an old French cinema (established after World War II). The venue seats 450 which is big enough to hold a good size audience and still within the bounds of keeping close audience-performer contact.

Performances are held on weekends 3–6 times a month and are always sold out in advance, with some audience members travelling 2–3 hours by car from Switzerland and France to see the show. Theatresports has hosted parties and even a wedding at the theatre.

The company's strength lies in its musical ability. They are very proud of their improvising musician Heiner Kondschak. Some of their 45 minute impro shows are all sung.

BELGIUM

Duffel

Although there is no Theatresports group as such in Belgium, improvisation is alive and living in various guises. Since 1990 the 'Belgische improvisatieliga' has been improvising 'French style' during breaks in ice-hockey games. Ivoor is the only company in Belgium experimenting with non-competitive improvisation. They have been playing since 1992 and performing Gorilla theatre since 1994. The Ivoor players were active in a TV impro show called 'Onvoorziene Omstandigheden.'

Ivoor plays about 30 performances a year all over the country, most of them Gorilla theatre. These performances draw 120–800 spectators, with the majority at about

Harlekin

Harlekin Theatre, Tübingen

300–400. There are four directors, each assigned to a specific task: comedy, music, truthfulness and soap. Directors rotate these tasks each performance. During each show there are several episodes of an improvised soap guided by the soap director. The company always plays with an experienced musical director who encourages the players to attempt musical scenes.

The company's other activities include improvisation training programs in schools, and community cultural centres. Players are also involved in business and corporate training programs. Future plans include a live improvised soap over a season of three nights.

FINLAND

Vantaa

Helsingin Improvisaatioteatteri–Stella Polaris Theatresports Finland began in 1990 when Keith Johnstone was invited to Espoo City Theatre to teach. Since then performances have been held in many venues, including weekly at the Arena Theatre Helsinki and twice a month in the Espoo City Theatre as well as gigs in venues all over Finland. Audiences range from 150–300 and are primarily a young audience who come to the show every week.

The company consists of professional actors who hold training sessions and workshops for new players, actors and interested general public. Workshops are also given in schools and universities and there is a growing corporate program.

Performances range from Theatresports to the Life game, Gorilla Theatre and nights of open impro. In spring 1996 the company will be improvising on their own weekly national television show.

Theatresports Finland keeps in close contact with Theatresports teams from Sweden, Denmark and Norway. Together they comprise Nordic Theatresports. A Nordic Championship Theatresports event is held every year.

NETHERLANDS

Rotterdam

Theatresports Lawine (Dutch for avalanche) began in 1988. The company comprise a group of professional clowns, drama teachers and actors who play Theatesports, Gorilla theatre and perform plays and improvisation shows for all ages. They have a rookie group, and teach beginners, trainers and theatre directors.

The company often perform in venues 'on the road'. They have travelled to international Theatresports tournaments in Edmonton, Orlando, Vancouver and have taught Theatresports groups in London, Germany, Slovenia, Belgium, Sweden and Denmark. They work as often as possible with Keith Johnstone and are regularly visited by other improvisors who travel to Holland.

JAPAN

Theatresports Japan

Tokyo

Japanese Theatresports is a combination of adopted traditions and new Japanese rituals. It is a collaboration between United Performers' Studio (UPS) and Pacific Link Communications. The first season was held in November 1994 in Tokyo. UPS invited a select group of actors, clowns, mime artists and singers to an intensive four week training process followed by a season of twelve performances with a bilingual finale for the Asia Screen Network Association.

Opening night in the Tsutsujigaoka studio was compered by Rome Kanda, with Sheila Takehara as time keeper and Satomi Taga on piano, synth and percussion. Ten players formed three teams: *Gokuraku monkiz* (Heavenly monkeys), *Yon piz* (Four people) and the overall season winners the *Panic Bombarz* (Panic bombers). Theatresports won Tokyo's heart.

From the moment Japanese television personality Kazuki Kosakai saw Theatresports he was hooked. He compered the follow-up season in March 1995 and a special finale performance at the Canadian Embassy. A third season at the Canadian Embassy Theatre followed in October 1995.

The audience love the Japanese Theatresports anthem (written by Yoko Narahashi and Satomi Taga) and being divided into cheer squads to learn their team chant. At each score update the audience supporting the highest scoring team is rewarded by Candy Marina chan, Japan's improvising, magical candy girl (Marina Okada). Performances usually have a compere and time keeper. Occasionally they are played with a single umpire who calls times and sets up scenes. The western coin-toss has been replaced with the traditional Japanese junken (scissors/paper/rock). This determines which team wins the challenge. These new rituals have become so popular with the audience that they shout their team chant every time their team plays, and players junken not only with their hands but with their whole bodies and faces.

Theatresports Japan

Marina Okada as Candy Marina chan, Japan

Most games and challenges are played as they are in the west with minor adjustments to support the Japanese language and culture. For instance, owing to the structure of the language, ONE-WORD-AT-A-TIME STORY must allow for two

Japan Times Weekly

Panic Bombarz — (left) Atsushi Yoshida and Yuri Kinugawa, Japan

words, and ALPHABET GAME has been adjusted because there are over 3000 letters in the Japanese alphabet. There are games which the Japanese have embraced and perform with inspired cultural flair. THE DIE GAME is a popular favorite and played at every public performance. In western scenes Theatresports players tend to kill each other. Japanese players prefer to kill themselves. The audience screams with laughter as the players spontaneously suicide with honour in hilarious and extraordinary ways. New games reflecting Japanese culture include KARAOKE VIDEO and SING ABOUT IT [see Program three].

Performances have been played in two team, Canadian style, untimed challenge rounds and the Australian four team, timed games style, and a combination of both. Teams comprise three to five players and with the growing number of rookie players, a rookie round at the top of the show has been added to give budding players stage time and experience. Successful rookies sometimes then play veterans in the main rounds. Three judges each give a score out of five in the usual three categories and in big venues such as the Canadian Embassy Theatre, the human scoreboard relays the scores to the audience.

The company holds regular workshops and is planning an education and corporate program. The players look forward to developing new ideas in a variety of styles and drawing together the global network with bilingual international playing.

appendices *and* indices

Appendix

appendix A LICENSED THEATRESPORTS CENTRES

Australia

Brisbane
Theatresports Queensland
The church hall
78 Enoggera Terrace
Paddington QLD 4064
phone (7) 3368 1700
fax (7) 3368 1711

Hobart
Theatre Now
77 Salamanca Place
Hobart TAS 7000
phone (3) 6237 400
fax (3) 6240 245

Melbourne
Flying Pig Theatre
St Martins Youth Arts Centre
28 St Martins Lane
South Yarra VIC 3141
phone (3) 9866 2703

Perth
Theatresports WA Inc
407 Guildford Road
Bayswater WA 6053
phone/fax (9) 272 2432

Sydney
Theatresports Inc
483 Riley St
Surry Hills NSW 2010
phone (2) 9318 0088
fax (2) 9318 0021

Austria

Graz
Theatresports Graz
Haupstr. 232
A-2391 Kaltenleutgeben
phone (2238) 7195

Vienna
A 1180 Wien Hans Sachs Gasse 21/4

Belgium

Duffel
Improvisatiegezelschap Ivoor
Wouwendonkstraat 133
B-2570 Duffel
phone/fax (15) 315 017

Brazil

Sao Paulo
Sociedade Pro'-Projeto Teatral Dano-Brasileiro
Alameda Barros, 186 ap. 101 01232-000
Sao Paulo - SP, Brazil
phone (11) 66 7297

Canada

Banff
Precipice Theatre Society
Box 1942
Banff, Alberta T0L 0C0

Calgary
Loose Moose Theatre Company
2003 McKnight Blvd
NE Calgary, Alberta T2E 6L2
phone/fax (403) 250 1414

Edmonton
Rapid Fire Theatre
PO Box 1933 Main Post Office
Edmonton, Alberta T5J 2P3
phone (403) 448 0695
fax (403) 439 7053

Quebec
On the spot improv company
4352 Marcil Avenue
Montreal, Quebec H4A 2Z8
phone (514) 482 1350

Finland

Vantaa
Stella Polaris
Länsisatamankatu 22 A 21
00180 Helsinki
phone/fax (0) 685 4346

Germany

Berlin
Theatresports Berlin
Richardplatz 12b
12055 Berlin

Dortmund
Emsherblut
Touché Theater
Bismarckstr. 29
44135 Dortmund
phone (231) 524 550
fax (231) 100 130

Munich
Fast Food Theatre

Tübingen
Harlekin Theater
Wilhelmstraße 103
72074 Tübingen, Germany
phone (7071) 23 858
fax (7071) 23 858

Japan

Tokyo
United Performers' Studio
1-32-17-201 Uehara
Sibuya-ku Tokyo, 151
phone (3) 3466 2041
fax (3) 3466 2074

Netherlands

Rotterdam
Theatersports Lawine
Quarantaineweg 1
3089 KP, Rotterdam, Netherlands
phone (10) 429 2518
fax (10) 495 4740

New Zealand

Auckland (national office)
PO Box 8154
Symonds Street
Auckland
phone/fax (9) 302 4146

Christchurch
The Court Theatre
20 Worcester Boulevard
Christchurch
phone (3) 379 5264
fax (3) 365 2493

Wellington
The Improvisors
PO Box 6273
Te Aro Wellington
phone (4) 384 6704
fax (4) 384 2317

Dunedin
Dunedin Improv
Theatreworks
PO Box 6260
Dunedin
phone (3) 477 1599

Norway

Oslo
TeatresportOslo
c/o Thorvald Meyers Gt.25
0555 Oslo 5

South Africa

Johannesburg
Market Theatre Laboratory
PO Box 8656
Johannesburg, 2000 South Africa
phone (11) 836 6499
fax (11) 836 6499

Sweden

Stockholm
Stockholms Improvisations Teatre
Sigtunagatan 12
113 22, Stockholm
phone (8) 306 242

USA

Boston
ImprovBoston
PO Box 965
Cambridge MA 02238
phone (617) 641 1710

Chatanooga
Chatanoodle
c/Dance Theatre Workshop
1222 Hanover Street
Chatanooga TN 37415
phone (615) 766 1942

Chicago
2528 W.Winnemac Ave
Chicago IL 60625
phone (312) 508 6969
fax (312) 989 7161

Columbia
Workshop Theatre of Columbia
c/Chris Pendleton
4006 Hickory St.
Columbia SC 29205

Denver
Denver Theatresports
c/John Klug
4565 King Street
Denver CO 80211

Dover
Come One See All Guerrilla Theatre
51 New York St.
Dover NH 03820
phone (603) 742 7307

Eureka
Humboldt Redwoods Theatresports
PO Box 2718
McKinleyville CA 95519
phone (707) 839 4153

La Jolla
Fourth of July Creek Productions
PO Box 3256
La Jolla CA 92038-3256
phone (619) 534 4488
fax (619)534 1078

Los Angeles
Los Angeles Theatresports
2145 Gower St.
Los Angeles CA 90068
phone (213)469 9689
fax (213) 464 1638

Maenasha
Comedic Services (Dairyland Theatresports)
504 River Way
Maenasha WI 54952
phone (414) 722 7404

Nashville
Nashville Theatresports
(The Comedy Company)
537 Tall Trees Lane
Nashville TN 37209
phone (615) 356 8571

New York
Freestyle Repertory Theatre
120 West 86 St, Suite 1a
New York NY 10024
phone (212) 642 8202
http://www.echonyc.com/~freestyle/frt.html

Orlando
SAK Entertainment
45 East Church Street
Orlando FL 32801
phone (407) 648 0001
fax (407) 648 1333

Palm Springs
Palm Springs Theatresports
68 395 Concupcion Road
Cathedral City CA 92234
phone (619) 779 8826

Pittsburgh
Pittsburgh Ensemble Theatre
307 S.Dithridge Street, #704
Pittsburgh PA 15213
phone (412) 682 3376

Portland
PDX Theatresports
PO Box 40833
Portland OR 97240
phone (503) 452 6544
http://www.teleport.com/~richieb/PDXTS/pdxts.html

San Diego
Grunion Productions
PO Box 9129
San Diego CA 92109
phone (619) 270 3409
http://www.trg2.saic.com/~jeff/misc/sdts.html

San Francisco
Bay Area Theatresports (BATS)
3435 Cesar Chavez (Army) St., Suite 224
San Francisco CA 94110
phone (415) 824 8220
fax (415) 695 1714
http://sfm.com/ppl/sara/bats.html
mailto://improbats@aol.com

Seaford (Long Island)
Theatresports Long Island
c/Bill Primavera
1799 Collins Street
Seaford NY 11783
phone (516) 781 1886

Seattle
Unexpected Productions
1428 Post Alley
Seattle WA 98101
phone/fax (206) 587 2414

Stanford
Stanford Improvisors (SIMPS)
c/Patricia Ryan Madson
Dept. of Drama/Stanford University
Stanford CA 94305
phone (415) 723 3512
fax (415) 584 0361

Ventura
Ventura Area Theatresports
6035 Cloverly
Ventura CA 93003
phone (805) 642 8041

Washington
1545 18 Street NW #709
Washington DC 20036
phone (202) 332 1077

Zimbabwe

Harare
Rooftop Promotion
c/Daves Guzha
20 Harare Drive Marlborough
Harare, Zimbabwe

appendix B

TOPICS AND TITLES

The function of the topic or title is to stimulate the process of imaging and give players a starting point for the scene. The suggestions are the first offer in the scene. They should give the players at least one of the following:

place — somewhere to be;
activity — something to do;
character — someone to be.

When players have a clear picture of at least one of these three, they have a solid beginning on which to build a single idea, give it focus, endow it and tell a story.

Keep them simple. Everyday topics spark wit, intelligence and emotion. If topics are too clever or funny they can block players rather than stimulate them. Begin with simple, clear topics and introduce specific content from general knowledge, current affairs and other parts of the curriculum to broaden content as the players' confidence and skills increase.

All the programs give specific starting points for training games, scenes and Theatresports performance games. Use the suggestions below to support these and to stimulate ideas further.

STARTING PLACES FOR SCENES

Suggestions for a first offer of place

Geographic locations

At Uluru
On the golf course
On the ocean floor
At the South Pole
In the Colosseum (wonders of the world etc)
On the moon
Planets/poles/monoliths/countries/rivers
At Stonehenge

Non-geographic locations

In the airport departure lounge
At the barbeque
By the booze bus
At the car wash
In a department store
In the ghost train
In a hot air balloon
In a lift
In a morgue
At the pit stop
In a public telephone booth
In a restaurant
In a rose garden
In a submarine
In a tree house
At the vending machine
At a wine tasting
Backstage
At the beach party
At the box office
In a casino
On a desert island
In the goal square
At the hot dog stand
In a manhole
On the operating table
At a play rehearsal
At a pyjama party
On a roller-coaster
In a sawmill
At the TAB
In the Turkish bath
At the video store
In a yacht
At the baggage carousel
At the blood bank
In the brewery
In the cockpit
At the dole office
At the hairdressers
At the laundrette
In a mirror maze
At the petrol station
At the polling booth
On a raft
On the roof
In a sewer
In a television studio
At the veterinary clinic
In a whale
At the zoo

Offers of place suggesting ritual and character

Anywhere a community meets that suggests ritual

In the ashram
At a burning at the stake
In church
At a funeral
In hell
At a scout or brownie group
At a synagogue
At a wake
In the bingo hall
At a christening
At an exorcism
At the gates of heaven
At a prayer group
At a stoning
On the temple altar
At a wedding

Characters — all characters fictional or non-fictional associated with the above at all levels of status

Angels
Dads
Fairies
Kids
Martyrs
Relatives - cousins, aunties
Sphinx-polishers
Toll collectors
Buddha
Devils
Gnomes
Kings/Queens etc
Mums
Saints
Spirits
Warlocks
Choir boys
Elves
God
Krishna
Nuns
Shiva
Stone-sellers
Witches

Places with a sense of mystique/occasion/ceremony

Around a bonfire
In court
In parliament
At a seance
In a convent
At the Logies/Academy Awards
At a pet cemetary
At a war memorial

Starting activities + place/environment — geographic and non geographic

Abandoning ship
Climbing Mount Everest
Discovering Tutankhamen's tomb
Fighting a fire/flood/cyclone
Landing on Mars
Renovating the bathroom
Tidying the bottom drawer
Boating on a river
Contacting Earth
Escaping from jail
Having a bath
Mowing the lawn
Selling the Taj Mahal/Uluru/Canberra
Writing graffiti in a subway

Starting activities plus object/person/relationship

Amputating a leg
Charming a snake
Delving into a lucky dip
Discovering your twin
Fighting a crocodile
Hanging a painting
Joining the army
Leaving home
Meeting a rock star
Moving a grand piano
Planting a tree
Putting up a sign
Sending a note in a bottle
Breaking mum's vase
Choosing a canary
Digging a grave
Disguising yourself
Firing a canon
Having a bath
Launching a spaceship
Making a bed
Meeting your penfriend
Mowing the lawn
Prospecting for gold
Putting up a tent
Talking to a dog
Changing a light bulb
Conducting a band
Discovering a lost tribe
Diving off a springboard
Flying a kite
Having a sauna
Learning to drive
Making toffee
Milking a cow
Opening for business
Pulling a tooth
Scaling fish
Throwing a lifeline

Training a flea
Waiting for a bus/letter/birth
Unwrapping presents
Walking an elephant/goldfish
Unveiling a statue
Washing a car

Indoor starting activities which imply place

Borrowing a book
Conducting an orchestra
Decorating the Christmas tree
Popping corn
Shoplifting
Cleaning windows
Counting the takings
Playing pool
Rug beating
Waiting for the telephone to ring

Outdoor starting activities which imply place

Butterfly catching
Finding a bird's nest
Parachuting
Raking leaves
Collecting the mail
Finding an oasis
Picnicking
Snorkelling

EVENTS

Domestic

Breaking an old family trinket
Bringing home the report card
Death of the family pet
Graduation ceremony
The arrival of the telephone bill
Visiting a retirement village
Bringing home a new baby
Christmas dinner
Family crisis
Mother's Day
The will reading
Winning Lotto

Political

Abdication
Election
Signing a treaty
Coronation
Revolution
War

Household objects

Bread board
Electric blanket
Light bulb
Television
Eggbeater
Iron
Potato peeler
Vacuum cleaner

Items of clothing

Bowler hat
Football jumper
Shoes
Veil
Feather boa
Pyjamas
Underwear
Wedding dress

Crimes

Arson
Fraud
Smuggling
Espionage
Impersonation
Theft

Quests

(something to search for)

- Eternal youth
- Nirvana
- The lost chord
- Truth

First line

- 1151, 1152...
- I'm starving to death on this diet
- You wouldn't say that if dad was here
- Every time we go out, you forget your wallet
- Yes, it works
- You're a genius, let's do it

Last line

- Congratulations my friend
- So that's the end of the story
- Plug it in, switch it on and off it goes
- There goes another poodle

Weather and environmental conditions

- All the elements (wind/fire/earth/water)
- Floods
- Plagues
- Famines
- Pests
- Volcanoes

Treasured possessions

- Bikes
- CDs
- Pets
- Rocks
- Books
- Diaries
- Photos
- Surfboards
- Cars
- Letters
- Rings
- Trophy

Riddle or problem to solve

- How Earth ran out of steam
- How the lounge chair got in the bottle

Famous personalities

- Cartoon and comic characters
- Music stars
- Spiritual leaders
- Characters from plays
- Politicians
- Super heroes
- Film stars
- Prophets
- Writers

People from history

- Artists
- Explorers
- Musicians
- Scientists
- Criminals
- Inventors
- Pioneers
- Religious leaders
- Doctors
- Martyrs
- Philosophers
- Warriors

Offer of scenario/event

- Bible stories
- Hansel and Gretel
- Myths/legends/fables
- Nursery rhymes/fairy tales
- Samson and Delilah
- David and Goliath
- Icarus
- Noah's Ark
- Romeo and Juliet
- The Trojan horse

And all the personalities and characters we associate with the above and the specific events we accept as part of a culture.

Titles for scenes

Amazon hunt
Cable car catastrophe
The curse of the kimono
Doing the midnight shift
First day on the job
Harry's hamburgers on wheels
Kevin the counterfeit king
The magic supermarket
Medical breakthrough of the century
The nanny's curse
On the other side of the river
The queen's amnesia
Sharky's big surprise
Tragedy on the monkey bars
Voyage through the human body
Bo Bo's big adventure
The case of the missing monk
Disaster on the assembly line
The face behind the veil
First landing on Earth
The home cooking demonstration
The lost tribe of Kilimanjaro
The man with 1000 voices
The mirror of truth
The Olympic swim
On the way home
Revenge of the mosquitoes
Siegfried's wish
Underneath the city
Your big brass bed

OPEN CHALLENGES

Types of scenes

Adventurous scene
Mysterious scene
Serious scene
Fantastical scene
Scary scene
Suspenseful scene
Love scene
Scene in the past/future
Tragic scene

ENDOWMENTS

Emotions

Anger
Calm
Disgust
Excitement
Greed
Happiness
Jealousy
Lust
Rage
Sadness
Bliss
Confusion
Empathy
Exhaustion
Grief
Hate
Joy
Melancholy
Regret
Shock
Boredom
Despair
Envy
Fear
Guilt
Horror
Love
Misery
Remorse
Sorrow

States of mind and being

Abandoned
Agonised
Anxious
Bad
Bold
Captivated
Childish
Adamant
Alienated
Apathetic
Beautiful
Brave
Charmed
Clever
Adequate
Ambivalent
Astounded
Betrayed
Burdened
Cheated
Competitive
Affectionate
Annoyed
Awed
Bitter
Capable
Cheerful
Condemned

Conspicuous	Contented	Contrite	Cruel
Crushed	Culpable	Deceitful	Defeated
Delighted	Delirious	Deluded	Desirous
Destructive	Determined	Different	Diminished
Discontented	Distracted	Distraught	Disturbed
Divided	Dominated	Doomed	Dubious
Eager	Ecstatic	Electrified	Empty
Enchanted	Energetic	Enjoyment	Evil
Exasperated	Exhilarated	Fascinated	Flustered
Foolish	Frantic	Freaked-out	Free
Frightened	Frustrated	Furious	Gay
Glad	Good	Gratified	Great
Guilty	Gullible	Heavenly	Helpless
High	Homesick	Honoured	Horrible
Hostile	Hurt	Hysterical	Ignored
Immortal	Impressed	Inadequate	Infatuated
Inferior	Inspired	Intimidated	Irritated
Isolated	Jumpy	Kind	Lazy
Lecherous	Left-out	Lonely	Longing
Low	Mad	Mean	Mystical
Naughty	Nervous	Obnoxious	Obsessed
Obsolete	Odd	Outraged	Overwhelmed
Pained	Panicked	Peaceful	Persecuted
Petrified	Pitiful	Pleased	Plucky
Pressured	Prim	Prissy	Proud
Quarrelsome	Queer	Rapturous	Refreshed
Rejected	Relaxed	Relieved	Remorseful
Resentful	Restless	Reverent	Righteous
Satisfied	Scared	Servile	Settled
Sick	Silly	Sceptical	Sleepy
Sneaky	Solemn	Spiteful	Spoiled
Startled	Stingy	Stunned	Stupefied
Stupid	Sure	Talkative	Tempted
Tenacious	Tense	Tentative	Tenuous
Terrible	Threatened	Thwarted	Tired
Trapped	Troubled	Ugly	Uncouth
Uneasy	Unloved	Unsettled	Unused
Vehement	Violent	Vital	Vivacious
Voluptuous	Vulnerable	Wacky	Warm
Weepy	Weird	Wicked	Wonderful
Worried	Worthless	Youthful	Zany

And all the possible permutations and combinations of these words and their effects on the human condition.

Occupations

Actor	Astronaut	Bar-tender	Beautician
Bricklayer	Cashier	Cook	Cow-boy/girl
Dentist	Designer	Doctor	Driving instructor
Farmer	Gardener	Judge	Kindergarten teacher
Lawyer/solicitor	Mechanic	Model	Mountaineer
Musician	Newspaper seller	Newsreader	Nurse
Opera singer	Optometrist	Orchestra conductor	Painter

Parking attendant	Parking inspector	Pearl diver	Pianist
Pick-pocket	Politician	Pop-singer	Religious (eg priest)
Sculptor	Taxi driver	Tight-rope walker	Truck driver
Used-car salesperson	Usher	Watchmaker	WP operator

Physical attribute/condition

(Be sensitive when choosing physical disabilities)

Acne	Arthritis	Bad back	Bad breath
Beautiful	Blind/deaf (senses)	Body odour	Breathes fire
Broken arm/leg	Charismatic	Elegant	Face on back of head
Haemophiliac	Hairy	Huge nose	Hunch back
Leaks oil	Long arms	Long tongue	Magical
Mystical	Naked	No/one leg/foot, etc	Pointed head
Pregnant	Short	Short/long sighted	Stutter
Tall	Tattooed	Toothless	Transparent
Weak bladder	Webbed fingers/toes	Weightless	Wooden leg/arm, etc

Styles/genres

Adventure (*Raiders of the lost ark*)
Agatha Christie (Poirot, Miss Marple)
Beach party (*Gidget, Summer holiday*)
Berkoff (*Greek, East, West*)
Brecht (*Caucasian chalk circle, The mother*)
Chaucer (*The Canterbury tales*)
Chekhov (*The cherry orchard, The three sisters*)
Children's television (*Play school, Here's Humphrey*)
Circus (clowns, trapeze artists, lion tamers)
DH Lawrence (*Women in love, Sons and lovers*)
David Williamson (*The removalists, The club*)
Dickens (*A Christmas carol*)
Disaster movie (*Earthquake, Towering inferno*)
Documentary (*The world around us*)
Fairy story (*Goldilocks, Aesop's fables, The pied piper*)
Fellini (*Satyricon*)
Film Noir (*The Maltese falcon*)
George Bernard Shaw (*Major Barbara, Pygmalion*)
Game show (*Wheel of fortune, Jeopardy*)
Gothic (*Dracula*)
Grand opera (*The magic flute, Carmen*)
Greek (Homer, Euripides, and all those gladiator movies)
Harold Pinter (*The homecoming, The birthday party*)
Horror/suspense (*The mummy's hand, Wait until dark*)
Ibsen (*Hedda Gabler, A doll's house*)
James Bond movies (*Octopussy, Gold finger*)
Japanese kabuki theatre
Japanese monster movie (*Godzilla*)
Melodrama
Molière/French Farce (*The imaginary invalid, Tartuffe*)
Musical (*Sound of music, Phantom of the opera*)
Mythical/Fantasy (*The dark crystal, The princess bride*)
News broadcast
Noël Coward

Oscar Wilde (*The importance of being Earnest*)
Pantomime
Puppetry
Religious Movie (*Nun's story, The ten commandments*)
Restoration Comedy (Congreve, Sheridan)
Rock & Roll; Country & Western; Blues; Gospel; Folk; Rock Opera
Romance (Mills and Boon)
Samuel Beckett (*Waiting For Godot, Endgame*)
Science fiction (*Forbidden planet, The day the earth stood still*)
Shakespeare
The Simpsons
Sitcom
Soap opera (*Neighbours, A country practice, Days of our lives*)
Splatter (*Nightmare on Elm Street*)
Street theatre/Busking
Strindberg (*Miss Julie*)
Teenage mutant ninja turtles
Tribal/Ritual
War Movie (*Battle of Britain, Gallipoli*)
Western

appendix C

SUGGESTED READING

Australian Theatre Design (1992) Australian Production Designers Association of NSW Inc

Barlow, W. (1973) *The Alexander Principle* Arrow Books Limited

Berry, C. (1973) *Voice and the Actor* George G. Harrap & Co. Ltd.

Berry, C. (1987) *The Actor and his Text* George G. Harrap & Co. Ltd.

Duchartre, P. L. (1964) *The Italian Comedy* Dover Publications Inc

Johnstone, K. (1981) *IMPRO Improvisation and the Theatre* London, Methuen

Johnstone, K. (1994) *Don't be prepared* Loose Moose Theatre Company

Laban, R (revised Ullmann) (1948) *Effort* Macdonald & Evans

Linklater, K. (1976) *Freeing the Natural Voice* Drama Book Specialists, New York

Litson, J. (1989) 'Thespian Gladiators and their Coliseum of Sport' *The Australian* August 2

Pierse, L. 'The State of the Sport' *New Theatre Australia* March 1988

Spolin, V. (1985) *Theatre Games for Rehearsal* Evanston, Northwestern University Press

Spolin, V. (1986) *Theatre Games for the Classroom* Evanston, Northwestern University Press

Spolin, V. (1987) *Improvisation for the Theatre* Illinois, Northwestern University Press

Spurgeon, D. (1991) *Dance Moves* Sydney, Harcourt Brace Jovanovich

Stanislavsky, C. (1968) *Building a Character* Methuen & Co. Ltd.

Index

index

ALPHABETICAL INDEX OF GAMES

• denotes classic

GENERAL INDEX

T

Robert McFarlane